About the Auth[illegible]

"In Martin Lings' lucid and sup[illegible] linary synthesis of metaphysical insig[illegible] poetic beauty, and mystical illumination, all the more striking considering the variegation of his work. This marvelous anthology draws on Lings' masterly exegeses of sacred texts and doctrines, his peerless lives of the Prophet and Shaykh Ahmad al-ʿAlawī, his elucidations of Shakespeare and the Sufi poets, his acute diagnosis of our contemporary spiritual malaise, and his reaffirmations of the perennial wisdom. A veritable treasure-house!"

—**Harry Oldmeadow**, author of *Frithjof Schuon and the Perennial Philosophy*

"We sense in the books of Martin Lings the imprint of his own unmistakable, elegant style, a certain flavour or taste (*dhawq*), bespeaking a particular spirit or inspiration. Reading his books, one is struck both by the unshakable certitude that pervades them, and by the almost tangible sense of the author's own effacement in the truths he so eloquently articulates."

—**Reza Shah-Kazemi**, author of *Paths to Transcendence: According to Shankara, Ibn Arabi & Meister Eckhart*

"The author of books on many subjects, including two collections of poetry, an interpretation of the major plays of Shakespeare, a study of Koranic calligraphy, and a biography of the Prophet Muhammad, Lings is especially prominent among scholars of Sufism, and he is widely recognized as a leading figure in the Perennialist or Traditionalist school of comparative religion."

—**James S. Cutsinger**, author of *Advice to the Serious Seeker: Meditations on the Teaching of Frithjof Schuon*

"Lings was a celestial intellectual and spiritual giant in an age of dwarfed terrestrial aspirations and endeavors. With a poet's pen, a metaphysician's mind, and a saint's concerns, Lings ... did in his life what he is urging the rest of us to do: return to the spirit."

—**Hamza Yusuf**, Zaytuna Institute

"I read it straight through, then I re-read it, almost in its entirety, fascinated."

—**Titus Burckhardt**, author of *Alchemy* and *Art of Islam*, on Lings' *Muhammad: His Life Based on the Earliest Sources*

"It is an extraordinarily rare experience in our age to read a book—especially a biography—in which the author, like some master craftsman of the Middle Ages, makes himself, as it were, anonymous in a work that nonetheless bespeaks his impeccable scholarship and quite remarkable narrative skill. If this sounds like a paradox, or an almost impossible literary feat, it has nonetheless been achieved by Martin Lings in this long awaited life of the Prophet of Islam, assembled from the traditional early accounts in Arabic.... Nothing remotely comparable exists in English, or in any other European language for that matter."

—***Studies in Comparative Religion***, on Lings' *Muhammad*

"An enthralling story that combines impeccable scholarship with a rare sense of the sacred worthy of his subject.... This is easily the best biography of the Prophet in the English language."

—**Victor Danner**, author of *The Islamic Tradition: An Introduction*, on Lings' *Muhammad*

"A masterly study of a man [Shaykh Aḥmad al-ʿAlawī] whose sanctity recalled the golden age of medieval mystics. In this well documented book Lings draws on many rare sources ... and has made some important original contributions."

—**A.J. Arberry**, renowned translator of the Qur'ān, on Lings' *A Sufi Saint of the Twentieth Century*

"Lings is a writer who knows his subject thoroughly and intimately and it has always been a characteristic of his writing that he goes straight to the heart of his subject."

—**R.W.J. Austin**, on Lings' *What is Sufism?*

"[Martin Lings] says more to reveal the quintessence of Shakespeare's greatness than the most laborious exposition could ever do."

—**Kathleen Raine**, author of *Defending Ancient Springs*, on Lings' *The Sacred Art of Shakespeare*

"I am particularly indebted to him for his book on Shakespeare, which I think of and return to again and again."

—**Wendell Berry**, author of *Jayber Crow*, on Lings' *The Sacred Art of Shakespeare*

"This book is unique.... [It] is the first book which comes anywhere near to doing justice to the two Koranic arts which are its theme. Its publication is a major event."

—**William Stoddart**, author of *Sufism*, on Lings' *The Qur'ānic Art of Calligraphy and Illumination*

"For those already interested in symbolism, particularly in relation to the Qur'ān, Lings' book will be immensely rewarding; for others who may not previously have grasped the importance of this subject, it cannot fail to be profoundly enlightening."

—**Gai Eaton**, author of *Islam and the Destiny of Man*, on Lings' *Symbol & Archetype*

World Wisdom
The Library of Perennial Philosophy

The Library of Perennial Philosophy is dedicated to the exposition of the timeless Truth underlying the diverse religions. This Truth, often referred to as the *Sophia Perennis*—or Perennial Wisdom—finds its expression in the revealed Scriptures as well as the writings of the great sages and the artistic creations of the traditional worlds.

The Essential Martin Lings appears as one of our selections in the Perennial Philosophy Series.

The Perennial Philosophy Series

In the beginning of the twentieth century, a school of thought arose which has focused on the enunciation and explanation of the Perennial Philosophy. Deeply rooted in the sense of the sacred, the writings of its leading exponents establish an indispensable foundation for understanding the timeless Truth and spiritual practices which live in the heart of all religions. Some of these titles are companion volumes to the Treasures of the World's Religions series, which allows a comparison of the writings of the great sages of the past with the perennialist authors of our time.

Cover:
Martin Lings, c. early 1990s

The Essential Martin Lings

Edited by

Reza Shah-Kazemi

World Wisdom

The Essential Martin Lings
Edited by Reza Shah-Kazemi

Library of Congress Cataloging-in-Publication Data

Names: Lings, Martin, author. | Shah-Kazemi, Reza, editor.
Title: The essential Martin Lings / edited by Reza Shah-Kazemi.
Description: Bloomington, Indiana : World Wisdom, 2023. | Includes
bibliographical references and index.
Identifiers: LCCN 2022058132 (print) | LCCN 2022058133 (ebook) | ISBN
9781936597741 (paperback) | ISBN 9781936597758 (epub)
Subjects: LCSH: Lings, Martin. | Islam. | Sufism. | Religions--Relations.
Classification: LCC BP88.L56 A2 2023 (print) | LCC BP88.L56 (ebook) | DDC
297.4--dc23/eng/20230211
LC record available at https://lccn.loc.gov/2022058132
LC ebook record available at https://lccn.loc.gov/2022058133

Printed on acid-free paper in the United States of America.

For information address World Wisdom, Inc.
P.O. Box 2682, Bloomington, Indiana 47402-2682
www.worldwisdom.com

CONTENTS

Editor's Preface

We can think of no better way of introducing an author of the stature of Martin Lings, also known as Shaykh Abū Bakr Sirāj al-Dīn (1909–2005), than by using his own words:

> The truly simple man is an intense unity: he is complete and whole-hearted, not divided against himself. To keep up this close-knit integration, the soul must readjust itself altogether to each new set of circumstances, which means that there must be a great flexibility in the different psychic elements: each must be prepared to fit perfectly with all the others, no matter what the mood. This closely woven synthesis, upon which the virtue of simplicity is based, is a complexity as distinct from a complication.[1]

We observe a reverberation of this "close-knit integration" in the fruits yielded by a "truly simple" soul. The writings which emanate from such a soul would also be an "intense unity", where each element "fit[s] perfectly with all the others" in a "closely woven synthesis". To extract from these writings those which are "essential" is, therefore, a very difficult task.

As a young man, before embracing the Sufi path, Martin Lings had already to a large extent refined his soul—in a properly alchemical sense—by cleaving to beauty as his sole "religion". As he often said: "We made a religion out of beauty". The Low Church Protestantism of his time was anything but beautiful, and he, together with his closest friends at Oxford University, Adrian Paterson and Peter Townsend, knew that religion without beauty could not be "true". They understood well the Platonic dictum: "Beauty is the splendor of the Truth." Lings therefore invited in the very core of his being the truth manifested by the splendor of beauty. He was thereby effectively purged of the dross of error and the impurity of ugliness by which early twentieth century European culture

[1] *Ancient Beliefs and Modern Superstitions* (London: Archetype, 2001), p. 11.

was poisoned. Beauty enabled him to concentrate on the essential—the transcendent Essence of beauty—with that which was essential within himself: the immanent beauty latent within his heart. The rest of his life can be seen as the unfolding of this alchemically transformative vision of truth as beauty: the gold of Heaven magnetizing and revealing the gold of the Heart. "Light upon Light", as the Qur'ān puts it (*nūr ʿalā nūr*).

Some of the material fruits of his vision of beauty's splendor can still be seen today, eighteen years after his death, in the flowers of his garden in Kent, England. Lings was an accomplished gardener who devoted years of his life carefully "anthologizing" flowers: selecting the flowers of his garden in full awareness of the alchemical symbolism of color. This awareness was itself cultivated and brought to fruition by the teachings of his master, Frithjof Schuon, according to whose intellectual inspiration and spiritual method he lived faithfully for over sixty of the ninety-six years of his life. To understand what made Lings the man that he was, it is necessary to relate his life and work to that inspiration. The books of Lings are replete with references to Schuon as his principal intellectual source. In the conclusion of the chapter entitled, "The Spirit of the Times", to quote just one telling example, we find Lings writing about the works of Schuon and their significance for the terminal age in which we are living: "We are conscious of all those positive qualities which belong to the end of an age, in particular of a supreme mastery of summing up and of putting everything in its right place. Again and again, about this or about that, one has the impression that Schuon has said the last word."[2]

* * *

The readiness with which Martin Lings makes use of symbols and doctrines from the great spiritual traditions of the world is but the outward intellectual expression of his inward spiritual loyalty to what Frithjof Schuon has called the "underlying religion", religion as such, or the *religio perennis*, summed up

2 *The Eleventh Hour: The Spiritual Crisis of the Modern World in the Light of Tradition and Prophecy* (London: Archetype, 2002), p. 83. The chapter, "The Spirit of the Times", is included in the present volume, pp. 94–120.

in the two elements of discernment between the Real and the illusory, and permanent attachment to the Real. It is his total commitment to this quintessential and timeless spirituality that above all characterizes the life, and by extension, the works of Martin Lings.

Before attempting to separate into clear-cut thematic divisions the unity of Lings' output, we can see a more general twofold division: there are certain works which clearly fall into the category of commentary upon, and introduction to, the writings of Frithjof Schuon and the other writers in the perennialist school; such works as *Ancient Beliefs and Modern Superstitions, Symbol and Archetype,* and *The Eleventh Hour.*[3]

Then there are books which are applications of the principles of the *sophia perennis* to specific delimited fields. Here, we observe his own particular affinities and, indeed, his genius. It is in this category of works that his books have excelled all other comparable works. First and foremost one must refer to his magisterial account of the life of the Prophet Muḥammad,[4] and his very first work, *The Book of Certainty*, a little gem which refracts some of the most essential elements of Sufi gnosis based on traditional Qur'ānic esoteric exegesis.[5] These are accompanied and complemented by his pioneering work on the Qur'ānic art of calligraphy and illumination;[6] by his book on the Shaykh Aḥmad al-ʿAlawī—arguably the finest biography of a Sufi in the English language;[7] by his majestic rendition into English of some of the finest Sufi poetry in the Arabic language;[8] and by a small monograph, *Mecca*, with his personal recollections and reflections on the *Hajj* or Islamic pilgrimage.[9]

[3] For full publication details of the books by Martin Lings, see the Bibliography, pp. 339–40.

[4] *Muhammad: His Life Based on the Earliest Sources.*

[5] Addressed originally to "one or two Egyptian friends", this book was not intended for publication in the West.

[6] *The Qur'ānic Art of Calligraphy and Illumination*; revised and expanded as *Splendours of Qur'ān Calligraphy and Illumination.*

[7] *A Sufi Saint of the Twentieth Century: Shaikh Aḥmad al-ʿAlawī: His Spiritual Heritage and Legacy.*

[8] *Sufi Poems: A Mediaeval Anthology.*

[9] *Mecca: From Before Genesis Until Now.*

His book on Shakespeare[10] and finally his verse, including some translations from Arabic and Lithuanian,[11] and his own poems culled discreetly, almost secretly "upon the edge of man's affairs", decade after decade, revealing his lifelong and profound relation with that "Muse" whom he had conjured in his youth, that he might "make for men some deep enduring utterance".[12]

In addition to his books, Lings was prolific as a contributor to scholarly publications of different kinds, writing articles for the *Encyclopedia of Islam*, the *Encyclopedia Britannica*, the *Cambridge History of Arabic Literature* and many journals. Towards the end of his life he was working on a translation of the Qur'ān, fragments of which have been collected in a posthumous edition.[13]

The apparent duality in a corpus combining perennialist writings with a distinct Islamic production has not failed to puzzle some readers, either among those who are for an exclusively formless esoterism or among the defenders of an exclusivist Islam. The key to the question is again furnished by Lings himself, as he masterfully gives an illuminating nuance to the oft-quoted symbol of the multiple radii connected to the centre of a circle; the different points on the circumference representing so many religious starting-points, the radii representing the mysticisms of the different religions and the centre standing for the Divine Essence: "Our image as a whole reveals clearly the truth that as each mystical path approaches its End, it is nearer to the other mysticisms than it was at the beginning. But there is a complementary and

[10] Originally *Shakespeare in the Light of Sacred Art*; subsequent editions were titled *The Secret of Shakespeare: His Greatest Plays Seen in the Light of Sacred Art*; *The Sacred Art of Shakespeare: To Take Upon Us the Mystery of Things*; and *Shakespeare's Window into the Soul: The Mystical Wisdom in Shakespeare's Characters.*

[11] Some of his translations from Arabic were published early on in the article on "Mystical Poetry" for the *Cambridge History of Arabic Literature* (1990). These were followed and consummated by the publication of *Sufi Poems*. His article on "The Symbolism of the Luminaries in Old Lithuanian Songs" (later a chapter of *Symbol and Archetype*) gave him the opportunity to translate from Lithuanian.

[12] His poetry, at some point hailed by C. S. Lewis as "true poetry" and "sheer inspiration", consists of one small single volume, *Collected Poems.*

[13] *The Holy Qur'ān: Translations of Selected Verses.*

almost paradoxical truth which it cannot reveal, but which it implies by the idea of concentration which it evokes: increase of nearness does not mean decrease of distinctness, for the nearer the centre, the greater the concentration, the stronger the 'dose'."[14]

This interpretation of the image furnishes us with a key for comprehending the Islamic works of our author taken as a whole: whether it be the Qur'ān, the Prophet, Sufi saints, Sufi doctrines—whatever be the subject at hand, his approach always carries the reader from the realm of forms to that of the Essence, from the particular to the Universal, from the symbol to the Archetype. In other words, the esoteric essence is always approached or intimated, by setting in motion a spiritual reverberation that, although starting out from an Islamic form, idea or symbol, always tends towards the essence of this form, and from thence to the Essence as such, which transcends all form. In adopting this mode of exposition, he is being altogether faithful to Schuon's conception of esoterism: "It would be completely false to believe that gnosis within a given religion presents itself as a foreign and superadded doctrine; on the contrary, that which in each religion provides the key for total or non-dualist esoterism is not some secret concept of a heterogeneous character, but it is the very presiding idea of the religion...".[15]

To the question that could have arisen: what can be added to Schuon's writings?, the books of Martin Lings themselves give an answer: faithful adherence to the principles enunciated, on the one hand, and creative application of these principles, on the other. We sense in the books of Martin Lings the imprint of his own unmistakable, elegant style, a certain flavour or taste (*dhawq*), bespeaking a particular spirit or inspiration. Reading his books, one is struck both by the unshakable certitude that pervades them, and by the almost tangible sense of the author's own effacement in the truths he so eloquently articulates. There is in his writings an intellectual power delivered with a certain lightness of touch; the books express in their own way that combination of spiritual authority and profound humility that so distinctly marked his personality, and so deeply

[14] *What is Sufism?* (Cambridge, UK: Islamic Texts Society, 1993), pp. 21–22.

[15] *Esoterism as Principle and as Way* (Bedfont: Perennial Books, 1981), pp. 25–-26.

impressed itself upon all those who came within the sphere of his guidance. We have elaborated on this master-disciple relation elsewhere,[16] and we shall thus now limit ourselves to an overview of the current volume.

* * *

As regards the selection and arrangement of the material in this volume, heartfelt thanks go to my esteemed collaborators in this project, Emma Clark and Juan Acevedo. The first essay in the anthology, "Oneness of Being", remains to this day—despite the many works connected with this subject that have appeared in the decades since the book was written—an unsurpassed distillation of the essence of this doctrine, associated with Ibn al-ʿArabī. Seyyed Hossein Nasr, in his lectures on Sufism, continues to refer to this chapter as the best summary of *waḥdat al-wujūd* in any western language. In the course of disabusing orientalists like Massignon and Nicholson of their various misconceptions on this score, Lings boldly claims that *waḥdat al-wujūd* is nothing short of "the Supreme Truth and therefore the ultimate goal of all mysticism".[17] He cites illuminating parallels to the Sufi formulations from diverse traditions, parallels which demonstrate, objectively, the true universality of this perspective, and which deepen, subjectively, one's orientation towards this "Supreme Truth".[18]

Under "Hermeneutics" we find some samples of Lings' mastery of the science of symbolism. In 1995 the first English edition of René Guénon's *Fundamental Symbols of Sacred Science* was published under the supervision of our author, who in his own writings, like *Symbol & Archetype*, seems to establish a bridge between the formal, objective approach to symbols and the more Schuonian approach where penetration into symbols is inextricably woven into the depths of the soul with a view to spiritual realisation.

[16] "*Martin Lings–The Sanctity of Sincerity*", originally a lecture at the Royal Asiatic Society, London, on 30 November 2009, and an ensuing article published in the *Temenos Academy Review*, 14 (both audio and printable text are available online from The Matheson Trust website).

[17] *A Sufi Saint of the Twentieth Century* (Cambridge, UK: Islamic Texts Society, 1993), p. 126.

[18] Thus we find Lao Tzu, Chuang Tzu, Angelus Silesius, D.T. Suzuki and Meister Eckhart cited alongside Hallāj, al-Ghazālī and al-Balyānī.

"Tradition and Modernity" includes works expounding an acute critique of modernity, and more particularly of the psyche of "fallen" man. This is of course closely related to the following section, "Traditional Psychology", where we get a glimpse of Lings' uncanny insights into that modern mind, and its struggles along the Lesser Mysteries so aptly portrayed in Shakespeare's works. In fact, it was Lings' fate to be a spiritual director for decades, guiding along the path of Sufism generations of seekers, and this section of the book reveals a little of this facet of his personality.

The section on "Islam", which, in line with the above quotations means also, naturally, Sufism, covers a wide range of interests. There are two complementary visions of Sufism: the biographical, through the portrait of Shaykh al-ᶜAlawī, and the more theoretical, explaining some basics of the Sufi path, the specialised introduction to the meanings of Qur'ānic calligraphy and illumination, and the lively narrative pages of the life of the Prophet. About the latter, and taking only one among many glowing reviews: "In reading Lings' *Muhammad*, we detect an alchemical effect in his narration and composition which so evenly combines scholarly accuracy with poetic passion. Lings is a scholar poet…".[19]

It is interesting to note that the final "Art and Poetry" section owes part of its rich texture to the fact that Lings was accomplished not only as a gardener, but also as a musician and as a stage director: working as a university lecturer in Cairo for many years, he had the opportunity to produce many of Shakespeare's plays with his students, thus gaining an intimate and very practical understanding which would eventually inform his lectures and work on Shakespeare.

It is our hope that readers will appreciate and benefit from the many internal echoing passages in the anthology, some of which are marked as cross-references in the footnotes, but most of which contribute to the inner cohesion of the corpus and testify discreetly to that "close-knit integration" mentioned above.

* * *

[19] Reviewed in *Hamdard Islamicus*, volume VII, no. 1.

Quite in the spirit of Guénon, Coomaraswamy and Schuon, Martin Lings was not concerned with his own biography. If, as Schuon has said, the Way is the path "from natural hypocrisy to spiritual sincerity", we might say that Lings was one who had undertaken that journey and, by the grace of God, reached its end. He had become truly holy, or "whole". Wholeness is etymologically connected to, and ontologically inseparable from, "holiness", Lings reminds us. Such considerations rightly throw into the background all biographical details, lending to the vicissitudes of life in this world a dreamlike quality. It cannot be otherwise, for Lings was a man of awakening whose poetry was "not written with ink but with the heart's blood".[20] Let us instead conclude by recourse to his own words, as he draws his Self-Portrait:[21]

Self-Portrait

Orpheus with his music made
The mountains tremble; he could persuade
The wind to veer, the earth to unfreeze,
The sap to rise up in the trees;
The waters, every living thing
Followed, to hear him play and sing.
But my soul from the dark pall
Of future ages he could not call,
That I might hear his minstrelsy:
The sticks and stones danced, but not I.

Nor was I with the dance possessed
When Indra with his dancers blessed
That land whose jungles are the haunt
Of tiger, peacock, elephant.
They came, their sacred art to unfold:
I was not present to behold
Those movements by no man invented,
To hear those ankle-bells new-minted
In Heaven, resound, as heavenly feet
With rhythmic step the earth did greet.

[20] From his own preface to *Collected Poems: Revised and Augmented* (London: Archetype, 2002), p. 9.

[21] *Ibid.*, pp. 51–53. For an analysis of this poem, see our *Martin Lings: The Sanctity of Sincerity.*

I saw not Rama: and I missed
The sight of Radha, to her tryst
Stealing at dusk for her Divine
Beloved. No; it was not mine
To share that beauty, that holiness,
Together my two hands to press in reverence, not mine to hear
What made five senses each an ear,
Thrilled every tree from crown to root,
The purity of Krishna's flute.

The sacrament I did not take
From the priest-king Melchizedek,
Nor stood I by that sacred well
With Abraham and Ishmael
In the Arabian wilderness,
Prayed not with them that valley to bless,
Stone on stone laid not, that house to build
Wherewith their prayers have been fulfilled.

I saw not Joseph in his glory;
I tell, but witnessed not, his story:
His brothers' guilt, how they did crave
Forgiveness and how he forgave,
And Jacob, Leah, all bowed down,
Eleven planets, sun and moon.
Their progeny scarce dared to glance
At Moses' dazzling countenance
When of the Burning Bush he told.
For me there was no need to hold
My lids half-shut: time was my veil,
Nor can I leap our nature's pale
To span the years with backward wing,
That I might hear the Psalmist sing,
Or gaze with Solomon entranced,
While Sheba's queen before him danced.

Years passed, but still beyond my reach
It was, to hear the Buddha preach,
And when he held up silently
That flower, he gave it not to me.

Of all the guests less than the least
I was not to that marriage feast
Bidden, at Cana in Galilee.

I did not hear, I did not see
The words and looks that passed between
The son and mother: she serene,
Gently prevailing, and he stirred
Infinitely deep, by the deep word
She uttered. But I dare surmise
That wine enough was in their eyes:
Wine upon wine those guests drank then.
Could any be the same again?

When half a thousand years and more
Had passed, and men allegiance swore
To the Arab Prophet, beneath the tree,
My willing hand was still not free
From bonds of time and space to be
Between his hands in fealty.

Such blessings missed, time was when I
Within myself would wonder why,
Half quarrelling with the book of fate
For having writ me down so late.
But now I no longer my lot
Can question, and of what was not.
No more I say: Would it had been!
For I have seen what I have seen,
And I have heard what I have heard.
So if to tears ye see me stirred,
Presume not that they spring from woe:
In thankful wonderment they flow.
Praise be to Him, the Lord, the King,
Who gives beyond all reckoning.

Reza Shah-Kazemi

METAPHYSICS

Oneness of Being

"Since Mysticism in all ages and countries is fundamentally the same, however it may be modified by its peculiar environment and by the positive religion to which it clings for support, we find remote and unrelated systems showing an extraordinarily close likeness and even coinciding in many features of verbal expression.... Many writers on Sufism have disregarded this principle; hence the confusion which long prevailed."

In the light of this timely remark by Nicholson,[1] no one should be surprised to find that the doctrine of the Oneness of Being (*Waḥdat al-Wujūd*), which holds a central place in all the orthodox mysticisms of Asia, holds an equally central place in Sufism.

As is to be expected in view of its centrality, some of the most perfect, though elliptical, formulations of this doctrine are to be found in the Qur'ān, which affirms expressly: *Wheresoe'er ye turn, there is the Face of God.*[2] *Everything perisheth but His Face.*[3] *All that is therein*[4] *suffereth extinction, and there remaineth the Face of thy Lord in Its Majesty and Bounty.*[5]

Creation, which is subject to time and space and non-terrestrial modes of duration and extent which the human imagination cannot grasp, is "then" (with reference to both past and future) and "there", but it is never truly "now" and "here". The True Present is the prerogative of God Alone, for It is no less than the Eternity and Infinity which transcends, penetrates and embraces all durations and extents, being not only "before" all beginnings but also "after" all ends. In It, that is, in the Eternal Now and Infinite Here, all that is perishable has "already"

[1] *A Literary History of the Arabs*, p. 384.

[2] II, 115.

[3] XXVIII, 88.

[4] In the created universe.

[5] LV, 26–7.

perished, all that is liable to extinction has "already" been extinguished leaving only God, and it is to this Divine Residue, the Sole Lord of the Present, that the word *remaineth* refers in the last quoted Qur'ānic verse. From this verse, amongst others, come the two Sufi terms *fanā'* (extinction) and *baqā'* (remaining)[6] which express respectively the Saint's extinction in God and his Eternal Life in God, or rather *as* God.

The doctrine of Oneness of Being is also implicit in the Divine Name *al-Ḥaqq*, the Truth, the Reality, for there could be no point in affirming Reality as an essential characteristic of Godhead if anything other than God were real. The word "Being" expresses this Absolute Reality, for it refers to That which is, as opposed to that which is not, and Oneness of Being is the doctrine that behind the illusory veil of created plurality there lies the one Divine Truth—not that God is made up of parts,[7] but that underlying each apparently separate feature of the created universe there is the One Infinite Plenitude of God in His Indivisible Totality.

The Treatise on Oneness[8] says: "When the secret of an atom of the atoms is clear, the secret of all created things both

[6] "The spiritual state of *baqā'*, to which Sufi contemplatives aspire (the word signifies pure 'subsistence' beyond all form), is the same as the state of *moksha* or 'deliverance' spoken of in Hindu doctrines, just as the 'extinction' (*al-fanā'*) of the individuality which precedes the 'subsistence' is analogous to *nirvana* taken as a negative idea" (Titus Burckhardt, *An Introduction to Sufi Doctrine*, p. 4, published by Muḥammad Ashraf, Lahore, 1959—a book which is almost indispensable to anyone who wishes to make a serious study of Sufism and who does not read Oriental texts).

[7] It is probably a failure to grasp this point which is at the root of most Western misunderstandings. Massignon for example says that *Waḥdat al-Wujūd*—which he unhappily translates "existentialist monism"—means that "the totality of all beings in all their actions is divinely adorable" (Encyclopaedia of Islam, *Taṣawwuf*). But there is no question here of the *sum* of things being any more divine than each single thing. The least gnat has a secret which is divinely adorable with total adoration. In other words, for those possessed of mystical vision, *there is the Face of God.*

[8] *Risālatu 'l-Aḥadiyyah*, also entitled *Kitāb al-Ajwibah* or *Kitāb al-Alif*. It is ascribed in some manuscripts to Muḥyi 'l-Dīn Ibn ʿArabī and in others to his younger contemporary ʿAbd Allāh al-Balyānī (d. 1287—see the prefatory notes to the French translation by ʿAbd al-Hādī in *Le Voile d'Isis*, 1933, pp. 13–4, and to the English translation by Weir, from which I quote, in the *Journal to the Royal Asiatic Society*, 1901, p. 809). It is one of the most important of all Sufi treatises. Hence the large number of existing manuscripts, although until now it has only been published in translations.

external and internal is clear, and thou dost not see in this world or the next aught beside God."[9]

If there were anything which, in the Reality of the Eternal Present, could show itself to be other than God, then God would not be Infinite, for Infinity would consist of God *and* that particular thing.[10]

This doctrine is only concerned with Absolute Reality. It has nothing to do with "reality" in the current sense, that is, with lesser, relative truths which the Sufis call "metaphorical". Ghazālī says: "The Gnostics rise from the lowlands of metaphor to the peak of Verity; and at the fulfilment of their ascent they see directly face to face that there is naught in existence save only God and that *everything perisheth but His Face,* not simply that it perisheth at any given time but that it hath never not perished.... Each thing hath two faces, a face of its own, and a face of its Lord; in respect of its own face it is nothingness, and in respect of the Face of God it is Being. Thus there is nothing in existence save only God and His Face, for *everything perisheth but His Face,* always and forever... so that the Gnostics need not wait for the Resurrection in order to hear the summons of the Creator proclaim: *Unto whom this day is the Kingdom?*

[9] We may compare the following Buddhist formulation: "When a blade of grass is lifted the whole universe is revealed there; in every pore of the skin there pulsates the life of the triple world, and this is intuited by *prajna*, not by way of reasoning, but "immediately". (D. T. Suzuki, *Studies in Zen*, p. 94.)

[10] This is implicit in the following formulation of *Waḥdat al-Wujūd* by Al-Ḥallāj, who literally takes the ground from beneath the feet of those who accuse the Sufis of localizing God (*ḥulūl*): "It is Thou that hast filled all 'where' and beyond 'where' too. Where art Thou then?" (*Dīwān*, p. 46, 1.4.)

The Shaykh Al-ʿAlawī quotes at some length (*Al-Nāṣir Maʿrūf*, pp. 112–5) Muḥammad ʿAbduh's formulations of the doctrine in question from pt. 2 of his *Wāridāt*, ending with the words: "Do not think that this is a doctrine of localization, for there can be no localization without two beings, one of which occupieth a place in the other, whereas our doctrine is: 'There is no being but His Being.'"

Over 2000 years previously the Taoist Chuang Tzu had said: "A boat may be hidden in a creek; a net may be hidden in a lake; these may be said to be safe enough. But at midnight a strong man may come and carry them away on his back. The ignorant do not see that no matter how well you conceal things, smaller ones in larger ones, there will always be a chance for them to escape. But if you conceal Universe in Universe, there will be no room left for it to escape. This is the great truth of things" (ch. 6, Yu-Lan Fung's translation).

Unto God, the One, the Irresistible,[11] for this proclamation is eternally in their ears; nor do they understand from His Utterance *God is Most Great* (*Allāhu Akbar*) that he is greater than others. God forbid! For there is nothing other than Himself in all existence, and therefore there is no term of comparison for His Greatness".[12]

This doctrine is necessarily present whenever there is explicit reference to the Supreme Truth—the Absolute, the Infinite, the Eternal. In Christianity the goal of mysticism is most often conceived of as union with the Second Person of the Trinity. Here the Supreme Truth is not explicit but implicit: who has Christ has indeed All; but for those who follow the path of love this Totality is not usually the direct object of fervour. Yet when it is conceived more directly, then in Christianity also[13] we find inevitably the doctrine of the Oneness of Being.

On the other hand, when the Supreme Truth recedes into the background, then in all religions this doctrine also necessarily recedes, since apart from the Infinite and Eternal Present it is meaningless. No one can hope to understand the formulations of the mystics without bearing in mind that there is liable to be a continual shifting of the centre of consciousness from one plane to another.

One of the first things that a novice has to do in the ʿAlawī Ṭarīqah—and the same must be true of other paths of mysticism—is to unlearn much of the agility of "profane intelligence" which an ʿAlawī faqīr once likened, for my benefit, to "the antics of a monkey that is chained to a post", and to acquire an agility of a different order, comparable to that of a bird which continually changes the level of its flight. The Qur'ān and secondarily the Traditions of the Prophet are the great prototypes in Islam of this versatility.

Three distinct levels of intelligence are imposed methodically twice a day in the three formulae of the ʿAlawī rosary which are (each being repeated a hundred times) firstly asking

[11] Qur'ān, XL, 16.

[12] *Mishkāt al-Anwār*, pp. 113–4 in *Al-Jawāhir al-Ghawālī* (Cairo, 1343 AH); in Gairdner's translation, which however I have not followed, pp. 103–5.

[13] "However vile the dust, however small its motes, the wise man seeth therein God in all His Greatness and Glory." (Angelus Silesius, *Cherubinischer Wandersmann*).

forgiveness of God, secondly the invocation of blessings on the Prophet, and thirdly the affirmation of Divine Oneness.[14] The first standpoint, which is at what might be called the normal level of psychic perception, is concerned with the ego as such. This is the phase of purification. From the second standpoint this fragmentary ego has ceased to exist, for it has been absorbed into the person of the Prophet who represents a hierarchy of different plenitudes of which the lowest is integral human perfection and the highest is Universal Man (*Al-Insān al-Kāmil*),[15] who personifies the whole created universe and who thus anticipates, as it were, the Infinite,[16] of which he is the highest symbol. The disciple aims at concentrating on perfection at one of these levels. From the third point of view the Prophet himself has ceased to exist, for this formula is concerned with nothing but the Divine Oneness.

All mysticism necessarily comprises these different levels of thought, because it is, by definition, the passage from the finite to the Infinite. It has a starting point and an End, and cannot ignore what lies between. It follows that the formulations of any one mystic are unlikely to be all from the same standpoint,[17] and this is especially true of the more sponta-

[14] According to Ḥasan ibn ʿAbd al-ʿAzīz, one of the Shaykh's disciples, this triple rosary is used in all branches of the Shādhilī Ṭarīqah (*Irshād al-Rāghibīn*, p. 31). The same formulae are also used, with some variations, by many branches of the Qādirī Ṭarīqah and others. See Rinn, *Marabouts et Khouan*, pp. 183–4, 252–3, 441, 503.

[15] See Titus Burckhardt's introduction to his *De l'Homme Universel* (translated extracts from Jīlī's *Al-Insān al-Kāmil*), P. Derain, Lyons, 1953.

[16] The first formula of the rosary may also open on to the Infinite, but in a negative sense, for the end of purification is extinction (*fanā'*). The Shaykh Al-ʿAlawī often quotes the saying attributed to Rābiʿah al-ʿAdawiyyah, one of the greatest women Saints of Islam (d. 801): "Thine existence is a sin with which no other sin can be compared" (*Minaḥ*, p. 41). It is this point of view which Al-Ḥallāj expresses in the words: "Between me and Thee is an 'I am' which tormenteth me. O take, by Thine Own *I am*, mine from between us" (*Akhbār Al-Ḥallāj*, Massignon's edition, no. 50).

[17] The refusal to see that mysticism is never a "system" and that mystics are consciously and methodically "inconsistent", taking now one standpoint, now another, has led to much confusion, especially as regards *Waḥdat al-Wujūd*. In his preface to his translation of *Mishkāt al-Anwār* (p. 61). Gairdner says: "The root question in regard to al-Ghazzali, and every other advanced mystic and adept in Islam, is the question of Pantheism (i.e. *Waḥdat al-Wujūd*, now usually translated, with some advantage, 'monism'): did he succeed in balancing himself upon the edge of the pantheistic abyss?... Or did he fail in

neous utterances such as those of poetry. But it is natural that spiritual Masters should stress *Waḥdat al-Wujūd* above all, because it is the Supreme Truth and therefore the ultimate goal of all mysticism, and also because, for that very reason, it is the point of view that is "furthest" from the disciple and the one he most needs help in adopting. Relentless insistence upon the doctrine has therefore a great methodic, not to say "hypnotic" value,[18] for it helps the disciple to place himself virtually in the Eternal Present when he cannot do so actually. *The Treatise on Oneness* says: "Our discourse (that is, the formulation of Oneness of Being) is with him who hath resolution and energy in seeking to know himself in order to know God, and who keepeth fresh in his Heart the image of his quest and his longing for attainment unto God; it is not with him who hath neither aim nor end."

It has been remarked—I forget by whom—that many of those who delight in the poems of ʿUmar ibn al-Fāriḍ and Jalāl ad-Dīn al-Rūmī would recoil from them if they really under-

this?" Massignon, for his part, has devoted much of his output to exculpating Al-Ḥallāj from the "unorthodoxy" in question, that is, to pinning him down to the dualism expressed in certain of his verses, and turning a blind eye to his affirmations of the Oneness of Being, or in other words denying that he ever made the transcension from what Ghazālī calls the metaphor of union (*ittiḥād*) to the truth of the realization of the Oneness (*tawḥīd—Mishkāt*, p. 115). Nicholson pleads for Ibn al-Fāriḍ (*Studies in Islamic Mysticism*, pp. 193–4). Gairdner, feeling that Ghazālī is in great "danger", pleads for him and by charitable extension for all other Muslim mystics on the grounds that they do not mean what they say! (*Ibid.*, pp. 62–3). The truth is that all the Sufis are "dualist" or "pluralist" at lower levels; but it is impossible that any of them should have believed that at the highest level there is anything other than the Divine Oneness, for though the Qur'ān changes the plane of its utterance more often even than the Sufis themselves, it is absolutely and inescapably explicit as regards the Eternal that *all things perish but His Face* and *all that is therein suffereth extinction, and there remaineth the Face of thy Lord in Its Majesty and Bounty*. This last word is a reminder that for the Sufis Oneness of Being is That in which there is no loss but only pure gain or, otherwise expressed, That in which all that was ever lost is found again in Infinite and Eternal Perfection. Therefore let those who shrink from this doctrine as a "pantheistic abyss" or what Nicholson calls "blank infinite negation" ask themselves if they really understand it.

[18] When Ibn ʿArabī for example criticizes some of the formulations of his great predecessors, such as Junayd and Al-Ḥallāj, as regards the Supreme State, it is clearly not because he thought that they had not attained to that State, but because the formulations in question are not sufficiently rigorous to be, in his opinion, methodically effective.

stood their deeper meaning. The truth is that if the author of this remark and Western scholars in general really understood the deeper meaning of such poetry, that is, if they really understood the doctrine of the Oneness of Being, they would cease to recoil from it. Massignon attacks it because it seems to him to deny both the Transcendence of God and the immortality of the soul. Yet in affirming the Transcendence and immortality in question he implicitly affirms the Oneness of Being. The difference between him and the Sufis is that he does not follow up his belief to its imperative conclusions, but stops half way. For if it be asked: "Why is the soul immortal?", the answer lies in Meister Eckhardt's "There is something in the soul which is uncreated and uncreatable.... This is the Intellect." The soul is not merely immortal but Eternal, not in its psychism but in virtue of the Divine Spark that is in it. The Shaykh Al-ᶜAlawī says in one of his poems: "Thou seest not who thou art, for thou art, yet art not 'thou'," and he quotes more than once Shushtarī's lines:

> After extinction I came out, and I
> Eternal now am, though not as I.
> Yet who am I, O I, but I?[19]

As to the Divine Transcendence, I will leave him to show that far from denying It, the doctrine of the Oneness of Being comes nearer than any other doctrine to doing justice to It.

Massignon writes[20] that this doctrine was first formulated by Ibn ᶜArabī. It may be that the term *Waḥdat al-Wujūd* was not generally used before his day, but the doctrine itself was certainly uppermost in the minds of his predecessors, and the more the question is studied the further it recedes along a purely Islamic line of descent. The already quoted passage in Ghazālī's *Mishkāt al-Anwār* is closely followed up by: "There is no he but He, for 'he' expresseth that unto which reference is made, and there can be no reference at all save only unto Him, for whenever thou makest a reference, that reference is unto Him even though thou knewest it not through thine ignorance of the Truth of Truths.... Thus 'there is no god but God' is the

[19] *Wa-man anā yā anā illā anā.*

[20] Encyclopaedia of Islam, *Taṣawwuf.*

generality's proclamation of Unity, and 'there is no he but He' is that of the elect, for the former is more general, whereas the latter is more elect, more all-embracing, truer, more exact, and more operative in bringing him who useth it into the Presence of Unalloyed Singleness and Pure Oneness."[21]

The Shaykh Al-ʿAlawī quotes[22] from the end the *Manāzil as-Sā'irīn* of ʿAbd Allāh al-Harawī (d. AD 1088) with regard to the third and highest degree of *Tawḥīd*: "None affirmeth truly the Oneness of God, for whoso affirmeth It thereby setteth himself in contradiction with It.... He, He is the affirmation of His Oneness, and whoso presumeth to describe Him blasphemeth (by creating a duality through the intrusion of his own person)".

This recalls the almost identical saying of Al-Ḥallāj (d. AD 922): "Whoso claimeth to affirm God's Oneness thereby setteth up another beside him."[23] Al-Kharrāz, in his *Book of Truthfulness*, quotes the Companion Abū ʿUbaidah (d. AD 639) as having said: "I have never looked at a single thing without God being nearer to me than it."[24]

Only one who stops short at the outer shell of words could maintain that there is a real difference between this and the following more analytical formulation from the thirteenth century *Treatise on Oneness*: "If a questioner ask: 'Supposing we see refuse or carrion, for example, wilt thou say that it is God?', the answer is: 'God in his Exaltation forbid that He should be any such thing! Our discourse is with him who doth not see the carrion to be carrion or the refuse to be refuse; our discourse is with him who hath insight (*baṣīrah*) and is not altogether blind."[25]

[21] pp. 117–18. Although written at the end of Ghazālī's life (he died in AD 1111), this treatise is about 100 years earlier than Ibn ʿArabī's *Fuṣūṣ al-Ḥikam*.

[22] *Al-Nāṣir Maʿrūf*, p. 99.

[23] *Akhbār*, no. 49.

[24] Arabic text, p. 59; Arberry's translation, p. 48.

[25] We may compare the following third century BC formulation: "asked Chuang Tzu: 'Where is the so-called *Tao*?' Chuang Tzu said: 'Everywhere.' The former said: 'Specify an instance of it.' 'It is in the ant.' 'How can *Tao* be anything so low?' 'It is in the panic grass.' 'How can it be still lower.'... 'It is in excrement.' To this Tung Kuo Tzu made no reply. Chuang Tzu said: 'Your question does not touch the fundamentals of *Tao*. You should not specify any particular thing. There is not a single thing without *Tao*.'" (Chuang Tzu, ch. XXII, Yu-Lan Fung's translation).

Al-Kharrāz's quotation, made about AD 850, spans the first two centuries of Islam with the Qur'ānic doctrine of Nearness–Identity–Oneness. We have seen that in the early Meccan Surahs the highest saints are referred to as the *Near*, and that what the Qur'ān means by "nearness" is defined by the words *We are nearer to him than his jugular vein.* In the following already quoted Holy Tradition this nearness is expressed as identity: "My slave seeketh unremittingly to draw nigh unto Me with devotions of his free will until I love him; and when I love him, I am the Hearing wherewith he heareth and the Sight wherewith he seeth and the Hand wherewith he smiteth and the Foot whereon he walketh." It cannot be concluded from this Tradition that this identity was not already there, for the Divinity is not subject to change. The "change" in question is simply that what was not perceived has now been perceived.[26] These two levels of perception are both referred to in the verse: *We are nearer to him than ye are, although ye see not.*[27] The lower of these two is perception of the merely relative reality of God's absence which is pure illusion in the face of the Absolute Reality of His Presence. For there is no question of relative nearness here. *We are nearer to him than his jugular vein* and *God cometh in between a man and his own heart*[28] mean that He is nearer to him than he is to his inmost self. The Oneness here expressed exceeds the oneness of union.

It may be convenient for certain theories to suppose that these flashes of Qur'ānic lightning passed unperceived over the heads of the Companions, and that they were only noticed by later generations; but is it good psychology? No men have been more "men of one book" than the Companions were, and there is every reason to believe that no generation of Islam has ever surpassed them in weighing the phrases of that book and in giving each one its due of consideration. They would have been the last people on earth to suppose that the Qur'ān ever meant *less* than it said. This does not mean that they would necessarily have interpreted as formulations of Oneness of Being all those Qur'ānic verses which the Sufis so interpret, for

[26] It has been perceived only because the agent of perception is God, not the mystic. "I am ... his Sight", or to use the Qur'ānic phrase: *The sight overtaketh Him not, but He overtaketh the sight* (VI, 103).

[27] LVI, 85.

[28] VIII, 24.

some of these verses admit more readily of other interpretations. But there are some which do not. If we take, for example, in addition to the already quoted formulations of "Nearness", the verse: *He is the First and the Last and the Outwardly Manifest and the Inwardly Hidden,*[29] it is difficult to conceive how the Companions would have understood these words other than in the sense of Ghazālī's, "there is no object of reference other than He", though they may never have formulated the truth in question except with the words of the Qur'ān itself, or with expressions such as Abū ʿUbaidah's: "I have never looked at a single thing without God being nearer to me than it," or the Prophet's: "Thou art the Outwardly Manifest and there is nothing covering Thee."[30]

[29] Qur'ān, LVII, 3.

[30] Muslim, *Daʿwāt*, 16; Tirmidhī, *Daʿwāt*, 19. This is not incompatible with other Traditions in which he speaks of "veils" between man and God. It is simply a question of two different points of view, the one being absolute and the other relative.

The Symbolism of the Letters of the Alphabet

The Shaykh mentions, as we have seen, the reeds of which a mat is woven as symbols of the Manifestations of the Divine Qualities out of which the whole universe is woven. We find a somewhat analogous but more complex symbolism in his little treatise *The Book of the Unique Archetype* (*Al-Unmūdhaj al-Farīd*) *which signalleth the way unto the full realization of Oneness in considering what is meant by the envelopment of the Heavenly Scriptures in the Point of the Basmalah.*[1]

He begins by quoting two sayings of the Prophet: "'All that is in the revealed Books is in the Qur'ān, and all that is in the Qur'ān is in the *Fātiḥah*,[2] and all that is in the *Fātiḥah* is in *Bismi 'Llāhi 'l-Raḥmāni 'l-Raḥīm*' and 'All that is in *Bismi 'Llāhi 'l-Raḥmāni 'l-Raḥīm* is in the letter *Bā'*, which itself is contained in the point that is beneath it.'[3]

"This Tradition[4] hath been bandied about from pen to pen, and sounded in the ears of the elect and generality, so that one and all they endeavour to probe its hidden mysteries. Nor had I the strength to stand aloof from the throng, which had fired the spirit of emulation within me, so I rose to my feet and groped for a snatch of some of its fragrance. My hands fell on the perfume at its very source, and I brought it out from among the hillocks of the dunes, and came with it before the wisest of

[1] The formula *Bismi 'Llāhi 'l-Raḥmāni 'l-Raḥīm* (literally "In the Name of God, the All-Merciful, the Merciful") with which the Qur'ān opens. Its "point" is the dot under the letter Bā'.

[2] The first chapter of the Qur'ān (literally "the Opening").

[3] These Traditions are quoted by ʿAbd al-Karīm al-Jīlī at the beginning of his commentary on them, *Al-Kahf wa 'l-Raqīm*, which was almost certainly the starting point of the Shaykh's treatise.

[4] Presumably he is referring to both Traditions. In the Arabic this preamble is in rhymed prose, from which the Shaykh is seldom far away in any of his writings.

the learned. They received it with all honour and magnification, and each one said: *This is none other than a noble Angel.*[5] I said: 'Indeed, it is above my station. It is the throw of a stone without a thrower.' Then the tongue of my state answered, and said: *Thou threwest not when thou threwest, but it was God that threw.*[6]

"Whenever, in this treatise, I mention one of the names of 'other than God', that is on account of the needs of expression. So let not thine imagination conceive 'the other' as being truly other, for then wouldst thou miss the good I am seeking to show thee. For verily we bring thee *great tidings*.[7] Incline then unto that through which thou mayest be o'erwhelmed in the Reality, and go thou forth from the relative unto the Absolute. Perchance thou wilt understand what is in the Point, though *none understandeth it save the wise*[8] *and none meeteth it face to face save him whose destined portion is immeasurably blessed*...[9]

"Whenever I speak of the Point I mean the Secret of the Essence which is named the Oneness of Perception (*Waḥdat al-Shuhūd*), and whenever I speak of the *Alif* I mean the One Who Alone *is* (*Wāḥid al-Wujūd*),[10] the Essence Dominical, and whenever I speak of the *Bā'* I mean the ultimate[11] Manifestation which is termed the Supreme Spirit, after which come the rest of the letters, then single words, then speech in general, all in hierarchy. But the pivot of this book turneth upon the first

[5] Said by the women of Egypt (Qur'ān, XII, 31) with reference to Joseph. [See p. 176, n. 74 of this volume.—Ed.].

[6] In the Qur'ān (VIII, 17) these words are addressed to Muḥammad with reference to his throwing a handful of gravel at the enemy during the Battle of Badr, an act which changed the tide of the battle in favour of the Muslims, who completely defeated a Meccan army three times as large as theirs. This was the first battle of Islam, AD 624.

[7] XXXVIII, 67.

[8] XXIX, 43.

[9] XLI, 35.

[10] It is here that he diverges from Jīlī, in whose treatise the Point stands for the Divinity in All Its Aspects, whereas the *Alif* is the Spirit of Muḥammad (Jīlī quotes the Tradition: "God created the Spirit of the Prophet from His Essence, and from that Spirit He created the entire Universe") that is, the Supreme Spirit, which for the Shaykh is symbolized by the *Bā'*. But beneath this divergence the doctrine remains the same.

[11] Ultimate, because this Spirit, which is none other than "Universal Man", contains the whole Universe.

letters of the alphabet on account of their precedence over the others. *The Foremost are the Foremost, it is they who are brought nigh.*[12] These are *Alif* and *Bā'*, and they hold in the Alphabet the place that is held by the *Basmalah* in the Qur'ān, for together they make up *Ab*[13] which is one of the Divine Names. By it would Jesus speak unto His Lord, and he used it when he said: 'Verily I go unto my Father and your Father,' that is, unto my Lord and your Lord. And now, if thou understandest that these two letters have a meaning that thou knewest not, be not amazed at what we shall say of the Point, and the rest of the letters.

"The Point was in its hidden-treasurehood[14] before its manifestation of itself as *Alif,* and the letters were obliterate in its secret essence until it manifested the inward outwardly, revealing what had been veiled from sight by donning the various forms of the visible letters; but if thou graspest the truth, thou wilt find naught there but the ink itself, which is what is meant by the Point,[15] even as one of us hath said:

> The letters are the signs of the ink; there is not one,
> Save what the ink hath anointed; their own colour is pure illusion.
> The *ink's* colour it is that hath come into manifest being.
> Yet it cannot be said that the ink hath departed from what it was.
> The inwardness of the letters lay in the ink's mystery,
> And their outward show is through its self-determination.
> They are its determinations, its activities,
> And naught is there but it. Understand thou the parable!
> They are not it; say not, say not that they are it!
> To say so were wrong, and to say 'it is they' were raving

[12] Qur'ān, LVI, 10–1.

[13] Father. It may be noted here incidentally how close the *Basmalah* is in reality to the *In Nomine*. The relationship between the two Names of Mercy in Islam, of which the second only is both Divine and human, is comparable to the relationship between the first two Persons of the Christian Trinity, while the Mercy Itself which is implied in the *Basmalah,* being from both *Al-Raḥmān* and *Al-Raḥīm*, that is, "proceeding from the Father and the Son", is none other than the Holy Ghost.

[14] Referring to the Holy Tradition: "I was a Hidden Treasure and I wished to be known; and so I created the world."

[15] The point and the ink are interchangeable as symbols in that writing is made up of a series of points of ink.

madness.
For it was before the letters, when no letter was;
And it remaineth, when no letter at all shall be.
Look well at each letter: thou seest it hath already perished
But for the face of the ink, that is, for the Face of His Essence,
Unto Whom All Glory and Majesty and Exaltation!
Even thus the letters, for all their outward show, are hidden,
Being overwhelmed by the ink, since their show is none other than its.
The letter addeth naught to the ink, and taketh naught from it,
But revealeth its integrality in various modes,
Without changing the ink. Do ink and letter together make two?
Realize then the truth of my words: no being is there
Save that of the ink, for him whose understanding is sound;
And wheresoe'er be the letter, there with it is always its ink.
Open thine intellect unto these parables and heed them!'[16]

"If thou hast understood how all the letters are engulfed in the Point, then wilt thou understand how all the books are engulfed in the sentence, the sentence in the word, the word in the letter, for we can say with truth: no letter, no word, and no word, no book. The word hath indeed no existence save through the existence of the letter. Analytical differentiation proceedeth from synthetic integration, and all is integrated in the Oneness of Perception which is symbolized by the Point. This is *the Mother* of every book. *God effaceth and confirmeth what He will,* and *with Him is the Mother of the Book.*[17]

"The Point is essentially different from the letters. *There is naught like unto Him and He is the Hearer, the Seer.*[18] Even so the Point, unlike the other signs, is not subject to the limitation of being defined. It transcendeth all that is to be found in the letters by way of length and shortness and protuberance, so that the sense cannot grasp it either visually or aurally as it graspeth the letters. Its difference from them is understood, but its presence in them is unknown save unto him whose sight *is like iron*[19] *or who giveth ear with full intelligence,*[20] for although the letters are its qualities, the Quality encompasseth not the

[16] ʿAbd al-Ghanī al-Nābulusī, *Dīwān al-ḥaqā'iq*, p. 435 (Cairo, 1889).

[17] Qur'ān, XIII, 39.

[18] XLII, 11.

[19] An echo of L, 22.

[20] L, 37.

Essence, not having the universality which is the Essence's own. The Essence hath incomparability as Its prerogative whereas the Qualities create comparisons.

"And yet to make a comparison is in reality the same as affirming incomparability by reason of the oneness of the ink, for though the letters are comparable each to other, this comparability doth not belie the incomparability of the ink in itself, neither doth it belie the oneness of the ink which is to be found in each letter. Here lieth the ultimate identity between striking comparisons and denying the possibility of comparison, for wherever there be any question of comparison, it is always in reality the ink itself which is compared with itself. *He it is who is God in Heaven and God on earth.*[21] Howsoever and wheresoever He be, He is God, so let not that which thou seest of Him in the earth of comparability prevent thee from conceiving of Him as He is in the Heaven of incomparability, for all things are made of both incomparability and comparability. *Wheresoe'er ye turn, there is the Face of God.* This is in virtue of the general Attribute which overfloweth from the Infinite Riches of the Point on to the utter poverty of the letters. But as to that which belongeth unto the Point's Own Mysterious Essence, it is not possible that it should undergo the least manifestation in the letters, nor can any letter, either in its form or its meaning, carry the burden of the Point's innermost characteristics.

"Seest thou not that if thou tracest some of the letters of the alphabet, as for example: ب ث ت thou wilt find for each letter another letter that resembleth it: ت is like ب, for example, and ث is like ت. Then if thou wishest to pronounce one of these letters, thou wilt find a sound that fitteth it exactly, whereas the Point hath no exteriorization that so fitteth it. If thou seekest to utter its truth, thou sayest *nuqṭatun,* and this utterance will force thee to submit unto letters which have nothing to do with the essence of the point—*nūn, qāf, ṭā'* and *tā'*. It is clear, then, that the Point eludeth the grasp of words. Even so is there no word that can express the Secret Essence of the Creator. Therefore whenever the Gnostic seeketh to denote the Divine incomparability in words, that is, when he seeketh to convey what is meant by the Plenitude of the Essence with all Its Attributes,

[21] Qur'ān, XLIII, 84.

there cometh forth from his mouth an utterance which goeth far wide of its mark by reason of the limitations of language.

"The Point was in its principial state of utterly impenetrable secrecy[22] where there is neither separation nor union, neither after nor before, neither breadth nor length, and all the letters were obliterate in its hidden Essence, just as all the books, despite the divergence of their contents, were obliterate in the letters. As to this reduction of books to letters, it can be perceived by all who have the least intuition. Examine a book, and thou wilt find that naught appeareth on its pages to convey their sense but the twenty-eight letters,[23] which in their manifestation of each word and meaning will be forever reassembling in new formations as the words and meanings vary, until God *inherit the earth and all who are on it*[24] and *all things come unto God.*[25] Then will the letters return unto their principial centre where nothing is save the Essence of the Point.

"The Point was in its impenetrable secrecy with the letters all obliterate in its Essence, while the tongue of each letter petitioned the length, shortness, depth or other qualities that its truth required. Thus the promptings unto utterance were set in motion according to the demands of the Point's attributes which lay hidden in its Essence. Then was determined the first manifestation.

"The Point's first manifestation, its first definable appearance, was in the *Alif*, which came into being in the form of incomparability rather than of comparability, so that it might exist qualitatively in every letter while remaining essentially aloof from them. Moreover, thou shouldst know that the appearance of the *Alif* from the Point was not caused, but the Point overflowed with it. Thus was the primal *Alif* not traced by the pen,[26] nor was it dependent upon it, but sprung from the

[22] *ʿAmā*, literally "blindness", with reference to the blindness of "other" than It, inasmuch as It is pure, unshared Perception (*Waḥdat al-Shuhūd*).

[23] It must be remembered that the purpose of a mystical treatise is always eminently "practical", and the practical purpose of this one is in fact indicated in its title (see p. 148). The Shaykh is here inviting his disciples to transpose this operation to the book of Nature in such a way as to see there the "letters" rather than the "words".

[24] Qur'ān, XIX, 40.

[25] XLII, 53.

[26] The pen symbolizes the Supreme Pen after which Sūrah LXVIII of the

outward urge of the Point in its principial centre. Whenever there streamed from it an overflow, there was *Alif*, naught else. It dependeth not upon the pen for its existence, nor needeth it any help therefrom in virtue of its straightness and its transcending all that is to be found in the other letters by way of crookedness or protuberance or other particularity. *He is not questioned as to what He doth, but they are questioned.*[27] As to the other letters, they need the movement of the pen upon them, nor could any of them have appearance except by means of it, on account of their concavity, roundness, and whatever else characterizeth them.

"It is true that the *Alif* also may be made to appear by means of the pen, while yet remaining independent of it and without any disparagement to the transcendence of its station, inasmuch as the pen hath its length and straightness from the *Alif*, nay, it *is* the *Alif*, whose penned appearance is thus through itself for itself.

"The *Alif* is a symbol of the One who Alone is, of Him whose Being no being precedeth. Thus the appearance of the Point as *Alif* is what is called 'Firstness'. Before its manifestation it was not so qualified, even as it was not qualified by 'Lastness'. *He is the First and the Last and the Outwardly Manifest and the Inwardly Hidden.*

"If the unique Firstness of the *Alif* be confirmed,[28] then of necessity must Lastness also be reserved for it alone.[29] Thus doth it declare unto the other letters *Unto Me is your return,*[30] one and all. Yea, *unto God come all things.*

"As to the Outward Manifestation of *Alif* in the letters, it is easily perceived. Consider the question well, and thou wilt find that there is no letter whose extension in space is not derived from the *Alif*: the *Ḥā'* for example is nothing other than a hunchbacked *Alif*, whereas the *Mīm* is a circular *Alif*, and such

Qur'ān is named. ʿAbd al-Karīm al-Jīlī (*Al-Insān al-Kāmil*, ch. 47), says: "The Prophet said: 'The first thing which God created was the Intellect' and he also said: 'The first thing which God created was the Pen.' Thus the Pen is the first Intellect, and they are two aspects of the Spirit of Muḥammad."

[27] Qur'ān, XXI, 23.

[28] "The *Alif*, unlike all other letters, is only one degree distant from the Point, for two points together make an alif" (Jīlī, *Al-Kahf wa 'l-Raqīm*, p. 7).

[29] In the inverse process of reintegration.

[30] Qur'ān, XXXI, 15.

is the manifestation of the *Alif* according to the dictates of its wisdom, in all the letters, but *the sight attaineth not unto Him,* and this is the meaning of the Inward Hiddenness, for it is clear that no one can perceive the existence of the *Alif* in the circle of the *Mīm* except after much practise, and naught hindereth us from perceiving it but its roundness, that is, its manifestation in a quality that we do not recognize. It itself is the veil over itself....

"The Outward Manifestation of the Truth may be stronger in some visible forms than in others, and this is not difficult to see for him who looketh. Canst thou not detect the *Alif* in some letters as not in others? Not far from its form is the form of the *Lām,* for example; and there is in the *Bā'* of the *Basmalah* that which revealeth the manifestation of the *Alif* therein. But few are they who can easily detect it in the other letters. As to the generality, they are ignorant of the rank of the *Alif*; some know it in its Firstness and are ignorant of it in its Lastness, and there are some who know it in both; but whoso knoweth it not in every letter, small and large, long and short, early in the alphabet and late, verily he seeth not aright, and his perception faileth. If thou hast understood that the *Alif* is manifest in every letter, tell me whether this causeth it to fall short of the dignity of its incomparability wherein it retaineth ever that which belongeth unto it alone. Nay, the essential truth of the *Alif* remaineth as it is, and I see no short-coming on account of its manifestation, which I see rather as one of its perfections. The short-coming—though God knoweth best—is in him who would confine it to one quality, not allowing it to reach out unto another, but constraining it, limiting it, refusing to know it, and reducing it to comparability by making of it a thing like other things. The truth of the knowledge which befitteth its station is that thou shouldst see the *Alif* manifest in every word of every book. All is *Alif*....

"The letter *Bā'* is the first form wherein the *Alif* appeared, and thus it manifested itself therein as never elsewhere. 'God created Adam in His Image';[31] and by Adam it is the First Man[32]

[31] Bukhārī, *Isti'dhān,* 1; and most other canonical books of Traditions.

[32] If God created the human being in His Image, He created a priori in His Image man's spiritual prototype, Universal Man, here called "the First Man", who was the first created thing, This prototype is what the *Bā'* represents; it is only remotely, and by extension, that *Bā'* can be said to represent Adam in the sense of earthly man, who was the final outcome of creation.

who is meant, and he is the Spirit of Being. It was in virtue of his having been created in His Image that He made him His representative on earth, and ordered the Angels to prostrate themselves to him.

> Had not His Beauty shone in Adam's countenance,
> The Angels never had bowed down prostrate before him.[33]

Was their prostration to other than Him? Nay, God pardoneth not him who is guilty of idolatry.

"The *Bā'* of the *Basmalah* differeth from the ordinary *Bā'* both in form as in function. *Verily thou art of a tremendous nature;*[34] and its greatness is none other than the greatness of the *Alif*. *Whoso obeyeth the Apostle obeyeth God.*[35] Seest thou not that elsewhere the *Bā'* is not lengthened, whereas in the *Basmalah* it is lengthened, and its length is none other than the elided *Alif*. *Bism* (بسم) was originally *bi-ism* (باسم), and then the *Alif* in *ism*[36] left its place vacant and appeared in the *Bā'*, which thus took on the form of the *Alif*, just as it fulfilled the function of the *Alif*. Even so did the Prophet say: 'I have a time wherein only my Lord sufficeth to contain me', and thou seest that the *Bā'* hath a time, namely in the *Basmalah*, wherein only the Alif sufficeth to contain it, both in its form and in its Point,[37] albeit the Point of the *Alif* is above it, whereas the Point of the *Bā'* is beneath it. Indeed the *Alif* is none other than the Point itself which is an eye that wept or a drop that gushed forth and which in its downpour was named *Alif*, without any detriment unto itself in virtue of the Integrity of the *Alif* and its flawless Transcendence wherein the Point remaineth in its Eternal Incomparability. *Verily we stand over them Irresistible.*[38] Full descent only took place at the manifestation of *Alif* as *Bā'*, followed by the other letters. If its form had been identical with that of the *Alif*, the *Bā'* would have lost its distinctive characteristics. But the *Bā'* is *Bā'* and the *Alif* is *Alif*: the *Alif*

[33] Jīlī, *ʿAiniyyat*.

[34] Qur'ān, LXVIII, 4 (addressed to Muḥammad).

[35] Qur'ān, IV, 80.

[36] An initial vowel is always written with *alif*.

[37] In many manuscripts of the Qur'ān the *hamzah* on an initial *alif* is indicated by a large dot.

[38] Qur'ān, VII, 127.

was manifested spontaneously, of its own free will, whereas manifestation was forced upon the *Bā'*. Hence the necessity of the difference between its form and that of the *Alif*, lest we should deny the latency of *Alif* in the other letters,[39] or lest we should think that freedom is altogether incompatible with obligation.[40]

"Moreover the Point, which is above the *Alif*, is beneath the *Bā'*, so let this be for us an illustration of the truth that the things of the lower worlds are manifestations of the Point even as are the things of the higher worlds, nor let the manifestation of the Point in the Essence prevent our recognition of it in the Qualities. The Prophet said: 'If ye lowered a man by a rope unto the nethermost earth, ye would light upon God.'[41] Even so doth the Point beneath the *Bā'* signify the effacement that underlieth all things. *Everything perisheth but his Face. He it is who is God in Heaven and God on earth.* The Point's being above the *Alif* instructeth us that the *Alif* is its state of manifestation; but the *Bā'* is its veil, and therefore doth it lie beneath the *Bā'*, like the hidden treasure beneath the wall that Al-Khiḍr feared would collapse.[42]

"When *Bā'* understood its true relation unto *Alif*, it fulfilled what was incumbent upon it both by definition and obligation.[43] It submitteth unto its definition by cleaving unto the other letters,[44] in as much as they are of its kind, unlike the *Alif*

[39] But for the mediation of the *Bā'* of the *Basmalah*, which on the one hand clearly suggests the *Alif* while on the other hand it is distinguished from it precisely by the lower curve which joins it to the other letters, it would not have been possible for us to see the *Alif* in the other letters. Otherwise expressed, but for the mediation of the Word made flesh, the latent Divinity in men could never be brought out.

[40] Lest we should think that the coexistence of free will and predestination in man is impossible. The *Bā'* is in fact an image of this coexistence, for its resemblance to the *Alif* symbolizes man's relative free will, whereas its difference from the *Alif* symbolizes man's predestination.

[41] A comment, by the Prophet, on the verse: *He is the First and the Last and the Outwardly Manifest and the Inwardly Hidden* (Tirmidhī, *Tafsīr Sūrat al-Ḥadīd*; Ibn Ḥanbal, VI, 370).

[42] A reference to Qur'ān, XVIII, 77–82.

[43] Referring to the Prophet's fulfilment of the normal functions of the human being, which were his by definition, and of his apostolic obligations.

[44] *Bā'* is joined to the letters on either side of it, *Alif* only to a letter that precedes it.

which standeth aloof from the letters when it precedeth them, though they attain unto it as a Finality; and verily *thy Lord is the Uttermost End.*"

HERMENEUTICS

The Truth of Certainty

Moses said to his household: Verily beyond all doubt I have seen a fire. I will bring you tidings of it or I will bring you a flaming brand that ye may warm yourselves. Then when he reached it he was called: Blessed is He who is in the fire and He who is about it, and Glory be to God the Lord of the worlds. (Qur'ān XXVII: 7–8)

In every esoteric doctrine there are references to three degrees of faith, and in Islamic Mysticism, that is, in Sufism, these three degrees are known as the Lore of Certainty (*ʿilmu 'l-yaqīn*), the Eye of Certainty (*ʿaynu 'l-yaqīn*) and the Truth of Certainty (*ḥaqqu 'l-yaqīn*). The difference between them is illustrated by taking the element fire to represent the Divine Truth. The lowest degree, that of the Lore of Certainty belongs to one whose knowledge of fire comes merely from hearing it described, like those who received from Moses no more than "tidings" of the Burning Bush. The second degree, that of the Eye of Certainty, belongs to one whose knowledge of fire comes from seeing the light of its flames, like Moses before he reached the Bush. The highest degree, that of the Truth of Certainty, belongs to one whose knowledge of fire comes from being consumed by it and thus becoming one with it, for this degree belongs only to the One. The realization of this Oneness is here implied for Moses in that he is summoned into the Divine Presence with which the Bush is surrounded. Entry into that presence is the equivalent of entering into the fire. *Blessed is He who is in the fire and He who is about it.*

In another chapter of the Qur'ān, also with reference to the Burning Bush, this supreme experience is confirmed by an additional symbolism: *And when he reached it, he was called: O Moses! Verily I am thy Lord. So take off thy sandals. Verily thou art in the holy valley of Tuwa.* (Q. XX: 11–12)[1]

[1] Since the Qur'ān is direct revelation, there can be no common measure between a translation and the original. A translation may serve to convey some of the meaning, but is of no value whatsoever for ritual purposes. The origi-

When Moses reached the Burning Bush his extinction in the Truth of Certainty is represented by his taking off his sandals, that is, by removing the very basis of his apparent existence apart from the Creator in the two created worlds, Heaven and earth. Nor could he do otherwise, for the name of the valley means, according to the commentary, "rolling up", as in the verse which describes the Last Day as: *The day when we shall roll up the heavens as at the rolling up of a written scroll.* (Q. XXI: 10)

To have been divested of all "otherness" is to have attained the degree of Universal Man (*al-insānu 'l-kāmil*), who is also called the Sufi. But strictly speaking, It cannot be considered as a degree at all, for It is no less than the Eternal and Infinite Oneness of God, the Certainty of Whose Truth effaces all except Itself. Therefore it is sometimes said that "the Sufi is not created",[2] since the Truth Itself is not created, and It has effaced in the Sūfi all that was created, leaving only Itself. This Identity of Universal Man with the Divine Truth is affirmed in a holy utterance (*ḥadīth qudsī*)[3] of the Truth Itself speaking through the mouth of the Prophet: "My slave ceaseth not to draw nigh unto Me through devotions of free-will until I love him; and when I love him, I am the Hearing Wherewith he heareth and the Sight Wherewith he seeth and the Hand Wherewith he fighteth and the Foot Whereon he walketh."

The same is also expressed in another utterance attributed by Sufis to the Prophet: "I am Aḥmad without the letter *mīm*. I am an Arab without the letter *ʿayn*. Who hath seen Me, the same hath seen the Truth."[4]

The letter *mīm* is the letter of death, that is, of ending, and the letter *ʿayn* is the letter of the source of creation, that is, of beginning, and in the Truth of Certainty all that has to

nal, which has been preserved exactly as it was transmitted to the Prophet by the Archangel Gabriel, holds in Islam the central place that is held in Christianity, not by the New Testament, but by Christ himself, who is likewise "the Word of God" (Q. III: 31, 45; IV: 171).

[2] *al-ṣūfī lam yukhlaq.*

[3] A distinction must be made between the *ḥadīth qudsī* in which the Divinity speaks directly, in the first person, and the *ḥadīth sharīf* (noble utterance), in which the Prophet himself speaks in the first person as a human individual.

[4] *ana aḥmadun bilā mīm; ana ʿarabiyyun bilā ʿayn; man ra'ānī faqad ra'ā 'l-ḥaqq. Aḥmad*, like *Muḥammad* (the Glorified) of which it is the superlative form, is one of the names of the Prophet. Another name is *Ṭā Hā*.

do with beginning and ending has been reabsorbed, leaving only That Which has neither beginning nor end, namely *aḥad*, One, and *rabbī*, my Lord. These words refer especially to that aspect of the Truth which is named Eternity after extinction (*al-baqā baʿd al-fanā'*), for all that is subject to change has been extinguished, and That which remains, the Eternal (*al-bāqī*), is beyond all change whatsoever. This Remainder is the Real Self, and the self which has a beginning and an end, and which corresponds to Aḥmad the Arab, is only an appearance. That the Real Self is none other than God is also affirmed in yet another utterance of the Prophet: "Who knoweth himself, the same knoweth his Lord"

The Self is All that is left to Universal Man in whom the veils of the self which hid It have been utterly consumed by the Truth. Thus it is said in the Chapter of the Cow: *We make no distinction between any of His Apostles.* (Q. II: 285) for in the Truth of Certainty each of them is nothing but the Self, and the Self is always One and the Same; and it was because of the Self above all that the Angels were told to prostrate themselves before Universal Man in the form of Adam.[5] The Self, Which is the Truth of Certainty, is One; but It is not one with the oneness of a single thing among many, but with Oneness Which Eternally annihilates all duality, and nothing can be added to It so as to make more than One, for It is already Infinite. This Infinite Unity (*al-aḥadiyyah*) is sometimes called He (*huwa*) or the Essence (*al-dhāt*). The Garden of the Essence is therefore the Highest of all the Paradises, or rather, in the Truth of Certainty, It is the One Paradise, the Paradise of Him, and nothing may enter It since Everything is already there. Thus if it be said that one has entered the Garden of the Essence, the meaning is that his self has been reduced to nothing and that he has thus been changed from one into nought, since only nought may enter It. This knowledge of the nothingness of oneself is what is called poverty (*al-faqr*) and it is implied in the utterance of Jesus: "It is easier for a camel to pass through the eye of a needle than for a rich man to enter the Kingdom of Heaven." In respect of poverty

[5] In Islam it is lack of spiritual courtesy (*adab*) to speak of a Prophet by his bare name. The original version reads "our liege-lord Adam (our liege-lord Jesus, etc.)—Peace be on him!" But we have reluctantly decided to conform in this to European custom, so as to avoid unnecessary strangeness.

one may see a further meaning in the words: "We make no distinction between any of His Apostles," considering this time not so much the Self as the selves of the Apostles; for though it is said in the Chapter of the Night Journey: *And We have favoured some of the Prophets above others, and unto David we gave the Psalms.* (Q. XVII: 55) these distinctions of favor only refer to what is below the Paradise of the Essence, whereas in the Essence Itself they are all equal in realizing the truth: *God is the Rich and ye are the poor.* (Q. XLVI:38)

It is in this equality that the Prophets are rated at their highest worth; for they are incomparably greater and richer by reason of their poverty than by reason of all their earthly and heavenly plenitudes, since this nothingness and poverty is the key by which alone one may have access to the Infinite Riches of the Truth; and yet since the being is utterly extinguished in the Truth he cannot be said to have gained possession of Its Riches, for in Reality He has never ceased to possess Them.

Before extinction, the being is veiled by the Qualities[6] from the Essence, that is, by multiplicity from Unity, and at extinction he is veiled by the Essence from the Qualities, whereas in Eternity after extinction He is veiled neither by the Qualities from the Essence, nor by the Essence from the Qualities, yet the Qualities are not other than the Essence. This Greatest of all Mysteries, the Mystery of the Infinitely Rich Who is One, is expressed in the Supreme Name *Allāh* (God, the Divinity), which signifies the Essence together with all the Qualities in Indivisible Unity. In view of this Mystery it is said: *Say: He, God, is One, God, the Eternally Sufficient unto Himself.* (Q. CXII: 1–2) lest in the weakness of human conception the Infinite Riches contained in God should as it were overflow into duality, the Supreme Name is safeguarded between two affirmations of His Unity, "He" signifying the Pure Essence in Itself without any differentiation as regards the Qualities. Then, to wipe away the stain of any idea of limitation or insufficiency that the human intelligence might conceive, the Name of Divinity is uttered again, and with it the Name of Absolute Plenitude, the Eternally Sufficient unto Himself (*al-ṣamad*).

The Truth is One, yet Its Unity implies, for the believer, no fear of any loss, since the Truth is also the Infinitely Good

[6] Such as, for example, His Mercy, Majesty, Beauty, Strength.

(*al-raḥmān*[7]) and the All-Bountiful (*al-karīm*). That which is taken away by extinction is restored in Eternity according to the Infinite measure of Its Real Self. The different beings are extinguished in the Truth as different colours that are reabsorbed into the principial whiteness of light. Yet as it were on the other side of the Whiteness are the True Colors, Each incomparably more distinct in the Eternal Splendor of Its Reality, as revealed in the Light of the Whiteness, than ever it was in its illusory self; and yet at the same time there is no duality, no otherness.

That Which is named the Garden of the Essence inasmuch as It is the Paradise of Him, is named Firdaws inasmuch as It is the Paradise of God. The Prophet said: "If ye ask a boon of God, ask of Him Firdaws for it is the midmost Paradise and the highest Paradise, and from it flow forth the rivers of Paradise." Here the Beloved[8] have attained to eternity after the extinction, which is the Divine Station (*al-maqāmu 'l-ilāhī*), the Station of Immutability; but lest their plurality should seem to imply a plurality in God, they are, when spoken of, as it were separated from the divinity being named "those who are brought nigh" (*al-muqarrabūn*). It is they who drink at Kawthar (Abundance), the Supreme River whence flow all others and of which the Prophet said: "There are on its banks as many cups of silver as there are stars in the firmament. Whoso drinketh thereof shall never thirst."

In Firdaws the nigh drink also from a Fountain which, like Kawthar, is perfumed with musk and which is named Tasnīm (Exaltation). Yet the name Tasnīm, in its expression of high-raisedness, is an understatement pregnant with significance, as is the name of the River in its expression of abundance, for Kawthar is no less than the flow of the Infinite Beatitude of the All-Holy (*al-quddūs*). Nor is it otherwise with the name of those who drink thereat in its expression of nearness, which must be measured in the light of the definition of the Nearness of God: *We are nearer to him (man) than his jugular vein.* (Q. L: 16) To speak of the Gardens and Fountains of Paradise, as also of Its Rivers, Fruits and Consorts, is to speak the truth, whereas

[7] This name denotes the Essential Source of Mercy, whereas its manifestation depends on the All-Merciful (*al-raḥīm*).

[8] They to whom may be applied the utterance: "... and when I love him, I am the Hearing Wherewith he heareth...."

to speak of such blessings in this world is only a manner of speaking, for the Realities are in Firdaws, and what we see in this world are only the remote shadows of Reality.

The Divinity, Immutable and Indivisible, is the Truth besides Which all other truths cease to exist. One such relative truth is that of the religious Law, and it is said that this truth may be expressed in the words "I and Thou", whereas the Truth of the Path, that is, the direct way of return towards God, may be expressed: "I am Thou and Thou art I". But the Truth Itself is: "There is neither I nor Thou but only He".[9]

Universal man realizes eternally in the Truth that he is nothing and yet that He is Everything. But such realization is beyond his human soul, and this is what is meant by the saying: "The slave remains the slave".[10] The slave cannot become God, since he is either the slave, as in appearance, or nothing at all, as in Reality. Universal man cannot make his human soul divine; like the souls of all other men, but with an outstanding difference of quality, it implies the illusion of an existence apart from God. It differs from them not in kind, but in what might almost be called an organic consciousness that this separate existence is in Truth no more than an illusion. There is a saying that "Muhammad is a man, yet not as other men, but like a jewel among stones." Albeit the soul remains the soul, just as night remains night, or else it vanishes and there is day. But though the soul of Universal Man cannot itself attain to the direct knowledge of the Truth of Certainty, yet unlike other souls it is touched in its centre by a ray of light proceeding from the sun of the Spirit of the Truth; for this perfect soul, represented in Islam by the soul of the Prophet, is none other than the Night of Power (*laylatu 'l-qadr*),[11] into which *descend the Angels and the Spirit*; and the Heart, that is, the point of this spiritual ray's contact, is as a full moon in the unclouded night of the perfect soul making it *better than a thousand months* of other nights, that is, peerless among all other souls. This Moon, from which the soul looks towards the Sun of the Spirit, is the Eye of Certainty; and its presence makes the soul at peace

[9] *al-sharīʿatu: anā wa anta; al-ṭarīqatu: anā anta wa anta anā; al-ḥaqīqatu: lā anā wa lā anta, huwa.*

[10] *al-ʿabdu yabqā 'l-ʿabd.*

[11] See Qur'ān, XCVII.

until the break of dawn, until the night vanishes, until the soul together with its peace is extinguished in the Light of Reality, leaving only the Absolute Peace of Unity.

Although the existence of any perfection or indeed of anything at all apart from God is an illusion, the illusory perfections of the created Universe may none the less serve as guides and incentives to one who has not yet attained to the Truth, inasmuch as they are images of His Perfection. Of these images the highest and fullest which can be readily conceived by one who has not passed beyond the limits of this world is the human perfection itself. Moreover this perfection, unlike other earthly perfections, is a state through which the traveller (*al-sālik*) must himself pass on his way to the Truth. Therefore the religions have greatly extolled the state of human perfection, setting it up as a lamp to mark the end of the first stage of the journey, just as one might tell a man who had long lived in darkness to look at the full moon, knowing that the light of the sun would serve at first rather to blind than to guide him; and so Universal Man, whose state is the End of the journey, is represented as having two perfect natures, the perfect human nature (*al-nāsūt*) being merely a reflection or image of the Divine Nature (*al-lāhūt*), besides Which in Reality it is nothing, though to the traveller it seems nearer and more accessible. In accordance with what has already been said, the two natures might be called the perfect self and the Perfect Self, the former corresponding to Aḥmad the Arab, and the Latter being the One Lord. The perfect human nature stands as it were between the traveller and the Divine Nature, in the sense that he must acquire the one before he may rise from it to the Other; and here lies one of the interpretations of the saying that no one may meet God if he has not first met the Prophet.

Universal man with his two natures is figured in the Seal of Solomon, of which the upper and lower triangles represent respectively the Divine and the human nature. In virtue of this duality he is the mediator between Heaven and earth, and it is owing to this function that he is sometimes referred to as "the isthmus"[12] (*al-barzakh*) as in the Chapter of the Distinct Revelation: *And He it is Who hath let loose the two seas, one sweet and fresh, the other salt and bitter, and hath set between them an isthmus, an impassable barrier.* (Q. XXV: 53) In His Heart alone does the sweet sea of the next world meet the salt sea of this; and by reason of this meeting his human nature itself is the noblest and best of all earthly things as is affirmed in the Chapter of the Fig: *Verily We created man in the fairest similitude.* (Q. XCV: 4) The nearness of Heaven, by reason of his presence, even causes sometimes the laws of earth to cease perceptibly, just as the moon grows pale at the approach of day; and it is at such moments that a miracle may take place, such as the changing of water into wine, or the step which leaves a print upon the rock and none upon the sand. As in the Seal of Solomon, his central function as mediator is also figured in the Cross,[13] which is another symbol of Universal Man in that the horizontal line represents the fullness of his earthly nature, whereas the vertical line represents his heavenly exaltation; and yet another of his symbols is the Crescent, for like a cup it indicates his function of receiving the Divine Grace, and at the same time, like the horns of the bull, it indicates his majesty, his function of administering this Grace throughout the whole Universe. *Blessed be He Who hath made the distinct revelation unto His servant, that he might be for all the worlds a warner.* (Q. XXV: 1)

[12] The isthmus, which has the same symbolic meaning as a bridge, recalls the ancient Roman title of *Pontifex*, "Bridgemaker" (between Heaven and earth).

[13] If Christians have the sign of the Cross, Muslims have its doctrine." This saying of the Shaykh ʿAbd al-Raḥmān ʿUlaysh al-Kabīr is quoted by René Guénon, *The Symbolism of the Cross* (London, 1958), chapter iii, note 2.

The Fall

Then Satan whispered unto him and said: "O Adam, shall I show thee the Tree of Immortality and a kingdom that fadeth not away?" (Qur'ān XX: 120)

In the centre of the Garden of Eden there is said to be not only a fountain but also a tree, at whose foot the fountain flows. This is the Tree of Immortality, and it is an outward image of the inward Tree of Immortality which grows in the Garden of the Heart, bearing as its fruits the universal and strange objects of perception. These are the objects of the perception of the Eye of Certainty, which is the Fountain of the Heart. Until the traveller has actually reached this fountain and the tree which is inseparable from it, he cannot be called the true man, nor can he be said to have safely finished the first part of his journey, for there is always the danger that he may still be swept back upon the general tide of degeneration and corruption which is personified by the devil himself. But once the traveller has drunk of the waters of the fountain and eaten of the fruit of the tree, and has thus gained the wisdom of the Eye of the Heart, which consists in direct contact with the Spirit, he is at last safe from all attacks of the devil and proof against all the powers of deception, this degree—that of the true man—being none other than the degree of the true slave of God: *Verily over my slaves thou, Satan, hast no power.* (Q. XVII: 65)

In considering therefore how Satan ever came to corrupt man, it may be concluded that at the time of the Fall, mankind in general, far from having actual knowledge of the Truth of Certainty, had begun to be born even without the knowledge of the Eye of Certainty, that is, without immediate access to the Tree and the Fountain of Immortality. Otherwise they could never have been deceived; and it is in fact clear from the above opening quotation that the Adam who fell had never seen the real Tree of Immortality. It would seem, then, that the perfection of mankind at the very end of the Primordial age was as it were a hereditary perfection, in that men continued to be born with primordial harmony in their souls after the cause of that harmony, the Eye of the Heart, had ceased to be theirs; and thus it may be imagined that the different psychic elements were still in their rightful places simply because there was as yet no actual reason for perversion, the faculties of particular earthly perception and desire remaining in the outer part of the soul, and the intuitive faculties which are the heavenly desires remaining near the centre in hopes of a vision of the Tree of Immortality. It is to these innermost faculties that the speech of Satan is addressed, since of all the soul's elements it is they alone which, from their abode at the boundary between the two Paradises, have leanings towards the universal and strange fruits of immortality and the kingdom of the next world that does not fade; and since he had in reality only the fruits of the Garden of the Soul to offer them, that is, the known and wonted objects of perception, being himself everlastingly barred from the Garden of the Heart, he could only tempt them with forgeries, giving the known and wonted objects of perception a semblance of strangeness by suggesting abnormal and irregular uses for them. Thus all his deception of mankind throughout the ages is summed up in the above verse; he ceaselessly promises to show man the Tree of Immortality, gradually reducing by this means the highest and most central faculties into the outer part of the soul so that he may imprison them there in attachment to the counterfeit objects which he has forged for their perception. It is the presence here of these perverted faculties, either in discontent in that they can never find real satisfaction or finally in a state of atrophy in that they are never put to their proper use, which causes all the disorder and obstruction in the soul of the fallen man, and which is mentioned in the Chapter of the Declining Day: *By the declining day, verily mankind is in ruinous loss, except they that believe and do good works, and exhort one another unto truth and unto patience.* (Q. CIII)

It is significant that the Qur'ān swears to this ruin by the declining day, that is, the time of day which comes immediately before the setting of the sun and which corresponds to the present age[1] in which man's intuitive faculties have reached

[1] According to the Hindus, and also the ancient Greek and Romans, each

their uttermost perversion. Moreover, since it is possible, as has already been explained, to apply what is said directly of the macrocosm to the microcosm also, this oath may be taken as a testification not merely to the ruin of man as a whole but also to the ruin of these particular faculties in man, since it is they in the microcosm which correspond precisely to the human race in the macrocosm. In the same way the following verses of the Chapter of the Fig: *Verily We created man in the fairest rectitude. Then cast We him down to be the lowest of the low.* (Q. XCV: 4–5) may be taken as referring to these faculties as well as to man himself. For just as man who was the highest of all earthly things becomes in his degeneration the lowest, so these faculties which were the most precious elements in his soul become the source of all its subsequent disorder, illustrating like man himself the truth which is expressed in the Latin proverb *corruptio optimi pessima*, the best when corrupted becometh the worst. Meanwhile, apart from the obstruction caused in the soul by the misplaced intuitions, the faculties of earthly perception and desire are also affected in themselves;

great cycle of time is divided into four ages, to which the Romans gave the name of Golden, Silver, Bronze and Iron, each age being spiritually inferior to the one which preceded it. The end of the Primordial Age (which is beyond the cycle) corresponds to the Fall, and the beginning of the Golden Age to the Relenting of God towards Adam. The end of the Iron Age, that is, the present age, which the Hindus call the Dark Age, is marked by the overthrow of the Antichrist by Christ at his second coming. As regards the intervening period, however, the correspondences are less obvious: the Hindu perspective is objective and historical, whereas the Islamic perspective is subjective and "practical". Instead of considering the great divisions of the cycle, the Qur'ān only mentions those few civilizations which were known to the Arabs by name. Moreover little or no distinction is made between the qualities of the different civilizations; the attention is always concentrated on the fact that after flourishing for a time each one of them came to ruin. For the Muslim, history is chiefly of value as evidence of the perishability of all earthly things.

The Hindu doctrine states that there are many great cycles, each one being made up of four ages; thus the end of the Dark Age is followed by a new Golden Age. According to the Jewish, Christian and Islamic perspectives, which consider time almost exclusively in its ruinous aspect, the whole span of the earth's existence is compressed into one cycle, so that the final ruin at the end of the present age is usually identified with the final ruin at the end of the world. But the tradition is strong, none the less, in these three latest religions, that the Messiah at his coming will rule for a certain time over the whole earth as king; and this is in accordance with the Hindu belief that Kalki (he who rides on the white horse), whose coming marks the end of the present Dark Age, will inaugurate a new Golden Age.

for the intuitive faculties were as channels by which the Fountain of the Lore of Certainty drew its waters from the Paradise of the Heart, and if the channels are corrupted the fountain itself is also necessarily corrupted. The particular desires cannot grow to fullness in that the particular objects of perception are desired only for themselves, being no longer prized as reflections of universal truths. At the same time, since unlike the heavenly desires these earthly desires do at least receive a certain satisfaction, they take on an undue importance, seeking to usurp the central place;[2] and with regard to the traveller's return, it will easily be understood that one of the purposes of fasting and of asceticism in general is to frighten these desires from this usurped position. Indeed, "fear is the beginning of wisdom", and the task of restoring order to the soul begins with the instilling of fear into the earthly desires, since it is they which immediately confront the traveller, the perverted intuitions being usually too remote from the centre of consciousness or too sunken in atrophy for him to be fully aware of their presence at first. It is only by exception that they are not definitely lost, as they are for the vast majority of the men of this age, in whom the plight of these higher faculties, analogous to that of mankind in general, is described in the Chapter of Yā Sīn: *Verily We have put shackles upon their necks even up to their chins, so that they are stiff-necked; and before them We have placed a barrier and behind them a barrier, and We have blindfolded them so that they see not. Alike is it to them whether thou warnest them or not, for they will not believe.* (Q. XXXVI: 8–10)

Rare indeed are those who have these faculties sufficiently unperverted for there to be the least flow of the Fountain of the Lore of Certainty in their souls, this degree of certainty being none other than that faith (*īmān*) which is referred to in the Chapter of the Inner Rooms: *The Arabs say: We believe. Say thou: Ye believe not. Say rather: "We have submitted",*[3] *for faith hath not entered your hearts.* (Q. XLIX: 14)

The believers are also referred to in the Chapter of the Declining Day, and the Lore of Certainty is the truth to which they exhort each other. But such belief by itself is not enough,

[2] Speaking of earthly desires, a Shaykh has said: "The spiritual man has desires; the profane man is his desires."

[3] *aslamnā*, that is, we have made submission (*islām*) to God.

and it is by a still greater exception that one may be born who not merely recognizes this truth but is actually drawn towards it, seeking to follow it in patience by "good works" which are "the devotions of free will" mentioned in an already quoted utterance of the Prophet. Only one who follows this path may be called a traveller (*sālik*); and the scarcity of such, even compared with the scarcity of the believers who recognize the truth, is affirmed in the commentary which says with regard to patience: "Verily it is easy to attain unto the truth, yet as for constancy unto it and patience with it through unerring perseverance in worship, these are rarer than the red sulphur and the white raven."

This rare virtue is none other than what is sometimes called excellence (*iḥsān*);[4] it implies the hope of regaining all that man has lost throughout the ages, and without it the traveller could never even begin his task through seeking by means of fear to make room in the centre of his soul for the return of the heavenly desires. But with *iḥsān* he will have patience to attempt this, and also patience to seek by the same means to detach these desires from the counterfeits of spiritual truth which have been forged for them in the outer part of his soul; and sooner or later he must pass through a phase complementary to that of fear, and this is the phase of love, since it is through spiritual love alone that the heavenly desires may actually be recalled to the centre of the soul, there as it were to await the opening of the Eye of the Heart. Moreover, this second phase may also serve indirectly the purpose of the first, since it is said that with the return of these higher desires to the centre the earthly desires retire[5] as if of their own accord into the outer part of the soul. These two phases may be more or less distinct or simultaneous, though in general that of fear precedes the other. But however they may take place, varying from one soul to another in accordance with the saying that there are as many different paths to the truth as there are souls of men, it is at least certain that until both phases be complete,

[4] For a fuller definition of this term, and also of the terms *īmān* and *islām*, see Frithjof Schuon, *Sufism, Veil and Quintessence* (Bloomington, Indiana, 1981), pp. 129–30.

[5] Very relevant to this is the saying of an Arab dervish, "It is not I who have left the world; it is the world which has left me", quoted by Frithjof Schuon, *The Transcendent Unity of Religions* (London, 1952), p. 74 note.

that is, until the true hierarchy be entirely restored to the soul, every element having been brought back to its proper place, the state of human perfection with its two Paradises cannot be regained.

The Symbol

Seest thou not how God citeth a symbol: "A good word is as good as a good tree, its root set firm and its branches in heaven, giving its fruit at every season by the leave of its Lord"? God citeth symbols for men that they may remember. (Qur'ān XIV: 24–25)

The Eternal (*al-bāqī*) is the All-Embracing (*al-muḥīṭ*): He is not only as it were after all time but also before all time, being the Ancient of Days (*al-qadīm*); and so the journey to extinction in the Truth of Certainty is likened to an act of remembrance. The same applies by analogy to the attainment of the lesser spiritual degrees, for each degree embraces or envelops the degrees which are below it. Thus time itself, which belongs to the lowest degree of all, that of earthly existence, is enveloped by all that lies above, so that the next world in its entirety, with all its spiritual degrees, is before time as well as after it; and this is expressed in an utterance of the Prophet referring to the creation of Adam's body which is at the beginning of time, and to his own prophethood which is of the next world: "I was a Prophet while Adam was still betwixt water and clay." It can thus be said that man has behind him not only a historical and "horizontal" past but also a spiritual and "vertical" past. A merely theoretic doctrinal knowledge is a horizontal remembrance: we remember what we have been taught in time; and apart from lessons in the narrower sense, the facts of the horizontal plane, that is, of this world, when looked at objectively, without prejudice, make us inclined to believe what the doctrine teaches us about the world beyond. But insofar as there is any certainty in this belief, a vertical element has been added to the horizontal; we are only certain about something because we have seen it to be true. Thus, even if we are unaware of it, the least particle of certainty that can be had about the next world must necessarily have come down from above; it does not belong to horizontal remembrance but to vertical remembrance which is nothing other than intellectual intuition or—what in a sense amounts to the same—spiritual love. We can thus add to what was said about love in the last chapter that the initial act of this way is to awaken, in the erring faculties of intuition, the vertical remembrance which is theirs by rights and which alone can draw them from the outer part of the soul to its centre, where the vertical is to be found in all its fullness, that is, in the Tree of Immortality. It is such remembrance[1] that is meant by the Arabic world *dhikr*, the general name given in Islam to all the different means of reminding man of his original state; and in every *dhikr* it is a symbol which is used to prompt the memory.

It has already been mentioned that the outer world of earthly existence corresponds in all its details to the inner world of man's soul, and that there is a similar correspondence between the Garden of the Heart and the Garden of the Soul; but these are only two particular instances of the general truth that all the different domains in the Universe correspond to each other in that each is an image of the Universe itself. The ancient sciences sprung from a knowledge of these correspondences, which was one of man's original endowments. For example, the sciences of medicine were based on a knowledge of the correspondences or likenesses between the domain of the body and other earthly domains such as those of plants and minerals. But the work of the spiritual path does not necessarily call for a knowledge of cosmic or "horizontal" likenesses such as these; when, in connection with the *dhikr*, the Qur'ān speaks of the *mathal*—"example" or "symbol"—it is referring to the essential or "vertical" likenesses between higher and lower domains, such as those already mentioned between the Heart and the soul. A symbol is something in a lower "known and wonted" domain which the traveller considers not only for its own sake but also and above all in order to have an intuitive glimpse of the "universal and strange" reality which corresponds to it in each of the hidden higher domains. Symbols are in fact none other than the illusory perfections of creation which have already been referred to as being guides and incen-

[1] This recalls the words of Jesus at the institution of the rite of the bread and wine: "Do this in memory of me." For his body, represented by the bread, is the fruit of the Tree of Immortality, just as his blood, represented by the wine, is the water of the Fountain.

tives to the traveller upon his journey, and they have power to remind him of their counterparts in higher worlds not through merely incidental resemblance but because they are actually related to them in the way that a shadow is related to the object which casts it. There is not the least thing in existence which is not such a shadow, as is implied in the Chapter of the Cow: *Verily God disdaineth not to cite as symbol even a gnat or something smaller.* (Q. 11:20)

Nor is there anything which is any more than a shadow. Indeed, if a world did not cast down shadows from above, the worlds below it would at once vanish altogether, since each world in creation is no more than a tissue of shadows entirely dependent on the archetypes in the world above. Thus the foremost and truest fact about any form is that it is a symbol, so that when contemplating something in order to be reminded of its higher realities the traveller is considering that thing in its universal aspect which alone explains its existence.

Thanks to the true relationship between this world and the next, the "known and wonted" objects have always, for the spiritual man, something of the marvellously "strange". Inversely, the Qur'ān tells us that the higher realities have, for the blessed souls in Paradise, something of the "known and wonted", inasmuch as those souls have had experience, on earth, of the shadows of the realities: *Whensoever they are given to eat of the fruits of the garden, they say: "This is that which was given us aforetime"; and it was given them in a likeness thereof.* (Q. 11:25)

What is true of earthly objects applies also to acts: an earthly act is the last of a hierarchy of corresponding shadows which spans the whole Universe. Figuratively speaking, if each series of corresponding shadows or reflections throughout the different worlds be likened to the series of the rungs of a ladder, an earthly act is as the lowest rung, or rather as the support upon which rests the foot of the ladder, and to stand at the foot in upward aspiration is precisely what constitutes an act of remembrance in the sense of the word *dhikr*. The traveller may thus sanctify all his acts[2] in seeking to remember,

[2] The intention to ritualize all one's actions necessarily means avoiding those actions which are too remote from the Truth to serve as reminders of it. For example, murder is in itself, that is, as an act of slaying, the shadow of a Reality. It is this Reality, expressed by His Name the Slayer (*al-mumīt*), which

through them, the Divine Qualities in which they are rooted. The fundamental acts of life which were given to man at his creation are as it were the primordial rites; but in view of human decadence Providence has added to these the rites revealed to the Prophets which are rites in the strict sense of the term. Each of these is as the foot of a ladder which the Divine Mercy has let down into the world as a vehicle of Grace and, in the upward direction, as an eminent means of remembrance. Such is the ladder which appeared in a dream to Jacob, who saw it stretching from Heaven to earth with Angels going up and down upon it; and it is also "the straight path" (*al-ṣirātu 'l-mustaqīm*), for indeed the way of religion is none other than the way of creation itself retraced from its end back to its Beginning.

The ladder as a symbol of the true rite and all that this rite implies recalls the tree which is mentioned in the opening quotation as a symbol of the good word; for indeed the best example of a good word is a Divine Name uttered as a *dhikr* in upward aspiration towards the Truth. The firm-set root of the tree is the *dhikr* itself uttered with firm-set purpose; the Heaven-reaching branches represent the tremendous impact of the *dhikr* as it passes upwards throughout the whole Universe; and the fruit of the tree is the Reality in Whose memory the *dhikr* is performed.

The images of the tree and the ladder may help to explain why the Revealed Books, which have been sent down directly from Heaven, necessarily admit of several different interpretations. These are in no sense contradictory, each being right at its own level.[3] Ranged in hierarchy like the rungs of a ladder,

makes possible the ritual sacrifice of an animal. But in Truth the Slayer is not to be separated from His other Names, whereas murder, unlike sacrifice, constitutes a kind of separation, reflecting nothing of the Divine Mercy, Benevolence and Serenity; the murderer is thus only a very indistinct and fragmentary shadow of the Slayer.

[3] In general only one interpretation of what is quoted from the Qur'ān is given here, the one most in conformity with this book's perspective. But it goes without saying that this interpretation is not exclusive of others.

As an example of different levels of interpretation, let us consider the story of the three messengers who were sent to a city to preach there the Truth (Q. XXXVI: 13–29). According to the literal historical meaning, the city is Antioch and the messengers are Peter and two others of the companions of Jesus. Also macrocosmic, but higher in virtue of its universality, is the interpretation according to which the city represents mankind, whereas the three they are what might be called the vertical dimension of the Book in question. This dimension is in the nature of things: like a star that falls from the sky, every Revelation leaves behind it a luminous trail of higher truths. A profane book, on the contrary, has only one meaning and therefore no vertical dimension at all. *A bad word is as a bad tree which lies uprooted on the surface of the earth.* (Q. XIV: 26)

messengers are Moses, Jesus and Muhammad. Higher still is the microcosmic interpretation—that of our commentator: the city is the human soul, its inhabitants the different psychic elements, and the three messengers the Heart, the Spirit and the Intellect.

The Seal of Solomon

Verily I am about to make on earth a viceregent. (Qur'ān II: 30)

Although everything on earth is a more or less direct reflection of a higher reality, it is only the most direct reflections which can be called truly symbolic. Such reflections are of two kinds, things of which the prototypes have been in this world from the very beginning, without owing their existence in any way to the intervention of fallen man, and things of which the prototypes were directly revealed at some later time.

The true symbol is figured in the lower triangle of the Seal of Solomon. But this triangle does not merely figure it as a direct reflection of the higher truth represented by the upper triangle; it also shows, by its inversion, that the symbol is an inverted reflection. As an example of inversion one may take this world which is inverted in relation to the next which it symbolizes; and a mark of its inversion may be seen at once in the fact that man, who is in this world the viceregent of God, appears last of all things in order of creation. This is expressed in the Seal of Solomon in which the apex of the upper triangle corresponds to the Creator from Whom all things emanate, whereas the apex of the lower one corresponds to man who is the final result to which all creation tends. This general law of inversion might have been inferred from what has already been said about the symbolism of the pairs. It will be remembered that the two terms of a complementary pair need not necessarily be on the same level of existence, and the two seas, representing either Spirit and soul or Heaven and earth, were given as an example of a pair whose terms are at different levels. In this case it may be noticed that the feminine term of the pair is the symbol of the masculine term, for the soul is the reflection of the Spirit, just as earth is of Heaven; and the same is in fact true of all pairs in which one term is lower than the other. The converse is also true, namely that a symbol and what it symbolizes may always be said to form a complementary pair in which the symbol is always the feminine term. It is this passivity in the face of activity, this being feminine in the face of what is masculine, negative in the face of what is positive, which is figured in the Seal of Solomon and which constitutes the inversion of the symbol in relation to what it symbolizes. Inversion may thus be seen as a law on which the harmony of the Universe is based, since from it results the complementary balance and mutual accord between a higher world and a lower world which is its symbol; or rather it may be seen as a law on which the Universe itself is based, since it is only by reason of its inversion, that is as an entirely negative reflection in the face of the Absolute Positive, that the Universe exists at all; and it is the prevalence of this law throughout the whole hierarchy of existence which causes eventually, in the lowest world of all, the reflection of an object in water to be inverted in relation to the object itself.

The highest earthly example of the true symbol is the true man himself; but before going on to consider his nature as illustrated by the lower triangle of the Seal of Solomon, there is yet another aspect of inversion to be explained, and for this purpose the Seal must first of all be considered once more in its highest meaning, that is, as a symbol of the Divine Majesty and Beauty. Among the Qualities of Majesty, Which are represented by the upper triangle, are all Those Which have to do with the Overwhelming and Irresistible Power of the Truth including the Oneness Itself in so far as It be considered in Its Aspect of Activity,[1] that is, as overwhelming with extinction all else beside It. Thus, when in the Chapter of the Believer a question is asked concerning the Divine Majesty: *Unto Whom on that*

[1] The Supreme Aspect of the Divine Unity (*al-aḥadiyyah*) is the Essence in Itself, whereas the Oneness (*al-waḥidiyyah*) is the Essence inasmuch as It is the Sum of all the Qualities. The Oneness may be said to have two Aspects, Singleness (or Wholeness) and Onliness: the creatures reflect It inasmuch as each is a single whole in itself and inasmuch as each is unique. It is thus the Source of all multiplicity (made up of an indefinite number of single entities) and differentiation. In Its Essential Absolute–Infinite Reality It includes both Majesty and Beauty, and Its Oneness is to be related to Majesty in as far as It excludes all plurality at the level of Itself while implying plurality, albeit an illusory one, at lower levels of existence. For further explanations see Titus Burckhardt, *An Introduction to Sufi Doctrine* (Wellingborough, 1976), pp. 60–1.

day belongeth the Kingdom? the King is immediately identified in the reply: *Unto God, the One, the Irresistible* (Q. XL: 16).

It is the Extreme Splendour of His Majesty Which makes it impossible for any other to stand beside Him, and on the other hand it is as it were by reason of His incomparability that He is King. In this connection it may be recalled that the upper triangle of the Seal of Solomon, as well as the vertical of the Cross, is a figure of fire, being in fact like a tongue of flame; and to what has already been said of this vertical element as a symbol of the Exaltation of His Majesty, it may be added that fire would be quite unable to burn if it were not also a manifestation of the All-Consuming Onliness, Which the upper triangle symbolizes by its contraction towards the single point of the apex. In the lower triangle, however, the dominating tendency is that of expansion towards the horizontal base, and the horizontal has already been mentioned as manifesting above all the Amplitude of the Divine Beauty. One Aspect of this Amplitude is Riches, Which under the title of Bounty takes the place of Beauty in His Name the Lord of Majesty and Bounty. It may thus be said that whereas an Aspect of His Majesty is in His Singleness and His Onliness, the corresponding Aspect of His Infinite Bounty and Beauty is in the Plurality and Variety of His Qualities. This must be reflected in all the pairs throughout the Universe, and so, in connection with what has already been said about symbolic inversion, it should be added that the symbol, as the feminine term of a pair, must not only be passive and negative in relation to its reality, but it must also have something of plurality and amplitude. This aspect of inversion which takes the form of multiplicity in the face of unity, of analytical expansion in the face of synthetic concentration, is illustrated by the Sufi saying that when the light first came before a mirror, it saw itself reflected in the form of a peacock with tail outspread. The light, with its impenetrable and concentrated whiteness, refers above all to the Secret of the Onliness of His Majesty, Whose Perfect Complement, namely the Full Display[2] of the

[2] This recalls the saying that in Paradise men will be clothed whereas women will be naked; for if it be taken in its highest sense, that is, as applied to the Gardens of Firdaws, its explanation is to be found in His Names "The Inwardly Hidden" (*al-bāṭin*), Which, suggesting His Secret, refers to His Perfection of Majesty, and "The Outwardly Manifest" (*al-ẓāhir*), Which refers to His Perfection of Beauty.

Infinite Riches and Variety of the Divine Beauty, is symbolized by the peacock. It is indeed thus that the true symbol, in imitation of the Divine Beauty, displays separately one by one the different aspects contained all together in the synthetic unity of what it symbolizes; and for an example of a symbol's fulfilling this function we may return once more to the true man, whose soul, at the presence of the light of the Intellect, amplifies itself outwards from the centre in all directions that it may be large enough to reflect all the realities hidden in the synthesis of the Eye of the Heart. These reflections appear as the virtues which are the ornaments of the true soul, and which, like the eyes in the peacock's tail, and like the higher spiritual realities themselves, symbolize above all the Divine Names and Qualities. Another example, parallel to this, is to be found in the riches and variety of the outer world itself; and here may be seen the extreme amplitude of the true man compared with other earthly creatures, for being the microcosm he corresponds not to any one of them but to the macrocosm which contains them all. They thus correspond to different qualities in his soul, each symbolizing a Divine Quality, whereas his soul symbolizes the Essence Which contains in Itself All the Qualities. Thus the Qur'ān testifies that man is the viceregent of God on earth, as does also the Old Testament in the words: "God created man in His Own Image"; for it is only in a far more limited sense that other creatures may be considered separately each as a little world in itself symbolizing the Whole Truth.

In like measure with expansive plurality, the other characteristics of the true symbol are also especially marked in the true man; for he alone of earthly creatures has direct knowledge of the higher realities, and the knowledge of these realities and of their excellence brings his soul to an extreme of plasticity and passivity in the desire to receive from them as full and pure a reflection as possible. It is this feminine perfection of his soul in its passivity and amplitude which is figured in the upturned base of the lower triangle of the Seal of Solomon.

So far we have considered only the passivity of the symbol in relation to the activity of what it symbolizes. But in the Seal of Solomon are to be found both the aspects which the symbol has in itself, figured in their relation to the two corresponding aspects of the higher reality. Thus if the upper triangle be taken to represent the Divinity, its apex will symbolize the Onliness of His Majesty and its base the Amplitude of His Beauty. The base of the lower triangle will then symbolize as before the amplitude of the true man's soul which is turned in passivity towards Heaven, reflecting the Passive Perfection, and the complement of this passivity, namely his majestic activity which is directed towards his kingdom, the earth, will be symbolized by the down-turned apex. The lower triangle as a whole is thus an image of the perfect human nature.

The active perfection of the true man as King of the Earth is the result of his passive perfection; for in the amplitude of his soul are reflected all the different possibilities of action, and from these he draws his inspiration to choose the one act perfectly suited to the particular circumstances. The fallen man, whose soul does not directly reflect the transcendent archetypes, has not this same possibility of inspiration, and is forced to rely too much on past experience. Thus his actions inevitably bear the traces of previous actions of the same kind, which means that they have a certain uniformity, being prevented by the fetters of habit from varying in proportion to the variation of the circumstances. The true man, on the other hand, has little need for memory of the past, which may be called "horizontal" memory. He is inspired by "vertical" memory in the sense of the word *dhikr*, and has the power to bring forth actions according to the process of the creation itself in descent from their spiritual source. Such an action is indeed a new creation specially made to fit particular circumstances, without the need to refer to previous actions, of which in its spontaneity it bears no trace, as if it were the first and only action of its kind. Thus the Onliness of the Divine Majesty finds Its shadow in the uniqueness of the true man's action. But by inversion, whereas the Archetype is the Cause of all passivity and contains in Itself all the different possibilities, the true man's action is the result of passivity and is itself contained among all the different possibilities of action.

To take another example on analogy with the last, if the upper triangle represents the Divinity in the Aspect of Providence, its apex will represent the Divine Free Will, Which is expressed in His Name "the Determiner" (*al-qādir*). The base will then represent the Passive Aspect of Providence Which is none other than the Mother of the Book (*ummu 'l-kitab*), the

Eternal Book in Which all things are written, and Which from the point of view of the creation may be called the Book of Destiny. Just as Destiny is Passive towards the Free Will Which is Its Cause, the true man is passive in the face of Destiny, and this passivity, represented by the upturned base of the lower triangle, is precisely what is meant by *islām* in the highest sense of the word, that is, not merely submission to the Law—the *islām* which contrasted with faith (*īmān*) and spiritual excellence (*iḥsān*)—but fully realized submission, that perfect acceptance of Destiny which is in fact a mark of sainthood, not to be attributed to the fallen man. As to the downturned apex of the lower triangle, it will represent the true man's relative freedom in action as the King of the Earth; and what was true in general of his activity in relation to his passivity is also true of this particular aspect of his activity; for by the law of inversion whereas the Absolute Free Will is entirely Active with regard to Destiny, the true man's relative free will is the result of his passivity in the face of Destiny. By reason of his extreme passivity towards Heaven he is far more free than any other earthly creature; and since this perfect passivity springs from his spiritual knowledge, that is, his vision of the Divine Qualities, one may see here an interpretation of the words of Jesus: "Get knowledge, for knowledge will make you free."[3] Indeed, the greater a man's knowledge, the more keenly he senses, beyond the purely human notion of good and evil, the Transcendent Beauty of the Divine Necessity and the harmony of the Universe which is Its shadow, and the more he shows his own relative freedom in giving thanks that everything is as it must be, his own destiny included, and in saying with all his soul: "Praise be to God, the Lord of the worlds!"

It is the true man's relative freedom, the full desire to do what he must do, which brings his activity to its extreme effectiveness; and this spontaneous activity, which in its emanation from unresisting passivity is symbolized by the lower triangle of the Seal of Solomon, is also symbolized by the element water, of which the inverted triangle is a figure; for just as water flows with irresistible penetration into a hollow in the rock, perfectly filling up every crevice down to its minutest

[3] In their highest sense these words refer to the Absolute Freedom which can only be regained by extinction in the Truth's Knowledge of Itself.

detail, even so the true man perfectly fills the hollow of each moment of his life, while in his outlook towards Heaven he remains like a calm and level surface upturned to the sky. Thus it is set down in the Book of the Way and Virtue (*Tao-Te-Ching*), revered by the Chinese as the most sacred of their scriptures: "The highest good is like water",[4] and again: "The weakest things in the world can overmatch the strongest things in the world. Nothing in the world can be compared with water for its weak and yielding nature; yet in attacking the hard and strong nothing proves better than it."[5] Water has these qualities because it is a direct reflection in the material world of the virtue of *islām*, which in its extreme passivity is the most penetratingly active of all earthly things.

[4] *Tao-Te-Ching*, translated by Ch'u Ta-Kao (London, 1959), chapter 8.

[5] *Ibid.*, chapter 78.

The Tree of the Knowledge of Good and Evil

And come not nigh this tree, for then would ye be transgressors. (Qur'ān II: 35)

The Qur'ān does not mention the name of the forbidden tree, but in the Old Testament it is named the Tree of the Knowledge of Good and Evil. The fallen man is in fact guided in action by memory of past experience, and from such "horizontal" memory is derived a general sense of what is desirable in action and what is to be avoided, which is none other than the knowledge of good and evil. But the true man's certainty enables him to go beyond this knowledge and to choose not merely a good action but the perfect action; thus when it is said in the Old Testament that before eating the fruit of the forbidden tree Adam was without the knowledge of good and evil, this does not imply any ignorance in him but on the contrary the possession of a higher knowledge in the synthesis of which the general sense of expediency remained undeveloped.

To save man from becoming subject to the merely human sense of expediency derived from experience, which is the knowledge of good and evil in its lowest form, such knowledge in its highest possible form was directly revealed in the religions represented by "the words" which Adam received from his Lord; and since for want of the Eye of Certainty the fallen man inevitably tends to become the slave of habits, the religions meet this necessity by prescribing the regular performance of rites, which become as it were sacred habits. Thus, through the Divine Mercy, the very limitations of the fallen man are made the vehicles of spiritual influence.

Like all else that is a direct reflection of spiritual truth, religion shows distinctly the two aspects figured in the lower triangle of the Seal of Solomon. But, in this, religion is not merely analogous to the true man; it actually is, in a sense, the true man, just as the true man, or more particularly the Prophet, is the incarnation of religion. The higher aspect of religion, corresponding to the passivity of the true man's soul in its outlook towards Heaven, is none other than this same outlook, abstracted from him and perpetuated. This higher aspect is universal and unchanging; in it each religion is necessarily identical with all the others, for with regard to the Divinity only one attitude is permissible, namely that of *islām*[1] (submission): *Verily before God religion is submission* (Q. III: 19). It is thus that the Qur'ān speaks of itself and the Gospel as confirming what was before it, and this inward identity of one religion with the rest is the clearest sign of its orthodoxy. On the other hand, in the formal or outward aspect of religion, the corresponding sign of orthodoxy lies in the extreme difference between the one particular set of outward forms and the others. For just as the true man's action is unique, the characteristic elements of a religion have a spontaneity and originality which give them also a certain uniqueness. The necessity for this outward difference between the religions is affirmed in the Chapter of the Table: *For each We have appointed a law and traced out a path, and if God had wished, verily He would have made you one people.* (Q. V: 48) whereas later in the same chapter these variations are as it were reabsorbed into the universal aspect of religion which is above all particular differences: *Verily they that believe, and those who are Jews, and the Sabaeans and the Christians—whosoever believeth in God and the last day and acteth piously—there shall come no fear upon them, neither shall they grieve.* (Q. V: 8)

The law of a religion is for a particular place and period, as a torch given to man to guide him on a moonless night; and to meet the fallen man's subjection to the knowledge of the forbidden tree, it makes a distinction between good, which corresponds to the narrow circle of light which it casts, and evil, which corresponds to the outer darkness. But the true man has no need of this torch; for him the circle of light which it casts is merged into one with the outer darkness by the light of the full moon. It is true that his spiritual vision enables him to see far more clearly than others the beauty of the religious laws as manifestations of the Will of Heaven, and thus his submis-

[1] The verb from which this verbal noun comes has as its present participle *muslim* (submitting, that is, practising *islām*).

sion to them is quite spontaneous. In other words he identifies them with his own certainty, and they become an expression of the Divine Will not only for a period and a people but for a particular moment and individual. But if by exception his certainty were not in accordance with these laws, it would necessarily take precedence over them, and so it is that the "transgressions" of the true man are "forgiven in advance". *Verily We have made thee victorious by a manifest victory, that God may forgive thee thy trespasses past and those which are to come.* (Q. XLVIII: 1)

What is Symbolism?

> *The seven Heavens and the earth and all that is therein glorify Him, nor is there anything but glorifieth Him with praise; yet ye understand not their glorification.* (Qur'ān: XVII, 44)

The above verse is an answer to the question asked by our chapter-heading; it also justifies to a certain extent, in its last sentence, the writing of the chapter, for a thing's glorification of God—which *ye understand not*—is precisely its symbolism. This may be deduced from the Islamic "holy utterance", so called because in it the Divinity speaks on the tongue of the Prophet: *I was a Hidden Treasure and I loved to be known, and so I created the world.*[1] Thus the universe and its contents were created in order to make known the Creator, and to make known the good is to praise it; the means of making it known is to reflect it or shadow it; and a symbol is the reflection or shadow of a higher reality.

The doctrine of symbolism may also be concluded from other verses in which the Qur'ān affirms that every single thing on earth has been sent down in finite measure from the Stores or Treasuries of the Infinite, sent down as a loan rather than a gift, for nothing herebelow can last, and everything must in the end revert to its Supreme Source. In other words, the Archetype is always the Heir who inherits back the symbol in which It manifested Itself: *Nor is there anything but with Us are the Treasuries thereof, and We send it not down save in known measure ... and verily it is We who give life and make to die, and We are the Inheritor* (XV: 21, 23). We may likewise quote the following Qur'ānic definition of the Divinity: *He is the First and the Last and the Outwardly Manifest and the Inwardly Hidden* (LVII: 3). The first, second and fourth of these Names are related to the Hidden Treasure. As to the *Outwardly Manifest*, the mystery of

[1] Italics are used throughout for all quotations from Scripture and by extension for such utterances as this.

the Divine Presence in the world of symbols is partly explained in the words *God created not the heavens and the earth and what lieth between them save from Truth and an appointed term* (XXX: 8). It can thus be said that the whole fabric of the universe is woven out of Eternity and ephemerality, Infinitude and finitude, Absoluity and relativity.

Man himself as he was created—True Man as the Taoists name him—is the greatest of earthly symbols. The universal doctrine that he was made *in the image of God* (Genesis 1:27) signifies this pre-eminence: man is the symbol of the sum of all the attributes, that is, of the Divine Nature in its Totality, the Essence, whereas the animate and inanimate creatures that surround him reflect only one aspect, or certain aspects of that Nature. Taken all together these symbols constitute the great outer world, the macrocosm, of which man, God's representative on earth, is the centre; and that centre is itself a little world, a microcosm, analogous in every respect to the macrocosm which is, like it, a total image of the Archetype.

It is through its centre that a world lies open to all that transcends it. For the macrocosm man is that opening; as to the microcosm, its centre is man's Heart—not the bodily organ of that name but his soul's central faculty[2] which, in virtue of its centrality, must be considered as being above and beyond the psychic domain. The openness of the Eye of the Heart, or the wake of the Heart as many traditions term it, is what distinguishes primordial man—and by extension the Saint—from fallen man. The significance of this inward opening may be understood from the relationship between the sun and the moon which symbolize respectively the Spirit and the Heart: just as the moon looks towards the sun and transmits something of its reflected radiance to the darkness of the night, so the Heart transmits the light of the Spirit to the night of the soul. The Spirit itself lies open to the Supreme Source of all light, thus making, for one whose Heart is awake, a continuity between the Divine Qualities and the soul, a ray which is passed from Them by the Spirit to the Heart, from which it is diffused in a multiple refraction throughout the various chan-

[2] The capital letter is used to denote the distinction. Moreover since this centre reflects a whole hierarchy of centres which transcend it, the term Heart is also sometimes used of the Spirit, and ultimately of the Supreme Centre, the Divine Self.

nels of the psychic substance. The virtues which are thereby imprinted on the soul are thus nothing other than projections of the Qualities, and inversely each of these projected images is blessed with intuition of its Divine Archetype. As to the mind with its reason, imagination and memory, a measure of the "moonlight" which it receives from the Heart is passed on to the senses and through them as far as the outward objects which they see and hear and feel; and at this furthest contact the ray is reversed, for the things of the macrocosm are recognised as symbols, that is, as kindred manifestations of the Hidden Treasure, each of which has its counterpart in the microcosm. Otherwise expressed, for primordial man everything, inward or outward, was transparent: in experiencing a symbol he experienced its Archetype. He was thus able to rejoice in being outwardly surrounded and inwardly adorned by Divine Presences.

The eating of the fruit of the forbidden tree was the attachment to a symbol for its own sake apart from its higher meaning. That violation of the norm barred man's access to his inward centre, and the consequent blurring of his vision made him no longer able to fulfil adequately his original function as mediator between Heaven and earth. But at the fall of the microcosm, the macrocosm remained unfallen; and though its symbols had become less transparent to man's perceiving, they retained in themselves their original perfection. Only primordial man does justice to that perfection; but at the same time he is independent of it, in virtue of being himself a symbol of the Divine Essence which is absolutely Independent of the Divine Qualities. Fallen man on the other hand has a lesson to learn from the great outer world which surrounds him, for its symbols offer him an enlightenment which will be of guidance to him on his path of return to what he has lost, inasmuch as their perfection can further the perfecting of their counterparts within him which have suffered from the Fall. The clouds of the macrocosm are never permanent; they come only to go, the luminaries still shine, and the directions of space have lost nothing of their measurelessness. But in fallen man the soul is no longer the vast image of the Infinite that it was created to be, and the inward firmament is veiled. That veiling is the decisive result of the Fall which did not sever the connection between soul and Spirit, between human perception and the Archetypes, but placed there a barrier that is more or less opaque—increasingly opaque as far as the majority is concerned, this increase being the gradual degeneration which inevitably takes place throughout each cycle of time. But in the context of our theme the barrier can and must be described as more or less transparent, since it would be pointless to speak of symbolism where there cannot be at least some intuition, however faint, of the Archetypes. Moreover the science of symbols is inextricably linked with the path of return which, being against the cyclic current, makes for an increase of transparency.

If the symbols of the macrocosm, taken collectively or separately, are reminders for the spiritual traveller of man's lost perfection, it might none the less be said that the most direct reminders will be microcosmic, that is, True Man himself, personified by the Prophets, the Saints and, more immediately, by the living Spiritual Master. But although there is no doubt a wealth of truth in this, it would be a simplification to reduce macrocosmic symbols to a second place in any absolute sense as regards their spiritual significance for man, since much will depend on the individual and on circumstances. Moreover otherness, as well as sameness, has its own special impact. The Qur'ān affirms the efficacy of both: *We shall show them Our signs on the horizons and in themselves* (XLI: 53).

Let us consider, to take a particular example, the virtue of dignity which might be described as majesty in repose, and which man, if he would be true to his nature, must seek to perfect in himself side by side with the other virtues which reflect the other Divine Qualities. The Swan incarnates just a particular aspect of dignity, but it does so to perfection, and by isolating that perfection it makes for man a powerfully clear-cut impression that is all the more irresistible for being presented in a non-human mode, that is, in a mode which is beyond our reach. That very beyondness can lend it wings, in the eye of the observer, for return to its Archetype. The same may be said of all the other great earthly symbols that are not human, such as sky, plain, ocean, desert, mountain, forest, river and what they encompass, each an eloquent "word" in this language that the members of the white, yellow and black races share in common.

Since nothing can exist except in virtue of its Divine root, does that mean that everything is a symbol? The answer is yes and no—yes for the reason just given, and no because "symbol" means "sign" or "token", which implies an operative power to call something to mind, namely its Archetype. In the light of the initially quoted verse *Nor is there anything but glorifieth Him with praise,* we could say that whether this or that can rightly be called symbolic depends on whether its "praise" is powerful or faint. The word symbol is normally reserved for that which is particularly impressive in its "glorification".

The distinction we have just made can be more clearly understood with reference to the spider's web as an image of the created universe,[3] an image that is all the more apt inasmuch as the web is woven out of the substance of its "creator". The concentric circles represent the hierarchy of the different worlds, that is, the different planes of existence; the more outward the circle, the lower its hierarchic degree, each circumference being in itself a disconnected outward (therefore "downward") projection of the centre. The radii of the web on the other hand are images of the radiance of the Divine Mercy, and they portray the relationship of connection between the centre and all that exists. But it is significant that even if on the basis of the web, a symbolic figure be drawn with the number of radii increased to the limit of what it is possible to set down on paper, there will still be, between the radii, gaps which increase in due proportion to the remoteness of the world in question from the "Hidden Treasure" which it was created to reveal. In the world of matter, which marks the lowest limit of the downward and outward radiation of the Divine Principle, there will therefore be wider "gaps" than anywhere else. Needless to say, there are in fact no voids, so that to justify our image it must be added that each radius has its own aura and that the intervening space between two radii is thus filled by the two presences in question. But not to be situated on the radius itself means necessarily not to be an outstandingly direct reflection of the transcendent Archetype; and the qualitative disparities between the various things of this world can be partly explained in the light of this image.

[3] This symbolism of the web has been admirably expounded by Frithjof Schuon, *In The Tracks of Buddhism* (London, 1989), pp. 26–7. See also his "*Atmā-Māyā*" in *Studies in Comparative Religion*, Summer 1973.

Since we are concerned with what is symbolic and what is not, it should be understood that we are not considering here disparities such as those between the animal, vegetable and mineral kingdoms or between different sections of the same kingdom—mammals, birds and insects, for example. The lion, the eagle and the bee are all true symbols, each being a summit in its own domain which means, in the language of our figure,[4] that it lies on one of the radii, whence its power to place us on that same ray of the creative Spirit so that our aspirations may thereby ascend inversely back to the Source. But not everything is capable of offering us this possibility; and the disparities we have been speaking of lie between true symbols and kindred beings which are considerably less well favoured.[5] It is in the nature of things that some of the contents of the world that is furthest from the Principle should bear signs of that remoteness.

By way of summing up, still with reference to the concentric circles and the radii of the web, it could be said that all created things are both disconnected projections of their creative Principle while being at the same time Its connected radiations. On this basis the symbol could be defined as that in which the relationship of connection predominates over that of disconnection, whereas the predominance of disconnectedness precludes, as it were by definition, any outstanding power to connect us with the Archetype, and it is that power which may be said to confer, on its possessor, the status of symbol.

To see that symbolism is inseparable from religion we have only to remember that the word religion indicates the

[4] No single symbol can possibly reflect all the aspects of its Archetype. While it figures the outward impetus set in motion by the creative act, the web has no downward dimension. In this respect it needs to be completed by the Biblical symbol of Jacob's ladder, or by the Sufi symbol of the Tree of the Universe which represents the different hierarchic levels by cedar-like layers of branches, one layer above the other.

[5] To take examples from the world of mammals in addition to the lion, with whom other members of the cat family are to be included, we may mention, as being truly symbolic in their different ways, the elephant, the camel, the horse and the wolf. On the other hand, in contrast with these sacred animals, the hippopotamus, the giraffe and the hyena are uninspiring, by which we mean, to revert to our liminal quotation, that their "praise" is too "faint" to earn for them, as such, the title of symbol in the higher and more exclusive sense of the word, though as animals, that is, in their life and consciousness, they are symbolic, as also in their very existence.

re-establishment of a ligament with the Supreme Archetype, and one has to resort to a symbol for that purpose. Primordial man, in virtue of being directly aware of his own connectedness, was the personification of the link which religion aims at restoring, whence his capacity to act as mediator between the Divinity and Its microcosmic and macrocosmic reflections which are, respectively, man (or the soul) and the earthly state in its entirety including its human centre.

If religion means spirituality, then primordial man was the embodiment of religion. But if this word be understood strictly in its etymological sense he cannot be said to have had any religion, for there is clearly no need to re-establish a connection which has never been impaired. Nor did he need, in any negative sense of that word, a science of symbols; but in virtue of his being a total image of the Divine, he could not fail to reflect the Hidden Treasure's joy—*I loved to be known*—at perceiving Itself mirrored in created things. Otherwise expressed, beneath the Supreme Beatitude of Gnosis, that is, the consciousness of identity with the Absolute Infinite One, his happiness as a soul in bliss coincided with symbolism, that of Paradise itself and of all that it contained including himself and other holy microcosms.

An essential aspect of every religion is the performance of rites. But if it be said that primordial man had no need of rites, it must be added that for him every act was potentially a rite in virtue of his awareness of its symbolic significance. The possession of a spiritual nature above his human nature enabled his consciousness to transcend the earthly state and with it the temporal condition. The domain of the Spirit encompasses the whole of time and is therefore as it were simultaneously "before" the creation of man and "after" his resurrection.[6] Seen from that angle, symbols have "already" been reabsorbed into their spiritual archetypes; but such a standpoint is beyond the reach of fallen man, except in theory, since he no longer has access to the Heart which is the gateway to the Spirit. In

[6] It is thus an error to suppose that blessed souls have to wait in Paradise for their bodies to join them after the resurrection, since if a soul has accumulated in life enough celestial gravity for it to be drawn towards Paradise as soon as it is liberated from its body at death, it will be reunited, once it has risen beyond the domain of time, with its "already" resurrected and transfigured body.

other words, the Saint is able to lend his wings to a symbol, and those wings, with which the primordial soul was naturally fledged, were lost at the Fall.

If the Saint does not, strictly speaking, need the prescribed rites of a religion, he can none the less rejoice in them, and he is their exemplary performer. But as to fallen man, inasmuch as they are Heaven's answer to his wingless predicament, he needs them imperatively above all things else. They could be defined as symbolic acts or enacted symbols, providentially endowed with wings for return to their Source, wings which the performer of the rite acquires by identifying himself with the act in question. Otherwise expressed, a rite is as a life-line thrown down from Heaven: it is for the worshipper to cling to the life-line; the rest is in the hands of the Thrower. Since a rite is always performed with a view to God, it amounts to a re-enactment of the connection between the symbol (in this case man) and the Supreme Archetype, a vibrating of that unsevered but dormant link, which needs the constant repetition of these vibrant acts to rouse it, once and for all, from sleep to wake.

In considering the relationship between rites and the categories of symbols already mentioned, it must be remembered that the Hidden Treasure may always radiate anew certain aspects of Itself in whatever degree of intensity is needed to overwhelm human limitations, and in whatever mode is best adapted to the particular receptivity of a given time and place. Such are the Divine interventions which establish the religions on earth, and without which no religion could take root. The altogether exceptional power with which Providence intervenes at these cyclic moments necessarily brings into being symbols for which the definitions already given will not suffice. It is true that every symbol has, as we have seen, a mysterious identity with its Archetype. But of symbols in general it can and must be said that they are merely symbols and not the Archetype. Being "of this world" they are subject to all its conditions and limitations. A Revelation also—together with the sacramental symbols with which it operates—being in this world, though not "of it", is bound to take on a finite form. It is none the less a "stranger" herebelow, for the whole point of its earthly existence is that it should amount to an other-worldly intrusion, that it should be a real presence of the Infinite in the finite, of the Transformal in the formal. Moreover what is true of Revelation, such as the Vedas, the Pentateuch and the Psalms, the Tao-Te-King, the Qur'ān, is likewise true of the descents of the Divine Word in human form such as the Hindu Avataras, including the Buddha, and by extension Jesus. Considering the part they are called upon to play in their various religions, it would indeed be pointless to say of any of these, within the context of the perspective in question, that they are "merely symbols". Therefore, in respect of our having said that a symbol worthy of the name is that in which the Archetype's radiation predominates over Its projection, it is necessary to add that the sacramental symbol proceeds from its Source, relatively speaking, by pure radiation. To express this distinction the words "begotten not made" can be transposed from the Christian creed and applied universally, for such symbols may well be said to be "of one substance" with the Archetype.

With regard to the Eucharist as an example of a sacramental symbol, it is worthy of note that the otherworldliness of its bread and wine is affirmed not only in Christianity but also, and even more absolutely, by the Islamic Revelation, which mentions the Last Supper—in a chapter that is named after it, "The Banquet"—as the immediate result of the following prayer of Jesus at the request of his disciples: *O God, our Lord, send down to us a banquet from Heaven which will be a feast for the first of us and the last of us,*[7] *and a sign from Thee* (V: 114). Also highly significant, as regards Revelation in general, is the Islamic dogma that the Qur'ān is "not created". The same identity of the sacramental symbol with its Archetype constitutes the basis of the universal esoteric rite of invoking the Divine Name. Hindu *japa-yoga* (union by invocation) and its equivalents, in all other esoterisms have, as their guarantee of efficacy, the truth which Sufism expresses with the words "the Name is the Named".

[7] That is, for the first and last generations of Christians.

The Decisive Boundary

The different degrees in the hierarchy of universal existence could be subdivided again and again. But what matters doctrinally is to be aware of the main divisions, starting from the Absolute Itself which is beyond existence and beyond Being, and which alone is Real, in the full sense of the word. This is the degree of the Transpersonal Self, which transcends all relativity. Below It, but still in the domain of Divinity, is the relative Absolute,[1] that is, the Personal God, the Creator from Whom proceeds all createdness, all existence.[2] Creation marks the division between the Divine and the existent, between Worshipped and worshipper. The subsequent great division in the hierarchy is the polarization of all existence into Heaven and earth, or Spirit and soul—from our point of view this world and the next, though the last word may be taken in a wider sense to include all that transcends this world, both created and Uncreated. Finally there is the division between soul and body, between the psychic world and the material world.

Each world in the hierarchy of the universe is a reflection of the one above it, and each of its contents reflects, in the higher world, a counterpart which is the immediate source of its existence but which, in its turn, is no more than the reflection of a yet more real counterpart from a yet higher plane of existence. There is thus, for each symbol in the world of matter, a whole series of archetypes one above the other, like the rungs of a ladder, leading up to the Supreme Archetype in

[1] We owe this indispensable term to Frithjof Schuon who, no doubt more than any writer of this century, has stressed the need for awareness of the distinction *in divinis* between the Absolute and the relative, a distinction which has always been known to esoterism, whatever the tradition, but which exoteric theology has refrained from divulging, more or less with impunity until now, when the widespread overactivity of minds makes its disclosure the lesser of two evils.

[2] The word is used here in its original sense of *ex-stare*, to stand out from (i.e. from an origin).

the Divine Essence. With regard to the term archetype however, we are obliged to make an important reservation, the reason for which can clearly be seen in the light of the significance of the *Symplegades*, the Clashing Rocks of Greek mythology. In his masterly article on these rocks,[3] Ananda Coomaraswamy shows that they have their equivalents in many other ancient traditions where the symbol takes also the form of clashing mountains, clashing icebergs, clashing waters, clashing portals and, in the temporal domain, the clashing together of day and night between which the two twilights offer narrow gates of passage. What is above all significant in our present context is the extreme difficulty and danger of the passage. It is virtually impossible to reach what lies beyond the rocks without the help of Heaven; and aspiration towards that beyond—so Coomaraswamy's article shows us—was a dominant factor in the lives of all the peoples of antiquity—we might say of all peoples except those who are typical of the modern civilization. The rocks are clearly the equivalent of the *strait gate* (Matt. VII: 13–14) of the Gospel; and like that gate they are situated precisely between the soul and the Spirit, where this world ends and the next world begins. To tell of the rocks is thus to affirm that the place where they operate is what might be called a particularly crucial rung in the ladder of existence. From the human point of view, that is indeed the decisive boundary; nothing of lasting value exists or can be achieved this side of the Symplegades, while beyond them there is no evil, no suffering and no death. It was the Fall which galvanised these rocks into activity, and they are in fact the equivalent of what barred the return of fallen man to Eden—in the words of Genesis;—*Cherubims and a flaming word which turned every way to keep the way of the tree of life* (III: 24). The Tree and the Fountain mark the centre of the earthly state; but a centre, since it is the point of access to higher realities, is always above the rest of its domain. Thus on the one hand Eden is the Terrestrial Paradise, while on the other hand it is spoken of as if it belonged to the next world, for like its central Tree and Fountain it is beyond the flaming sword and the clashing rocks. So, analogously, is the Heart the centre of the soul; but the soul as such, together with its body,

[3] See *Studies in Comparative Religion*, Winter, 1973. For a brief analysis, see Martin Lings, *The Eleventh Hour* (Cambridge 1987), pp. 85–8.

is on this side of the barrier. It ranks above the body, which is its shadow or reflection; but it shares with the body the limitation of being natural and not in any sense supernatural.

It follows by way of consequence that although every material symbol reflects its counterparts in the soul—and it may reflect more than one at different levels of the psychic domain—such counterparts are not normally referred to as archetypes. This term is strictly reserved, in traditional practice, for what lies beyond the crucial barrier that is represented by the rocks which Athene held apart for the Argonauts to pass, by *the strait gate* of which it is said *few are they that find it*, and by the waters of the Red Sea[4] which opened for the children of Israel on their way to the Promised Land but which closed upon Pharaoh and his host who had no warrant to pass.

There is more than one imperative practical reason—and for practical we might say methodic—why such words as archetype should not be squandered on the psychic domain. The prefix "arch" signifies both exaltation and primacy, which confers on it also a sense of finality from the mystical standpoint of looking towards our first origins with a view to reintegration, whereas the soul is, from the same standpoint, that which has to be surpassed. There can be no advancing upon the spiritual path unless all one's aspirations and energies be concentrated on what lies beyond the ego. But there is something in the soul which shrinks, not unnaturally, from the ordeal of the dread passage, and which will snatch at any pretext for putting off "the evil day", and for enticing the spiritual traveller into its own seemingly endless labyrinthine recesses. Moreover the microcosm's fear of surpassing itself finds an ally in the unwillingness of the macrocosm, that is, all that lies on this side of the barrier, to allow any part of itself to escape from its hold. Nor, to say the least, is it for nothing that the Fall unleashed for mankind a downward and outward impetus which makes any approach to the decisive boundary a difficult upstream movement. The personifier of that impetus, whether he be called demi-urge or devil, will not fail to exploit the above mentioned disinclinations as a means of obstructing the path of return to our origins.

[4] That is, if the Exodus be interpreted, beyond its literal sense, according to its esoteric or anagogical significance as an image of the spiritual path, of which the ultimate goal is symbolized by the Promised Land.

The modern world presents another obstacle for him to exploit, one which did not previously exist, inasmuch as psychology—in all but name—was in the hands of spiritual men. In traditional civilizations it was the priest or his equivalent, and no one else, who was thought qualified to give advice about the soul, which was never considered independently of man's final ends, that is without reference to the higher degrees of reality. The ego could not turn a blind eye to its own limitations because it was never allowed to forget its place in the hierarchy of existence. Moreover those responsible for "the cure of souls" could take for granted a general knowledge of the doctrine of original sin. It was as if every patient had been told in advance, to use the language of our theme, "you are on the wrong side of the boundary, and until you are able to reach the other side you will continue to be somewhat subhuman and must expect the consequences." All advice was given on that basis of realism.

Modern psychology, on the contrary, dismisses the doctrine in question and with it the "rocks". The higher reaches of the universe are relegated to the realm of mere supposition, and the microcosm, soul and body, is isolated from all that transcends it. The soul is thus treated as the highest known thing. The average psychoanalyst may not deliberately set out to inflate it with self-importance, but in fact his so-called science acts like a conspiracy in that direction. Another closely related illusion inculcated by it is that of being self-sufficient and normal. The soul is made unrealistically expectant of freedom from problems which are bound to beset it, and the absence of which would be discreditable.[5]

The point to be made here however, is that although modern psychology is eager to throw metaphysics to the winds, it is not prepared to impoverish its own vocabulary by abstention from high-sounding words of metaphysical import. Consequently "archetype" and "transcendent", to mention only two examples,[6] are currently used in relation to things which,

[5] See, in this respect, Frithjof Schuon, *Survey of Metaphysics and Esoterism* (Bloomington, Indiana, 1986), p. 197.

[6] We are not considering here the words "intellect" and "intellectual", since these have already been in misuse since the so-called "Enlightenment". Modern psychology did not inaugurate this violation, though it can be blamed for failing to react against it.

while being higher than others, none the less belong to the domain of nature which is by definition untranscendent and therefore not capable of being the repository of archetypes.[7]

[7] Jung is particularly insidious in his misuse of this term—see Titus Burckhardt, *Mirror of the Intellect* (Cambridge, 1987), pp. 58–67.

The Symbolism of the Pairs

> *Glory be to Him who hath created all the pairs, of that which the earth groweth, and of themselves, and of that whereof they know not.* (Qur'ān, XXXVI: 36)

Creation means manifestation, by the Creator, of His own unmanifested attributes, as is clear from the already quoted Holy Tradition: *I was a Hidden Treasure and I loved to be known, and so I created the world.* But the title of this chapter may raise the question: "What of the Divine Oneness? Should not this be dwelt on, before there is any consideration of duality?" The answer is that the symbolizing of the One is too obvious to need exposition at any length. On the one hand this Archetype is reflected in the unity which everything possesses in itself; on the other hand the One's exclusive aspect of One-and-Onliness imprints uniqueness on each single one of Its manifestations so that no two things can possibly be identical, however similar they may be. Nor can any of the dualities which are the theme of this chapter escape from the One, for the very notion of "pair" implies complementarity, which is a condition and an anticipation of Union.

The particular aspect of creation referred to in the opening Qur'ānic verse may be said to have its roots in the Divine Name, Possessor of Majesty and Bounty (*Dhū l-Jalāli wa l-Ikrām*), which indicates a polarity of complements mysteriously hidden in the Oneness of the Creator. On the basis of this polarity a distinction is made in Islamic doctrine between the Majestic Names and the Beautiful Names. Bounty and Beauty are closely related aspects of what the Taoists term Passive Perfection (*K'un*), of which the complement is Active Perfection (*Ch'ien*). The Hindu terms *Purusha* and *Prakriti* denote the same archetypal pair. They themselves are unmanifested, but it is from them that manifestation (creation) proceeds or, more precisely, it is born from the womb of *Prakriti* under the influence of *Purusha*. The great symbol of *Prakriti* is water.

The same symbolism but at a lower level, within the domain of creation, is used in Genesis. *The Spirit of God moved upon the face of the waters* (1: 2) and from the subsequent division of the waters results the pair Heaven and earth, and their personal analogue Spirit and soul. A figure universally used to portray such "vertical" polarity in which one term transcends the other is the Seal of Solomon. It expresses this relationship at every level, and in particular it frequently serves to denote the pair Creator–creation, or God–man. Its close-knit symmetrical beauty, which often figures in the decorative arts of many different traditions, goes hand in hand with its symbolic power, for it expresses not only direct analogy—man made in the image of God—but also inverse analogy by reason of which the First is reflected on earth above all by the last in order, of creation, just as, on the plane of matter, the top of a mountain is seen at the bottom of a pool of water that reflects it. The Seal is also expressive of the mysterious interpenetration between the higher and lower poles of a vertical pair, and because of this it is used as a symbol of the two natures of Christ, Divine and human. But its significance is by no means limited to relationships at different levels, since the upturned apex of one triangle and the upturned base of the other, that is, the predominance of dynamic contraction in one and of static expansion in the other, make them respectively symbols of activity and passivity, or male and female. The Seal is thus a figure of the union of the Active and Passive Perfections, and of the Divine Name, Possessor of Majesty and Bounty.

Pre-eminent amongst the created pairs are the polarizations of the different persons of the Spirit, each one of which has inevitably both a masculine and a feminine aspect. According to Hinduism, *Buddhi* (Spirit, Intellect) is the summit and the synthesis of all manifestation, being the manifested offspring of *Purusha* and *Prakriti*. It corresponds to the Logos in its created aspect, and it has three persons, Brahmā, Vishnu and Shiva, each of which has its *Shaktī* (productive will), that is, its feminine consort. These are, respectively, Sarasvatī, Lakshmī and Parvati.[1] There is also an apotheosis of Sita and Radha, the earthly consorts of Rama and Krishna, the seventh and eighth

[1] In his chapter on *Buddhi* in *Man and his becoming according to the Vedānta* (London, 1945), René Guénon draws our attention to the equivalent triad Wisdom, Beauty, Strength which figures in Masonic doctrine.

Avatāras (descents) of Vishnu, who are thus frequently invoked by the two-fold names Sita–Ram and Radha–Krishna. We are reminded, despite the difference of human relationship, of the name Jesu–Maria.

The starting point of esoterisrn is the soul's consciousness of its need to regain the lost Paradise of Eden wherein it had access, through the Tree of Life and the Waters of Life, to the Spirit. In other words, the initial aspiration is a longing of the soul for the Spirit—"for God" we might say, for the Spirit opens onto the Divinity. If the seeker is a man, in order to enlist more easily all the powers of the soul for the spiritual path, the Spirit, considered in its complementary feminine aspect, may be personified by a woman. An example is to be found in Dante's *Divine Comedy*, where Beatrice, the beloved of Dante, symbolizes an aspect of the Spirit. From the Earthly Paradise, on the top of the Mountain of Purgatory, it is she who guides him through the Heavens.

Since no symbol can account for every aspect of its archetype, the Seal, for all its remarkable symbolic scope, can be instructively supplemented by another figure which may be obtained from it by turning the two triangles upside down so that their apexes meet in a point. The upturned lower triangle, like a pair of Christian hands in prayer, expresses the upward aspiration of the soul towards the Spirit, while in a parallel way it stands for the Mountain of Purgatory. The down turned upper triangle is an image of Mercy and Grace. As a whole, the figure is a diagram of the two seas—Heaven and earth or Spirit and soul—mentioned in the Qur'ān (XXV: 53 & LV: 19–20) as meeting but unable to overpass the barrier which prevents them from encroaching upon each other. Also powerfully figured, in the central point where the apexes meet, is the *strait gate* of the Gospels.

Despite the inequality of Spirit and soul, their mutual relationship maybe considered none the less as "conjugal" in view of our final ends. The soul itself is virtually spiritual, being no less than a projection of the Spirit into the psychic domain from which it will be, normally speaking, reabsorbed into its transcendent source. The "glorious body of the resurrection" is so named because the body is at that moment in the process of being reabsorbed into the soul, and with the soul, by sublimation into the Spirit.

Virtually equivalent to the polarity Spirit/soul, but less unequal and more horizontal, is the pair Heart and soul which may be said to comprise the whole human individuality. The Heart, which is the microcosmic Fountain of Life, is the gateway to the Spirit and as such it transcends the soul in the way that the centre transcends the circumference, though from a certain point of view they are at the same level of existence. The soul itself has likewise two poles: "As all active knowledge belongs to the masculine side of the soul, and all passive being to its feminine side, thought-dominated (and therefore clearly delimited) consciousness can in a certain sense be ascribed to the masculine pole, while all involuntary powers and capacities connected with life as such appear as an expression of the feminine side."[2]

The harmonious reunion of these two poles of the psychic substance is termed in alchemy the chemical marriage, and it is a preliminary step in the direction of "the mystical marriage", that higher union by which the soul is reunited with the Spirit and thus regains all that was lost at the Fall: "The marriage of the masculine and feminine forces finally merges into the marriage of Spirit and soul, and as the Spirit is the 'Divine in the human'—as is written in the *Corpus Hermeticum*—this last union is related to the mystical marriage. Thus one state merges into another. The realization of the fullness of the soul leads to the abandonment of the soul to Spirit, and thus the alchemical symbols have a multiplicity of interpretations. Sun and Moon can represent the two powers of the soul (Sulphur and Quicksilver); at the same time they are the symbols of Spirit and soul."[3]

The subdivisions are endless: each faculty of the soul may be said to have two aspects, active and passive, masculine and feminine. The same applies at all lower levels: the body is one but it has two ears, two eyes, two nostrils, two lips, two arms and two legs. Every separate thing is a unity penetrated by duality: a single flower comprises a central "eye" and a circumference of petals, by which it symbolizes, on the human plane, the individual as such, that is, the polarity Heart–soul.

[2] Titus Burckhardt, *Alchemy: Science of the Cosmos, Science of the Soul* (Shaftesbury, Dorset, 1986), p. 15.

[3] Ibid., p. 155.

In some cases of symbolic duality it is a question of two entities becoming isolated from a larger group. There are more than two elements, but fire, and water none the less form a pair which is one of the great symbols of complementarity. Analogously, amongst the five senses, sight and hearing form a distinct pair that is comparable to fire and water. It is in the nature of sound to spread, and listening involves, for the aural faculty, a dilation that induces an expansion of the whole psychic substance in receptivity. On the other hand sight concentrates itself—and with itself the soul—upon the object of vision.

The senses and what they sense are particular modes of a duality which is always with us and which concerns each one of us at every moment of consciousness. This is the pair subject–object. As we have seen, the complementary pairs may be termed male and female, active and passive, dynamic and static, or contractive and expansive. Each of these twofold designations is analogous to the others though each may be more immediately apt with regard to one particular pair. It is evident that the subject and the object are respectively active and passive, dynamic and static. They can also be termed male and female, but in this connection let it be remarked once again that every single thing in existence, therefore every pole of a duality, is bound to have in itself two complementary aspects. In the case of the conjugal pair, each of the two will always be the subject in respect of his or her "male" dynamic and active pole, and each will be the object in respect of his or her "female" expansive and passive pole. Thus the woman as subject beholds the display of the man's masculinity and not its secret, not the root of his ego which, being hidden and purely subjective, could never serve as object. But she has this as it were non-feminine experience within the framework of being herself the purely feminine pole of the marriage of male and female.

To revert once more to our initial quotation, we have seen that the immediate source of duality lies in the two complementary aspects that are to be found in the Creator Himself. But this is not its primal source: neither the Name Creator nor the Dominical Name, Lord, can be placed at the level of the Pure Absolute, because of their implicit involvement with relativity, for a lord has his subjects just as a creator has his creatures. In Islamic doctrine a distinction is made between non-essential Names—such as these two and most of the others—[4] and the names of the Essence which are purely Absolute such as the Truth, the One, the Self-Sufficient, the Independent, the Living, the Holy. Analogous distinctions are made in Hinduism and other esoterisms; and if we wish to trace the pairs to their ultimate Origin and End, we must therefore go back to the Essence Itself. There could be no complementary duality inherent in the Creator without a purely Absolute Precedent. In other words the plenitude of all complementarity can only lie in the Absolute Oneness of the Divine Selfhood, and it is here, beyond the creative Principle, that the Supreme Archetype of the pairs must be sought.

A question may arise at this point in connection with subject and object, a pair which is closely related to the personal pronouns. The third of these, He (*Huwa*) is commonly used in Islam as one of the Essential Names to denote the Absolute Truth, and an equivalent use is made in Hinduism of the demonstrative "That" (*Tad*). But it will be clear to our readers that the Archetype of the pair subject–object is, primarily, not the Essential He but the Essential I–Thou. We say primarily because the first and second persons belong to each other and readily merge into oneness, whereas the third person has always been of indispensable value to theology as a means of expressing the Divine Incomparability and it has, for our minds, a powerful primary association with the idea of otherness.

The Supreme Subject is the Absolute in His Pure Selfhood. But the Absolute could not possibly be deprived of an object, nor could the I–Thou relationship exist as the vehicle of love throughout the universe if it were absent from That which is the Source of all things. In other words, it is a metaphysical necessity that the Divine Selfhood should possess intrinsically, as complement to the subjective Secret, an objective mode of display, and this is Infinitude. Nor can there be any particular aspect of joy or wonderment in any subject–object relationship

[4] The Majestic Names and the Beautiful Names belong to this non-absolute category. But in themselves the Names of Majesty and Beauty cannot be excluded from the highest level, and the same must be said of the Active Perfection and the Passive Perfection of Taoism.

whatsoever which does not have its archetypal plenitude in the Absolute–Infinite Oneness.

Here lies the highest meaning of the Far-Eastern symbol *Yin–Yang* which ranks with the Seal of Solomon as one of the most powerfully expressive figures of complementarity. The Absolute is white whereas the Infinite, so often symbolized by night, is black; as to their Oneness, apart from the unity of the figure as a whole, the black circle in the centre of *Yang* signifies the Infinite as an intrinsic dimension of the Absolute, and the white circle in the centre of *Yin* signifies the Absolute as an intrinsic dimension of the Infinite. Oneness or Union is also expressed in the mutual attraction between *Yang* and *Yin*, inasmuch as each has something which the other lacks and without which it cannot be complete. Like the Seal, this figure also has its applications at every level of the universe and, in a vertical sense, at two different levels.

What then of the third person? Absolute–Infinite Oneness excludes the possibility that there should be anything "other" than Itself. But otherness is not the only signification of he, she or it, which can be used to express that which the first and second persons possess in common; and this is its original sense, that is, what it signifies in the Oneness of the Absolute I–Thou. A more precise answer to the question here raised may be deduced from the following formulation: "God is Absolute, and being the Absolute, He is likewise the Infinite; being the Absolute and the Infinite, intrinsically and without duality, He is also the Perfect."[5] Perfection is thus what the Absolute is conscious of sharing with the Infinite and what the Infinite is conscious of sharing with the Absolute; and since there is no duality, and therefore no separation or division between the Subject and the Object of Consciousness, Reality may be expressed in either subjective or objective terms, which gives rise to He or That as an alternative to I. Selfconsciousness is fraught with the implicit question "What am I?", which could also be worded as a self-addressed "What art thou?" At the highest level the answer is "I am (or Thou art, or We are) Absolute Infinite Perfection" or simply "I am That", or "I am

[5] Frithjof Schuon, *From the Divine to the Human* (Bloomington, Indiana, 1982), p. 73.

It" which becomes in Islam "I am He",[6] for want of a neuter in Arabic. The Qur'ān says *there is no god but I* and *there is no god but He*, and there is a constant easy fluctuation between the first and the third persons, when used of God, throughout the revealed book.

As the Supreme Archetype of the pairs, Absolute Infinite Perfection may be conceived of as a single Perfection that is mysteriously endowed with two aspects, as in the Taoist perspective. But it is also possible, as we shall see in the next chapter, to consider this threefold term as expressive of the Supreme Archetype of all the triads in existence.

[6] It may also become She inasmuch as the word *Dhāt* (Essence) is feminine.

TRADITION & MODERNITY

The Past in the Light of the Present

Would the peoples of old have changed their attitude towards their earliest ancestors if they had known all that modern scientists now know?

This is in some ways equivalent to another question: Is there any real incompatibility between religion and science?—for the opinions of our forefathers were largely based on religion.

Let us take one or two examples of "stumbling-blocks", considering them in the light of both religion and science, and not in the darkness of either.

Does religion claim that pre-historic events can be dated on the basis of a literal interpretation of figures mentioned in the Old Testament, and that the approximate date of the Creation itself is 4,000 BC? It could hardly make such a claim, for "a thousand years in Thy Sight are but as yesterday" and it is by no means always clear, when days are mentioned in sacred texts, whether they are human days or whether they are Divine Days each consisting of "a thousand human years", that is, a period which bears no comparison with a human day.

Can science allow that the earth was created about 6,000 years ago? Clearly it cannot, for evidence of various kinds shows beyond doubt that at that date the earth and man were already old.

If science seems here to refute the letter of the Scriptures, it does not refute their spirit, for even apart from archaeological and geological evidence there are directly spiritual reasons for preferring not to insist on the letter of Genesis chronology. This does not mean that our mediaeval ancestors, many if not most of whom did accept a literal interpretation, were less spiritual or less intelligent than ourselves—far from it. But although, as we shall see later, they almost certainly had a more qualitative sense of time than we have, that is, a keener sense of its rhythms, they no doubt had less sense of time in a purely quantitative way; and it did not strike them, as it can scarcely fail to strike us, that there is something spiritually incongruous in the idea of an All-Powerful God's creation being so remarkably unsuccessful that within a very short space of time the Creator saw the need to drown the whole human race, except for one family, in order to be able to start afresh. But even apart from questions of time, the men of the Middle Ages were too conscience-stricken to reason as we do, too overwhelmed by a sense of human responsibility—to their credit be it said. If what had happened was incongruous, not to say monstrous, all the more blame to man. This way of thinking certainly comes nearer to the truth than some more modern trends of thought do, but it does not correspond to the whole truth; and we who tend to look at the question more "detachedly" cannot help seeing that God has His responsibilities also. None the less it remains for each one of us to ask himself exactly how sublime his own detachment is, always remembering that a man who is standing idly down in the plain sometimes has a better view of certain aspects of a mountain than have those who are actually climbing it.

Whatever answers we may give to this question, the fact remains that our sense of what is to the Glory of God and what is not fits in less well, as regards bare chronology, with the perspective of mediaeval Christendom than it does with the perspective of the Ancient World, according to which it is only after having granted mankind many thousands of years of spiritual well-being that God has allowed it to pass through a relatively short period of decay, or in other words allowed it to "grow old". In any case this more ancient perspective cannot lightly be brushed aside. Its basis, the tradition of the four ages of the cycle of time which the Greeks and Romans named the Golden, Silver, Bronze and Iron Ages, is not merely European but is also to be found in Asia, among the Hindus, and in America among the Red Indians. According to Hinduism, which has the most explicit doctrine on this subject, the Golden Age was by far the longest; the ages became increasingly shorter as they were less good, the shortest and worst being the Dark Age, which corresponds to the Iron Age. But even this last and shortest age, the age we live in, stretches back more than 6,000 years into the past. What modern archaeologists call "the Bronze Age" bears no relation to the third age of the four, and what they call "the Iron Age" merely happens to coincide with a fraction of the fourth age.

The ancient and world-wide tradition of the four ages does not contradict the Book of Genesis, but, like the evidence of science, it does suggest an allegorical rather than a literal interpretation. It suggests, for example, that certain names indicate not merely single individuals but whole eras of pre-history, and that the name Adam in particular may be taken as denoting not only the first man but also the whole of primordial humanity, spanning a period of many thousands of years.

* * *

But is it necessary for religion to maintain that at some time in the past man was created in a state of surpassing excellence, from which he has since fallen?

Without any doubt yes, for if the story of the Garden of Eden cannot be taken literally, it cannot, on the other hand, be taken as meaning the opposite of what it says.[1] The purpose of allegory is, after all, to convey truth, not falsehood. Besides, it is not only Judaism, Christianity and Islam which tell of the perfection of Primordial Man and his subsequent fall. The same truth, clothed in many different imageries, has come down to us out of the prehistoric past in all parts of the world. Religions are in fact unanimous in teaching not evolution but devolution.

Is this religious doctrine contrary to scientifically known facts? Must science, in order to be true to itself, maintain the theory of evolution?

In answer to this last question let us quote the French geologist Paul Lemoine, editor of Volume V (on "Living Organisms") of the *Encyclopédie Française*, who went so far as to write in his summing up of the articles of the various contributors: "This exposition shows that the theory of evolution is impossible. In reality, despite appearances, no one any longer believes in it.... Evolution is a sort of dogma whose priests no longer believe in it, though they uphold it for the sake of their flock."

Though undeniably exaggerated in its manner of expression—that is, as regards its sweeping implications of hypoc-

[1] To this obvious fact Teilhard de Chardin turned a blind eye, and here lies one of the weaknesses of his standpoint.

risy on the part of the "priests" in question—this judgement, coming where it does, is significant in more than one respect. There is no doubt that many scientists have transferred their religious instincts from religion to evolutionism, with the result that their attitude towards evolution is sectarian rather than scientific. The French biologist Professor Louis Bounoure quotes Yves Delage, a former Sorbonne Professor of Zoology: "I readily admit that no species has ever been known to engender another, and that there is no absolutely definite evidence that such a thing has ever taken place. None the less, I believe evolution to be just as certain as if it had been objectively proved." Bounoure comments: "In short, what science asks of us here is an act of faith, and it is in fact under the guise of a sort of revealed truth that the idea of evolution is generally put forward."[2] He quotes, however, from a present day Sorbonne Professor of Palaeontology, Jean Piveteau, the admission that the science of facts as regards evolution "cannot accept any of the different theories which seek to explain evolution. It even finds itself in opposition with each one of these theories. There is something here which is both disappointing and disquieting."[3]

Darwin's theory owed its success mainly to a widespread conviction that the nineteenth-century European represented the highest human possibility yet reached. This conviction was like a special receptacle made in advance for the theory of man's sub-human ancestry, a theory which was hailed without question by humanists as a scientific corroboration of their belief in "progress". It was in vain that a staunch minority of scientists, during the last hundred years, persistently maintained that the theory of evolution has no scientific basis and that it runs contrary to many known facts, and it was in vain that they pleaded for a more rigorously scientific attitude

[2] *Le Monde et la Vie*, November 1963. [Given that the first edition of this book saw the light in 1965, it may be necessary to comment, half a century after, on the current significance of some outdated references to the ever thriving evolutionist controversy. The author's own observation below comes apropos: "What has changed is not so much knowledge of facts as the sense of values." The discerning reader will surely have noticed that Lings is as far from joining the polemics about "the facts", as he is intent on making the case for a return to a traditional "sense of values".—Ed.]

[3] *Le Monde et la Vie*, March 1964.

towards the whole question. To criticize evolutionism, however soundly, was about as effective as trying to stem a tidal wave. But the wave now shows some signs of having spent itself, and more and more scientists are re-examining this theory objectively, with the result that not a few of those who were once evolutionists have now rejected it altogether. One of these is the already quoted Bounoure; another, Douglas Dewar, writes: "It is high time that biologists and geologists came into line with astronomers, physicists and chemists and admitted that the world and the universe are utterly mysterious and all attempts to explain them [by scientific research] have been baffled";[4] and having divided evolutionists into ten main groups (with some subdivisions) according to their various opinions as to what animal formed the last link in the chain of man's supposedly "pre-human" ancestry, opinions which are all purely conjectural[5] and mutually contradictory, he says: "In 1921 Reinke wrote: 'The only statement, consistent with her dignity, that science can make [with regard to this question] is to say that she knows nothing about the origin of man.' Today this statement is as true as it was when Reinke made it."[6]

If science knows nothing about the origins of man, she knows much about his prehistoric past. But this knowledge—to revert to our opening question—would have taught our ancestors little or nothing that they did not already know, except as regards chronology, nor would it have caused any general change in their attitude. For in looking back to the past, they did not look back to a complex civilization but to small village settlements with a minimum of social organization; and beyond these they looked back to men who lived without houses, in entirely natural surroundings, without books, without agriculture, and in the beginning even without clothes. It would be true then to say that the ancient conception of early man, based on sacred scriptures and on age-old traditional lore handed down by word of mouth from the

[4] *The Transformist Illusion* (preface) (Dehoff Publications, Tennessee, 1957). [For a review of this book, see the Appendix of the original work by Martin Lings.—Ed.]

[5] Because "no evolutionist who values his reputation will name *any known fossil* and say that, while not human, it is an ancestor of *Homo sapiens*" (p. 114).

[6] p. 294.

remote past, was scarcely different, as regards the bare facts of material existence, from the modern scientific[7] conception, which differs from the traditional one chiefly because it weighs up the same set of facts differently. What has changed is not so much knowledge of facts as the sense of values.

Until recently men did not think any the worse of their earliest ancestors for having lived in caves and woods rather than houses. It is not so long ago that Shakespeare put into the mouth of the banished Duke, living in the forest of Arden "as they lived in the golden world":

> "Here feel we but the penalty of Adam,
> The seasons' change...
> And this our life, exempt from public haunt,
> Finds tongues in trees, books in the running brooks,
> Sermons in stones, and good in everything.
> I would not change it."

These words can still evoke in some souls an earnest echo, an assent that is considerably more than a mere aesthetic approval; and behind Shakespeare, throughout the Middle Ages and back into the furthest historical past, there was no time when the Western world did not have its hermits, and some of them were among the most venerated men of their generation. Nor can there be any doubt that these exceptional few who lived in natural surroundings felt a certain benevolent pity for their brethren's servile dependence upon "civilization". As to the East, it has never broken altogether with the ancient sense of values, according to which the best setting for man is his primordial setting. Among the Hindus, for example, it is

[7] This word means what it says and is used here: (a) To exclude the bestial features which in the illustrations to so many school books are attributed to our remote ancestors. As the palaeontologist Professor E. A. Hooton remarks: "You can, with equal facility, model on a Neanderthaloid skull the features of a chimpanzee or the lineaments of a philosopher. These alleged restorations of ancient types of man have very little, if any, scientific value, and are likely only to mislead the public (quoted by Evan Shute in *Flaws in the Theory of Evolution*, Temside Press, London, Canada, 1966, p. 215). (b) To include evidence too often passed over in silence such as that of the Castenedolo and Calaveras skull, which point to the existence of "men of modern type" at a period when, according to the evolutionists, *Homo sapiens* had not yet evolved. (See Dewar, *ibid.*, pp 117–29, and Shute *ibid.*, ch. XXI).

still an ideal—and a privilege—for a man to end his days amid the solitudes of virgin nature.

For those who can readily grasp this point of view, it is not difficult to see that agriculture, after a certain degree of development had been reached, far from marking any "progress" became in fact "the thin end of the wedge" of the final phase of man's degeneration. In the Old Testament narrative, this "wedge", consisting no doubt of hundreds of human generations, is summed up in the person of Cain, who represents agriculture as distinct from hunting or herding, and who also built the first cities and committed the first crime. According to the Genesis commentaries, Cain "had a passion for agriculture"; and such an attachment, from the point of view of the nomadic hunter-herdsman and casual tiller of the ground, was a sharp downward step: professional agriculture means settling in one place, which leads to the construction of villages, which develop sooner or later into towns; and in the ancient world, just as the life of a shepherd was always associated with innocence, towns were always considered, relatively speaking, as places of corruption. Tacitus tells us that the Germans of his time had a horror of houses; and even today there are some nomadic or semi-nomadic peoples, like the Red Indians for example, who have a spontaneous contempt for anything which, like agriculture, would fix them in one place and thus curtail their liberty. "The red man has no intention of 'fixing' himself on this earth where everything, according to the law of stabilization and also of condensation—'petrification' one might say—is liable to become 'crystallized'; and this explains the Indian's aversion to houses, especially stone ones, and also the absence of a writing, which according to this perspective, would 'fix' and 'kill' the sacred flow of the Spirit."[8]

This quotation brings us from the question of agriculture to that of literacy; and in this connection we may remember that the Druids also, as Caesar tells us, held that to commit their sacred doctrines to writing would be to desecrate them. Many other examples could be brought forward to show that the absence of writing, like the absence of agriculture, can have a positive cause; and in any case, however accustomed we

[8] Frithjof Schuon, *Language of the Self*, p. 220 (Luzac & Co., London, for Ganesh, Madras, 1959).

may be to thinking of linguistic prowess as inseparable from literacy, a moment's reflection is enough to show that there is no basic connection between the two, for linguistic culture is altogether independent of the written alphabet, which comes as a very late appendix to the history of language as a whole. As Ananda Coomaraswamy pointed out with reference to what he calls "that whole class of prophetic literature that includes the Bible, the Vedas, the Edda, the great epics, and in general the world's 'best books'": "Of these books many existed long before they were written down, many have never been written down, and others have been or will be lost."[9]

Countless altogether illiterate men have been masters of highly elaborate languages. "I am inclined to think that dialect the best which is spoken by the most illiterate in the islands ... men with clear heads and wonderful memories, generally very poor and old, living in remote corners of remote islands, and speaking only Gaelic."[10]

"The ability of oral tradition to transmit great masses of verse for hundreds of years is proved and admitted.... To this oral literature, as the French call it, education is no friend. Culture destroys it, sometimes with amazing rapidity. When a nation begins to read ... what was once the possession of the folk as a whole becomes the heritage of the illiterate only, and soon, unless it is gathered up by the antiquary, vanishes altogether."[11]

"If we have to single out the factor which caused the decline of English village culture we should have to say it was literacy."[12]

In the New Hebrides "the children are educated by listening and watching ... without writing, memory is perfect, tradition exact. The growing child is taught all that is known.... Songs are a form of story-telling.... The lay-out and content in the thousand myths which every child learns (often word perfect, and one story may last for hours) are a whole library ... the hearers are held in a web of spun words."

[9] A. K. Coomaraswamy, *The Bugbear of Literacy*, p. 25 (Denis Dobson, London, 1949).

[10] J. F. Campbell, *Popular Tales of the West Highlands*.

[11] G. L. Kittredge in his introduction to F. G.Childe's *English and Scottish Popular Ballads*.

[12] W. G. Archer, *The Blue Grove*, preface (G. Allen & Unwin, London, 1940).

They converse together "with that accuracy and pattern of beauty in words that we have lost... The natives easily learn to write after white impact. They regard it as a curious and useless performance. They say: 'Cannot a man remember and speak?'"[13]

In addition to these quotations, all of which I have taken from Coomaraswamy, it may be remarked that among the pre-Islamic Arabs it was the custom of the nobles of Mecca to send their sons to be brought up among the Bedouins of the desert because these entirely illiterate nomads were known to speak a purer Arabic than their more "civilized" brethren of the town.

There is no doubt that, in general, "civilization" takes the edge off man's natural alertness and vigilance, qualities which are most necessary for the preservation of language. In particular, literacy lulls men into a sense of false security by giving them the impression that their everyday speech is no longer the sole treasury in which the treasure of language is safeguarded; and once the idea of two languages, one written and one spoken, has taken root, the spoken language is doomed to degenerate relatively fast and to drag down with it, eventually, also the written language—witness the new English translation of the Bible.

In the West of today, the degeneration of the spoken language has reached a point where, although a man will take more or less trouble to set down his thoughts in writing, pride of speech is something almost unknown. It is true that one is taught to avoid certain things in speaking, but it is for purely social reasons which have nothing to do with richness of sound or any other positive quality that language may have. And yet the way a man speaks remains a far more significant factor in his life than the way he writes, for it has an accumulative effect upon the soul which a little spasmodic penning can never have.

Needless to say, the purpose of these remarks is not to deny that the written alphabet has its uses. Language tends to degenerate in the natural course of events, even among the illiterate, and accidents such as exile or foreign domination can cause all sorts of things to be forgotten in a surprisingly short space of time. How much of the spiritual heritage of the Jews might have been lost, for example, but for written records?

[13] T. Harrison, *Savage Civilization*, pp. 45, 344, 351, 353 (1937).

In any case, the manifest inspiration of some of the world's calligraphic arts suggests that when men began to record the spoken word in writing, they did so "by order of God", and not merely "by permission of God". It is not, after all, writing but printing that is responsible for having turned the world into the great rubbish-heap of books that it is today. None the less, writing cannot be said to confer any superiority on man, to say the very least, and it would no doubt even be true to say that it only became necessary, as the lesser of two evils, after a certain point of human degeneration had been reached.

Speech on the other hand was always considered to be one of the glories of man. In Judaism, as also in Islam, we find the doctrine that by Divine Revelation Adam was taught the true language, that is, the language in which the sound corresponded exactly to the sense. This conception of man's primordial speech as having been the most perfectly expressive or onomatopoeic of all languages is undoubtedly beyond the reach of any philological verification. None the less philology can give us a clear idea of the general linguistic tendencies of mankind, and in doing so it teaches us nothing which in any sense weighs against the traditional report. On the contrary, every language known to us is a debased form of some more ancient language, and the further we go back in time the more powerfully impressive language becomes. It also becomes more complex, so that the oldest known languages, those which are far older than history itself, are the most subtle and elaborate in their structure, calling for greater concentration and presence of mind in the speaker than do any of the later ones. The passage of time always tends to diminish the individual words both in form and in sonority, while grammar and syntax become more and more simplified.

It is true that although time tends to strip language of its quality, a language will always have, quantitatively speaking, the vocabulary that its people needs. A vast increase of material objects, for example, will mean a corresponding increase in the number of nouns. But whereas in modern languages the new words have to be artificially coined and added on from the outside, the most ancient known languages may be said to possess, in addition to the words in actual use, thousands of unused words which, if required, can be produced organically, as it were, in virtue of an almost unlimited capacity for word-forming which is inherent in the structure of the language. In this respect it is the modern languages which could be called "dead" or "moribund"; by comparison the more ancient languages, even if they be "dead" in the sense that they are no longer used, remain in themselves like intensely vital organisms.

This does not mean that the ancient languages—and those who spoke them—were lacking in the virtue of simplicity. True simplicity, far from being incompatible with complexity, even demands a certain complexity for its full realization. A distinction must be made between complexity, which implies a definite system or order, and complication which implies disorder and even confusion. A corresponding distinction must be made between simplicity and simplification.

The truly simple man is an intense unity: he is complete and whole-hearted, not divided against himself. To keep up this close-knit integration, the soul must readjust itself altogether to each new set of circumstances, which means that there must be a great flexibility in the different psychic elements: each must be prepared to fit perfectly with all the others, no matter what the mood. This closely woven synthesis, upon which the virtue of simplicity is based, is a complexity as distinct from a complication; and it has its counterpart in the complexity of the ancient languages to which the term "synthetic" is generally applied to distinguish them from modern "analytical" languages. It is only by an elaborate system of grammatical rules that the different parts of speech, analogous to the different elements in the soul, may be inflected so as to fit closely together, giving to each sentence something of the concentrated unity of a single word. The simplicity of the synthetic languages is in fact comparable to that of a great work of art—simplicity not necessarily of means but of total effect; and such no doubt, in an altogether superlative degree, was the simplicity of the primordial language and, we may add, of the men who spoke it. That at any rate is the conclusion to which all the available linguistic evidence points, and language is of such fundamental importance in the life of man, being so intimately bound up with the human soul of which it is the direct expression, that its testimony is of the highest psychological significance.

One of the legacies from the far past which has entered with exceptional fullness into the present, and which is therefore well qualified to serve as a "touchstone", is the Arabic language. Its destiny has been a strange one. When the Arabs first appear in history they are a race of poets, with a wide and varied range of metrical forms, almost their only prose being their everyday speech. They possessed a somewhat rudimentary script, which only a few of them could use, but in any case they preferred to pass down their poems by living word of mouth, and until the coming of Islam they were probably the most illiterate of all Semitic peoples. No doubt this explains, at least in part, why their language was so remarkably well preserved: although linguistic evidence shows it to be a falling away from an even more archaic, that is, an even more complex and more fully sonorous language, Arabic was still, in AD 600, more archaic in form and therefore nearer to "the language of Shem" than was the Hebrew spoken by Moses over two thousand years previously. It was Islam, or more particularly the need to record every syllable of the Qur'ān with absolute precision, which imposed literacy on the seventh-century Arabs; but at the same time, the Qur'ān imposed its own archaic language as a model, and since it was to be learned by heart and recited as much as possible, the detrimental effect of literacy was counteracted by the continual presence of Qur'ānic Arabic upon men's tongues. A special science was quickly evolved for recording and preserving the exact pronunciation; and language-debasement was also checked by the sustained efforts of Muslims throughout the centuries to model their speech upon the speech of their Prophet. As a result, his language is still living today. Inevitably dialects have been formed from it in the course of time through leaving out syllables, merging two different sounds into one, and other simplifications, and these dialects, which vary from one Arab country to another, are normally used in conversation. But the slightest formality of occasion calls at once for a return to the undiminished majesty and sonority of classical Arabic, which is sometimes spontaneously reverted to in conversation also, when anyone feels he has something really important to say. On the other hand; those few who on principle refuse to speak the colloquial language at all are liable to find themselves in a dilemma: either they must abstain altogether from taking part in an "ordinary conversation" or else they must run the risk of producing an incongruous effect, like street urchins masquerading in royal robes. Idle chattering, that is, the quick expression of unweighed thoughts, must have been something comparatively unknown in the far past, for it is something that ancient languages do not lend themselves to; and if men thought less glibly, and took more trouble to compose the expression of their thoughts, they certainly took more trouble to utter them. Sanskrit tells the same story as Arabic: each, with its marvellous range and variety of consonantal sounds, leaves us no option but to conclude that in the far past man's organs of articulation and hearing were considerably finer and more delicate than they are today; and this is fully confirmed also by a study of ancient music, with all its rhythmic and melodic subtlety.[14]

If philology cannot reach the origins of language, it can none the less survey, in one unbroken sweep, thousands of years of linguistic history which means also, in a certain respect, thousands of years of the history of the human soul, a history that is one-sided, no doubt, but remarkably definite as far as it goes. In the light of this vista, which takes us far back into what is called "prehistory", we are forced to take note of a relentless trend; and this trend is itself simply one aspect of a more general tendency which, as Dewar remarks, most physicists, chemists, mathematicians and astronomers are agreed upon, namely that "the universe is like a clock which is running down." So far religion and science stand together. But religion adds—as science cannot without going beyond the scope of its function—that there is a way of escape for individuals from the collective downstream drift, and that it is possible for some to resist it, and for some even to make upstream headway against it, and for a few to overcome it altogether by making their way, in this life even, back as far as the source itself.

[14] See, for example, Alain Daniélou, *Introduttion to the Study of Musical Scales*, Royal India and Pakistan Society, London, 1943.

The Spirit of the Times

According to world-wide tradition, the "life" of the macrocosm consists of thousands of years of spiritual prosperity leading gradually down, from Golden Age to Silver Age to Bronze Age, until it reaches a relatively short final period[1] in which the prosperity is increasingly marred by its opposite. This period, the Iron Age or, as the Hindus term it, the Dark Age, is the late autumn and the winter of the cycle, and it roughly coincides with what is called "historic" as opposed to "prehistoric". All old age, both macrocosmic and microcosmic, has its ills. But normal old age has also its wisdom; and half hidden behind the negative signs which we see on all sides, our day has also something positive to offer which is characteristic of no previous era and which is, as such, yet another sign of the times.

Needless to say, this is not a claim that old age alone is endowed with wisdom, or that, analogously, our times excel in that respect—far from it. Humanity is the heart of the macrocosm and the four ages of the cycle are what they are according to the state of mankind. The pre-excellence of the Golden Age derives from the spirituality—which implies wisdom—of mankind in general. This whole was subsequently reduced to being no more than a majority which was then reduced to a minority, ultimately a small one. It can none the less be said that there is a mode of wisdom which belongs to old age in particular, and which is even susceptible of being assimilated, to a certain degree, by those who were not wise in youth and middle age. The old age of the cycle is bound to be a congenial setting for it; and the following passage gives us a hint of a collective or

[1] According to Hinduism, which has the oldest and most explicit doctrine of the cycles, the first age is the longest and the fourth is the shortest. The Genesis commentaries and the Jewish apocryphal books make it clear that there is no mutual contradiction between the perspective of the monotheistic religions and the pre-biblical doctrine of four ages (see *Ancient Beliefs and Modern Superstitions,* pp. 20–22).

macrocosmic wisdom which belongs to our times precisely by reason of their lateness.

"The usual religious arguments, through not probing sufficiently to the depth of things and moreover not having previously had any need to do so, are psychologically somewhat outworn and fail to satisfy certain requirements of causality. If human societies degenerate on the one hand with the passage of time, they accumulate on the other hand experiences in virtue of old age, however intermingled with errors these may be. This paradox is something that any pastoral teaching intended to be effective should take into account, not by drawing new directives from the general error, but on the contrary by using arguments of a higher order, intellectual rather than sentimental."[2]

In the phrase "human societies" the plural reminds us that the modern world is not the only human world that has degenerated with the passage of time. Each of the four ages may be said to constitute in itself a lesser cycle, beginning with a "youth" and ending with an "eld": and there are yet lesser cycles within them—for example, the civilization of ancient Egypt, or that of ancient Rome. In all these lesser cycles there must have been in some degree, towards the end, an accumulation of "experience in virtue of old age". The twentieth century, together with the decades which immediately follow it, would appear to constitute the final phase of that particular human society which may be said to have been established in Europe—with eventual prolongations—about 1500 years ago. It is also, in a parallel way, the final phase of many other societies—Hindu, American Indian, Jewish, Buddhist and Islamic—which have been partially merged into one with the Western world by the super-imposition of its way of life over their own traditional differences from it and from each other. But at the same time we are living at the very end of one of the four ages; and since it is the last of the four, its end will be the end of the great cycle of all four ages taken as a whole. In other words, we are now participating in the extreme old age of the macrocosm, which is to be followed by a new cycle of four ages.

[2] Frithjof Schuon, *In the Face of the Absolute*, pp. 89–90.

It may be objected that in view of the immense length of the cycle the macrocosm could be said to have reached its old age long before the twentieth century. That is true, but the old age in question was overlaid by the youth of subsidiary cycles. Two thousand years ago, the incipient twilight of the great cycle receded before the dawn of Christianity, which was followed later by the dawn of Islam; and even as recently as 700 years ago there took place what has been called the "second birth" of Christianity: it was the time of the building of the great cathedrals and the founding of many of the orders of mysticism. Christendom had been allowed a "fresh flowering", precariously set though it was within the old age of the great cycle. It could not last: all too quickly and easily it was drawn into the main cosmic current of degeneration. The same applies to the already mentioned "second birth" of Islam[3] which partly coincided in time with that of Christianity inasmuch as Christendom took considerably longer to develop than the civilization of Islam. It is true that the younger religion still retained something of its youth when its elder sister could no longer be called young in any sense. But today there is nothing to modify the greater cycle's old age which is, on the contrary, reinforced by the old age of all the lesser cycles which it contains. It can therefore be said, macrocosmically speaking, that all men alive today, whatever their years, are "old"; and the question arises, for each individual, which aspect of old age, the positive or the negative, will he or she represent in the macrocosm, that is, in the human collectivity taken as a whole, and how active or passive will each be in this respect.

As regards what Schuon says about pastoral teaching that is no longer effective, the dogma that there is only one valid religion, namely "ours", may serve as an example of an argument that is "psychologically somewhat outworn". Such teachings "fail to satisfy certain requirements of causality" because they are now seen to defeat one of the main ends of religion which is to bestow a sense of the Glory of God. Modern man cannot help having a broader view of the world than his ancestors had, partly through the destruction of the protective walls of

[3] The seventh century of Islam—and let us include with it also the eighth—could no doubt be said to correspond to the latest and therefore most accessible point of non-degeneration for the Islamic world. See *The Eleventh Hour*, p. 51.

the different traditional civilizations—in itself a tragedy—and partly through the enormously increased facilities of travel and the corresponding increase of information which is poured into his mind through various channels. This broader view may enable him to be impressed by religions other than his own, and at the very least it compels him to see that their existence makes the world-wide spread of his own religion impossible. If they were false, what of the Glory of Him who allowed them to establish themselves, with their millennial roots, over so vast an area?

For those who are not prepared to sacrifice that Glory to human prejudices, it has become abundantly clear that none of the so-called "world religions" can have been intended by Providence to establish itself over the whole globe. The question does not arise with those forms of worship like Hinduism and Judaism which are specifically for one people only. But Buddhism, Christianity and Islam, though each is virtually open to everybody, have also beyond doubt their particular sectors of humanity; and though the frontiers may be difficult to define, and though Islam, the most recently revealed of the three, is in the nature of things likely to continue gaining ground in many directions, it seems probable to say the least that the three sectors will remain largely the same until the end of the age. But if such an objective view of religion is widespread, this is not for the most part due to an increase of acuity in the intelligence, but rather to the fact that an "old man" cannot help being "experienced". Otherwise expressed, it is due to a mainly passive participation in the positive aspects of the present age. For anyone who is intellectually active however, this universal outlook is a secondary accompanying asset—albeit none the less necessary—of what may be called "the spirit of the times".

To see what is meant by this, let us consider in more detail the characteristics of old age. To speak of the "old age" of the macrocosm is not merely to speak in metaphor. According to a doctrine that is to be found, variously expressed, in all religions, there is a real analogical correspondence between macrocosm and microcosm, a correspondence which is implicit in these terms themselves, "great world" and "little world". This universal doctrine enables us to grasp certain elusive aspects of the macrocosm through the corresponding aspects of the microcosm; and the ambiguous, dividedly dual nature of our times can be better understood if we consider in more detail the old age of the microcosm or, more precisely, of the normal microcosm, for he alone is the true counterpart of the macrocosm.

The word normal is used here in its strict sense, as the epithet of that which is a norm: only man as he was created, or one who has regained the primordial state, True Man as the Taoists call him, can be considered as a full microcosm, whose life corresponds to the "life" of the macrocosm, that is, to the cycle of time which is now nearing its close; and by extension from True Man, that is, from the Saint, we might include in the human norm every truly spiritual man who has at least a virtual wholeness, even if it be not yet fully realized.

Like the macrocosm, the normal microcosm is subject in old age to the tension of two opposite tendencies, a contradiction which in the first part of life was relatively latent and from which, in the Earthly Paradise, man was altogether exempt. This contradiction is due to the imprisonment of an immortal soul in a mortal body, a soul which is moreover in communion with the Spirit. The body is an image of the soul, of which it is also a prolongation. In youth, generally speaking, the body appears as a purely positive symbol and there is perfect harmony between it and the soul. Analogous to this is the harmonious homogeneity of the earlier ages of the macrocosmic cycle. But gradually, in the microcosm, the body begins to show that it is merely a symbol, and that "merely" becomes more and more aggravated with the passage of time. On the one hand, therefore, there is a gradual bodily deterioration which ends with death; on the other hand there is a mellowing of spirituality. The serene and objective wisdom which is the central characteristic of normal old age outweighs, by its transcendence, the many ills which are the inevitable result of increasing decrepitude,[4] and in a certain sense it may be said to thrive on them. The corresponding ills of the macrocosm likewise create a climate which is not unfavorable to wisdom on condition that they are seen as ills. Detachment is an essential feature of the sage, and this virtue, which in better times could

[4] By way of example we may consider on the one hand the blindness which befell both Isaac and Jacob in extreme old age, and on the other hand their inward illumination.

only be acquired through great spiritual efforts, can be made more spontaneous by the sight of one's world in chaotic ruins.

There is yet another feature of normal old age, the most positive of all, which likewise has its macrocosmic equivalent, in virtue of which our times are unique. It is sometimes said of spiritual men and women at the end of their lives that they have "one foot already in Paradise". This is not meant to deny that death is a sudden break, a rupture of continuity. It cannot but be so, for it has to transform mortal old age into immortal youth. None the less, hagiography teaches us that the last days of sanctified souls can be remarkably luminous and transparent. Nor is it unusual that the imminence of death should bring with it special graces, such as visions, in foretaste of what is to come. The mellowing of spirituality, which is the highest aspect of old age in itself, is thus crowned with an illumination which belongs more to youth than to age; and it is to this synthesis, or more precisely to its macrocosmic counterpart, that the title of our chapter refers; for analogously, in the macrocosm, the nearness of the new Golden Age cannot fail to make itself mysteriously felt before the end of the old cycle; and, as we shall see later, such an anticipation has been predicted in various parts of the globe. We have here, in this junction of ending with beginning, yet another reason, perhaps the most powerful of all, why "the last shall be first".

The decrepitude of the macrocosm in its old age is the theme of the two preceding chapters of this book; and to those ailments already mentioned we may add the many pseudo-esoterisms and heresies with which the modern world is rife, and which make it easier to go astray than ever before. Despite these, thanks to what is most positive in this day of conflicting opposites, the highest and deepest truths have become correspondingly more accessible, as if forced to unveil themselves by cyclic necessity, the macrocosm's need to fulfill its aspect of terminal wisdom. This same need—for to speak of wisdom is to speak of esoterism—was bound to cause an inward movement away from error and towards these truths. That it has in fact done so is shown, apart from more direct but less accessible signs, by the greatly increased publication of relevant books, for a minority no doubt but none the less on a scale to which esoterism has long been unaccustomed. The complex nature of the spirit of the times can explain facts which could otherwise be difficult to account for. In this meeting of estuary and source, finality derives from primordiality a certain aspect of abruptness, an initiative which is not typical of old age itself. Needless to say, the movement in question could not be lacking in the necessary traditional continuity; but neither could it be a smooth transition, an ordinary sequel from something that has gone before; and this explains also the widespread lack of preparation for it. Amongst those who in themselves are truly qualified for an esoteric path, it is inevitable that not a few should stand in need of a certain initial enlightenment by reason of their upbringing and education in the modern world.

This applies in yet greater measure to others, less qualified and more numerous, who in an earlier age would probably have remained in exoterism and who appear to owe their eventual qualification for esoterism partly to the fact of their birth in the present age. The following quotation will help to explain this paradox: "Exoterism is a precarious thing by reason of its limits or its exclusions; there comes a moment in history when all kinds of experiences oblige it to modify its claims to exclusiveness, and it is then driven to a choice: escape from these limitations by the upward path, in esoterism, or by the downward path, in a worldly and suicidal liberalism. As one might have expected, the civilizationist exoterism of the West has chosen the downward path, while combining this incidentally with a few esoteric notions which in such conditions remain inoperative."[5]

This lower choice, officially ratified by Vatican II for the Catholic Church and already characteristic of the other Churches of Western Europe, does not prevent individuals from choosing the upward path, that of esoterism. Some of those who would not have been qualified in the past are now given access to it in virtue of a truly positive attitude, severely put to the test by the present spiritual crisis, and amply verified

[5] Frithjof Schuon, *Esoterism as Principle and as Way*, pp. 19–20. By way of example, the acceptance of religions other than one's own is esoterically operative if it be based on intellectual discernment between the true and the false, that is, if it be recognition of orthodoxy to the exclusion of everything else. But acceptance of other religions on the basis of the widely predominant sentimental pseudo-charity of our day is not merely inoperative in any positive sense but it is exceedingly harmful, for where discernment is not the guiding factor the door to error is inevitably opened, and the true religions are dishonored by being placed on a level with heretical sects.

by the choice of the higher rather than the lower. On the one hand, the foundering of certain exoteric vessels is bound in the nature of things to enlarge the responsibilities of esoterism, which cannot refuse to take onboard those in the sea about it who ask for a lifeline to be thrown to them and who have no means of salvation else. On the other hand, obtusenesses which in the past would have proved to be disqualifications can be modified or even partially dissolved by the virtues inherent in "old age". Whatever the circumstances may be, a suppliant hand held out from the modern chaos in the direction of right guidance is an indication that its owner cannot be relegated to the spiritually passive majority.

In connection with the widespread need for initial enlightenment, it must be remembered that esoterism presupposes the sense of the Absolute. More precisely, since there is no soul which is not virtually imbued with this sense, esoterism presupposes that it be actual and operative, at least to a certain degree. On that basis it can be further actualized by indirect contact with the Absolute, that is, with Its "overflows", if one may use such a term, into the various domains of this world. One such "overflow" is the esoteric doctrine itself, and this is indispensable; but its effect upon the soul may be reinforced by other earthly manifestations of the Absolute. The argument of beauty, for example, may be a powerful ally to the arguments of truth.

In the theocratic civilizations, the spiritual authority and the temporal power saw to it that the beauty of nature was not unduly desecrated by man, and that parallel to nature there were objects of sacred art that conformed to a style which had come as a gift from Heaven, and which was never a merely human invention. In the rigorous sense of the term, which is all we are considering here, sacred art is as a crystallization of sanctity, a spiritual presence which has power to purify and to enlighten and which, unlike ascetic practices of a similar power, make no demands of man which run counter to his natural bent.

"It[6] sets up, against the sermon which insists on what must be done by one who would become holy, a vision of the cosmos

[6] Sacred art, and in particular the architecture of medieval Christendom.

which is holy through its beauty; it makes men participate naturally and almost involuntarily in the world of holiness."[7]

Today, despite the desecrations, nature still remains an inexhaustible treasury of reminders to man of his true heritage, reminders which may become operative in the light of the doctrine; and parallel to virgin nature, even if the Christian civilization may have gone without possibility of recall, many of its landmarks still remain. Some of these, the cathedrals for example, are monuments of overwhelming beauty which bear witness to the spiritual exaltation of the age which produced them. In addition to their power as sacred art, they are eloquent exponents—and never more so than when seen from today's abyss—of spirituality's universal rule: "Seek ye first the Kingdom of Heaven and all the rest shall be given unto you," and its parallel "Unto him that hath shall be given." At the same time, their presence is yet another demonstration of the truth that "from him that hath not shall be taken away even that which he hath." As material objects, they proclaim the spiritual man's mastery over matter, whereas the inability of the modern world to produce anything like them betrays the materialist's impotence precisely where he might have been expected to excel. He it is "that hath not", having rejected the Transcendent; and "that which he hath", namely matter, is taken away from him in the sense that he cannot really be said to possess it, having no qualitative dominion over it. We have only to approach a town like New York to have an alarming impression that matter has taken possession of man and quantitatively overwhelmed him. But standing in front of Durham, Lincoln or Chartres Cathedral we see that our mediaeval ancestors were able to dominate matter to the point of compelling it to excel itself and to become vibrant with the Spirit.

What has been said about Christian art applies also to the arts of other sacred civilizations; and for the great loss of the experience of a traditional way of life, there can now be, for those capable of taking it, a certain compensation in the gain of access to the spiritual riches of traditions other than one's own. Religions in their outermost aspects have often been represented as different points on the circumference of a circle,

[7] Titus Burckhardt, *Sacred Art in East and West*, p. 46. The message of this book is centrally typical of the wisdom of the age both in virtue of its universality and of its finality.

the centre of which is the Divine Truth. Every such point is connected to the centre by a radius which stands for the esoterism of the religion in question. The more a radius approaches the centre, the nearer it is to the other radii, which illustrates the fact that the esoteric paths are increasingly close to each other, however far the respective exoterisms may seem to be; and sacred art, although it does not withhold its blessings from any sector of the community, is in itself a purely esoteric phenomenon, which means that it is central and therefore universal. Needless to say, there are degrees to be observed in this respect; but all that is best in sacred art virtually belongs to everyone who has "eyes to see" or "ears to hear", no matter what his faith or his race; and this virtuality can be actualized today as never before.

The nearer a work is to the centre the more universal it is, but also, at the same time, the more concentratedly it represents the world of its own particular provenance. What could be more universal than the Bharata Natyam temple dancing of India and the music that accompanies it, the landscape paintings of China and Japan, the Romanesque and Gothic cathedrals of Western Europe, and the mosques of Andalusia, Egypt, Persia and Turkestan, to mention only a few examples? And what, respectively, could give us a more concentrated sense of the unique spiritual fragrance of each of the four ways in question, Hinduism, Taoism, Christianity and Islam? To add a fifth, exactly the same may be said of the statuary of Buddhism, from Ajanta to Kyoto. Taken together, the summits of sacred art give us in little, that is, in an easily assimilated form, a faithful view of the immense variety of the great religions and their civilizations, a pageant which can be for some as a semi-transparent veil that both hides and reveals the Transcendent Source of these wonders.[8] This comprehensive view may be considered as an aspect of that wisdom which is the theme of our chapter; for although it is a potential feature of every sage, no matter when he lives, it withheld itself as an actuality from all other epochs, and offers itself now to him who seeks.[9]

[8] In the Islamic litany of the 99 Names of God, one of the names which this context recalls is *al-Badīʿ*, the Marvellously Original.

[9] The quantities of lavishly illustrated books now available, and their equivalents for the auditive arts, are yet another sign of the times inasmuch as they spring from what might be called the archival aspect of finality, a question we will return to later.

What has been said about the crystallization of holiness in art may be said to hold good for incarnations of holiness, the sainthoods which exemplify the primordial nature that is hidden in fallen man by second nature. Some men can be initially penetrated and won more easily by a personal perfection, a human summit, than by any other mode of excellence; and there can now be added, to the Saints of one religion's calendar, their glorious counterparts from every other religion. We are speaking here of an initial penetration, and of indirect contacts with holy men such as can be made through the reading of hagiographies. It goes without saying that at a later stage the living personal perfection of the Spiritual Master[10] will necessarily take precedence, while at the same time it will make these other examples of sainthood more accessible.

As to the doctrine, it is indispensable both in itself and to throw its light on other motivations. It is also needed today as a protection: if esoteric truths continued to be kept secret as in the past on account of their danger, this would not prevent the spread of pseudo-esoterism, a poison to which the best antidote is true esoterism whose dangers are thus outweighed by its powers to safeguard against its own counterfeits; and beyond these it is needed for the refutation of more general errors. "We live in an age of confusion and thirst in which the advantages of communication are greater than those of secrecy; moreover only esoteric theses can satisfy the imperious logical needs created by the philosophic and scientific positions of the modern world.... Only esoterism ... can provide answers that are neither fragmentary nor compromised in advance by a denominational bias. Just as rationalism can remove faith, so esoterism can restore it."[11]

In order to follow an esoteric path it is not necessary to make a quantitative study of the doctrine; it is enough to know the essentials, which are centered on the nature of God and the nature of man. The symbolism of the elementary numbers is always enlightening, and in this case it is the number three which holds, as it were, the keys to understanding the rela-

[10] It is a universal axiom that anyone who is truly qualified to follow an esoteric path will find, if he "seeks" and if he "knocks", the Master he needs. For more ample consideration on this subject, see "Answers to Questions About the Spiritual Master", in *The Eleventh Hour*, p. 98.

[11] Frithjof Schuon, *Esoterism as Principle and as Way*, pp. 7–8.

tionship between the Creator and His human image. The presence of certain triads in the world, such as that of the primary colors, is the proof of a triplicity in the Divine Nature Itself, the Supreme Archetype of all that exists. In *From the Divine to the Human*, Schuon dwells at some length on this triplicity which is nothing other than the Absolute Infinite Perfection of God Himself, these three supreme transcendences being the intrinsic dimensions of Divine Reality. Perfection is, as he remarks, "the Sovereign Good"; and having reminded us of St Augustine's saying that "the good tends essentially to communicate itself," he adds: "As Sovereign Good, the Absolute-Infinite cannot not project the world."[12] But he goes on to remind us that It remains in Itself totally unaffected by this projection: "Being what it is, the Absolute cannot not be immutable, and It cannot not radiate. Immutability, or fidelity to itself; and Radiation, or gift of Itself; there lies the essence of all that is."[13]

The Absolute Infinite Perfection is One. It transcends all multiplicity while being its root, and it is only at a lower level that we can begin to differentiate between the three terms of the triad. This is the level of what Schuon has called "the relative Absolute"—a term which is applicable to the Christian Trinity and to Hinduism's analogous ternary Being-Consciousness-Beatitude.[14] At the same level, in Jewish and Islamic doctrine, are the non-essential Divine names such as Creator, which already implies the duality Creator-creature. Without being as yet manifested, the "Hidden Treasure" is on the way to manifesting Itself.

If the Good is that which is to be manifested or communicated, the means of radiation is derived from the Infinite. These two intrinsic aspects of Reality are reflected by the Second and Third Persons of the Trinity, and, for Hinduism, by the corresponding Consciousness and Beatitude. "It could be asked what relationship there is between the Good and Consciousness (*Chit*); now the Good, from the moment that It springs as such from the Absolute—which contains It in an undifferentiated or indeterminate manner—coincides with the

[12] This same truth is expressed in Islam as the already quoted tradition: "I was a hidden treasure, and I loved to be known, and so I created the world."

[13] p. 42.

[14] *Sat-Chit-Ānanda.*

distinctive Consciousness which the Absolute has of Itself; the Divine Word, which is the 'Knowledge' that God has of Himself, cannot but be the Good, God being able to know Himself as Good only."[15]

The Divine triplicity is reflected throughout the Universe in innumerable ways,[16] being especially intense in man himself. "Man, 'made in the image of God', has an intelligence capable of discernment and contemplation; a will capable of freedom and strength; a soul, or a character, capable of love and virtue."[17] In the light of the quotation which precedes this, it is clear that intelligence corresponds to Perfection, the Sovereign Good. The same applies to doctrine, the content of the intelligence; all theology derives from the Divine Perfection by way of the Divine Word. Will and soul are rooted in the Absolute and the Infinite respectively. The psychic substance is the "space" in which man deploys his faculties, and the primordial soul is no less than a vast presence. As to the primordial will—the will that is "for God" in the most powerful sense of these words—it is irresistibly overwhelming:[18] no obstacle can stand in its way.

"Man may know, will and love; and to will is to act. We know God by distinguishing Him from whatever is not He and by recognizing Him in whatever bears witness to Him; we will God by accomplishing whatever leads us to Him and by abstaining from whatever removes us from Him; and we love God by loving to know and to will Him, and by loving whatever bears witness to Him, around us as well as within us."[19]

Man's three faculties, intelligence, will and soul, thus correspond to the equally interdependent ternary of doctrine, method, morals, or faith, practice, virtue, or "comprehension

[15] Ibid., p. 39.

[16] Since the primary colors have been mentioned, we may say, in passing, that it is the right of the Absolute that we should know which is its color before we have time to think. As to the Infinite, its right is, with regard to the same question, that our thoughts should unfold in the direction of its two great earthly symbols, the sky and the ocean. Nor is it difficult to see that Perfection, the Sovereign Good, is the Supreme Archetype of gold.

[17] Frithjof Schuon, *Esoterism as Principle and as Way*, p. 101.

[18] Even when perverted, the will retains something of the imprint of the Absolute, whence the terrible dangers inherent in ambition.

[19] Ibid., pp. 95–6.

concentration,[20] conformation". It follows from the above quotations that to be effective the doctrine's initial appeal to the intelligence must include within its scope also the will and the soul. There can be no spirituality—or in other words no microcosm worthy of the name—without wholeness, that is, without sincerity, which means the harmonious co-operation of all these three faculties towards the common end. Nor indeed can there be any advance upon the esoteric way if the truth that is addressed to the mind does not lead to practice, and if both are not supported by virtue.

"Obviously the most brilliant intellectual knowledge is fruitless in the absence of the realising initiative that corresponds to it and in the absence of the necessary virtue; in other words, knowledge is nothing if it is combined with spiritual laziness and with pretensions, egoism, hypocrisy. Likewise the most prestigious power of concentration is nothing if it is accompanied by doctrinal ignorance and moral insufficiency; likewise again, natural virtue is but little without the doctrinal truth and the spiritual practice which operate it with a view to God and which thus restore to it the whole point of its being."[21]

The movement towards the inward, which we are considering here, may be said to represent the highest aspect of the extreme old age of the macrocosm. As such, in virtue of all that the times stand for in a positive sense, the esoterism in question could not be other than what the Hindus call *jnāna-marga*, the way of knowledge or, more precisely, of gnosis. It was fated to be so, for such a way presupposes a perspective of truth rather than love,[22] and it is objective regard for truth which characterizes the wisdom of old age.[23] It is beyond doubt significant in this respect that the last religion of the cycle,

[20] The quintessence of esoteric practice is concentration on the Real. One of the most direct methodic supports for this is the invocation of the Divine Name, an orison said by Hinduism to be, for the whole of the Dark Age, the greatest means of Deliverance (*moksha*) and thus of Union (*yoga*) with the Divine Self, the One Real "I" of which all subjectivities are reflections.

[21] Ibid., p. 169.

[22] Needless to say. it is not a question of mutually exclusive alternatives but of emphasis. Both elements must be present in every spiritual path.

[23] Even the many pseudo-esoterisms with which the modern age is rife purport to be ways of knowledge, no doubt in the awareness that otherwise they would be without attraction for contemporary seekers.

Islam—and therefore Sufism its esoteric dimension—should be dominated by the perspective of truth.

The mention of *jnāna* does not necessarily mean, in this context, a movement towards Hinduism. For each seeker the way in question could be, in principle, anyone of the orthodox esoteric paths which are now operative. But before a way can be followed there must be an aspiration, and the word "movement" is used here to mean the initial setting in motion of individuals in search of spiritual guidance and not the way itself, though this is bound to follow if the aspiration be a true one.

The seeming paradoxes and contradictions of our day are perhaps nowhere more apparent than in the literature of this most literate of all ages. On the one hand, like an old man who has become irrepressibly garrulous in his senility, the human race produces a ceaseless flow of books, and we may be certain that incomparably more is written than what reaches the stage of print. No period of history can come near to competing with this output either in terms of quantity or in terms of profanity and pointlessness—lack of the sense of reality, one might say. Most of these writings are in fact without pretension, for they claim to be no more than a means of lightly passing the day, and they have little hope of not being quickly superseded by others of their kind. They share with the mass media the blame of distracting man from the essential,[24] but they are far less dangerous than the writings of those literary, philosophic and scientific "heroes" of the hour which serve to indoctrinate their readers with error in various forms and in general to imprison them within the limitations of the modern outlook.

At the same time, there are those many publications which reflect the already referred to archival aspect of finality. A general sense of the need to place everything on record—a sense that seems to be more collective than individual—has brought forth not only a spate of encyclopaedias but also a wealth of translations. The labour involved in making these records is for the most part no more than a passive participation in the wisdom of the age. The motives are largely academic; but

[24] There is also the blame of modern man's lack of sense of royal responsibility for his vegetable kingdom. It has been calculated that about 15,000 fine forest trees are cut down to make enough paper to publish one issue only of one of the leading New York daily newspapers, almost all of which is thrown away the next day as rubbish.

some of the classics[25] in question are of great spiritual value, and their present availability is a providential setting for those twentieth century works which may be considered as actively and centrally representative of our day in its best aspect,[26] and which no other age could have produced.

Amongst these signs of the times we will mention first of all *Man and his Becoming according to the Vedānta*[27] by René Guénon. As the title suggests, this book is a definition, in Hindu terms, of the whole nature of man and of the supreme spiritual possibilities which lie open to him. Although the author himself had already found a spiritual path in the esoterism of Islam, that is, in Sufism, he preferred, with characteristically impersonal reckoning, to take as the basis for his exposition something still further removed from Christianity than just another monotheism. This does not however prevent him from continually referring to the three Abrahamic traditions. It is significant, in view of what was cyclically needed, that the Advaita Vedanta has the advantage, shown by its altogether direct manner of expression, of never having had to speak in veiled terms in order to avoid a conflict with the limitations of exoterism. Moreover, as we have already seen, Hinduism possesses, like other religions of antiquity, the full doctrine of the *samsara*: it does not simplify the multiple reality of the great round of innumerable states of individual existence by narrowing it down to this one state of earthly life.

Another advantage of Hinduism as a basis for the exposition of universal truth is the comprehensive breadth of its structure. On the one hand, like Judaism and Islam, it depends on direct revelation and makes a rigorous distinction between what is revealed and what is merely inspired. On the other hand, like Christianity, it depends on the *Avatāra*, that is, the descent of

[25] One of the first examples that comes to mind is *Hōnen, the Buddhist Saint* by Shunjō.

[26] It is indeed ironical that the true nature of our times should so completely elude the comprehension of the most ardent champions of the twentieth century, including all those would-be artists, a majority alas, who are exclusively bent on producing works that reflect the age we live in. Instead of seeing a husk of decrepitude which envelops a luminous kernel of wisdom—and it is the kernel that any true art of our day would reflect—they see only the husk, which they refuse to recognize as such. There is no need to dwell on the result.

[27] *L'Homme et son devenir selon le Vêdânta*, first published in 1925.

the Divinity into this world; and for the maintenance of the tradition there is a succession of no less than ten *Avatāras*. As far as historic times are concerned, the seventh and eighth of these, Rama and Krishna, are the most important for Hinduism itself. The ninth, specifically non-Hindu (literally "foreign"), is generally considered to be the Buddha; and the tenth, Kalki, "the rider on the white horse", will have the universal function of closing this cycle of time and inaugurating the next, which identifies his descent with the second advent of Christ.

Hinduism's breadth of structure is matched by its unequalled length of span across the centuries as a fully valid way of worship, by reason of its providential escape from the degeneracy which other religions of its own age suffered in the normal course. This brings us to the Aryan affinity which it has with the Western world as a whole. The fact that European languages are Indo-Germanic and therefore cognate with Sanskrit means, at a deeper level, that the religions of the ancient Greeks, Romans, Germans and Celts must have been originally so many counterparts or parallels of Hinduism. To make this most ancient religion the basis of a doctrinal exposition is thus to offer the Western world, for those few who are capable of taking it, a mysterious and purely positive renaissance of a relatively primordial heritage which has long been out of reach.

This question of affinity must not however be exaggerated. It means that there may be something in the European soul which is naturally open to the voice of Hinduism and predisposed to listen to its altogether objective approach to the doctrine. But it cannot be considered in a more operative sense, nor had Guénon any intention along those lines.[28] The great purpose behind *Man and his Becoming* and all his other writings is to open his readers to the possibility of following an esoteric path, a possibility which, in the case of vocation becomes a necessity; but he does not recommend anyone traditional line more than another. His motto was expressly *Vincit omnia veritas* "Truth conquers all"; it was also, in fact, "Seek and ye shall find" and "Knock and it shall be opened unto you." Implicit in his writings is the certainty of their author that they will providentially come to the notice of those qualified to receive

[28] In letters to those who asked his advice—for he kept up a wide correspondence—he tended to be discouraging with regard to Hinduism as a possible spiritual path for the Western seeker.

his message, which will prove irresistible to them in the sense that they will be compelled to seek, and thus to find, a spiritual path. His books and articles are therefore, in intention and in fact, a treasury of information about what an intellectual—or one who is virtually so—needs to be made aware of; and a feature of Guénon's greatness is his remarkable grasp of the twentieth-century situation and his consequent ability to put his finger on the crucial gaps in modern man's understanding.

One of these gaps is the already mentioned failure to make a rigorous distinction between Intellect and reason, a distinction which he frequently emphasizes. Moreover to read the main part of his writing is to study metaphysics, which is concerned with the whole hierarchy of those states of being which transcend the human state, including those which transcend creation itself. One of his definitions of the qualification to follow an esoteric path is "having the presentiment of one's higher states", which clearly takes us beyond the rational or mental domain. Guénon is also an unsurpassed master of the science of symbolism, and a whole section of his work is devoted to that theme. The consciousness that the fabric of this world is woven out of symbols is not something that modern man acquires in the course of his education; and another closely related gap in his understanding has to do with the performance of sacred rites which are symbols enacted. The relationship between rite and symbol, at the best only partially understood, needed to be explained in greater depth. The following passages, from a chapter entitled "The Language of the Birds", are representative of Guénon in more ways than one:

"There is often mention, in different traditions, of a mysterious language called 'the language of the birds'. The expression is clearly a symbolic one since the very importance which is attached to the knowledge of the language—it is considered to be the prerogative of a high initiation—precludes a literal interpretation. The Qur'ān for example says (XXVII, 15): 'And Solomon was David's heir and he said: O men we have been taught the language of the birds, and all favours have been showered upon us.' Elsewhere we read of heroes, like Siegfried in the Nordic legend, who understand the language of the birds as soon as they have overcome the dragon, and the symbolism in question may easily be understood from this. Victory over the dragon has, as its immediate consequence, the conquest of immortality which is represented by some object, the approach to which is barred by the dragon, and the conquest of immortality implies, essentially, reintegration at the centre of the human state, that is, at the point where communication is established with the higher states of the being. It is this communication which is represented by the understanding of the language of the birds and, in fact, birds are often taken to symbolise the angels and thus, precisely, the higher states. That is the significance, in the Gospel parable, of the grain of mustard seed, of 'the birds of the air' which came to lodge in the branches of the tree—the tree which represents the axis that passes through the centre of each state of being and connects all the states with each other. In the mediaeval symbol of the Peridexion (a corruption of *Paradision*) one sees birds on the branches of a tree and a dragon at its foot."[29]

In the same article Guénon says, in speaking of the rhythmic formulae which are termed *dhikr*[30] in Sufism and *mantra* in Hinduism: "The repetition of these formulae is intended to bring about the harmonization of the different elements of the being and to cause vibrations which, by their repercussions throughout the whole hierarchy of the states, are capable of opening up a communication with the higher states. This is moreover, generally speaking, the essential and primordial purpose of all rites."[31] Elsewhere he says: "Rite and symbol are basically two aspects of the same reality, namely the correspondence[32] which connects with each other all the degrees of universal existence. Through this correspondence, our human state can be put in communication with the higher states of the being."[33]

One of the points which is especially stressed by Guénon is the need for the rite of initiation, without which there can be no question of an esoteric path. What is generally known in the West as "the chain of apostolic succession" is merely

[29] *Fundamental Symbols,* p. 39.

[30] Literally "remembrance", which must be understood in the light of what has already been said about "Platonic remembrance" with regard to the power of the symbol to recall its archetype.

[31] Ibid., p. 40.

[32] He means the symbol-archetype correspondence.

[33] *Aperçus sur l'initiation,* p. 122.

one example, in a relatively outward domain, of something which all esoterisms have in common. The initiatic rite serves to attach fallen man, through the chain which goes back to the founder of the religion himself, to a new ancestral line. Without this true and effective renewal of primordial heredity, there could be no hope of regaining one's first nature, except by a miracle which no one has the right to expect, least of all one who had had the presumption to refuse to follow the normal course.

In addition to his writings on esoterism, Guénon also wrote books which are mainly concerned with the errors of the modern world,[34] though here also esoterism is always present in the background as "the one thing necessary", the indispensable corner-stone for any restoration of the world to normality. A note which is sounded in all his writings is the need for orthodoxy, a term which has become, in academic use, almost a synonym for narrow and fanatical exoterism, but which Guénon re-establishes in its true sense, while extending its guarantee of rightness beyond the limits of one religion only. In his perspective it takes on a vast significance, to include, for all seekers of religious truth, every form of worship that has its origin in Divine intervention and has been faithfully transmitted from generation to generation by an uninterrupted process of tradition.

With Guénon mention must also be made of Ananda Coomaraswamy.[35] In most respects they cover the same ground, for the writings of both are centered on metaphysical principles and both, from this same standpoint, wrote pertinent and devastating criticisms of the modern world. In particular Coomaraswamy was also, like Guénon, a master of symbolism; but there is a whole aesthetic dimension in Coomaraswamy that is lacking in Guénon, who was not an authority on art. Needless to say, it is their similarities rather than their differences which bring them into the present context; but within the general framework of terminal wisdom, it cannot be denied

[34] *The Crisis of the Modern World,* for example and *The Reign of Quantity and the Signs of the Times.*

[35] Coomaraswamy's *The Bugbear of Literacy* is an example which may be added to the two books of Guénon mentioned in the previous note.

that there is a certain complementary relationship between the two.[36]

A typical example of Coomaraswamy's writing is his article "Symplegades", so entitled because its starting point is "The Clashing Rocks" of Greek mythology. These rocks have, as he shows, many different parallels in other traditions, in particular the various forms of "The Active Door", that is, the gateway through which it is difficult and dangerous to pass because the two leaves of the portal, in some cases represented as "razor-edged", are liable to snap suddenly together. This side of the "narrow gate" is the domain of earthly nature and of man; beyond it lies the Transcendent. Sometimes the passage is made in order to bring a celestial object to earth as when, for the quest of the Golden Fleece, Jason's boat Argo is driven by Athene, Goddess of Wisdom, between the Clashing Rocks which she holds apart. More often however it is a question of the spiritual path of no return, and of the passage from mortality to Immortality. But in any case, none can pass safely between the rocks or the door-leaves by merely human resource. Divine aid is needed—for example, a God-given incantation or invocation. In some Eskimo legends the souls of men are represented by birds, in particular geese migrating to the South at the onset of Winter, and it is only "the fast fliers" (that is, as Coomaraswamy remarks, those who have duly received initiation, the mandate of Heaven) who escape being crushed to death by "the clapping mountains" which are a form of "the clashing rocks". Another form is that of "the clashing waters", if the Exodus be interpreted in its esoteric sense, "the crossing of the Red Sea from the Egyptian darkness of this world to a Promised Land". Yet another form, to be found in a Greenland myth, is that of "two clashing icebergs".

The Symplegades have also a temporal significance: "An unmistakable reference to the Clashing Rocks is to be found

[36] This is well brought out in the A. K. Coomaraswamy Centenary Issue of *Studies in Comparative Religion* (Summer, 1977), in the article "Coomaraswamy: the Man, Myth and History" by Whitall Perry, whose monumental *A Treasury of Traditional Wisdom* may be mentioned here as another of those works which only this age could have produced. Its undertaking was inspired, so the author tells us, by Coomaraswamy's remark: "The time is coming when a Summa of the Philosophia Perennis will have to be written, impartially based on all orthodox sources whatsoever."

in Rgveda, VI, 49.3, where the 'Rocks' are times, viz. Day and Night, described as 'clashing together and parting'." He quotes also from the *Kauṣītaki Brāhmana:* "Night and Day are the Sea that carries all away, and the two Twilights are its fordable crossings; so he sacrifices [performs the sacrifice to Agni] at Twilight... Night and Day, again, are the encircling arms of Death; and just as a man about to grasp you with both arms can be escaped through the opening between them, so he sacrifices at Twilight... this is the sign of the Way-of-the-Gods, which he takes hold of, and safely reaches Heaven."

Coomaraswamy gives far more examples than those few mentioned here; and while basing his exposition mainly on the sacred books of Hinduism, he quotes also copiously from an immense variety of other sources, Buddhist, American Indian, Jewish, Pythagorean, Hermetic, Platonic and Neo-Platonic, Christian,[37] and Islamic, with additional references to world-wide "folklore" survivals from more ancient traditions.

In conclusion he says: "It remains only to consider the full doctrinal significance of the Symplegades. What the formula states literally is that whoever would transfer from this to the Otherworld, or return, must do so through the undimensioned and timeless 'interval' that divides related but contrary forces, between which, if one is to pass at all, it must be 'instantly'... It is, then precisely from these 'pairs' that liberation must be won, from their conflict that we must escape, if we are to be freed from our mortality... Here, under the Sun, we are 'overcome by the pairs' (*Maitri Upanishad,* III, 1): here 'every being in the emanated-world moves deluded by the mirage of the contrary-pairs, of which the origin is in our liking and disliking... but those who are freed from this delusion of the pairs... freed from the pairs that are implied by the expression 'weal and woe', these reach the place of invariability (*Bhagavad Gītā,* VII, 27–8 and XV,5)." He adds, from St Nicholas of Cusa: "The wall of the Paradise in which Thou, Lord dwellest, is built of contradictories, nor is there any way to enter but for one

[37] The Christian sources include Dionysus, St Augustine, St Thomas Aquinas, Dante, Eckhardt, Ruysbroeck, St Nicholas of Cusa, Boehme and Angelus Silesius, not to mention numerous references to the mediaeval romances of Chrétien de Troyes and others.

who has overcome the highest Spirit of Reason[38] who guards its gate (*De Visione Dei*, chapter IX, to end)."

These paragraphs will at least serve to give some inkling of the great interest of this article in itself, which "proves" the existence of a universal consciousness, going back to incalculably early times, of the need to transcend our human state, and of the impossibility of doing so without the help of the Transcendent, the "mandate of Heaven". "Symplegades" is moreover merely one example amongst many others which display the same qualities. Again and again Coomaraswamy goes out to meet the modern world's so-called intelligentsia on their own ground, that is, the ground of what they would call "purely objective scholarship", which alone they respect. It is as if he had said: "You ask for scholarship and nothing but that, so let us have it; but let it be the real thing, in fullness and in depth, not merely a surface smattering." Having thus as it were thrown down the gauntlet, he takes some theme of basic importance for religion in general and proceeds to expound his thesis with a mastery which no modern authority of learning could fail to recognize—we might even say, at which no such authority could fail to feel dwarfed, for the writings of Coomaraswamy have evoked in many minds, both before and since his death in 1947, the question as to whether any other equally great scholar has ever existed. However that may be, his books and articles demonstrate amongst other things that beneath the superficial differences and apparent contradictions at which most modernist minds tend to stop short, there lies a complete traditional unanimity the world over for all that is of essential significance, a unanimity of far reaching implications which cannot be disregarded.

If we were to sum up the work of Coomaraswamy as "truth", that of Guénon could be summed up with the word "orthodoxy". In reading Guénon we are scarcely ever allowed to lose sight of the driving force behind his pen, the already mentioned purpose or hope of enabling and impelling a qualified minority to take effective spiritual action. This purpose

[38] The plane of reason is, precisely, the plane of opposites, and to overcome the one is to overcome the other. But this can only be achieved by the Intellect which is supraratational and, in its highest reaches, Divine, and which alone can conquer the dualism to which man became subject through eating the fruit of the forbidden tree.

was no doubt also present in Coomaraswamy, but the reader is less aware of it. One's immediate impression is of a vast canvas of metaphysical and cosmological truth which stretches the intelligence towards its limits, enlarging it and enlightening it, and thus predisposing it for the spiritual work which is the methodic complement of doctrine—a complement which tends to be no more than implicit in Coomaraswamy, whereas in Guénon it is altogether explicit.

The mention of these two writers recalls the great commandment: "Thou shalt love the Lord thy God with all thy Heart, and with all thy soul, and with all thy mind, and with all thy strength."[39] It was part of their function to recall the forgotten truth, affirmed by traditions all over the world, that the Heart is the throne of the Intellect. As to the rest of the commandment, the tendency of Western religious authorities in recent centuries had been to sacrifice almost totally "with all thy mind" for the supposed benefit of "with all thy soul" and "with all thy strength". In consequence, piety had become more and more sentimental, and minds, set free for other things, had worked themselves up into an unparalleled state of unrest. The modern civilization is largely the result. But it has been the function of Guénon and Coomaraswamy to recall some minds from the profane to the sacred, and to awaken others which were half asleep for want of a true object. The writings of these two sages, which could not have been expected by any chain of worldly causality, are indeed so opportune as to be suggestive of something in the nature of a mission. This does not mean that we are claiming for either the status of prophethood, which both would have disclaimed. But it may none the less be relevant to remember, in connection with them, the promise contained in the closing words of the Old Testament: "Behold I will send you Elijah the prophet before the coming of the great and dreadful day of the Lord: And he shall turn the heart of the fathers to the children, and the heart of the children to their fathers, lest I come and smite the earth with a curse."[40]

In connection with this passage, in an article about the function of Elijah—or Elias, as he is called in the New Testament—Leo Schaya remarks that the relationship between "fathers"

[39] St Mark, XII: 30.

[40] Malachi, IV, 5–6.

and "children" signifies the "tradition", the religious teaching which is passed from the one to the other. He adds: "The 'heart of the fathers' is the central inward aspect, the essence of the tradition, its esoteric spiritual and universal nucleus; it is also the doctrines, methods and influences which are derived from it. The 'heart of the children' or believers is their spiritual receptivity, their inward acceptance and reception of what is given them by their 'fathers'.... This acceptance or reception is expressed in Hebrew by the word *Qabbalah* which has become synonymous quite specifically with the esoteric tradition in which Elias is the invisible Master, he who descends secretly to this lower world, not only towards the end but each time, ever since his ascension, that the tradition has needed reviving from within."[41] Schaya also says: "When he returns towards the end of time ... Elias will raise his voice so loud, says Jewish tradition, that it will be heard from one end of the earth to the other. This means that Elias' mission is not confined to Israel, but will spread to all peoples and thereby to all religions." The Gospel likewise reiterates the promise that Elias will come again before the end: "Elias shall truly first come and restore all things."[42] But Jesus adds that he has also already come in the person of John the Baptist; and Gabriel foretold to Zachariah that his son would proceed "in the spirit and power of Elias."[43] Schaya concludes: "Elias therefore means not only a prophet sent to Israel but also a universal function which may be exercised by several persons both within Judaism and within other traditions."

We will come back later to the question of Elias. Meantime he has been mentioned here because the works of Guénon and Coomaraswamy are precisely, in a very full sense, a turning of "the heart of the fathers to the children" in order to operate a turning of the "heart of the children to their fathers". This, together with the almost prophetic suddenness of the Guénon-Coomaraswamy phenomenon, is a powerful indication that they were destined to inaugurate, for this cyclic moment, the workings of "the Eliatic function".

[41] "The Eliatic Function" in *Studies in Comparative Religion,* Winter-Spring, 1979, p. 15.

[42] St Matthew, XVII, 11.

[43] St Luke, I, 17.

Their writing leads up to that of Frithjof Schuon. It could be said, again at the risk of simplification, that if Coomaraswamy represents truth in which commitment is implicit, and if Guénon represents both truth and commitment, it was left to Schuon to add his insistence on the need for total commitment, while at the same time, as regards doctrinal truth, his works are a self-sufficient whole. It could also be said that if the writings of Guénon lead to initiation, those of Schuon lead both to it and beyond it, for they contain a dimension of method which it was not the function of his two predecessors to give.

"Knowledge saves," says Schuon, "only on condition that it enlists all that we are: only when it is a way which tills and which transforms, and which wounds our nature as the plough wounds the earth.... Metaphysical knowledge is sacred. It is the right of sacred things to demand of man all that he is."[44]

It was necessary that Guénon and Coomaraswamy should do concentrated justice to "with all thy mind", and this they did, even to the point of partially neglecting "with all thy soul". Some enthusiasts of Guénon have wrongly concluded from his works that the whole esoteric path depends on the assimilation of doctrine and the correct performance of orthodox rites, and on nothing else, as if the virtues were not also essential. Guénon himself, if asked, would certainly have affirmed their necessity. His avoidance of the moral issue may have been deliberate, in view of a generation in full reaction against unintelligent moralism. However this may be, the reaction none the less called for an answer; and Schuon gives it by speaking of the moral dimension in a new, unmoralistic and more intellectually convincing way, with a stress on the importance of outward beauty, whether it be of nature or of art, as a prolongation of the inward beauty of virtue. In general the absence of the element "with all thy soul" in Guénon and Coomaraswamy may not be unconnected with the extreme objectivity of their writings which was carried to the point of excluding any intrusion of their own individualities into what they wrote. Schuon is no less objective, where objectivity is required, than they are; but in reading him, one is conscious of a subject that is adequate to the cyclic significance of the writing itself. Nor can it be doubted that the living inwardness which penetrates his works

[44] *Spiritual Perspectives and Human Facts,* pp. 144–5.

does much to bestow on them their remarkable, integrating power—the power to draw both the mind and the soul in the direction of the Heart. To the many quotations already made from Schuon throughout this book we will simply add here a paragraph which is particularly relevant to our immediate context: "The virtues, which by their very nature bear witness to the Truth also possess an interiorizing quality according to the measure in which they are fundamental; the same is true of beings and things that transmit the messages of eternal Beauty; whence the power of interiorization that belongs to virgin nature, to the harmony of creatures, to sacred art, to music.... If we wish to withdraw into the Heart in order to find there the total Truth and the underlying pre-personal Holiness, we must manifest the Heart not only in our intelligence but also in our soul in general, by means of spiritual attitudes and moral qualities; for every beauty of the soul is a ray coming from the Heart and leading back to it."[45]

As is clear from its title, the recent work from which these words are taken has a very direct bearing on the theme of this chapter,[46] but his other writings[47] are no less fully representative of the spirit of the times. On the one hand we are conscious of all those positive qualities which belong to the end of an age, in particular of a supreme mastery of summing up and of putting everything in its right place. Again and again, about this or about that, one has the impression that Schuon has said the last word. On the other hand we are conscious of the meeting of extremes and of a light that is primordial as well as terminal.

[45] *Esoterism as Principle and as Way*, p. 234.

[46] [The author refers here to an appendix with some reflections on Schuon's *Sufism: Veil and Quintessence*.—Ed.]

[47] [A full bibliography is available from the Frithjof Schuon Archive at www.frithjofschuon.info —Ed.]

Do the Religions Contradict One Another?

The answer to this question is emphatically no inasmuch as every religion is a manifestation of the One Supreme Reality. It needs nonetheless to be answered in some detail, since most of us have heard it said more than once over the years: "How is it possible to believe in religion since the different religions contradict each other?" The motive behind such remarks can never be profound, but it may vary between a would-be self-justification for not practicing religion and the desire to be thought intelligent or up to date. As to other motives given such as the mistaken supposition that the Darwinian theory of evolution has been scientifically proved to be true, whereas it has in fact no scientific basis at all, I have written about this at some length already elsewhere,[1] so I will not repeat myself here.

I am bound however to repeat in our present context what I have already said more than once elsewhere about the complete dependence of every religion upon the Divine Word, which may manifest Itself either as Book or Man. In Christianity the Word is Christ, and the New Testament is not Revelation but an inspired sacred history of the life and teaching of the Word made Flesh, whereas Judaism and Islam are based on the Word made Book. The basis of Judaism is the Pentateuch, the first five books of the Old Testament which were revealed to Moses, together with the Psalms which were revealed to David, and the basis of Islam is the Qur'ān which was revealed to Muhammad. In the ancient religions, of which Hinduism appears to be the sole fully surviving example, there was room for both these Divine Manifestations: the Vedas were the Word made Book, and the Avataras of Vishnu are the Word made Flesh.

[1] *The Eleventh Hour*, ch. 3; *Ancient Beliefs and Modern Superstitions*, ch. 1. [The latter chapter is to be found in this volume, pp. 81–93.—Ed.]

It must however be clearly understood that in the religions which are based on the Word made Book, the Messenger to whom the Book is revealed is thereby to be ranked at the highest degree of sanctity, which means that some of his utterances are bound to proceed from the level of the Divine Word, even if the structure of the religion does not allow him to be worshipped. It is therefore possible for every Divine Messenger to make a statement which amounts to the same as the words of Christ, "None cometh to the Father but through me"; and there is in Islam a saying attributed to the Prophet Muhammad to the effect that there can be no meeting with God which is not preceded by a meeting with himself. Moreover St. Thomas Aquinas says that the fact of a Divine Person having manifested Itself in one human nature does not prevent It from doing so in another human nature.[2] We are thus enabled to speak symbolically of the Word as a precious stone of many facets. It is true that the above quoted words of Christ are altogether central to Christianity, whereas the equivalent saying of Muhammad cannot be said to have the same place in Islam. We did not however quote them to distinguish this from that, but on the contrary to identify each with the other. Both are expressions of the truth that there is no way to God except through His Word. There is therefore no question here of contradiction between two religions.

We will briefly mention here another point which might seem to some of our readers to be contradictory. The Buddha is not mentioned in the Qur'ān at all, but the Qur'ān states that for every people God has sent a messenger (X: 47), and that some of these have been mentioned whereas others have not (XL: 78; IV: 164); and since the Buddha established a religion over two thousand years ago which to this day remains in possession of a large part of the East, he must have been a messenger in the full sense of the Arabic word *rasūl*. Can it not then be said that the absence in Buddhist doctrine of any word which can reasonably be translated by the word "God" constitutes a kind of inter-religious contradiction? The answer is that Buddhism's insistence on the One Absolute Infinite Eternal Reality brings it into agreement with all other religions.

[2] *Summa Theologiae*.

Let us now pass on to an apparent contradiction which cannot be dismissed so easily. If the religion of Islam depended on the beliefs of the average Muslim, then there would indeed be a contradiction; but Islam depends on the Qur'ān, not on human opinion that is based on Qur'ānic verses taken out of their context.

It is a fact that most Muslims believe that Christ was not crucified, whereas Christians consider the Crucifixion to be as it were the foundation stone of their religion. Many aspects of their religion have been questioned and rejected by certain Christians: already in very early Christianity a number of differing schools of thought were hurling anathema at each other;[3] but I have never heard of any Christian that denies the Crucifixion and rejects the sign of the Cross. The Muslim denial of the Crucifixion is based on a Qur'ānic statement isolated from its setting, combined perhaps with a natural readiness to accept what appears to be good news. The idea that God would allow one of His Messengers to be crucified is hard to accept, nor is the Christian doctrine of the Redemption easy to understand. I have heard it said: "Are we not all included in God's redemption of Adam?"

As to the whole of the Qur'ānic passage in question, having been blamed for their calumny of Mary and their denial of the Virgin birth of Christ, they are then blamed for having said: *Verily we have slain the Messiah Jesus the Son of Mary, the Messenger of God.* The Qur'ān then adds the words: And they did not slay him and they did not crucify him, but it seemed to them that they had done so.

Now we must bear in mind that when the Prophet Muhammad was once asked: "When did you become a Prophet", he answered: "I was a Prophet when Adam was between water and clay." In other words, Prophethood is not of this world, but transcends time and space. As we have seen, every Messenger has two natures, one which is transcendent and one which is human. There is never any question in Christianity of the Divine Nature of Christ having been crucified. As for the Jews, they looked on him as a man who falsely claimed to be the Messiah. But instead of saying "we have slain this usurper", they said, with typical Jewish sarcasm: "We have

[3] See Frithjof Schuon, *Islam and the Perennial Philosophy*, p. 36.

slain the Messiah". The Qur'ān denies this possibility, and then adds what are, in our context, the all important words: *But it seemed to them that they had done so*. Why did it seem to them that they had done so? Precisely because they had seen the dead body of Christ's human nature before them on the Cross. There is therefore no mutual contradiction between Christianity and Islam on this point.

In this context it should perhaps be mentioned that exoterism as opposed to esoterism is a domain in which there are bound to be apparent contradictions—apparent but not real, because exoterism is no more than the result of a gradual falling away from an esoterism which alone can be considered as the full reality of the religion in question. I once, not recently, attended an inter-religious congress in Delhi, and the speaker who had been invited to represent Christianity was insistent that since the Crucifixion the only valid religion was Christianity with its Trinity of Father, Son and Holy Ghost who are, taken all together, One God. Moreover he seemed pleased to have the opportunity of being able to preach what he believed to be the one and only truth to such a diversity of non-Christians; but unknown to himself, he could hardly have chosen a less receptive setting than this for his particular theme.

The congress, being where it was, had in the nature of things been organised by Hindu Brahmins who considerably outnumbered the single representatives of the other religions. They were all of the Advaita Vedantist school and knew well that the age-old doctrine of Hinduism affirms a Divine Trinity which corresponds to the Christian Trinity but which is still in the domain of *Māyā* (illusion), being transcended by *Ātmā*, the Self, which is the One-and-Only Reality. Moreover these Hindus were particularly insistent upon the transcendence in question.

When the talk had come to an end, during the brief period in which others are allowed to speak, I felt obliged to point out that more than one of the greatest Christian Saints had insisted, with no little vehemence, that beyond the Trinity there is the Supreme Reality of Absolute Infinite Eternal Perfection. Among the best known of these, to name only two, are Meister Eckhart and Angelus Silesius; and if others, no less great, remained silent on this point, it was no doubt through consideration for the vast majority of their fellow Christians for whom two different levels of Divinity, one above the other, would inevitably amount to two Gods. In mentioning this danger, Frithjof Schuon also reminds us that the main purpose of religion is to save souls rather than to convey metaphysical truths. Needless to say, he is not denying that the truth has its rights, but simply remarking that in the present state of the world certain errors have to be accepted by official representatives of religion as half-truths for fear of causing even greater errors. But in his own writings, which are addressed to metaphysicians and to those who are capable of accepting metaphysical truths as Divine Mysteries even if they cannot yet clearly understand them, he is so insistent on mentioning the truth in question that he goes so far as to speak of "the Relative Absolute"—which is, as he fully admits, something of a contradiction in terms—in order to distinguish the less higher aspect of Divinity (academically sometimes known as the Personal God) from the Supreme Summit which transcends it.

The Brahmins showed such interest in what I had said that I took the opportunity of informing these representatives of the oldest living esoterism that the final esoterism of this cycle of time, namely Sufism, the esoterism of Islam which I had been invited to represent, is in entire agreement with Hinduism in reserving a place, at the summit of the hierarchy, for Absolute Infinite Oneness which excludes all question of duality.

In Islam it is often said that God has a hundred Names, but this saying is not to be taken too literally because more than one list has been handed down to us by tradition. These Names are not all at the same level, and the chief criterion as to the level of any particular Name is whether or not it implies any plurality. The Names Lord (*al-Rabb*) and King (*al-Malik*) suggest respectively the existence of slaves and subjects. But the highest Names, those of the Divine Essence, such as *al-Ḥaqq* the Truth (in its widest sense of Absolute Reality), *al-Qayyūm* the Absolutely Independent, *al-Aḥad* the One-and-Only, and *al-Ṣamad* the Self-Sufficient, are beyond any such implication.

It is also possible for a Divine Name which usually expresses plurality to be used at the level of the Essence. It could be said that in the opening words of the Holy Tradition "I was a Hidden Treasure and I loved to be known," the Divine Name *al-Shākir*, the Grateful, is implicitly present in its supreme sense as a Name of the Essence expressing the Gratitude of the Absolute Infinite Perfection to Itself for being what It is.

Certain Names of the Essence are less obviously so, and as such they are highly informative, as for example *al-Ḥayy* the Living, which tells us that such life as we have on earth is not ours but a brief loan from the Living Himself, immensely reduced to the level of our transitory earthly existence. Analogously the certitude that each one of us has of being "myself", of being "I", is just such a loan from *Anā* (the Arabic word *anā* denotes the first personal pronoun). In the Qur'ān God not only says "No god but God" and "no god but He" but also "no god but I". This brings us back to the Sanskrit word *Ātmā*, the One and Only Self of Hindu doctrine.

To revert to our chapter heading, it will, I think, have been clearly understood that difference by no means necessarily coincides with contradiction. Muslims are forbidden to drink wine, for example, though they are promised it for the higher Paradises of the Hereafter. The Eucharist, on the other hand, which consists of bread and wine, may be considered as the basic rite of Christianity, and there is a chapter in the Qur'ān of which the title, "The Table", signifies the farewell supper at which Christ established the rite of the Eucharist. The Qur'ān affirms the Christian doctrine of the transubstantiation of what the Christian Apostles ate and drank at the table by stating that the whole meal was sent down from Heaven as a sign which would be perpetual for all Christians throughout the centuries (V, 112–5).

Al-Muhaymin, the Protector, the Watcher-over, is one of the Names of God, and this Name is used in the Qur'ān of the Qur'ān itself in relation to what preceded it. The Qur'ānic passage about the Eucharist that we have just mentioned is an example of that protection. It may be said to reaffirm the essence of Christianity in the face of doubts which certain heretical sects and many individuals who claim to be Christians have cast upon the idea of transubstantiation.

Conversely it should be made known to both Christians and Muslims of today that at the time of the Last Supper, and possibly even at the Supper itself, Christ predicted the revelation of the Qur'ān. It was moreover inevitable that he should do so. Without making any quotation, Frithjof Schuon has remarked in general: "It is inconceivable that Christ, when speaking of the future, should not have mentioned the one Divine Manifestation which was to take place between his two comings".

The passage in question which undoubtedly refers to the Revelation of the Qur'ān to Muhammad is as follows: "I have yet many things to say unto you, but ye cannot bear them now. Howbeit when he, the Spirit of Truth is come, he will guide you into all truth: for he shall not speak of himself, but whatsoever he shall hear, that shall he speak; and he will show you the things to come."[4]

It is however an undeniable fact that not all prophesies are made primarily for the sake of those who first hear them and record them. Not without importance in this context are the words "But ye cannot bear them now". In any case Christ would have known that the majority of those who surrounded him thought that his second coming would be soon and that what he said about the Spirit of Truth was therefore bound to be identified with something far more immediate than the coming of Muhammad some six hundred years later. It was in fact identified with the miracle of Pentecost. The descent of the tongues of flame might be said in a certain sense to indicate a coming of the Spirit of Truth, but it does not fully correspond to the words, "He shall not speak of himself, but whatsoever he shall hear, that shall he speak" which clearly refer to the Prophet's foundation of the religion of Islam, not on his own initiative of personal ideas, but on the verses of the Qur'ān which he heard revealed to him, passage by passage, throughout the rest of his life. Moreover towards the end of the preceding chapter of St. John which contains the first mention of the Spirit of Truth, the words "he will tell you all things"[5] correspond perfectly to the Qur'ānic verses. Unlike the New Testament which providentially fulfils the Christian need for an inspired record of the life and teachings of the Word made Flesh, the Qur'ān does in fact "guide us into all truth" by telling us much that we did not know about the lives of Messengers and Prophets whom God has sent into the world, about the different religions and their foundation, about human nature, and above all about the Nature of God in Whose image man's nature was made.

[4] St. John, XVI: 12-15.

[5] St. John, XV: 26.

It is not illegitimate to suppose that Christ would have known also that the full meaning of his words as recorded by St. John was not destined to be understood until over a thousand years had passed since the actual coming of the Spirit of Truth. Otherwise expressed, he would have known that the identification of his words with the miracle of Pentecost was destined to be more or less exclusively accepted by Christians until the present day.

We have more than once quoted Schuon's timely remark that "if human societies degenerate on the one hand with the passage of time they accumulate on the other hand experience in virtue of old age, however intermingled with error their experience may be".[6] It is true that the world was already in extreme old age two thousand years ago, but that old age lay hidden under the youth of Christianity and then, subsequently, also under the youth of Islam. Nonetheless, its unseen presence below the surface has now precipitated those two latest religions towards itself, that is, in the direction of old age. I myself, having briefly summed up what has just been said, have even ventured to say in more than one recent lecture given in London, "Everyone in this room, including those who are young in years, is old, and as such we have a choice between two attributes offered us by old age, namely senility and wisdom. Despite the fact that the vast majority of our contemporaries have chosen the former of these—whence the present state of the world—it is nonetheless possible and even inevitable that some will choose wisdom, a wisdom that is calm and objective, free from the passionate prejudices which have previously been too dominant in human souls with regard to religions other than their own, a wisdom which cannot fail to rejoice in the certitude of this prediction by Christ of the coming of the Prophet of Islam. Nor can we fail to rejoice in the honour that it is directly to us, men and women of the eleventh hour, that Christ is addressing this message more than to any others."

We will close this chapter with words from the Qur'ān which in a sense sum up all that we have been saying, words which might be called the Islamic equivalent of the Christian *Credo*, compared with which they have a striking simplicity.

[6] See *Form and Substance in the Religions*, p. 222.

On the one hand they are more authoritative than the *Credo* because the Qur'ān, unlike the Christian *Book of Common Prayer*, is direct Revelation from God. But on the other hand, unlike the Credo, they have no distinct place in the liturgy of Islam, and the average Muslim is ignorant of their existence. They give us nonetheless a definite statement, on the authority of the Word made Book, of the faith of the Prophet and of those who may be considered as the most spiritual of his Companions. *They believe, all of them, in God and His Angels and His Books and His Messengers. And they say: "We make no distinction between any of His Messengers"* (II, 285).

Let us add, by way of commentary on the final sentence, two utterances of the Prophet, evoked on different occasions by disregard of the principle in question: "Say not that I am better than Moses" and "Say not that I am better than Jonah".

TRADITIONAL PSYCHOLOGY

Thou hast spoken right, 'tis true.
The wheel is come full circle; I am here.
V, 3, 171–77

At a cursory reading of the play these speeches are almost embarrassing to some of us. Our reaction is spontaneously rationalistic. We ask ourselves what is the meaning of these reiterated assertions that the gods are just. Can Shakespeare have forgotten for the moment that the world is full of injustice? Or is he simply making Edgar and Albany express a rather primitive and unintelligent point of view which he does not hold himself? The answer to both questions is certainly "No". Our medieval ancestors did not believe in chance. When a worldly event seemed just, they immediately recognised the workings of Providence. But their faith remained quite unruffled in the face of triumphant and prosperous wickedness, for they knew that any apparent injustices in this world would be made good in the next. The remarks of Albany and Edgar are simply spontaneous comments on events, equivalent to some ejaculation such as "Praise be to God". If they jar on the humanist, it is because he wrongly suspects an attempt to justify the ways of God to man. In other words he attributes to Albany and to Edgar something of a modern psychology, a sort of primitive rationalism, cruder and less fully developed than his own. He fails to realize how little store was set in the Middle Ages, despite all their dialectic, by logical proof.

Shakespeare, unlike Milton, has no illusions about the scope of reason. He knew that since reason is limited to this world it is powerless to "justify the ways of God". Milton may have known this in theory, but in practice he was very much a son of the Renaissance, very deeply under the spell of humanism. *Paradise Lost* cannot be called an intellectual poem. Milton portrays the next world by sheer force of human imagination. His God the Father, like Michelangelo's, is fabricated in the image of man; and the purely logical arguments which he puts into the mouth of God to justify His ways inevitably fail to convince us. Now Shakespeare also seeks to justify the ways of God to man. That is, beyond doubt, the essence of his purpose in writing. But his justification is on an intellectual plane, where alone it is possible; and this brings us back to the theme of his plays, for the intellect is none other than the lost faculty of vision which is symbolised by the Holy Grail and by the Elixir of Life.

In considering how Shakespeare conveys his message to us we must remember that the true function of art is not didactic. A great drama or epic may contain little or much teaching of a didactic kind, but it does not rely on that teaching in order to gain its ultimate effect. Its function is not so much to define spiritual wisdom as to give us a taste of that wisdom, each according to his capacity. We may quote in this connection a profound remark which has been made about sacred art in Christianity: "It sets up against the sermon which insists on what must be done by one who would become holy, a vision of the cosmos which is holy through its beauty; it makes men participate naturally and almost involuntarily in the world of holiness."[1] In its original context it is the great Norman and Gothic Cathedrals, the sanctuaries in which the sermon is preached, which immediately spring to mind as examples of art which reveals a vision of the cosmos. But drama can also yield such a vision; and to reveal the beauty and thereby the harmony of the universe is to justify the ways of God.

The first spectators of Shakespeare were probably more receptive than we are. We tend to take art less seriously than they did. For modern man the supreme distinction is between "fiction" and "truth", as we say, between art on the one hand and "reality" on the other. Now naturally our medieval ancestors made the same distinction, but for them it was not so sharp. They were not in the habit of speaking and thinking of life as "truth". By truth, by reality, they meant something different; for them the supreme distinction was not between life and art, but between the next world, that is, Truth, and this world, which is the shadow of Truth. The sharpness of that distinction took the edge off all other distinctions. Moreover, art for them was not merely a copy of life, that is, it was not merely the shadow of a shadow; it was also by inspiration, partly and in some supreme cases even almost wholly—a direct copy or shadow of the "substance" itself. The distinction between art and life is therefore not so much between a shadow and a reality as between two shadows. This sounds exaggerated, and no doubt the divergence in outlook between then and now was

[1] Titus Burckhardt, *Sacred Art in East and West*, p. 46.

far slighter for the vast majority than might appear from what has just been said. But it went certainly further than a mere verbal quibble over the meaning of the word "reality", and it would have been enough to make an appreciable difference to the attitude of an audience towards a play. By attributing a less absolute reality to life, they attributed more reality to art. They no doubt entered into it more wholeheartedly. But the difference is relative. We also can enter in. Let us consider what actually happens.

In life we have no view of the whole: we see only bits and pieces here and there, and our view is quite distorted. What is near to us we look at with feverish subjectivity: what is not near we look at with more or less cold objectivity. Above all we fail to see the pattern. It is as if life were a great piece of tapestry and as if we looked at it from the wrong side, where the pattern is obscured by a maze of threads, most of which seem to have no purpose. Now a play of Shakespeare's is like a much smaller piece of tapestry, partly copied from the other but also, in virtue of an aspect of what we call his secret, copied from the transcendent Original of the other, that Divine Harmony of which the temporal and spatial cosmos is a reflection, but of which it is merely a reflection, whence the superficial discords which, for fallen man, give the lie to the profound beauty of the image as a whole—a totality which he cannot see, being, by definition, cut off from the vision of it. The remarkable intensity of Shakespeare's copy is redoubled by the corresponding intensity of those who hear it and see it. The dramatist is highly privileged with a privilege that he shares with no other artist, except the composer of music, namely the extreme passivity of his audience. It is in the nature of things that people go to a play in the hope that they will be spellbound. Shakespeare holds out this smaller piece of tapestry to us in the theatre, between ourselves and him. He is on the right side of it and we are again on the wrong side just as, unlike him, we are on the wrong side of the great tapestry of life. To begin with we look at the rather chaotic maze of threads with the same cold objectivity with which we view the threads of our neighbours' lives. But little by little, as the play goes on, we are drawn into it and become more and more bound up with its threads. Our cold objectivity vanishes and we feel the warmth of subjectivity. So it is with any dramatic piece, one may say. That is true; but with most drama what is the benefit to be gained? It is simply a question of exchanging one's ordinary subjectivity for another one which is no better and which may be worse. But when a drama is created as an image of the whole universe, and when the hero represents a great soul which is being purified of all its faults, and being developed towards the limits of human possibility, then it is no light thing to be drawn into the web of the tapestry and to become identified with its central figure. But that is not all: the purification of the hero is in view of an end. By the close of the play we have become objective once more, but with a higher objectivity which is completely different from the initial one; for Shakespeare has drawn us right through the tapestry and out at the other side, so that we now see it as it really is, a unity in which all the parts fit marvellously together to make up a perfect whole. Having been given a taste of the hero's purification we are now given one of the spiritual wisdom to which it leads: and just as Shakespeare's small tapestry merges mysteriously with the great tapestry of life, so our view of the harmony and beauty of the one is also, in a sense, a view of the harmony and beauty of the other. We "participate naturally and almost involuntarily in the world of holiness." It is only a momentary glimpse, and it does not last. But it does make an imprint upon the soul, which may not be easily effaced.

Shakespeare's being from the outset on the right side of the small tapestry he holds out to us in the theatre is part of his secret as an artist; his being on the right side of the great tapestry of life is part of his secret as a man. This higher objectivity is directly mentioned by King Lear at the beginning of the last scene of the play. He is now almost at the end of the quest, and he imagines what it would mean to be altogether united with Cordelia who, according to the deeper meaning of the play, is herself a personification of the same objectivity which can, to use her own words, "outfrown false fortune's frown" (V, 3, 6). In an already quoted speech, the King says that they will live together in prison

> And pray, and sing, and tell old tales, and laugh
> At gilded butterflies, and hear poor rogues
> Talk of court news; and we'll talk with them too,
> Who loses and who wins; who's in, who's out;

And take upon's the mystery of things
As if we were God's spies.
V, 3, 12–17

Alone the eye of the intellect, the eye of the angels who are "God's spies", can perceive the justice of the workings of Providence. It is clearly from the standpoint of this higher objectivity that the maturer plays were written; and when at the end, having passed through the tapestry, we stand side by side with Shakespeare himself, we also for the moment have in a sense taken upon ourselves "the mystery of things".

Let us consider this in a slightly different way. The fall of man is represented traditionally as the acquisition of the knowledge of good and evil. The intellectual knowledge of Absolute Good is lost and is replaced by a purely mental knowledge which is only capable of grasping a relative good, that good which is the opposite of evil. We have thus the illusion that the devil is the opposite of God, whereas in reality nothing at all can stand in the scales against Divine Providence. In the course of *Othello*, for example, as also in the course of *King Lear*, Shakespeare has shown us the extremities of relative good and evil; but by the end it is as if for the moment he has taken out of our mouths the taste of the fruit of the Forbidden Tree. The knowledge of good and evil is there, but it no longer blinds us to the Absolute Good. We no longer ask ourselves that most difficult of all questions "Why does God allow evil?" for we have mysteriously felt the answer to it, where alone the answer lies, upon the plane of the intellect. We accept everything with serenity and would change nothing. We feel in an inexplicable way that all is well, not according to human justice which in any case is fragmentary, being largely based on ignorance, but according to "poetic justice", which is none other than Divine Justice. But it is not only sorrow that can work this wonder in us: just as we accept the endings of *Othello* and *King Lear*, so also we accept the endings of *Cymbeline* and *The Winter's Tale*. It is not the same with the happy endings of *Twelfth Night* and *As You Like It*, for example. Nor is the total effect of *Romeo and Juliet* comparable to that of the great tragedies. The best of the pre-*Hamlet* plays, *Romeo and Juliet* and *A Midsummer Night's Dream* included, have a total effect of undeniably exalting and peacegiving harmony, but this is something less transcendent than the harmony of the Universe itself, nor can it come near to making us forget "the knowledge of good and evil" or to justifying the ways of God.

But once he has succeeded in justifying those ways, Shakespeare does so not only once but again and again, which suggests that his own life was patterned upon the pattern of his plays, and that he was writing about what he himself knew. There is nothing really extravagant in such a claim, for according to the traditional conception of poetry, a poet should be no less than a seer, *vates*; and the Garden of Helicon, the abode of Apollo and the Muses, the only source of true poetic inspiration, is as Dante tells us none other than the Garden of Eden, where grows the Tree of Life whose fruit is the only antidote to the poison of the knowledge of good and evil.

Always allowing that there are many different degrees of being inspired, the explanation of what Shakespeare is able to do to us can only lie in his inspiration or, if one prefers it, in his intellectuality, which according to the true sense of the word really amounts to the same. It is certainly not a mere question of the power of language, neither is it merely a question of the feelings of pity and terror, as might be concluded from Aristotle's all too inexplicit references to catharsis. The verse of Webster's *Duchess of Malfi* is fine enough, like that of Shelley's *Cenci*; nor are the elements of pity and terror lacking, to say the least. Yet these two plays leave us rather with feelings of horror than with visionary acceptance and serenity. The key to what Aristotle meant by catharsis lies above all in the example he gives, and it is clear from this that the "purification" in question is no less than what has been described here in other terms, for the effect upon us of Sophocles' *Oedipus* is in fact essentially the same as that of *King Lear*.

Many secondary features of Shakespeare's plays suggest that the poet had power to draw upon the transcendent. Characters like Hamlet and Cleopatra for example are not so much fabrications as "creations". There is something almost miraculously alive about them as if they had been brought down ready made from above. An analogous remark could be made about his coining of words.[2] Created also rather than

[2] Macbeth's anguish was so intense that ordinary language could not suffice to express it. His sudden spontaneous coining of two new words in "... this my hand will rather the multitudinous seas incarnadine" strikes us as marvellously right—nothing else would do—while bearing witness to the high degree of Shakespeare's inspiration.

fabricated are the worlds in which the plays are set: each is like a unique sphere of existence with its own atmosphere which makes it quite distinct from all the other Shakespearean macrocosms. But contact with a transcendent source is above all suggested by the constant repetition of a transcendent total effect. That contact is a secret, for it belongs to the domain of the Mysteries; but the true and original purpose of art—the primal reason for its existence—is precisely to communicate secrets, not by blurting them out but by offering them as it were with half open hand, by bringing them near and inviting us to approach.

It is generally agreed that in *The Tempest*, Prospero's magic, aside from its other meanings, is intended to represent Shakespeare's own powers as an artist; and truly inspired art is indeed a kind of white magic which casts a spell over man and momentarily changes him, doing as it were the impossible and making him quite literally excel himself.

Why "With All Thy Mind"?

It could be said that one of the criteria of orthodoxy in a religion is that it should provide adequate means for the fulfilment of the following commandment in all its aspects: "Thou shalt love the Lord thy God with all thy heart, and with all thy soul, and with all thy mind, and with all thy strength."[1]

The most essential part of the commandment is clearly its opening. The heart is the organ of faith, whose higher possibilities are certainty, intellection, gnosis. It is called "heart" because it is as central and vital to the soul as the physical heart is to the body. The function of a centre is always that of attraction and radiation, on the one hand to draw towards it the outlying parts and to keep them knitted together as an integral whole, and on the other to transmit to them, according to the measure and the mode of their varying capacities, what it receives from worlds which lie above and beyond it. To "love with all thy heart" means total love. Mind and soul, which depend ultimately on the heart for love of God, needed separate mention in the commandment only because their domination by the centre was reduced at the Fall to being no more than a virtuality, and because on the path of return to the primordial state of loving "with all thy heart", mind-love and soul-love have a function of cause—or so it seems—in the process of re-awakening heart-love, though they could never be fully realized except as a result of that re-awakening. The give and take in question correspond to the interaction of human initiative and Divine Grace. However much the manner of expression may vary, religions are in agreement that a minimum of effort from mind or soul in the direction of

[1] St. Mark, XII, 30. In Deuteronomy VI, 5, to which this is a reference, the element "mind" is not mentioned, which makes no fundamental difference since the mind is strictly speaking a psychic faculty, and is therefore implicit in the word "soul". In St. Matthew, XXII, 37, on the other hand, the element "strength" is absent, which again makes no difference inasmuch as energy and endurance are dominated by the will, which is also a psychic faculty.

the heart, that is, the Transcendent, is guaranteed to call down upon itself a vivifying and growth-promoting force out of all proportion to the gesture that released it. But that human gesture needs to be continually repeated.

Loss of direct contact with the heart meant loss of that inward attraction which alone could counterbalance the centrifugal tendencies of the lower faculties. Left to their own resources, they were bound to move further and further from the centre and therefore from each other. This process of disintegration, although checked and even partially reversed for brief periods by repeated Divine interventions throughout the course of time, is inevitably now near to reaching its extremities, inasmuch as all traditions agree that we are approaching the end of this temporal cycle; and one of the most striking features of the general disintegration characteristic of modern man is an unparalleled mental independence by reason of which many minds are feverishly active and almost "acrobatically" nimble. The same lack of anchorage makes also for an abnormally hurried superficiality of judgements and conclusions.

It is this mental independence which makes so timely and so necessary the chapter on "Understanding and Believing" in Frithjof Schuon's *Logic and Transcendence*.[2] The author focuses our attention on the monstrous yet now not uncommon phenomenon of understanding metaphysical truths in the mind without any assent of belief from the soul, let alone the heart. The only remedy is re-integration, since only if the different faculties are knit closer together can the soul be brought within near enough reach of the mind to respond to the light of the doctrine, which is addressed to the mind directly. But mental understanding followed by re-integration are as a second and third stage in the path of return. In the present context we are concerned with the preliminary stage of removing obstacles. Even in the innermost aspects of religion there can be affirmations which are unattractive to the mind. But at the esoteric level all that is needed to transform that unattractiveness to its opposite is a fuller explanation. By way of example, the supreme aim and end of religion, which in Christianity is sometimes termed Deification, is perhaps in general more often

[2] Ch. XIII (Harper and Row, 1975).

referred to as the Supreme Identity; and at the beginning of the path, after a certain very relative progress has been made, there is a danger that the novice in question, greatly overrating that progress, may fall into the trap (which is precisely what the enemy of mankind wants above all) of deifying his own ego rather than God. For this reason we find, in Sufism for example, the not infrequent insistence on referring to the Divine Self by the third personal pronoun rather than the first. It has more than once been said that the most perfect formulation of the Supreme Truth is "He is He". But other Sufis have seen that each of the three personal pronouns has its limitations. The Shaykh al-'Alawī, while admitting the inadequacy of "I" and "Thou", points out that the third of the three has also a disqualifying limitation that makes it incapable of expressing the Absolute Reality, and this is its lack of inclusiveness.[3] To go back to our starting point, the mind, far from being totally enamoured of "He is He" feels as it were "left out in the cold". But one of the greatest of the early Sufis, Abū Saʿīd al-Kharrāz, gives us implicitly a most satisfying solution in his answer to the question "Through what sign knowest thou God?" He said: "Through His Union of Opposites",[4] after which he added the following quotation from the Qur'ān: *He is the First and the Last, and the Outward and the Inward* (LVII, 3).

If we consider the latter of these two pairs, the Outward and the Inward, in one of its aspects, namely Objectivity and Subjectivity, we see that on the plane of Supreme Reality, He (Objectivity) and I (Subjectivity) are inseparably One, while remaining nonetheless absolutely objective and subjective; and an aspect of that inseparability is Thou, the Archetype of the second personal pronoun, for nothing positive exists in manifestation which is not already present in its Divine Source. It is through Thou that I and He converse with each other, and that communion is an aspect of the Divine Self-Sufficiency expressed by the Name *al-Ṣamad*.

As to the outer aspects of religion, the rights of intelligence have by no means always been upheld by the authorities in question. The mental faculties need to be appeased and reassured; and to this end religion has no option but to sacrifice

[3] Martin Lings, *A Sufi Saint of the Twentieth Century*, p. 206.

[4] William C. Chittick, *The Sufi Path of Knowledge*, p. 67.

certain half-truths, not to speak of mere suppositions and conjectures, which in the past were considered as powerful motives for loving God "with all thy soul and with all thy strength".

A religion's claim to unique efficacy must be allowed the status of half-truth because there is, in fact, in the vast majority of cases, no alternative choice.[5] In the past it would have been as pointless for a religion to dwell on the validity and efficacy of other religions as it would be for an announcement to be made from an all-capacious lifeboat to those struggling in the waters about it that five miles away there was an equally good lifeboat. The lack of any such acknowledgement did not cause minds to falter in their worship, because each traditional civilization lived for the most part in high-walled isolation from other sectors of humanity. Moreover, there is nothing questionable in the general notion that certain religions are defunct and have been superseded by Divine intervention. Nor can it be doubted that pseudo-religion is a possibility, since the scriptures themselves speak of false prophets. A mediaeval Christian, for example, was therefore not mentally compromised because he classed Judaism as a superseded religion or because he classed Islam as a pseudo-religion. Everyone has a right to be ignorant or mistaken about what takes place in worlds other than his own.

But in the present age the isolating walls have for the most part been broken down. Otherwise expressed, the lifeboats are mostly within reach of each another, and lifelines even cross; and minds are inevitably troubled by thoughts which would never have assailed them in the past. In a word, it becomes difficult to dedicate the mind to the worship of God when religious authorities make claims which the intelligence sees to be in direct contradiction with what religion teaches about the nature of God.

It may be objected that if the present situation is new, globally speaking, it none the less existed in the past, if only

[5] As Frithjof Schuon has remarked, for those who come face to face with the founder of a new religion, the lack of alternative choice becomes as it were absolute in virtue of the correspondingly absolute greatness of the Divine Messenger himself. But with the passage of time there is inevitably a certain levelling out between the new and the less new, the more so in that the less new may have special claims on certain peoples.

for relatively small minorities who lived at the frontiers which separated one theocratic civilization from another. For the last thirteen hundred years and more, Christians and Muslims have lived side by side in the Near East, with ample opportunities for seeing that "the other religion" is, in fact, just as genuine as their own. But until recent times the vast majority, including intellectuals, were none the less able, in all peace of mind, to live out their lives in the conviction that their religion alone was truly valid. Why should not the same exclusivism still be compatible with mental serenity?

The answer is partly that the frontiers which separate one perspective from another are not merely geographical. In a theocratic civilization, men are perpetually surrounded by reminders of God and the Beyond; and this produces an "inwardness" which is both individual and collective, and which is itself a kind of isolating wall.[6] The destruction of such walls is an evil; but the virtues they helped to maintain are indispensable and must be supported by other means. We have already quoted in a previous chapter[7] what Frithjof Schuon says about the positive aspect of old age with regard to a certain collective wisdom which human societies accumulate through experiences, despite the errors that result from degeneration. But we did not mention his remark that the representatives of religion should take advantage of all that is positive in being experienced and should change their way of presenting religion by using arguments of a higher order, intellectual rather than sentimental.

Mental dilemma is a more or less inevitable consequence of seeking to maintain, in the modern world, all the details of the average religious perspective which characterized one's pious ancestors. A striking example of this is to be seen in an article on Jesus which a Jewish Rabbi was invited to write in

6 "Aloof" and "introspective" are the epithets applied by Kenneth Cragg to the Eastern Churches, whom he severely criticizes in *The Call of the Minaret* for having done practically nothing throughout the centuries to convert the Islamic East to Christianity. It does not seem to occur to him that the qualities in question, though inconvenient for missionaries, are nearer to virtue than to vice. Moreover, the "aloofness" may well be in part a subconscious unwillingness to "rush in where angels fear to tread".

7 [See "Do the Religions Contradict One Another?", pp. 121–29 of this volume.—Ed.]

one of our leading newspapers, the purpose of the invitation being to have an opinion which was representative of Jewry as a whole. The Rabbi's exposition is based on the question: What prompted Jesus to claim that he was the Messiah? A Jew, he maintains, is well qualified to answer this question in virtue of his special knowledge of the history of his own people, from which he knows that expectations of the Messiah had never been so strong as they were at that particular time. There was a kind of collective wishful thinking in the air which made it almost inevitable that someone would persuade himself and others that he was, in fact, the Lord's Anointed. The Rabbi goes on to speak appreciatively of Jesus as a man, acknowledges his excellent human qualities, emphasizes his good intentions, and excuses him for his Messianic claims.

As a purely psychological explanation of how the Christian religion came into existence, this article opens up the way for someone else to demolish Judaism by exactly the same type of argument. Another point to be noticed is that the author, so it seems, does not dare to think beyond early first century Palestine either in time or in space. He speaks almost as if the crucifixion had only just been perpetrated, closing forever, as it must have seemed to not a few, one of many chapters in the chronicle of false Messianic claims. But what of world history in the last two thousand years? What of the fact that this "false Messiah" has taken possession, spiritually speaking, of three continents and half possession of a fourth, while making considerable inroads into the fifth? And what of the God who has allowed this wide-spread, long-lasting, deep-rooted deception to take place?

In other words, a would-be demonstration of the falsity of another religion proves to be a boomerang which comes back to strike at the very heart of one's own religion. For God is the heart of every religion; and a god who would allow deception on such a colossal scale would not be worth worshipping, even by the "chosen people" whom he had protected against that deception.

On such a basis, belief can only be kept up by not following certain trains of thought which demand to be followed, and by refusing to draw certain obvious conclusions—in fact by no longer being equipped "with all thy mind", let alone loving God. Such belief is exceedingly precarious; and even if the believer in question can live out his own life in orthodoxy to the end, he has little means of fortifying others, and he is in perpetual danger of finding any day that his sons and his daughters have lapsed into agnosticism or atheism. The anti-spiritual pressures of the modern world being what they are—and this applies especially to modern education—the scales are heavily weighted against finding the only true solution, namely a more universal spiritual perspective, which means moving nearer to the Spirit and therefore "upstream" and "against the current". On the other hand, the false solution of agnosticism is simply the next easy step down from misgivings about religion that are based on rationalism and pseudo-logic.

It seems to the Jew that to admit the Messianic claims of Jesus would amount to admitting that Judaism has been superseded—and Christians are waiting at the door to tell him that this is indeed the case. He wrongly imagines himself to be faced, practically speaking, with a choice between Judaism and Christianity. But it would be possible—and this is certainly a solution which some orthodox Jews have individually[8] found for themselves—at least to reserve judgement about Jesus, or even to accept in his first coming a foretaste of the final and all-fulfilling Messianic advent, while continuing to cling to the God-given certainties of the Pentateuch and the Psalms. For Jews who were not swept into Christianity on the crest of its initial wave, the fact that the Messianic mission has not yet been altogether fulfilled can be taken as a sign that Judaism has not yet been superseded and as a justification for remaining faithful to the religion of Moses.

It is relatively easy for the Jew to go half way towards the perspective of *religio perennis* simply by reserving judgement about other religions. Since Judaism is not a world religion he can, with a clear conscience, leave other sectors of humanity to Providence in the certainty that It will take care of them. The Christian on the other hand feels himself to be the chosen instrument of Providence in this respect, as indeed he is, but within limits. The Church's refusal to see these limits results in a perspective which, in the modern world, runs dangerously close to the precipice of disbelief.

[8] For the ideal collective attitude of Judaism to Christianity, and for the reasons why it could never be realized, see Frithjof Schuon, *Islam and the Perennial Philosophy*, pp. 58–9.

It is now some years since the already mentioned book *The Call of the Minaret* was published, and there is reason to think that the views of its author have moved since that time in a more universal direction. It is none the less a faithful mirror of the dilemma which faces many Christians, in particular clergymen and more especially missionaries, who come into close contact with Islam, and who cannot help being deeply impressed by its strength and its fullness as a religion. It is impossible for them to persist in calling Muhammad a "false prophet". On the other hand they will not, or as the case may be, dare not, give up their claim that the Passion of Jesus is the sole means of man's redemption. The point of the book's title is that the muezzin's call should be for Christians as a summons to duty, "the duty of restoring to Muslims the Christ that they have missed." The author adds: "The Christ Jesus of the historic faith is an inescapable figure. It is He we must present to the world of Islam ... yet how we are to do this remains a problem and a burden!" These last words are an understatement. It is almost impossible to make adult Muslims accept the Christian doctrine of Redemption, for they already have a full doctrine of Divine Grace and Mercy in another form, and the historic Jesus plays no part in it, although he remains a most benevolent and glorious onlooker. The Qur'ān calls him the Word of God and a Spirit from God; and Muhammad testified to his second coming. In the days of the Caliphate, one of the traditional ways of wishing long life to a Caliph was to say to him: "May you live long enough to give your government into the hands of Jesus, the son of Mary—Peace be on them both!" But it would be impossible to introduce Jesus into the inner structure of Islam, for the building is already complete and perfect. Providence has not been waiting nearly fourteen hundred years for some Christian missionary to lay the foundation stone.

The author in question seems to have certain suspicions along these lines, and sparks of exasperation—or something akin to that—fly out from time to time: "Islam has proved in history the supreme displacer of the faith of Christ", and "The rise of Islam will always be a painful puzzle to the Christian mind". But although he speaks of "transcending difficulties", there is nothing really transcendent in the book from beginning to end, and that is its weakness. On such a basis, there can clearly be no question of "loving with all thy mind".

The same criticisms cannot be made of *A New Threshold*[9] by the Bishop of Guildford, because there is at least one remarkable outlet onto universality in a timely quotation from St. Justin Martyr's *Apology*, where the uniqueness of Christ as Redeemer is expounded at the level of the Logos and not allowed to trespass upon lower domains which are subject to multiplicity. From this point of view, the act of Redemption belongs to the Divine Nature of Jesus, not to his human nature, and since it thus transcends time and space, it cannot be limited to any historical event. "We have been taught that Christ is the First-begotten of God, and have testified that He is the Intellect (*logos*) of which every race of man partakes. Those who lived in accordance with Intellect are Christians, even though they are called godless, such as, among the Greeks, Socrates and Heraclitus and others like them.... Those who lived by Intellect, and those who so live now, are Christians, fearless and unperturbed."[10]

In recalling St. Justin's standpoint as a legitimate one for Christians to take with regard to adherents of other religions, the Bishop of Guildford thereby implicitly assents to its inescapable corollary, that the act of Redemption operates in other modes as well as the specifically Christian mode of the Passion. The contrary claim, that in a world subject to multiplicity the Divine Mercy, by definition Infinite, should be limited to one single effective act is in principle something that a metaphysician cannot readily accept, quite apart from the overwhelming factual evidence against it. Admittedly the majority cannot be sacrificed to a minority; but certain claims which may have "worked" in the past are of an increasingly dubious value for the majority while being lethal to the intellectual minority. There are Christians for whom the Bhagavad Gita comes next to the Gospels and the Psalms as their most revered book; and this Hindu scripture bears a most eloquent and irrefutable witness to a redeeming Divine Incarnation other than Jesus in the person of Krishna and, by extension, of other Hindu *Avatāras*, including the Buddha.

[9] This booklet, with the subtitle, *Guidelines for the Churches in their relations with Muslim Communities* has recently been published to coincide with the World of Islam Festival.

[10] *First Apology*, Section 46. For the word "Reason", as translation of logos, we have substituted "Intellect".

As Frithjof Schuon remarks: "Every exoteric doctrine is in fact characterized by a disproportion between its dogmatic demands and its dialectical guarantees; for its demands are absolute as deriving from the Divine Will and therefore also from Divine Knowledge, whereas its guarantees are relative, because they are independent of this Will and based, not on Divine Knowledge, but on a human point of view, that of reason and sentiment. For instance, Brahmins are invited by Christian missionaries to abandon completely a religion that has lasted for several thousand of years, one that has provided the spiritual support of innumerable generations and has produced flowers of wisdom and holiness down to our times. The arguments that are produced to justify this extraordinary demand are in no wise logically conclusive, nor do they bear any proportion to the magnitude of the demand; the reasons that the Brahmins have for remaining faithful to their spiritual patrimony are therefore infinitely stronger than the reasons by which it is sought to persuade them to cease being what they are. The disproportion, from the Hindu point of view, between the immense reality of the Brahmanic tradition and the insufficiency of the religious counter arguments is such as to prove quite sufficiently that had God wished to submit the world to one religion only, the arguments put forward on behalf of this religion would not be so feeble, nor those of certain so-called 'infidels' so powerful; in other words, if God were on the side of one religious form only, the arguments put forward on behalf of this religion would be such that no man of good faith would be able to resist it."[11]

The title of this chapter makes the many references to Frithjof Schuon inevitable because his writings lead the way in giving the mind its due in respect of religion. Not that they are limited to the mind, any more than the mind, in the context of "with all thy mind", can be limited to itself, since to be fully operative its higher reaches depend directly on the heart. It is to the mind, to the intermediary intellective faculties, and to the heart that Frithjof Schuon's writings are above all addressed. To avoid giving a false impression, however, it must be added, as regards the soul, that while demolishing certain outworn human arguments which have in the past served

[11] *The Transcendent Unity of Religion* (Harper and Row, 1975), p.14.

the cause of "with all thy soul", he puts other arguments of a higher order in their place. Few writers, if any, have so clearly demonstrated the importance of sacred art in this respect. And who in recent centuries has written so profoundly and unmoralistically about the necessity of virtue?

To the passage written for Christians in affirmation of the validity of Hinduism, let us add the following affirmation of Islam: "... that God could have allowed a religion that was merely the invention of a man to conquer a part of humanity and to maintain itself for more than a thousand years in a quarter of the inhabited world, thus betraying the love, faith, and hope of a multitude of sincere and fervent souls—this is contrary to the Laws of the Divine Mercy, or in other words, to those of Universal Possibility.... If Christ had been the only manifestation of the Word, supposing such a uniqueness of manifestation to be possible, the effect of His birth would have been the instantaneous reduction of the earth to ashes."[12]

To consider now the limitations of Muslim exoterism, it must be remembered that from its stronghold of finality as the last religion of this cycle of time, Islam, unlike Judaism and Christianity, can afford to be generous to other religions. Moreover its position in the cycle confers on it something of the function of summer-up, which obliges it to mention with justice what has preceded it, or at the least to leave an open door for what it does not specifically mention. *Verily We have sent messengers before thee.*[13] *About some of them have We told thee, and about some have We not told thee.* (XL, 78)

We may quote also: *Verily the Faithful*[14] *and the Jews and the Sabians*[15] *and the Christians—whoso believeth in God and the Last Day and doeth deeds of piety—no fear shall come upon them neither shall they grieve.* (V, 69) There is a place for both Judaism and Christianity within the Islamic civilization, and Muslims are obliged to protect the synagogues and churches and other

[12] Ibid, p. 20.

[13] Muhammad.

[14] Muslims.

[15] There is no general consensus of opinion as to what religion is referred to, and certain Muslim rulers, in India and elsewhere, have made the name in question a loophole for tolerance towards their non-Muslim, non-Christian and non-Jewish subjects.

Jewish and Christian sanctuaries. It was a calamity for Spanish Jews when the Christians conquered Spain.

It has to be admitted, however, that the authorities of Islam have been no less ready than their counterparts in other religions to risk "with all thy mind" for the sake of "with all thy soul and with all thy strength". Muslims have been encouraged to believe, and the majority have been only too eager to believe, that Islam has superseded all other religions and that it is therefore the sole truly valid religion on earth. But however absolute the claims of Muslim theologians and jurisprudents may be, they are shown in fact to be relative by the tolerance which Islam makes obligatory towards Judaism and Christianity. Taken with that "grain of salt"—though few are fully conscious of it—the claims in question are not necessarily unpalatable to the intelligence, and are not bound to prevent an intellectual from loving God with all his mind, provided he remain within the walls of the Islamic civilization, which stop him from seeing the full implications of this exclusivism.

But once outside these walls, the situation is different. The most that a sound intelligence can accept are the claims which naturally result from the fact that Islam represents the most recent Divine intervention upon earth. But these claims, though considerable, are relative, not absolute;[16] and a Muslim intellectual in the modern world will not find peace of mind except by assenting to this. It should not however be difficult for him to do so, for a glance at those passages of the Qur'ān on which the theologians' exclusivism is based shows that the verses in question call for a deeper and more universal interpretation than is generally given.

One of these passages is the following: *He it is who hath sent His Messenger with guidance and the religion of Truth, that He may make it prevail over all religion, though the idolaters be averse.* (IX, 33) This verse can be given a narrower or a wider interpretation. Its more immediate meaning is clearly the narrower one: the *Messenger* is Muhammad, *the religion of Truth* is the Qur'ānic message and the *idolaters* are the pagan Arabs and certain other

[16] An orthodox Jew, for example, deeply in love with the Hebrew Psalms, would be justified in hesitating to give up his religion for one that was based on a Revelation in a language he did not know; and he could use Qur'ānic arguments to justify himself.

pagans. To the words *that He may make it prevail over all religion* must be added "in your part of the world".

Whatever the disadvantages of modern education, it serves to implant a more global concept of world history and geography than is normally held by members of traditional civilizations which tend, as we have seen, to be "aloof" and "introspective". The wider knowledge is a mixed blessing, but where it exists it must be taken into account. An intelligent Muslim, living in the modern world, is bound to realize sooner or later, suddenly or gradually, not only that the Qur'ānic message has not been made *to prevail over all religion* in a wider sense, but also that Providence itself is directly responsible for the "shortcoming". The shock of this realization may shatter his belief, unless he is enabled to understand that the verse in question has a wider significance. In the narrower sense, *all religion* can only be taken to mean "all religion in your part of the world". But if *all religion* be interpreted in an absolute sense, and if *idolaters* be made to include such people as the Germans and Celts, many of whom were still pagan at the outset of Islam, then *the religion of Truth* must also be given its widest application, and the words "once again" must be understood (i.e. *He it is who hath sent once again His Messenger...*), for the Divinity has sent messengers before, and never with anything other than *the religion of Truth.* These last four words, like the term Islam itself, can be taken in a universal sense, to include all true religion. The Qur'ān makes it clear that the religions of Adam, Noah, Abraham, Moses and Jesus may be called "Islam" in its literal meaning of "submission to God". In this sense Islam may be said to have been made to *prevail over all religion.*[17] But in its narrower sense Islam has only been allowed to *prevail over all religion* in a limited part of the world. It is now fourteen hundred years since the revelation of the Qur'ān and Providence has allowed non-Qur'ānic modes of *the*

[17] The verse we are considering is parallel to the words of Christ, "This Gospel of the Kingdom shall be preached in all the world. Then shall the end come", which likewise admit of both a limited and a universal interpretation, according to what is understood by "world". In its wider sense (as well as the narrower one) the first part of this prophecy has now come true inasmuch as every people on earth is now within easy reach of the gospel of the Kingdom, that is, the religion of Truth, in at least one of its modes.

religion of Truth to remain as barriers to the Qur'ānic message in more than half the globe.

In the same context, verses affirming that Muhammad has been sent *for all people* (XXXIV, 28) have to be understood in a less monopolizing way than they have been throughout the centuries by Muslims with little or no general knowledge about other religions and their distribution. What the Qur'ān tells us here is that Islam, unlike Judaism or Hinduism, is a world religion. But it is not denying that Buddhism and Christianity are also world religions, that is, open to everybody, at least in principle. These last words are important, for *God doth what He will* (II, 253), and our only means of knowing His Will in this respect are by the results.[18] With regard to the world as it has been in its geographical distribution of peoples for the last two thousand years, it will not escape the notice of an observant Muslim any more than an observant Christian that there is, spatially speaking, a certain sector in which Providence has worked wonders for Buddhism and done relatively little for either Christianity or Islam. The same Muslim will also notice that there is another sector in which Providence has worked wonders for Christianity and done little for the other world religions; and the fact that between these two sectors there is a third in which Islam has been favoured beyond all other religions will not be enough to exonerate him from changing this perspective. For if, as he had been led to believe, God had truly wished Islam (in the narrower sense) to spread over the whole world, why did He construct such impregnable barriers to it in so vast an area?[19]

[18] That is, the great and lasting results which have been put to the test by centuries of time.

[19] The answer of some Muslim theologians to this question has been, in all seriousness, that Almighty God has evidently decided to send the larger part of humanity astray, and that it is not for us to question His Wisdom. But faith on this basis can never be more than fragmentary. By such logic the mind surreptitiously robs itself of love, while turning a blind eye to some of the most essential Attributes of the Object of love. Another "explanation", shared also by Christians, *mutatis mutandis*, is that the "religion of Truth" (understood in a non-universal sense) will in fact prevail over the whole world. *Veritas omnia vincit*. But if only one religion had been valid in the eyes of Heaven for the last thousand years or more, the expectation of a sudden total triumph of that true religion at the end of the cycle could not be enough to appease the mind, that is, it could not convincingly "exonerate" Providence from having allowed false religion to triumph so far and wide for so long.

To take the nearest example, Providence was putting an end to paganism in England at the very time when the Qur'ān was being revealed. *The religion of Truth,* in its Christian mode, was being made to *prevail over all religion,* although the idolaters were averse; and since a Divine intervention is never mediocre, Christianity was being established on the firmest foundations, so that not even the Qur'ānic message, at the height of the power of the Islamic civilization, could come near to prevailing against it. And yet it would have been easy for Providence to have waited a few years and converted England to the new religion instead of setting up there such a resistance to it. The answer to the "problem", if anyone considers it to require an answer, lies in the following verse, which many consider to be among the last Revelations received by the Prophet and which in any case belongs to the period which marks the close of his mission. As such it coincides with a cyclic moment of extreme significance—the last "opportunity"[20] for a direct message to be sent from Heaven to earth during what remains of this cycle of time. Many of the last Qur'ānic Revelations are concerned with completing and perfecting the new religion. But this verse is a final and lasting message for mankind as a whole. The Qur'ān expressly addresses the adherents of all the different orthodoxies on earth; and no message could be more relevant to the age in which we live and, in particular, to the mental predicament of man in these latter days. *For each of you We have appointed a law and a way. And if God*[21] *had so willed He would have made you one people. But (He hath willed it otherwise)*

[20] *God doth what He will.* But it is clearly in the interests of man that a Divine intervention which founds a new religion should be overwhelmingly recognizable as such. The accompanying guarantees must be too tremendous, and too distinctive, to leave room for doubts in any but the most perverse, which means that certain kinds of things must be kept in reserve as the special prerogative of such a period. The Qur'ān refers to this "economy" when it affirms that questions which are put to God during the period of Revelation will be answered (V, 101), the implication being that after the Revelation has been completed, questions will no longer be answered so directly. It is as if a door between Heaven and earth were kept open during the mission of a Divine Messenger, to be closed at other times.

[21] The change from first to third person with regard to the Divinity is frequent in the Qur'ān, and in fact, as we have already seen, I and He, at the highest level, are inseparable.

that He may put you to the test in what He has given you.[22] *So vie with one another in good works. Unto God will ye be brought back, and He will inform you about that wherein ye differed.* (V, 48)

[22] If He had sent only one religion to a world of widely differing affinities and aptitudes, it would not have been a fair test for all. He has therefore sent different religions, specially suited to the needs and characteristics of the different sectors of humanity.

ISLAM

The Spiritual Master

Many legends grew up around those few months during which the Shaykh visited Tunis, Tripoli and Istanbul.[1] Consequently an article published in *Revue Africaine*[2] two years after his death tells us: "He spent ten years of his life in the East, travelling in Egypt, Syria, Persia and India.[3] This remains the most mysterious and least known part of his life." But although these ten years in the East were no more real than a dream, I think there can be little doubt that this dream corresponds to what the Shaykh would have chosen for himself if his destiny had allowed it. The urgency with which he sought to escape from his function shows at any rate that he would not have chosen to spend the rest of his life beneath the weight of the responsibility that was to be his, and one of his motives, possibly the chief, is no doubt to be understood in the light of what he says about the learning which he "felt the need for".

Berque writes: "I knew Shaykh Bin-ʿAlīwah from 1921 until 1934. I saw him slowly grow old. His intellectual enquiringness seemed to become sharper each day, and to the very end he remained a lover of metaphysical investigation. There are few problems which he had not broached, scarcely any philosophies whose essence he had not extracted."[4]

[1] [These pages follow on from the last paragraphs of Shaykh al-ʿAlawī's autobiography, which comes to a close with the Shaykh's return to Algeria in 1910. —Ed.]

[2] 1936, pp. 691–776, "Un Mystique Moderniste" by A. Berque. The title is a strange one, for Berque's quotations are in themselves enough, as we shall see, to show that the Shaykh was essentially very conservative. His so-called "modernism" appears to have been nothing other than the great breadth of his spiritual interests.

[3] Sidi Muḥammad al-Hāshimī writes to me that the Shaykh certainly never went to India, and that apart from what he describes in his autobiography his only visit to the Near East was shortly before his death when he made the Pilgrimage and went on from Mecca and Medina to Jerusalem and Damascus and from there back again to Mostaganem.

[4] Ibid., p. 693.

From his writings, as also from the testimony of those who knew him, one has the impression of a vast and penetratingly active intelligence of which the higher or central part was utterly and eternally satisfied—he speaks of "remaining inwardly forever steeped in drunkenness"[5]—and of which the circumference, that is, the earthly or mental part, in so far as it had any respite from the demands made on him by his thousands of disciples, found ample sustenance in meditating on the Qur'ān and the Traditions and in exploring some of the Sufi treatises,[6] in particular those of Ibn ʿArabī and Jīlī. Moreover he was a great lover of poetry, especially of the odes of ʿUmar ibn al-Fāriḍ, long passages of which he seems to have known by heart. But although it does not appear directly in his writings, and although it is relatively most unimportant, it is evident from what Berque says of the Shaykh's thirst for information about other religions that at the extreme edge of this circumference there was a certain "nostalgia" for something which he would never have found unless he could have come into some kind of contact with representatives of other religions who were on a spiritual level with himself, such as, for example, his slightly younger Hindu contemporary, Sri Ramana Maharshi of Tiruvannamalai, whose teaching was essentially the same as his own. But he seems to have had no knowledge of Hinduism, and none of Taoism or Buddhism, nor had he any intellectual exchanges with the Qabbalists of Judaism, and as regards Christianity, with which he always maintained a certain contact, it is extremely doubtful whether he ever met any representative of it who was even remotely comparable to himself.

Here, however, he would in any case have needed an exception, for generally speaking Christianity scarcely admits of mutual understanding with other religions. Even the Christian mystic, though he may not reject other religions as false,[7]

[5] *Al-Minaḥ al-Quddūsiyyah*, p. 22.

[6] He says: "I do not think I am exaggerating if I say that there are amongst the Sufis men whose intelligences, each taken separately, would almost outweigh the combined intelligences of all the writers of this present age." (*Risālat al-Nāsir Maʿrūf*), p. 20).

[7] Unless one is content to imply that God is a monstrosity of injustice, caprice and ineffectuality, the words "None cometh to the Father but by Me" must be considered to have been spoken by Christ as the Logos, the Divine Word,

is indifferent to them, legitimately so, for the method of "the straight and narrow path" of love scarcely admits of looking either to the right or to the left.[8]

But although all mystic paths are "straight and narrow" in a certain sense, this description is not immediately apt as regards Islamic mysticism, for *wheresoe'er ye turn, there is the Face of God.*[9] In Islam, as we have seen, it is the vista of knowledge which predominates over that of love, and the Sufi is essentially a Gnostic. Sufism is not so much a path hedged by temptations and distractions on both sides as a passage across a wilderness, each stone of which is liable to be transformed in an instant from barren poverty to Infinite Riches. In one of the Shaykh's poems, the Creator is represented as saying:

> "The veil of creation I have made
> As a screen for the Truth, and in creation there lie
> Secrets which suddenly like springs gush forth."[10]

He also continually quotes the saying of the Prophet: "Lord, increase me in marvelling at Thee." The alchemy of Gnosis does not leave things at their face-value, but reduces them to nothingness or reveals them as aspects of the Face of God.

The full Islamic perspective, that is, the Qur'ānic perspective, is far too vast for the average Muslim. The words: *For each*

of which not only Jesus but also, for example, the Hindu Avataras, including the Buddha, are manifestations; and just as these are "the Word made flesh", so the Vedas, the Torah and the Qur'ān are "the Word made book". But since so many people, especially Europeans and Semites, are incapable of following seriously a religion unless they believe it to be the only one or to be exceptionally privileged, it is clearly providential that the above saying of Christ should be taken by most Christians in an exclusive sense as referring to one manifestation of the Word only (see Frithjof Schuon, *The Transcendent Unity of Religions*, ch. II, §6–8), and that the average Muslim, while not denying other religions, is inclined to relegate their validity to pre-Islamic times.

[8] Unless one is compelled to do so in virtue of some special function, or other exceptional circumstances. A great contemporary of the Shaykh, Pope Pius XI, said in confidence to Cardinal Facchinetti whom he had just appointed Apostolic Delegate to Libya: "Do not think that you are going among infidels. Muslims attain to Salvation. The ways of Providence are infinite." These words, spoken so many years ago, have only been made public recently, in *L'Ultima*, Anno VIII, 75–76, p. 261 (Florence, 1954).

[9] Qur'ān, II, 115.

[10] *Dīwān*, p. 10.

of you We have appointed a law and traced out a path, and if God had so willed, He would have made you one community[11] remain for him little more than a dead letter, and the same may be said of many other verses such as: *For every community there is a Messenger,*[12] and the already quoted *Verily We have sent Messengers before thee. About some of them have We told thee, and about some have We not told thee,* and *Verily the Faithful*[13] *and the Jews and the Sabians and the Christians—whoso believeth in God and the Last Day and doeth deeds of piety—no fear shall come upon them, neither shall they grieve.*[14] But the Sufi, who methodically seeks to permeate his whole being with the Qur'ān, cannot fail to be interested, potentially, in all other Heaven-sent religions as manifestations of Divine Mercy, as God's *Signs on the Horizons.*[15] I say "potentially" because he may never come into direct contact with other religions, and in any case he will be more or less bound to retain outwardly the prejudices of the great majority of his co-religionaries so as to avoid creating a scandal. But in so far as these prejudices are his own, they will be like fetters of gossamer upon his outlook, ready to be brushed away at a mere touch.

According to Berque, "the Shaykh was always hungry for knowledge about other religions. He seemed to be quite well informed as regards the Scriptures and even as regards the patristic tradition. The Gospel of St. John and the Epistles of St. Paul appealed to him in particular. As an extremely subtle and penetrating metaphysician, he was able to reconcile plurality with unity in the Trinitarian conception of three persons in a consubstantial identity... He rejected it none the less, but his understanding of it made some people think that he adhered to it."[16]

At the time when the Shaykh left the ʿĪsāwī Ṭarīqah, and when he and his friend Al-Ḥājj Bin-ʿAwdah were searching for a spiritual path, there were several different branches of the

[11] Qur'ān, V, 48.

[12] X, 47

[13] Muslims.

[14] V, 69.

[15] *We shall show them Our Signs on the horizons and in themselves until it be clear to them: He is the Truth* (XLI, 53).

[16] Berque, p. 739. He was in fact accused by some of his enemies of believing in the Trinity (*Ibid.,* p. 735).

Darqāwī Ṭarīqah[17] firmly established in the province of Oran to which Mostaganem belongs, not to mention many branches of other orders. Yet he says: "Although we considered it an absolute necessity to take as a guide someone who was generally recognized as a Master by those who could judge, we had little hope of finding such a one."[18] Fifteen years later, at the death of the Shaykh Al-Būzīdī, there was still the same quantity rather than quality among those who offered guidance.

In one of his poems he declares:

> I hid the truth[19] on a time and screened it well
> And whoso keepeth God's Secret shall have his reward.
> Then when the Giver vouchsafed that I might proclaim it,
> He fitted me—and how I know not—to purify souls,
> And girded upon me the sword of steadfastness,
> And truth and piety, and a wine He gave me,
> Which all who drink must needs be always drinking,
> Even as a drunk man seeketh to be more drunk.
> Thus came I to pour it, nay, it is I that press it.
> Doth any other pour it in this age?[20]

The sight of the relatively wasted efforts of so many fervent souls unconsciously following "blind guides" made the Shaykh more and more outspoken as regards his own function and indirectly—sometimes even directly—as regards the false pretentions of others.[21]

There is little doubt that he felt himself to be the renewer (*mujaddid*) which the Prophet had promised for every cen-

[17] According to Depont and Coppolani, *Les Confréries religieuses musulmanes*, pp. 510–1, there were over 9500 members of this brotherhood in Algeria at that time. In Mostaganem itself there were three Darqāwī *zāwiyahs*, and it was no doubt from one or more of these that the Shaykh Al-Būzīdī met with opposition on his return from Morocco. Berque wrongly says that he was a member of the Habrī branch of the Darqāwīs, whereas in actual fact he was not a descendant of Shaykh Muḥammad al-Habrī but as it were his younger brother, both being disciples of Muḥammad ibn Qaddūr of Morocco.

[18] *Rawḍah*, p. 12.

[19] The truth of his own supreme spiritual realization.

[20] *Dīwān*, p. 35. The whole poem, "The Wine", is translated on pp. 330–33.

[21] For lines which he addressed to a spiritual impostor, see his poem "The Impostor", in *A Sufi Saint of the Twentieth Century*, Islamic Texts Society, Cambridge, 1993, p. 215.

tury.[22] The last one had been unquestionably the great Shaykh Al-Darqāwī himself. The Shaykh Al-ʿAlawī says: "I am the pourer, the renewer,"[23] and: "Proclaim, O chronicler, the name of ʿAlawī after Darqāwī, for God hath made him his successor."[24] His poems were not published until just after the first world war, though they had a wide circulation in manuscript. But the jealousy of the various heads of *zāwiyahs* was probably roused not so much by anything he said or wrote as by the fact that they found themselves being deserted by their own disciples.

The Shaykh was at this time in his early forties. Berque who met him about ten years later says: "A remarkable radiance emanated from him, an irresistible personal magnetism. His glance was quick, clear and extraordinarily attractive... He was very affable and courteous, unassertive, full of tact and delicacy, anxious to avoid any friction... and at the same time one was conscious of a great tenacity of purpose in him, a subtle flame which consumed its object in a few moments."[25] One of his disciples wrote: "When he was talking he seemed almost negligent, as though he was relying upon help from outside, and at the same time he mastered men's hearts and brought them by force to the point of what he was saying."[26] Another wrote: "He spoke to everyone according to his intellectual capacity and particular disposition, and when he was speaking it seemed as if the one he was speaking to was the only one he cared for in all the world."[27] His presence was such that when he went out he was liable to draw men irresistibly after him down the street.[28]

As might have been expected, the greatest opposition to him came at first from the heads of the Darqāwī *zāwiyahs* in the neighbourhood. This was brought to a climax when after about five years he decided to make himself independent of

[22] "God will send to this community at the head of every hundred years one who will renew for it its religion" (Abū Dā'ūd, *Malāḥim*, 1).

[23] *Dīwān*, p. 30, 1.6.

[24] *Dīwān*, p. 45, 1.6.

[25] pp. 692–3.

[26] *Shahā'id*, p. 137.

[27] *Shahā'id*, p. 141.

[28] *Ibid.*, p. 95.

the mother *zāwiyah* in Morocco and thus distinct from the other Algerian branches of the order, and to name his branch *Al-Ṭarīqa al-ʿAlawīya al-Darqāwīya al-Shādhilīya.*

One of his motives for taking this step was that he felt the need to introduce, as part of his method, the practice of *khalwah*, that is, spiritual retreat in the solitude of an isolated cell or small hermitage. There was nothing very drastic in this, for if remembrance of God be the positive or heavenly aspect of all mysticism, its negative or earthly aspect is retreat or drawing away from other than God. The Tradition "Be in this world as a stranger, or as a passer-by" has already been quoted, and one of the most powerful aids to achieving this permanent inward spiritual retreat is bodily withdrawal which, in some form or another, perpetual or temporary, is a feature of almost all contemplative orders. In some Sufi brotherhoods—the Khalwatī Ṭarīqah, for example—it was the tradition to make retreat in a special hermitage. But in the Shādhilī Ṭarīqah and its branches, the spiritual retreat had usually taken the form of withdrawal to the solitudes of nature, after the pattern of the Prophet's retreats in the cave on Mount Hira, and though inevitably the *khalwah* must have been used on occasion, to introduce it as a regular methodic practice was something of an innovation for the descendants of Abu 'l-Ḥasan al-Shādhilī. However the Shaykh no doubt found this form of retreat more practicable than any other in view of the conditions in which most of his disciples lived. We have already seen that he himself had suffered for want of a definite place where he could be alone, and that it was part of his method to supervise at times very closely the invocation of his disciples, which presupposed that the disciple in question would be within easy reach of him.

ʿAbd al-Karīm Jossot[29] quotes the Shaykh as having said to him: "The *khalwah* is a cell in which I put the novice after he has sworn to me not to leave it for forty days if need be. In this oratory he must do nothing but repeat ceaselessly, day and night, the Divine Name (*Allāh*), drawing out at each invocation the syllable *āh* until he has no more breath left.

"Previously he must have recited the Shahādah (*lā ilāha illa 'Llāh*, there is no god but God) seventy-five thousand times.

[29] [Né Gustave-Henri Jossot (1866–1951).—Ed.]

"During the *khalwah* he fasts strictly by day, only breaking his fast between sunset and dawn.... Some *fuqarā* obtain the sudden illumination after a few minutes, some only after several days, and some only after several weeks. I know one *faqīr* who waited eight months. Each morning he would say to me: 'My heart is still too hard', and would continue his *khalwah*. In the end his efforts were rewarded."[30]

His action in making himself independent seems to have created, for the moment, a disproportionately violent ill-feeling. Every obstacle was put in his way, and no effort was spared to detach from him the Shaykh Al-Būzīdī's former disciples, now his by oath of allegiance. Moreover he had no time to earn his living and was extremely poor, sometimes to the point of having to sell his household goods, for he could not bring himself to ask his disciples for anything and they did not always perceive that he was in difficulties. But although some of the Shaykh Al-Būzīdī's disciples did in fact fall away from him, new disciples began to flock to him from elsewhere, including even one or two heads of *zāwiyahs* together with their followers. His opponents among the Darqāwīs must have been somewhat disconcerted when the great-grandson of Mawlāy Al-ʿArābī al-Darqāwī himself came from the mother *zāwiyah* in Morocco and took the Shaykh as his Master. Here follows an extract of a letter from him:[31]

"What I saw in the Shaykh and his disciples compelled me to cleave to his presence, and in longing for a possible means of opening my inward eye I asked his permission to invoke the Supreme Name. Until then I had simply been an initiate of the order and nothing more, but I had heard that my ancestors used to rely on the *Ṭarīqah* as a means of direct attainment, not merely of attachment to a spiritual chain. After I had practised the invocation of the Name according to his instructions, I had certain experiences which compelled me to persevere in it, and before long I had direct knowledge of God.... If I served the Shaykh as a slave for ever and ever, I should not have given him back a tenth part of a tenth of what I owe him. In a word, it was what compelled my great-grandfather to follow Sidi Mawlāy ʿAlī al-Jamal which compelled me to follow Shaykh

[30] Berque, pp. 753–4, quoting Jossot's *Le Sentier d'Allah*.

[31] Muḥammad ibn al-Ṭayyib al-Darqāwī.

Sidi Aḥmad Bin-ʿAlīwah.... I paid no attention to those of my family who blamed me for following him, for they did not know the truth of the matter.... But when I explained things to my uncle, Sidi Mawlāy,[32] he showed no opposition to my following the Shaykh. On the contrary, he often gave me to understand that he had no objection."[33]

The ill-feeling against the Shaykh on the part of other *zāwiyahs* was short-lived, and only went on here and there spasmodically in the case of one or two hereditary marabouts who were in danger of losing their influence altogether. But he had now to face the attacks of the enemies of Sufism, and before long he became one of their chief targets. The publication of his poems was the signal for a general attack, in various newspapers and periodicals, on him and on the *Ṭarīqah* in particular and on Sufism in general. As regards himself, hostility seems to have concentrated especially on a passage in one of the early poems written many years before the death of his Master. He says of it: "Everything has a cause, and the cause of those verses was that one day I was overwhelmed by a great longing for the Prophet. Then I fell asleep, and in my sleep I saw him in front of me. I was at that time in a state very different from the one in which you see me now, and he stood there, haughty and aloof, whilst I, in all abasement and humility before him, addressed him with those verses, and when I woke I wrote them down."[34] The offending verse was: "If I should die of longing, rejected, what excuse will save thee?"

He was accused of disrespect towards the Prophet for daring to address him with anything in the nature of a threat. In view of the utter devotion expressed in the poem as a whole the accusation can scarcely have been in good faith, but the Shaykh seems to have felt that he had in fact been guilty of a certain impropriety. The offending passage was left out of the second edition, and although several of his disciples wrote vigorous defences for the press, he would not allow any of

[32] The head of the mother *zāwiyah*.

[33] *Shahā'id,* pp. 151–3. When he left Mostaganem, the Shaykh said to him: "If you owe me anything, pay me back by giving your family their due, especially with your uncle" (*Ibid.,* note 5).

[34] *Shahā'id,* p. 56, note 1.

these to be published,[35] nor would he himself answer any of the personal attacks. The nearest he came to doing so was to write to the editor of one of the hostile papers, *Al-Najāḥ* (after greetings): "You have unsheathed your blade and thrust at my honour and reputation with the vigour of a man whom nothing will daunt, and I took it all as springing from jealousy for the religion and the desire to defend it, until the writer was led on to abuse and insults. And all these too I accept and place upon my head, if they were truly meant in defence of the honour of the Prophet. *If God knoweth good in your hearts, He will requite you with good,*[36] but if not, then *I submit my case unto God. Verily God is the Seer of His slaves.*"[37]

It was in the same year, 1920, that he wrote the first of his vindications of Sufism.[38] This was in answer to a pamphlet entitled *A Mirror to Show Up Errors* by a teacher in the Religious College at Tunis, whose criticisms were so petty and childish that one might be surprised that the Shaykh should have bothered to answer them at all. But he no doubt realized that they had a significance which went far beyond their immediate author and that they were nothing less than particular crystallizations of a general hostility which could not be ignored. Since most people are apt to be irritated by what they do not understand, any critic of mysticism, however crude and unintelligent his arguments may be, can be almost certain today that his words will awaken a chorus of agreement from quite a large portion of the community, not only from those who are anti-religious but also—and perhaps above all—from a certain class of believers.

It is one of the excellencies of Islam that there is no laity and that every Muslim is in a sense a priest, spiritual authority

[35] Several years later, however, he allowed one of his Tunisian disciples to publish a large collection of testifications as regards himself by Muslims of note and authority from various Islamic countries, together with many extracts from letters in praise of him and the ʿAlawī *Ṭarīqah* in general. It was compiled by Muḥammad ibn ʿAbd al-Bārī', entitled *Kitāb al-Shahā'id wa'l-Fatāwi*, and published at Tunis in 1925.

[36] Qur'ān, VIII, 70.

[37] Qur'ān, XL, 44. *Shahā'id*, p. 214, note 1. This was published in *Al-Najāḥ* itself, which later published a long article in praise of the Shaykh and his disciples (*Shahā'id*, pp. 55–61).

[38] *Al-Qaul al-Maʿrūf*. The quotations from it which follow are from pp. 38–76, with omissions.

being shared by the community as a whole. On the other hand it is one of the excellencies of Christianity that it has a definitely constituted spiritual authority consisting of a small minority of men whose lives are dedicated to religion, the other-worldliness of their office being stressed in various ways and in general by the fact that its function does not extend to the domain of the temporal power, inasmuch as Christ said: "My Kingdom is not of this world." But although these excellencies have been responsible, or partly responsible, for centuries of spiritual well-being in both religions, they come in the end to cast their shadows, which are in Christianity the stifling and choking of the spiritual authority by the laity, who push it further and further into a remote corner of the community from which it can barely function and from which it sometimes seeks to emerge by pandering to mundane triviality, and in Islam the existence of a large number of very limited individuals who imagine that the whole religion is within their grasp and that what lies outside the scope of their own meagre understanding is necessarily outside the pale of Islam itself. The author of the *Mirror* is a striking example of the extreme exoterism that any Muslim mystic is liable to be confronted with. One of his tirades ends with the words: "Islam is nothing other than the Book of God and the Wont of His Messenger." To this the Shaykh replied: "Who told you that the Sufis say that Islam is based on any principles other than these? They say, however, that in the Book of God there is doctrine which is beyond most men's attainment. The Sultan of the Lovers[39] said: 'There lieth a lore beneath the words of the text too subtle to be grasped by the farthest reach of sound intelligences.'[40]

"It may well be that one who cleaves to externals can see nothing in the Book of God but what his own intelligence, such as it is, can apprehend and that he may belie what goes beyond this without realizing that in knowing the outside of the Book only he is as one who knows a fruit by nothing but its peel—and beyond that lies 'what no eye hath seen and what no ear hath heard and what the heart of man cannot conceive.' Let him examine himself: if what his heart hides is more precious than what his tongue tells of, then he is *one whom his Lord hath*

[39] The Egyptian Sufi ʿUmar ibn al-Fāriḍ.

[40] "*Al-Tā'iyyat al-Kubrā*", 1. 675

made certain;[41] but if not, then he has missed far more than he has gained.... The Prophet said: 'Knowledge of the inward is one of the Secrets of God. It is wisdom from the treasury of His Wisdom which He casteth into the heart of whomsoe'er He will of His slaves'[42] and 'Knowledge is of two kinds, knowledge in the Heart which is the knowledge that availeth, and knowledge upon the tongue which is God's evidence against His slave'.[43] This shows that secret knowledge is different from the knowledge that is bandied about.

"Abū Hurairah said: 'I have treasured in my memory two stores of knowledge which I had from God's Apostle. One I have divulged; but if I divulged the other ye would cut my throat'.[44]

"In saying: 'Islam is nothing other than the Book of God and the Wont of the Apostle', it is as if you said: 'Islam is what *I* understand of the Book and the Wont, and no more' ... which means that you set your own innermost perceptions on a level with the innermost perceptions of the Companions—nay, of the Prophets!...

"The Prophet said: 'The earth shall never be found lacking in forty men whose Hearts are as the Heart of the Friend[45] of the All-Merciful.'[46] One has only to study the traditions to find that they tell us explicitly that there is within the community an elect to whom God has revealed the secrets of the Book and the Wont, and where else is this body of men to be found save amongst the Rememberers, who are marked out for having devoted their lives to God? It was of such as them that Dhu'n-Nūn al-Miṣrī[47] said: 'In my travels I met a slave girl and asked her whence she came. She said: "From men *whose sides shrink away from beds.*"[48] Then I asked her whither she was

[41] Qur'ān, XI, 17.

[42] Suyūṭī, *Al-Jāmi*ʿ *al-Ṣaghīr.*

[43] *Ibid.*

[44] Bukhārī, ʿIlm, 42.

[45] Abraham.

[46] This Tradition is given by Suyūṭī (*Al-Jāmi*ʿ *al-Ṣaghīr*) in a slightly different form.

[47] An Egyptian Sufi, d. 860.

[48] Qur'ān, XXXII, 16.

going, and she said: "To *men whom neither bartering nor selling diverteth from the remembrance of God*"'."[49]

Like many others before him, the author of the "Mirror" did not fail to criticize the Sufi practice of dancing, not only because it had not been the practice of the Prophet and his Companions but also on the grounds that the Prophet had forbidden dancing altogether. Opinions differ about this last point; but although we do not know exactly what the Companions did in their Sessions of Remembrance, or Circles of Remembrance as they are called in some Traditions, it seems unlikely that they had any deliberate practice resembling the sacred dance described by Dr Carret.[50] None the less, it is difficult to believe that they did not make some spontaneous rhythmic movements of the body while reciting their various litanies and invoking the Divine Name. Given the Arab genius for rhythm, a practice so simple and elemental as the Darqāwī-ʿAlawī *dhikr* could have crystallized in one generation;[51] and

[49] Qur'ān, XXIV, 37.

[50] [A biographical sketch by Dr Marcel Carret was used by Martin Lings as ch. 1 of *A Sufi Saint of the Twentieth Centuty*.—Ed.]

[51] This possibility was brought home to me by the following incident. I was driving from Mecca to Medina with a group of lecturers and students from the Universities of Cairo and Alexandria. Some of the students were "Muslim Brothers". The founder of their movement, Shaykh Ḥasan al-Bannā', had a respect for the Sufis, but many of the younger generation tended to be not unlike the author of the "Mirror" in their conception of Islam, and only a few days previously I had been drawn into an argument with some of them about Sufism, which I had felt bound to defend against their criticisms. As we drew near to Medina one member of the party began to chant an invocation of Blessings upon the Prophet. Soon we all joined in, and then four or five of these Muslim Brothers who were sitting together began to sway rhythmically from side to side. At first it was not very noticeable, but gradually the rhythm of the chant became more and more marked and the swaying more and more purposeful and vigorous. Finally the driver called out that if they did not stop they would overturn the car. They had almost certainly never performed such a *dhikr* before and probably never would again, unless they made another visit to Medina. But the Sufis visit Medina in spirit every morning and evening. In this connection it may be regarded in passing—for it is very significant as regards the place of Sufism in the religion as a whole—that the average Muslim pilgrim becomes, in his practices, something of a Sufi for the brief period of his pilgrimage. This is particularly noticeable on the Day of Arafat, for every tent on the sacred hill-top is like a *zāwiyah* and the very air vibrates with the perpetual murmur of the Qur'ān and litanies on every tongue. But when they return to their various countries they relapse for the most part into "ordinary life", not having that aspiration to nearness which sustains the Sufi upon his path and makes every day for him a "Day of Arafat".

once such practices had been established as they were bound to be, in the natural course of events, it is understandable that certain Shaykhs, as for example Jalāl al-Dīn al-Rūmī, the founder of the Mawlawī Order of Sufis who are better known to the West as "the Whirling Dervishes", should have incorporated into the *dhikr* some of the movements, together with the music, of traditional local dances which by heredity flowed as it were in the blood of his disciples and had therefore a more immediate appeal for them.

None the less, the subjection of the body to a rhythmic motion is never, for the Sufis, any more than an auxiliary; its purpose is simply to facilitate *dhikr* in the fullest sense of remembrance, that is, the concentration of all the faculties of the soul upon the Divine Truth represented by the Supreme Name or some other formula which is uttered aloud or silently by the dancers. It was explained to me by one of the Shaykh's disciples that just as a sacred number such as three, seven or nine, for example, acts as a bridge between multiplicity and Unity, so rhythm is a bridge between agitation and Repose, motion and Motionlessness, fluctuation and Immutability. Fluctuation, like multiplicity, cannot be transcended in this world of perpetual motion but only in the Peace of Divine Unity; and to partake of this Peace in some degree is in fact that very concentration which the *dhikr* aims at. Knowledge of this virtue of rhythm[52] is part of man's primordial heritage, and all men possess it instinctively whether they are aware of it or not.

The sacred dance of the Sufis enters into a more general category of practices which are summed up in the Arabic word *tawājud*. In defence of them the Shaykh quotes from one of the more eminent exoteric authorities of Islam, Ibn Qayyim al-Jawziyyah:[53]

[52] Rhythm, like other cosmic and potentially sacred forces, such as those used in magic for example, is capable of being perverted into the wrong direction. It is therefore of vital importance to distinguish between "white rhythm" and "black rhythm" and there is no doubt as to which of the two is more familiar to the modern Western World. Needless to say the words "white" and "black" are used here without any ethnological significance. To judge from what little one has the opportunity of hearing, the rhythm of most Africans in their native state is eminently "white".

[53] d. AD 1350. In his youth he had been a violent critic of the Sufis, but towards the end of his life he came to venerate them. The change appears to

"*Tawājud* is seeking to induce a state of ecstasy (*wajd*) through deliberate effort, and opinions differ as to whether it is legitimate or not. The truth is that if one's effort is for the sake of enhancing one's reputation it is wrong, but if it is for the sake of obtaining a *ḥāl* (the partial and transitory realization of a spiritual degree) or *maqām* (the integral and permanent realization of a spiritual degree), it is justified."[54]

Ibn Qayyim quotes in defence of legitimate *tawājud* the saying of the Prophet: "Weep, and if ye weep not, then try to weep"[55] which makes one think of the Jews wailing at the "Western Wall" and the Red Indians going out into the wilds of nature to lament,[56] and similar modes of *tawājud* in other religions. It would be true to say, however, that in the aspen-like soul of the mystic there is nearly always some spiritual motion, however slight, so that the effort in question, instead of being a new departure, is in most cases merely the exaggeration of an initial degree of ecstasy which the mystic fears to lose and wishes to increase. *Tawājud* thus means, "rushing out to meet ecstasy half way", and that is why the Shaykh makes no distinction between the effort and the achievement in his reply to the criticisms of the *Mirror*.

He says: "God commended the people of the Book[57] for their rapture, mentioning one of its aspects with the highest praise: *When they hear what hath been revealed unto the Prophet, thou seest their eyes overflow with tears from their recognition of the Truth.*[58] Does not this point to a sudden impact of movement within the believer through his remembering God and

have taken place during a period which he spent in prison, where "he busied himself with reciting the Qur'ān and pondering and meditating, whereby much good was opened up to him and he had many spiritual intuitions and veritable ecstasies. It was in virtue of this that he ventured to expound the doctrine of the Gnostics" (quoted from Ālūsī's life of Ibn Qayyim by Rashīd Riḍā in his preface to *Madārij al-Sālikīn*, II, p. 6).

[54] This is a paraphrase of Ibn Qayyim. The full text in question is on p. 43 of pt. 3 in the Manār edition of the *Madārij*.

[55] Ibn Mājah, Iqāmah, 176.

[56] A mystic contemporary of the Shaykh, a man only 6 years older than him but very far removed in space, said in an unforgettable description of the Red Indian ritual lamentation: "Until now I had only been trying to weep, but now I really wept…" (*Black Elk Speaks*, by J. G. Neihardt, p. 187).

[57] The Jews and Christians.

[58] Qur'ān, V, 83.

listening to His words? Has He not said moreover: *If We caused this Qur'ān to descend upon a mountain, thou wouldst see the mountain lying prostrate with humility, rent asunder through fear of God....*[59] Why then can you not excuse hearts for being rent and bodies for swaying from side to side at what causes the rending of mountains? It is simply because you do not find within yourself what others find, for there are hearts, as indeed He has mentioned, as *hard as stones or even harder*;[60] or else it is because you have mentioned the Name of God and recited His Book merely by rote.... The Imam Al-Shāfiʿī heard someone reciting: *This is a day on which they speak not, nor are they permitted to proffer excuses?*[61] whereupon he fainted and was carried to his house. But such occurrences do not call for much explanation, seeing that awe and rapture have caused even the death of many of our pious ancestors....[62] Have you never read or heard His Words: *Only those are believers whose hearts thrill with awe at the remembrance of God,*[63] and did you not know that the Prophet mentioned as being amongst his people 'folk who enter Paradise and whose hearts are as the hearts of birds.'[64] Where are we to find those referred to in these utterances if not among the Rememberers? No doubt you tell yourself that you are one of them. So answer me this, with God as your witness: Are you one of *those who remember God much,*[65] or of those *whom neither bartering nor selling diverteth from the remembrance of God,* or of those *whom neither their possessions nor children divert from the remembrance of God,*[66] or of those *who remember God standing and sitting and reclining upon their sides,*[67] or of those *whose hearts thrill with awe at the remembrance of God,* or of *those whose eyes overflow with tears when they hear what hath been revealed unto the Prophet;* or of those about whom the Prophet said: 'The solitary ones take

[59] Qur'ān, LIX, 21.

[60] Qur'ān, II, 74.

[61] Qur'ān, LXXVII, 35–6.

[62] See Hujwīrī, *Kashf al-Maḥjūb*, ch. XXV; in Nicholson's translation, pp. 396–7.

[63] Qur'ān, VIII, 2.

[64] Muslim, *Jannah*, 27; Ibn Ḥanbal, II, 331.

[65] Qur'ān, XXXIII, 35.

[66] Qur'ān, LXIII, 9.

[67] Qur'ān, III, 191.

precedence, they who are utterly addicted to the remembrance of God,'[68] or of those who are called mad through acting on the Prophet's injunction: 'Multiply remembrance of God until they say: "Madman!"'[69] or of those who are called pretenders because they act on his injunction: 'Multiply remembrance of God until the hypocrites say: "Verily ye are pretenders"'?[70] Tell me, I beg you, which group you belong to. Are you one of the sayers or the said?...

"If the grace of ecstasy is beyond you, it is not beyond you to believe that others may enjoy it.... None the less I do not say that dancing and manifestations of ecstasy are among the essentials of Sufism. But they are outward signs which come from submersion in remembrance. Let him who doubts try for himself, for hearsay is not the same as direct experience."

The Prophet is said to have considered that of all his family the one who resembled him most was his cousin Jaʿfar to whom on one occasion he said: "Thou art like me both in looks and in character,"[71] whereupon no words could express Jaʿfar's pleasure, and he danced in the Prophet's presence.

One of the last precepts given to the Shaykh Al-Darqāwī by his Master, Shaykh ʿAlī al-Jamal, was that he and his followers should continue to follow the example of Jaʿfar ibn Abī Ṭālib in dancing to the Glory of God.[72]

Against the *Mirror*'s affirmation that "anyone who considers dancing to be legal is an infidel," the Shaykh Al-ʿAlawī mentions the dancing of Jaʿfar, and also the dancing of a delegation of Abyssinians before the Prophet on one occasion in the mosque at Medina. But he adds: "Do you imagine that the Sufis hold dancing to be absolutely lawful, just as you hold it to be absolutely unlawful?... It behoves the learned man not to pass any judgement about it until he knows what is the motive behind it, lest he forbid what God has allowed."

[68] This Tradition is to be found, with very slight variations, in nearly all the canonical books, e.g. Muslim, *Dhikr*, 1.

[69] Ibn Ḥanbal, III, pp. 68 and 73.

[70] Suyūṭī, *Al-Jāmiʿ al-Ṣaghīr*.

[71] Ibn Ḥanbal, I, 108.

[72] For a list of these last precepts, see Rinn, *Marabouts et Khouan*, p. 233.

Then, since going to meet ecstasy halfway is in reality answering a Divine Summons, he dismisses the question with the following verses, which are attributed to Ibn Kamāl Pasha:

In wooing rapture there is no blame,
And none in swaying to and fro.
Thou risest if one call thy name
And on thy feet dost hurrying go.
He whom his Lord hath summoned
May then go hurrying on his head.

He continues: "Every lover is shaken at the mention (*dhikr*) of his beloved ... and if love crept through the marrow of your bones, you would long to hear the mention of God, even from an infidel, and you would say, as the Sultan of the Lovers said:

'Mention of her is sweeter to me than all words else,
Even when alloyed by my censurers with their blame of me.'[73]

"Then you would know what it is to thrill with awe, and you would see whether you could retain the mastery over yourself or not. Have you not read in the Book of God about the women who cut their hands when Joseph came before them. *They said: Peerless is God's Glory! This is not of humankind.*[74] Now if such as this could happen through contemplating created beauty, why should not something of the kind happen at the contemplation of the Beauty of its Creator, when He appears in all the Splendour of His Greatness?

"Remembrance is the mightiest rule of the religion.... The law was not enjoined upon us, neither were the rites of worship ordained but for the sake of establishing the remembrance of God. The Prophet said: 'The circumambulation round the Holy House, the passage to and fro between Ṣafā and Marwah,[75] and

[73] Ibn al-Fāriḍ's "*Mīmiyyah*" which begins *Adir dhikra man ahwā*, 1.3.

[74] Qur'ān, XII, 31. The Qur'ān tells here how Potiphar's wife invited some of the women of Egypt to her house so that, having seen Joseph for themselves, they would understand why she loved him and would excuse her. When he appeared before them they were so amazed at his beauty that they cut their hands in mistake for their food.

[75] Two rocks in Mecca (the wall of the Great Mosque comes near to Ṣafā, after which one of its gates is named) between which Hagar passed in search of

the throwing of the pebbles were only ordained as a means of remembering God';[76] and God Himself has said: *Remember God at the Holy Monument.*[77] Thus we know that the rite of stopping there was ordained for remembrance and not especially on account of the monument itself, just as the stay at Mina was also ordained for remembrance, not on account of the valley, for He has said: *Remember God during the appointed days.*[78] Moreover concerning the ritual prayer He has said: *Perform the prayer in remembrance of Me;*[79] and you will find other examples if you look through the Book. In a word, our performance of the rites of worship is considered strong or weak according to the degree of our remembrance of God while performing them. Thus when the Prophet was asked what spiritual strivers would receive the greatest reward, he replied: 'Those who remembered God most'. Then when questioned as to what fasters would be most rewarded he said: 'Those who remembered God most', and when the prayer and the almsgiving and the pilgrimage and charitable donations were mentioned, he said of each: 'The richest in remembrance of God is the richest in reward'."

Among the already referred to last precepts given by the Shaykh ᶜAlī al-Jamal to the Shaykh Al-Darqāwī was the recommendation that he and his disciples should follow the example of the Prophet's Companion Abū Hurayrah and wear their rosaries round their necks. The Shaykh Al-ᶜAlawī made an exception for his more Oriental disciples and allowed them, if they wished, to carry their rosaries in their hands in conformity with the general practice of their countries. But he himself and his Algerian and Moroccan disciples, like the other Darqāwīs, continued to follow the injunction of the Shaykh ᶜAlī al-Jamal. Their large flat wheel-shaped wooden beads make strikingly

water for herself and Ishmael. To pass between them seven times is one of the subsidiary rites of the Pilgrimage.

[76] Tirmidhī, Ḥajj, 64.

[77] Qur'ān, II, 198. This is a mound at a place called Muzdalifah where the Pilgrims spend the night after the day on Mount Arafat, and where each gathers 49 pebbles with which to stone Satan, represented by 3 stone pillars in the valley of Mina (between Arafat and Mecca) where they spend the next three days.

[78] Qur'ān, II, 203.

[79] Qur'ān, XX, 14.

virile necklaces, very different from the smaller more delicate round-beaded Middle-Eastern rosaries which are often made of amber or mother-of-pearl and which are usually carried in the hand.

Both Western and Eastern rosaries have usually ninety-nine beads with a piece at the end called the *alif*, about the length and shape of a finger, to make up the hundred, this being the number most often specified by the Prophet for the recitation of formulae. When a formula is to be repeated a thousand times the Sufis often put ten pebbles or other objects in front of them, one of which they remove after each hundred. As to the shorter litanies each formula is usually repeated thirty-three times, and to facilitate this most rosaries have a small *alif* or other shaped division mark after the thirty-third bead and another after the sixty-sixth.

Beads were not used in the time of the Prophet, and therefore the author of the *Mirror* added the rosary to his list of "reprehensible innovations."

"What is the difference," replied the Shaykh, "between counting with date-stones (for which you say there is a precedent) and counting with beads or any other ritually clean objects? You have affirmed that some of the Companions counted with pebbles instead of date-stones. Perhaps you object to beads because they are strung on a cord. But tradition reports that Abū Hurayrah had a knotted cord[80] with a thousand knots in it and that he did not go to sleep until he had told it. Does not this come very near to the bead-strung rosary that is used today? And do you think that Abū Hurayrah would have left his rosary behind if he had gone on a journey, for example, or that if the Prophet had seen him carrying it in his hand, or wearing it round his neck he would have censured him? Personally I do not think so—but God knoweth best.

[80] Necessity is the mother of invention, and since the Prophet continually recommended the repetition of formulae a specific number of times (the canonical books abound in Traditions to that effect), and since all are not equally good at counting on the fingers, as the Prophet himself appears to have done, without being distracted by the effort of counting from the formula itself, it would be strange if not a single one of the Companions had been able to devise so simple and practical an expedient as a knotted cord. There is no need to look further than this for the origin of the rosary in Islam.

"You complain that the rosary is shaped like a cross. By all that is marvellous, what has the form of a rosary to do with the cross? However, 'the eye of hatred ferrets out faults.' But if a man must needs avoid, in what he eats and drinks and beholds, anything that comes anywhere near to being shaped like a cross, then your own form, in virtue of which you are a human being, comes far nearer to a cross than a rosary does. For you said of the rosary: 'If the two division marks are long, then its resemblance to the cross shows up very clearly indeed.'[81] But however long they may be, your own resemblance to the cross shows up far more clearly. If you stand up and stretch out your arms sideways, you will have no need to look for the cross in the rosary, for you will find it in yourself,[82] and then you will be obliged to put an end to your own existence or at least take care never to see yourself, lest your sight should fall upon something that resembles a cross. But if God doomed you to make comparisons as regards the rosary, why did you liken it to the cross rather than to the garlands with which the Arabs used to garland both themselves and whatever they intended to give as an offering when they visited the Holy House of God, as a sign to prevent anyone from doing harm to the wearer of them. These garlands are ropes made of plaited rushes and the like, and God has praised the Arabs for this practice."[83]

The *Mirror* went on to qualify as hypocrites all those who use rosaries. The Shaykh replied: "Even if we admit that there is no lack of hypocrites amongst those who use rosaries for glorifying God, there is certainly no lack of sincere worshippers either, so how can we possibly pass a general judgement? Have you everyone's conscience within your grasp? Probably if you asked the possessor of a rosary what is his intention in wearing it round his neck, he would say: 'I find it prevents me from

[81] To look anything like a cross, they would have to be not only much longer, but also exactly level.

[82] For many Muslims the cross is just something in the nature of an enemy flag; but for the Sufis it is a symbol of the highest significance. René Guénon dedicated his *Symbolism of the Cross* (Luzac & Co., 1958) to the memory of an older contemporary of the Shaykh Al-ʿAlawī, an eminent Egyptian Shādhilī Shaykh, ʿAbd al-Raḥmān ʿUlaysh, to whom, as he (Guénon) says: "I owe the first idea of this book." Later he quotes him as having said: "If Christians have the sign of the Cross, Muslims have its doctrine."

[83] Qur'ān, V, 97.

keeping company with fools and from entering places of ill repute, so I have put it here as a fetter upon my soul, for it says to me as clearly as if it could speak: 'Keep thy duty unto God. Thou are not one to commit flagrant acts of disobedience.' Is this anything but a pious intention? Similarly, if you questioned one who carries a rosary in his hand, he would probably say: 'I hold it so that it may remind me of God whenever I forget to remember Him; for I have heard that the Prophet said: 'How excellent a remembrancer is a rosary!'"[84] Is this anything but a pious intention?... Similarly there are those who carry rosaries by way of imitating devout men, hoping to be eventually of their number, and this also is a pious intention. Then there are a few of those whom you described as hypocrites, *and they only remember God a little.*[85]

"It is such verses as this last which compel the Sufis to steep themselves in remembrance and to be quite open about it and to abound in it, so that they may pass out of the category of 'little' into that of 'much', thus escaping altogether from the qualification of hypocrites which is remembering God only a little. May God inspire both us and you to remember Him much—and to think well of His Saints!

"Then you started a new chapter: 'Another error is imitating the infidels' ... and you mentioned a number of innovations which are indeed to be avoided ... but it was clear to me that you were just treading out the ground for an onslaught, with all your fury, upon the tombs of the righteous and those who visit them. If you had really aimed at stopping the imitation of the infidels, you would have written a chapter urging the need to guard against the scourge of foreign customs which now holds us in its grip and which is taking its unresisted course amongst our sons and our womenfolk. You would have urged us to keep to Islamic precedents and Arab ways, but instead of this you made pronouncements which for the most part could serve no purpose except to stir up discord amongst us.

"As to your pretext for stopping visits to tombs on the ground that the average Muslim believes that the dead Shaykh who is visited has power to give or withhold, etc., I do not

[84] Quoted from Daylamī's *Musnad al-Firdaws* by Suyūṭī in his *Al-Minḥah fi 'ttikhādh al-subḥah.* See *Al-Ḥāwī li 'l-Fatāwī,* II, pp. 139–44.

[85] Qur'ān, IV, 142. It is the Shaykh who adds this Qur'ānic definition of hypocrisy.

think that such a belief exists in any single member of the community. Muslims in general simply believe that there are intermediaries between them and God, and they seek their help in time of need,[86] for they have not yet reached the spiritual state you claim to have reached yourself, in which all mediation is abolished, and so they have recourse to what is nearer to God than they are, and that is all.

"As evidence of the profitlessness of visiting the dead you quoted the words of Ibn ʿArabī: 'Verily the dead man is of no avail, for to avail is to act, and his action hath been suspended.' Now I do not say that there is any mistake in these words of his, but I do say that there is a mistake in your understanding of what he meant. The dead man is of no avail as regards the training of the disciple and his furtherance upon the path of God. It is scarcely possible to receive the benefit of guidance without the companionship of a living man. But as to the benefit which is sought when one takes as intermediaries and intercessors with God the elect of His creatures, and when one seeks blessings at their shrines, this the Law gives us no option but to acknowledge, for the Law-giver has on the contrary allowed us to seek grace through what is altogether lifeless, such as the Black Stone and the Holy House, let alone forbidden us to do so through undefiled spirits and bodies whose substance is pure light.

"At any rate, you have played your part most dutifully; for having gone beyond all bounds in reviling the members of the Sufi brotherhoods and in cautioning people against keeping company with them, and having demonstrated that no good can come of associating with them while they are still alive, you were afraid lest someone might imagine that there might be some benefit in visiting them when they were dead, so you said: 'Ibn ʿArabī said: "Verily the dead man is of no avail."' Then it became clear—and it is in fact the gist of your whole

[86] For example, round the tomb of Al-Ḥusayn (the younger of the Prophet's two grandsons) near the Azhar in Cairo there revolves a circle of suppliants and pilgrims from early morning until late at night. Parents frequently bring sick children into the sanctuary and pass their hands over the outside of the shrine and then over their children's faces and heads. None of them asks the Saint himself to work the cure. But one often hears the prayer: "O Lord Ḥusayn, ask thy mother to ask her father to ask God to cure my child."

treatise—that both alive and dead they are good for nothing. This is your judgement; and the Final Judgement is God's."

Many of the features of the Shaykh's few months' travel after his Master's death are very typical of his life as a whole, and this is especially tru of his visit to Tunis, with the somewhat furtive entry into the town to avoid meeting profane acquaintances, the dream about members of the Sufi brotherhoods coming to him, his staying four days in the house until they actually came, and his finally going out with them and meeting and teaching many others. Particularly characteristic is his lack of plans as regards detils and his continual reliance upon inspiration, in one form or another, to tell him what to do. Thus although he was by nature exclusive and aloof, and disinclined to mix with those who were not *fuqarā*, he never allowed a general rule to interfere with the particular law of each moment which came to him through the dictates of the Spirit, and it was certainly these dictates rather than his own inclination that imposed upon him a function which went far beyond the confines of his *zāwiyah*.

The Originality of Sufism

The great Andalusian Sufi, Muḥyi 'd-Dīn Ibn ʿArabī, used to pray a prayer which begins: "Enter me, O Lord, into the deep of the Ocean of Thine Infinite Oneness",[1] and in the treatises of the Sufis this "Ocean" is mentioned again and again, likewise by way of symbolic reference to the End towards which their path is directed. Let us therefore begin by saying, on the basis of this symbol, in answer to the question "What is Sufism?": From time to time a Revelation "flows" like a great tidal wave from the Ocean of Infinitude to the shores of our finite world; and Sufism is the vocation and the discipline and the science of plunging into the ebb of one of these waves and being drawn back with it to its Eternal and Infinite Source.

"From time to time": this is a simplification which calls for a commentary; for since there is no common measure between the origin of such a wave and its destination, its temporality is bound to partake, mysteriously, of the Eternal, just as its finiteness is bound to partake of the Infinite. Being temporal, it must first reach this world at a certain moment in history; but that moment will in a sense escape from time. *Better than a thousand months*[2] is how the Islamic Revelation describes the night of its own advent. There must also be an end which corresponds to the beginning; but that end will be too remote to be humanly foreseeable. Divine institutions are made *for ever.*[3] Another imprint of the Eternal Present upon it will be that it is always flowing and always ebbing in the sense that it has, virtually, both a flow and an ebb for every individual that comes within its scope.

There is only one water, but no two Revelations are outwardly the same. Each wave has its own characteristics according to its destination, that is, the particular needs of

[1] British Museum Ms. Or. 13453 (3).

[2] Q., XCVII: 3.

[3] Exodus, XII: 14.

time and place towards which and in response to which it has providentially been made to flow. These needs, which include all kinds of ethnic receptivities and aptitudes such as vary from people to people, may be likened to the cavities and hollows which lie in the path of the wave. The vast majority of believers are exclusively concerned with the water which the wave deposits in these receptacles and which constitutes the formal aspect of the religion.

Mystics on the other hand—and Sufism is a kind of mysticism—are by definition concerned above all with "the mysteries of the Kingdom of Heaven"; and it would therefore be true to say, in pursuance of our image, that the mystic is one who is incomparably more preoccupied by the ebbing wave than by the water which it has left behind. He has none the less need of this residue like the rest of his community—need, that is, of the outward forms of his religion which concern the human individual as such. For if it be asked what is it in the mystic that can ebb with the ebbing wave, part of the answer will be: not his body and not his soul. The body cannot ebb until the Resurrection, which is the first stage of the reabsorption of the body—and with it the whole material state—into the higher states of being. As to the soul, it has to wait until the death of the body. Until then, though immortal, it is imprisoned in the world of mortality. At the death of Ghazālī, the great eleventh-century Sufi, a poem which he had written in his last illness was found beneath his head. In it are the lines:

> A bird I am: this body was my cage
> But I have flown leaving it as a token.[4]

Other great Sufis also have said what amounts to the same: but they have also made it clear in their writing or speaking or living—and this is, for us, the measure of their greatness—that something in them had already ebbed before death despite the "cage", something incomparably more important than anything that has to wait for death to set it free.

[4] British Museum Ms. Or. 7561, f. 86. See our translation and commentary in *Sufi Poems* (Islamic Texts Society, Cambridge, UK, 2004), p. 56. The whole poem is translated in Margaret Smith's *Al-Ghazālī the Mystic* (Luzac, 1944), pp. 36–7.

What is drawn back by spiritual realisation towards the Source might be called the centre of consciousness. The Ocean is within as well as without; and the path of the mystics is a gradual awakening as it were "backwards" in the direction of the root of one's being, a remembrance of the Supreme Self which infinitely transcends the human ego and which is none other than the Deep towards which the wave ebbs.

To use a very different image which will help to complete the first, let us liken this world to a garden—or more precisely, to a nursery garden, for there is nothing in it that has not been planted there with a view to its being eventually transplanted elsewhere. The central part of the garden is allotted to trees of a particularly noble kind, though relatively small and growing in earthenware pots; but as we look at them, all our attention is caught by one that is incomparably finer than any of the others, which it far excels in luxuriance and vigour of growth. The cause is not naked to the eye, but we know at once what has happened, without the need for any investigation: the tree has somehow been able to strike root deep into the earth through the base of its receptacle.

The trees are souls, and that tree of trees is one who, as the Hindus say, has been "liberated in life", one who has realised what the Sufis term "the Supreme Station;" and Sufism is a way and a means of striking a root through the "narrow gate" in the depth of the soul out into the domain of the pure and unimprisonable Spirit which itself opens out on to the Divinity. The full-grown Sufi is thus conscious of being, like other men, a prisoner in the world of forms, but unlike them he is also conscious of being free, with a freedom which incomparably outweighs his imprisonment. He may therefore be said to have two centres of consciousness, one human and one Divine, and he may speak now from one and now from the other, which accounts for certain apparent contradictions.

To follow the path of the mystics is to acquire as it were an extra dimension, for this path is nothing other than the dimension of depth.[5] Consequently, as will be seen in more detail later, even those rites which the mystic shares with the rest

[5] Or of height, which is the complementary aspect of the same dimension. The Tree of Life, of which the Saint is a personification, is sometimes depicted as having its roots in Heaven, lest it should be forgotten that depth and height are spiritually identical.

of his community, and which he too needs for the balance of his soul, are not performed by him exoterically as others perform them, but from the same profound esoteric point of view which characterises all his rites and which he is methodically forbidden to forsake. In other words he must not lose sight of the truth that the water which is left behind by the wave is the same water as that which ebbs. Analogously, he must not forget that his soul, like the water that is "imprisoned" in forms, is not essentially different from the transcendent Spirit, of which it is a prolongation, like a hand that is held out and inserted into a receptacle and then, eventually, withdrawn.

If the reason for the title of this chapter is not yet apparent, this is partly because the word "original" has become encrusted with meanings which do not touch the essence of originality but which are limited to one of its consequences, namely difference, the quality of being unusual or extraordinary. "Original" is even used as a synonym of "abnormal" which is a monstrous perversion, since true originality is always a norm. Nor can it be achieved by the will of man, whereas the grotesque is doubly easy to achieve, precisely because it is no more than a chaos of borrowings.

The original is that which springs directly from the origin or source, like pure uncontaminated water which has not undergone any "side" influences. Originality is thus related to inspiration, and above all to revelation, for the origins are transcendent, being beyond this world, in the domain of the Spirit. Ultimately the origin is no less than the Absolute, the Infinite and the Eternal—whence the Divine Name "The Originator", in Arabic *al-Badīʿ* which can also be translated "the Marvellous". It is from this Ocean of Infinite Possibility that the great tidal waves of Revelation flow, each "marvellously" different from the others because each bears the imprint of the One-and-Only from which it springs, this imprint being the quality of uniqueness, and each profoundly the same because the essential content of its message is the One-and-Only Truth.

In the light of the image of the wave we see that originality is a guarantee of both authenticity and effectuality. Authenticity, of which orthodoxy is as it were the earthly face, is constituted by the flow of the wave, that is, the direct provenance of the Revelation from its Divine Origin; and in every flow there is the promise of an ebb, wherein lies effectuality, the Grace of the Truth's irresistible power of attraction.

Sufism is nothing other than Islamic mysticism, which means that it is the central and most powerful current of that tidal wave which constitutes the Revelation of Islam; and it will be clear from what has just been said that to affirm this is in no sense a depreciation, as some appear to think. It is on the contrary an affirmation that Sufism is both authentic and effectual.

As to the thousands of men and women in the modern Western world who, while claiming to be "Sufis", maintain that Sufism is independent of any particular religion and that it has always existed, they unwittingly reduce it—if we may use the same elemental image—to a network of artificial inland waterways. They fail to notice that by robbing it of its particularity and therefore of its originality, they also deprive it of all impetus. Needless to say, the waterways exist. For example, ever since Islam established itself in the subcontinent of India, there have been intellectual exchanges between Sufis and Brahmins; and Sufism eventually came to adopt certain terms and notions from Neoplatonism. But the foundations of Sufism were laid and its subsequent course irrevocably fixed long before it would have been possible for extraneous and parallel mystical influences to have introduced non-Islamic elements, and when such influences were finally felt, they touched only the surface.

In other words, by being totally dependent upon one particular Revelation, Sufism is totally independent of everything else. But while being self-sufficient it can, if time and place concur, pluck flowers from gardens other than its own. The Prophet of Islam said: "Seek knowledge even if it be in China."

The Universality of Sufism

Those who insist that Sufism is "free from the shackles of religion"[1] do so partly because they imagine that its universality is at stake. But however sympathetic we may feel towards their preoccupation with this undoubted aspect of Sufism, it must not be forgotten that particularity is perfectly compatible with universality, and in order to perceive this truth in an instant we have only to consider sacred art, which is both unsurpassably particular and unsurpassably universal.[2] To take the example nearest our theme, Islamic art is immediately recognizable as such in virtue of its distinctness from any other sacred art: "Nobody will deny the unity of Islamic art, either in time or in space; it is far too evident: whether one contemplates the mosque of Cordova or the great madrasah of Samarkand, whether it be the tomb of a saint in the Maghreb or one in Chinese Turkestan, it is as if one and the same light shone forth from all these works of art."[3] At the same time, such is the universality of the great monuments of Islam that in the presence of any one of them we have the impression of being at the centre of the world.[4]

Far from being a digression, the question of sacred art brings us back to our central theme, for in response to the

[1] So it is in a way, but not in the way that they have in mind.

[2] This emerges with clarity from Titus Burckhardt's *Sacred Art in East and West: its Principles and Methods* (Sophia Perennis, 1967), as does also the close relationship between sacred art and mysticism.

[3] Titus Burckhardt, "Perennial Values in Islamic Art" in *Mirror of the Intellect*, ch. 22 (Quinta Essentia, 1987).

[4] This idea has been borrowed from Frithjof Schuon's masterly demonstration of the difference between sacred art and art which is religious without being sacred. I have also taken the liberty of transposing it from its Christian setting. The original is as follows: "When standing in front of a Romanesque or Gothic cathedral, we feel that we are at the centre of the world; when standing in front of a Renaissance, Baroque or Rococo church we are merely conscious of being in Europe." (*The Transcendent Unity of Religions*, The Theosophical Publishing House, 1993, p. 61).

question "What is Sufism?", a possible answer—on condition that other answers were also forthcoming—would be simply to point to the Taj Mahal or to some other masterpiece of Islamic architecture. Nor would a potential Sufi fail to understand this answer, for the aim and end of Sufism is sainthood, and all sacred art in the true and full sense of the term is as a crystallisation of sanctity, just as a Saint is as an incarnation of some holy monument, both being manifestations of the Divine Perfection.

According to Islamic doctrine, Perfection is a synthesis of the Qualities of Majesty and Beauty; and Sufism, as many Sufis have expressed it, is a putting on of these Divine Qualities, which means divesting the soul of the limitations of fallen man, the habits and prejudices which have become "second nature", and investing it with the characteristics of man's primordial nature, made in the image of God. Thus it is that the rite of initiation into some Sufi orders actually takes the form of an investiture: a mantle (*khirqah*) is placed by the Shaykh over the shoulders of the initiate.

The novice takes on the way of life of the adept, for part of the method of all mysticisms—and of none more than Islamic mysticism—is to anticipate the end; the adept continues the way of life he took on as novice. The difference between the two is that in the case of the adept the way, that is, Sufism, has become altogether spontaneous, for sainthood has triumphed over "second nature". In the case of the novice the way is, to begin with, mainly a discipline. But sacred art is as a Divine Grace which can make easy what is difficult. Its function—and this is the supreme function of art—is to precipitate in the soul a victory for sainthood, of which the masterpiece in question is an image. As a complement to discipline—we might even say as a respite—it presents the path as one's natural vocation in the literal sense, summoning together all the souls' elements for an act of unanimous assent to the Perfection which it manifests.

If it be asked: Could we not equally well point to the Temple of Hampi or to the Cathedral of Chartres as to the Taj Mahal as a crystallisation of Sufism? the answer will be a "yes" outweighed by a "no". Both the Hindu temple and the Christian cathedral are supreme manifestations of Majesty and Beauty, and a would-be Sufi who failed to recognise them and rejoice in them as such would be falling short of his qualification inasmuch as he would be failing to give the signs of God their due. But it must be remembered that sacred art is for every member of the community in which it flowers, and that it represents not only the end but also the means and the perspective or, in other words, the way opening onto the end; and neither the temple nor the cathedral was destined to display the ideals of Islam and to reveal it as a means to the end as were the great mosques and, on another plane, the great Sufis. It would certainly not be impossible to point out the affinity between the particular modes of Majesty and Beauty which are manifested in both these Islamic exemplars, that is, in the static stone perfections and in their dynamic living counterparts. But such an analysis of what might be called the perfume of Islamic spirituality would be beyond the scope of a book of this nature. Suffice it to say that the Oneness of the Truth is reflected in all its Revelations not only by the quality of uniqueness but also by that of homogeneity. Thus each of the great theocratic civilisations is a unique and homogeneous whole, differing from all the others as one fruit differs from another and "tasting" the same all through, in all its different aspects. The Muslim mystic can thus give himself totally, without any reserve,[5] to a great work of Islamic art; and if it be a shrine he can, by entering it, put it on as the raiment of sanctity and wear it as an almost organic prolongation of the Sufism which it has helped to triumph in his soul. The same triumph could be furthered by the temple or the cathedral; but he could not "wear" either of these—at least, not until he had actually transcended all forms by spiritual realisation which is very different from a merely theoretic understanding.

Sacred art was mentioned in that it provides an immediately obvious example of the compatibility between the universal and the particular. The same compatibility is shown by

[5] That is, without fear of receiving any alien vibration, for two spiritual perspectives can be, for doctrinal or methodic reasons, mutually exclusive in some of their aspects while converging on the same end. But sacred art is an auxiliary and does not normally constitute a central means of spiritual realisation. Any danger that might come from the sacred art of a traditional line other than one's own is thus incomparably less than the dangers inherent in practising the rites of another religion. Such a violation of spiritual homogeneity could cause a shock powerful enough to unbalance the soul.

the symbolism of the circle with its centre, its radii, and its circumference. The word "symbolism" is used here to show that the circle is being considered not as an arbitrary image but as a form which is rooted in the reality it illustrates, in the sense that it owes its existence to that reality, of which it is in fact an existential prolongation. If the Truth were not Radiant there could be no such thing as a radius, not even a geometric one, let alone a spiritual path which is the highest example. All radii would vanish from existence; and with this vanishing the universe itself would vanish, for the radius is one of the greatest of all symbols inasmuch as it symbolises that on which everything depends, namely the connection between the Divine Principle and its manifestations or creations.

Everyone is conscious of "being at a point" or of "having reached a point", even if this be no more than consciousness of having reached a certain age. Mysticism begins with the consciousness that this point is on a radius. It then proceeds by what might be described as an exploitation of this fact, the radius being a Ray of Divine Mercy which emanates from the Supreme Centre and leads back to it. The point must now become a point of Mercy. In other words, there must be a deliberate realisation or actualisation of the Mercy inherent in the point which is the only part of the radius which one can as yet command. This means taking advantage of those possibilities of Mercy which are immediately available, namely the outer formal aspects of religion which, though always within reach, may have been lying entirely neglected or else only made use of exoterically, that is, considering the point in isolation without reference to the radius as a whole.

The radius itself is the religion's dimension of mysticism; thus, in the case of Islam, it is Sufism, which is seen in the light of this symbol to be both particular and universal—particular in that it is distinct from each of the other radii which represent other mysticisms and universal because, like them, it leads to the One Centre. Our image as a whole reveals clearly the truth that as each mystical path approaches its End it is nearer to the other mysticisms than it was at the beginning.[6]

[6] It reveals also, incidentally, the ineffectuality of dilettantism, which corresponds to a meandering line that sometimes moves towards the centre and sometimes away from it, crossing and recrossing various radii but following none with any constancy while claiming to follow a synthesis of all. The

But there is a complementary and almost paradoxical truth which it cannot reveal,[7] but which it implies by the idea of concentration which it evokes: increase of nearness does not mean decrease of distinctness, for the nearer the centre, the greater the concentration, and the greater the concentration, the stronger the "dose". The concentrated essence of Islam is only to be found in the Sufi Saint who, by reaching the End of the Path, has carried the particular ideals of his religion to their highest and fullest development, just as the concentrated essence of Christianity is only to be found in a St Francis or a St Bernard or a St Dominic. In other words, not only the universality but also the originality of each particular mysticism increases in intensity as the End is approached. Nor could it be otherwise inasmuch as originality is inseparable from uniqueness, and this, as well as universality, is necessarily increased by nearness to the Oneness which confers it.

While we are on this theme, it should be mentioned that there is a lesser universality as well as the greater one which we have been considering. All mysticisms are equally universal in the greater sense in that they all lead to the One Truth. But one feature of the originality of Islam, and therefore of Sufism, is what might be called a secondary universality, which is to be explained above all by the fact that as the last Revelation of this cycle of time it is necessarily something of a summing up. The Islamic *credo* is expressed by the Qur'ān as belief *in God and His Angels and His Books and His Messengers*.[8] The following passage is also significant in this context. Nothing comparable to it could be found in either Judaism or Christianity, for example: *For each We have appointed a law and a path; and if*

self-deceivers in question are, to quote a Sufi of the last century (the Shaykh al-Darqāwī) "like a man who tries to find water by digging a little here and a little there and who will die of thirst; whereas a man who digs deep in one spot, trusting in the Lord and relying on Him, will find water; he will drink and give others to drink" (*Letters of a Sufi Master*, Fons Vitae, 1998, p. 29).

[7] A symbol is by definition fragmentary in that it can never capture all the aspects of its archetype. What escapes it in this instance is the truth that the Centre is infinitely greater than the circumference. It therefore needs to be complemented at the back of our minds by another circle whose centre stands for this world and whose circumference symbolises the All-Surrounding Infinite.

[8] II: 285.

God[9] *had wished He would have made you one people. But He hath made you as ye are that He may put you to the test in what He hath given you. So vie with one another in good works. Unto God ye will all be brought back and He will then tell you about those things wherein ye differed.*[10] Moreover—and this is why one speaks of a "cycle" of time—there is a certain coincidence between the last and the first. With Islam "the wheel has come full circle", or almost; and that is why it claims to be a return to the primordial religion, which gives it yet another aspect of universality. One of the characteristics of the Qur'ān as the last Revelation is that at times it becomes as it were transparent in order that the first Revelation may shine through its verses; and this first Revelation, namely the Book of Nature, belongs to everyone. Out of deference to this Book the miracles of Muḥammad, unlike those of Moses and Jesus, are never allowed to hold the centre of the stage. That, in the Islamic perspective, must be reserved for the great miracle of creation which, with the passage of time, is taken more and more for granted and which needs to be restored to its original status. In this connection it is not irrelevant to mention that one of the sayings of the Prophet that is most often quoted by the Sufis is the following "Holy Tradition" (*ḥadīth qudsī*),[11] so called because in it God speaks directly: "I was a Hidden Treasure and I loved to be known, and so I created the world."

It is no doubt in virtue of these and other aspects of universality that the Qur'ān says, addressing the whole community of Muslims: *We have made you a middle people*;[12] and it will perhaps be seen from the following chapters, though without there being any aim to demonstrate this, that Sufism is in fact something of a bridge between East and West.

[9] The Qur'ān speaks with the voice of the Divinity not only in the first person (both singular and plural) but also in the third person, sometimes changing from one to the other in two consecutive sentences as here.

[10] V: 48.

[11] The word "Tradition" will be used throughout with a capital letter when it translates *ḥadīth*, literally "a handed-down saying" (by the Prophet himself or by one of his Companions, with reference to him).

[12] II: 143.

The Heart

"Today[1] Sufism (*taṣawwuf*) is a name without a reality. It was once a reality without a name." Commenting on this in the following century, Hujwīrī adds: "In the time of the Companions of the Prophet and their immediate successors this name did not exist, but its reality was in everyone. Now the name exists without the reality."[2] Similarly, but without being so absolute either in praise or in blame, Ibn Khaldūn remarks that in the first three generations of Islam mysticism was too general to have a special name. But "when worldliness spread and men tended to become more and more bound up with the ties of this life, those who dedicated themselves to the worship of God were distinguished from the rest by the title of Sufis".[3]

The word *ṣūfī* means literally "woollen" and by extension "wearer of wool", and there can be little doubt that woollen dress was already associated with spirituality in pre-Islamic times. Otherwise the Prophet would hardly have thought it worth mentioning that Moses was clothed entirely in wool when God spoke to him. Nonetheless, the wearing of wool does not appear to have ever been a general practice among the mystics of Islam. The most likely explanation of the name is that it was first aptly applied to a small group who did wear wool and that it was then indiscriminately extended to all the mystics of the community in order to fill a void; for they had as yet no name, and since they were becoming a more and more distinct class, it was becoming more and more necessary

[1] In the tenth century, some three hundred years after the Prophet. The speaker is Abū 'l-Ḥasan Fushanjī.

[2] *Kashf al-Maḥjūb*, ch. III.

[3] *Muqaddimah*, ch. XI. The final word stands for two words in the original, *ṣūfiyyah* and *mutaṣawwifah*, the English "Sufi" being commonly used to translate both *ṣūfī* and *mutaṣawwif* (of which the above Arabic terms are the plurals). Strictly speaking, they denote respectively one who is at the end of the path and one who is on the path. There is also a third term, *mustaṣwif*, one who aspires to be a *mutaṣawwif* (see Victor Danner, "The Necessity for the Rise of the Term Sufi" in *Studies in Comparative Religion*, Spring, 1972).

to be able to refer to them. The extremely rapid spread of the name Sufi and its subsequent permanence are no doubt to be explained partly in view of this need and also in virtue of the suitability, in more than one respect, of the term itself. The difficulty which people have always had in explaining it is not the least of its advantages since for the majority Sufism itself, by its very nature, is something of an enigma, and as such it calls for a name that is partially enigmatic. At the same time, its name should have venerable associations and profound implications; and the Arabic root, consisting of the three letters *ṣad–wāw–fā'*, which has the basic meaning of "wool", has according to the science of letters a secret identity[4] with the root *ṣad–fā'–wāw* which has the basic meaning of "purity" in the sense of what has been sifted, as grain is sifted from chaff. Moreover this root yields a verbal form which, when written without vowels as is normal in Arabic, is identical to the eye with *ṣūfī* and which means "he was chosen as an intimate friend", the implication being that the chooser was God, as in the case of *al-Muṣṭafā*, the Elect, the Chosen, one of the names of the Prophet, which is also from this root. The name given to the mystics of Islam is near enough to these other words to be apt, but remote enough for the mystics to accept it without seeming vainglorious. As often as not, however, they speak of themselves as "the poor", *al-fuqarā'*, plural of *faqīr*, in Persian *darvīsh*, whence the English "fakir" and "dervish".

The poverty in question is the same as in the Beatitude: "Blessed are the poor in spirit, for theirs is the Kingdom of Heaven". But the origin of the Sufi term is the verse of the Qur'ān: *God is the Rich and ye are the poor.*[5] Unlike the Beatitude, it refers to mankind in general, expressing a fact from which none can escape. The Sufis apply the verse to themselves because it is they alone who draw from it, as we shall see, the ultimate conclusions. Indeed, Sufism could almost be defined as an exploitation of the fact in question—the double fact, in what concerns God as well as man. Moreover the name *faqīr* has an operative value in that it serves as a precious reminder;

[4] In virtue of the fact that each letter of the alphabet has a particular numerical value, and the letters of both these roots add up to the same total number.

[5] XLVII: 38; and also XXXV: 15: *O men, ye are the poor unto God, and God—He is the Rich, the Object of all Praise.*

and in ending a letter for example, a Sufi will often precede his name with the words: "from the poor unto his Lord...".

If the Qur'ān does not address the Sufis specifically in the words *Ye are the poor*, it does, as we have seen, refer to the Saints, that is, to the fully realised Sufis, as *the slaves of God* in certain contexts where not only the fact of slavehood (which concerns everyone) but also the full consciousness of it is indicated; and the two concepts of slavehood and poverty are inextricably connected. We have also seen that the Sufis, or rather the best of them, are *the foremost* and *the near*. But of all those Qur'ānic terms which may be said to refer to them and to no one else except *a priori* the Prophets, the most significant as well as the most recurrent is probably the somewhat enigmatic phrase *those who have hearts*; and mention of this has been reserved until now because it is important enough to be the central theme of a chapter. For what indeed is Sufism, subjectively speaking, if not "heart-wakefulness"?

In speaking of the majority, the Qur'ān says: *It is not the eyes that are blind but the hearts*.[6] This shows—and it would be strange if it were otherwise—that the Qur'ānic perspective agrees with that of the whole ancient world, both of East and of West, in attributing vision to the heart and in using this word to indicate not only the bodily organ of that name but also what this corporeal centre gives access to, namely the centre of the soul, which itself is the gateway to a higher "heart", namely the Spirit. Thus "heart" is often to be found as a synonym of "intellect", not in the sense in which this word is misused today but in the full sense of the Latin *intellectus*, that is, the faculty which perceives the transcendent.

In virtue of being the centre of the body, the heart may be said to transcend the rest of the body, although substantially it consists of the same flesh and blood. In other words, while the body as a whole is "horizontal" in the sense that it is limited to its own plane of existence, the heart has, in addition, a certain "verticality" for being the lower end of the "vertical" axis which passes from the Divinity Itself through the centres of all the degrees of the Universe. If we use the imagery suggested by Jacob's Ladder, which is none other than this axis, the bodily heart will be the lowest rung and the ladder itself will repre-

[6] XXII: 46.

sent the whole hierarchy of centres or "Hearts"[7] one above the other. This image is all the more adequate for representing each centre as separate and distinct from the others and yet at the same time connected with them. It is in virtue of this interconnection, through which the centres are as it were merged into one, that the bodily heart receives Life from the Divinity (according to Sufi doctrine all Life is Divine) and floods the body with Life. In the opposite direction the bodily heart may serve as a focal point for the concentration of all the powers of the soul in its aspiration towards the Infinite, and examples of this methodic practice are to be found in most forms of mysticism and perhaps in all. It is also in virtue of the same interconnection that "Heart" may be used to indicate the topmost rung of the ladder, that is, the Infinite Self, as in the following Holy Tradition:[8] "My earth hath not room for Me, neither hath My Heaven, but the Heart of My believing slave hath room for Me." Another example is to be found in the poem of the Sufi Ḥallāj which begins: "I saw my Lord with the Eye of the Heart. I said: 'Who art thou?' He answered: 'Thou'."

From this last point of view, "Heart" can be considered as synonymous with "Spirit", which has a Divine as well as a created aspect; and one of the great symbols of the Spirit is the sun which is the "heart" of our universe. This brings us back to the significance of the name Sufi. We have seen that the word means "wearer of wool" and that wool is associated with spirituality. But what is the reason for this association? The answer to this question is clearly to be sought for in the science of symbols and in the knowledge that it gives us of mysterious equivalences; and it emerges, as if by chance, from a remark made by René Guénon[9] about the profound connection between two symbols of the Spirit, namely the tree and the sun (represented here by its metal, gold): "The fruits of the Tree of Life are the golden apples of the Garden of the Hesperides; the golden fleece of the Argonauts, which was also placed on a tree and guarded by a serpent or a dragon, is another symbol

[7] For the sake of clarity, this word will be written with a capital letter wherever it denotes a transcendent centre.

[8] See above, p. 193.

[9] Better known in Egypt as ʿAbd al-Wāḥid Yaḥyā. He was, by *ṭarīqah*, a Shādhilī.

of the immortality which man has to reconquer."[10] Although he does not mention it, Guénon was certainly aware that this second symbol is solar not only on account of the gold but also on account of the fleece. Like the lion, the sheep has always been especially sacred to the sun;[11] and so to wear a woollen garment is to put on the raiment of that "Heart-wakefulness" which is symbolised by the sunlight and which is a central aspect of all that the Sufi sets out to reconquer. The Qur'ānic term *those who have hearts* has thus a relationship even with the name of Sufism as well as being directly expressive of its essence.

So far we have considered the Heart mainly as a centre which includes all its "vertical" prolongations. But when the term "Heart" is used in Sufism (as in other mysticisms) of one particular centre as distinct from others, it normally denotes neither the highest nor the lowest but the next to the lowest, that is, the centre of the soul. In the macrocosm, the Garden of Eden is both centre and summit[12] of the earthly state. Analogously the Heart, which in the microcosm corresponds to the Garden, is both centre and summit of the human individuality. More precisely, the Heart corresponds to the centre of the Garden, the point where grows the Tree of Life and where flows the Fountain of Life. The Heart is in fact nothing other than this Fountain, and their identity is implicit in the Arabic word *ʿayn* which has the meaning of both "eye" and "spring". The extreme significance of this penultimate degree in the hierarchy of centres is that it marks the threshold of the Beyond, the point at which the natural ends and the supernatural or transcendent begins. The Heart is *the isthmus* (*barzakh*) which is so often mentioned in the Qur'ān[13] as separating *the two seas* which represent Heaven and earth, *the sweet fresh-water sea* being the domain of the Spirit whereas *the brackish salt sea* is the domain of soul and body; and when Moses says: I will not cease until I reach the meeting-place of the two seas,[14] he

[10] *The Symbolism of the Cross*, p. 52.

[11] Astrologically, the sun is said to be "in dignity" in the sign of *Leo* and "in exaltation" in the sign of *Aries*.

[12] As such it is often represented as being on top of a mountain.

[13] As for example XXV: 53.

[14] XVIII: 60. The Fountain is here replaced by the celestial sea whose waters are the Waters of Life.

is formulating the initial vow that every mystic must make, implicitly if not explicitly, to reach the lost Centre which alone gives access to transcendent knowledge.

One of the Qur'ānic keys to inner meanings is the verse: *We will show them Our signs on the horizons and in themselves.*[15] This draws our attention to the correspondence between outer phenomena and inner faculties, and in considering what is meant by the Heart it is particularly instructive to consider which of "the signs on the horizons" is its symbol. We have already seen that as the Centre of our whole being, the Heart is the inward Sun. But it is so only in virtue of its "conjunction" with the Spirit; in its own right, as centre of the soul and threshold of Heaven, it corresponds to the moon. In a fourteenth-century Sufi commentary[16] on the Qur'ān the sun is interpreted as signifying the Spirit; light is gnosis; day is the Beyond, the transcendent world of direct spiritual perception; and night is this world, the world of ignorance or, at its best, the world of indirect reflected knowledge symbolized by moonlight. The moon transmits indirectly the light of the sun to the darkness of night; and analogously the Heart transmits the light of the Spirit to the darkness of the soul. But it is the moonlight that is indirect; the moon itself, when it shines in the night sky, is looking directly at the sun and is itself not in night but in daylight. This symbolism reveals the transcendence of the Heart and explains what is meant when it is said that the Heart is the faculty of direct spiritual (or intellectual) vision. But in fallen man this faculty is veiled; for to say that when man was compelled to leave the Earthly Paradise he lost contact with the Fountain of Life amounts to saying that he no longer had direct access to the Heart. The soul of fallen man is thus comparable to a clouded night; and this brings us to a question of fundamental importance for Sufism: if it be asked what qualification is necessary for entry into a Sufi order, or what is it that impels anyone to seek initiation, the answer will be that the clouds in the night of the soul must be thin enough to allow at least some glimmer of Heart-light to penetrate the gloom. A Shaykh of this century, when asked how it was that would-be novices came to him although his disciples made no

[15] XLI: 53.

[16] By ʿAbd al-Razzāq al-Kāshānī, wrongly attributed also to Ibn ʿArabī.

attempt to proselytise, replied that they came because they were "haunted by the thought of God".[17] In other words, they came because the clouds were not thick enough to keep out the awareness of spiritual reality. We may also reflect, in this context, on the phrase "to have a presentiment of one's higher states". This presentiment was mentioned by Guénon as a valid motive for seeking to embark on a spiritual path and as a criterion of qualification for the path. The higher states are the spiritual degrees which are centred in hierarchy, one above the other, along the Axis of the World which is none other than the Tree of Life, the Ray of Light which connects the inward Sun with the inward Moon, the Spirit with the Heart; and the crown of this presentiment is the sense, however remote it may be, of what the same author translated as the "Supreme Identity"[18]—in other words, a foretaste of the truth expressed in the lines which have just been quoted from Ḥallāj.

The word "foretaste" enters in here with a view to the Arabic *dhawq* (taste), a term much used by the Sufis following the Prophet to denote the directness of Heart-knowledge as opposed to mind-knowledge. Ghazālī in fact defines Sufism as *dhawq*; and in order to understand how this knowledge which belongs to the summit of the soul and the threshold of Heaven can have need of a term borrowed from the knowledge which is experienced at the soul's lower boundary, the threshold of the body, it is necessary first to understand the universal law of which this "need" is a particular application.

When it is said that God is Love, the highest meaning this can have is that the Archetypes of all the positive relationships—conjugal, parental, filial and fraternal—are Indivisibly One in the Infinite Self-Sufficing Perfection of the Divine Essence.[19] A less absolute meaning is that the central relationship, namely the conjugal one on which the others depend and in the background of which they are already present, has its Archetype in the polarisation of the Divine Qualities into Qualities of Majesty and Qualities of Beauty. It results from this Archetype that mutual concord depends on likeness and unlikeness, affinity and complementarity. Both the Majesty and

[17] Shaykh Ahmad al-ʿAlawī. See *A Sufi Saint of the Twentieth Century*, p. 21.

[18] In Arabic *tawḥīd*, literally "realisation of Oneness".

[19] The Divine Name which expresses this Self-Sufficiency is *al-Ṣamad.*

the Beauty are Infinite and Eternal, whence their affinity. But one is Active Perfection and the other is Passive Perfection,[20] whence their complementarity. On earth the human pair have affinity through their vice-regency for God, and they are complementary through being man and woman. The harmony of the universe depends on analogous samenesses and differences not only between individuals but also between worlds. The relationship may be "horizontal" where both poles are on the same plane as in the examples already given, or it may be "vertical" as between a higher world and a lower world which is its manifestation or symbol. In this latter case the parental-filial relationship is stressed, but by no means exclusively; the conjugal relationship is always there inasmuch as the Divine Immanence can never be excluded. Thus it is possible to speak of "the Marriage of Heaven and Earth"; and it is also in virtue of the Divine Immanence,which puts the Lover virtually on a level with the Beloved, that the Sufi poems addressed to the Divinity under the name of Layla[21] are love poems in the most central sense. The all-embracing example of the vertical relationship is to be found in the already quoted Holy Tradition "I was a Hidden Treasure and I loved to be known and so I created the world". There is nothing in the world which has not its Divine Archetype. But harmony demands also that the world shall be a complement, and complementarity implies invertedness. Thus man, whose Archetype is the Divine Being Itself from which everything derives, is the last of all created things, the finality towards which all creation tends. It is this precedent that causes, on the lowest plane of all, the reflection of an object to be a faithful yet inverted image of the object itself. The mountain whose top appears to be at the bottom of the lake which reflects it is a natural prototype of the Seal of Solomon, the world-wide symbol of the Union of the Active and Passive Perfections and by extension the symbol of all the pairs which are the images of this Union throughout the worlds of the universe.[22]

[20] Active and Passive Perfection are the Taoist equivalent of the Sufi terms Majesty and Beauty.

[21] This name of one of the greatest heroines of the Near East has the literal meaning of "night" and is used by the Sufis to denote the Mystery of the Divine Essence.

[22] See in this connection Abū Bakr Ṣirāj ad-Dīn, *The Book of Certainty* (The Islamic Texts Society, 1992), ch. 13.

The perfect balance of the primordial soul depends on the harmonious union of the domains of inner and outer man. If we take the apex of the upper triangle of the Seal of Solomon to represent the Heart's direct experience of Spiritual Truths which are the fruits of the Tree of Life, the down-turned apex of the lower[23] triangle will represent taste in the literal sense, whereas the two interpenetrating bases will represent the indirect mind-knowledge which derives from the two direct experiences. The Seal's message here is that if we want to know what Heart-knowledge is like we must consult the senses rather than the mind, at any rate as regards directness. But our symbol also figures the gulf which separates the senses from the Heart: sense-knowledge, being the lowest mode of perception, is the most deeply submerged in space and time and other earthly conditions and is therefore narrower and more fleeting than mind-knowledge, whereas the inner "taste" escapes from these conditions in virtue of its exaltation and is thus of all experiences the vastest and most enduring.

The Seal of Solomon is a key to the interpretation of many texts which have eluded the comprehension of those who are ignorant of the laws of symbolism, and amongst such texts are the Qur'ānic descriptions of Paradise. It is true that spiritual bliss is often indicated simply by an affirmation that there is no common measure between earthly and heavenly joys, or by such words as *Verily thy Lord shall give and give unto thee and thou shalt be satisfied.*[24] But in descriptive passages, the Qur'ān speaks in terms of the pleasures of the senses, because these direct pleasures are in fact the earthly projections or shadows of the Paradisal archetypes which it is seeking to convey. Having their roots in these archetypes, the sensations have power to recall them, for the "tether" which attaches the symbol to its reality not only traces the path by which the symbol came into existence but can become, in the opposite direction, a vibrating chord of spiritual remembrance.

These Qur'ānic descriptions, while serving to remind the soul that Paradise is intensely desirable,[25] serve also to re-

[23] The outer is "below" the inner.

[24] XCIII: 5.

[25] Fallen man, if left to his own resources, is in something of a quandary between mind-knowledge and sense-knowledge: he knows that mind knowledge is higher than sense-knowledge and that it must be rated accordingly;

endow life on earth with a lost dimension; and here lies a significant aspect of Sufism, already hinted at in connection with Islam's claim to be a restoration of the primordial religion. It goes without saying that this claim is above all justified—we might even say only justified—in virtue of Islamic mysticism. Every form of mysticism begins with a quest for the "primordial state", since this state means human perfection which is the only basis for the spiritual ascent. But the perfection envisaged, although essentially always the same, is not always "primordial" in its details. What distinguishes Islamic mysticism from many others is that it looks for its ideal to man as he was created, that is, to a perfection which would accord with the Earthly Paradise. As an image of the primordial soul, the Seal of Solomon with its two triangles pointing in opposite directions figures an intense extroversion balanced—and dominated—by an intense introversion, the pull of the outer world being balanced by the pull of the Heart. We have already seen how the Prophet of Islam personifies this harmonious resolution of opposites. The "pull of the Hour" which was mentioned in this connection may be said to coincide with the magnetism of the Heart inasmuch as consciousness of both lies in the Heart. Moreover it is the Hour which actually reintegrates symbols into their archetypes, and one of the functions of Heart-knowledge is to anticipate this reintegration by continually referring outward objects back to the inner realities they symbolise. Typically representative of the primordial religion is one of the best known utterances of the Prophet: "Perfume and women have been made dear to me, and coolness hath been brought to mine eyes in the prayer".[26]

An analogous inward outwardness is characteristic of the Message which as Messenger he received and transmitted. Coming at the end of the cycle of time, it holds out to mankind once more the Book of Nature, the Primordial Revelation

but he knows also that the lower knowledge has an intensity and directness that the higher knowledge lacks. The doctrine of Heart knowledge explains everything; but failing this, and failing its prolongation, faith, and the virtues that go with faith, in particular patience at what one does not understand and unpretentious trust in Providence, something appears to be wrong; and the soul finds itself at the brink of a dilemma between hypocrisy and sensuality.

[26] "Coolness of the eyes" is a proverbial Arabic expression signifying intense pleasure. The passive tense is important here; it is as if the Prophet had said: It has been my destiny to love perfume and women and prayer.

whose hieroglyphs are man and the animals, the forests and the fields, the mountains, seas and deserts, sun, moon and stars. One of the Qur'ān's most central teachings is: "Do not look on the things of this world as independent realities, for they are all in fact entirely dependent for their existence on the Hidden Treasure whose Glory they were created to reveal." In its own words: *The seven heavens and the earth and all that is therein extol Him, nor is there anything which doth not glorify Him with praise; yet ye understand not their glorification.*[27] And one of the "refrains" of the Qur'ān is to address the visionaries or potential visionaries among men and bid them meditate on these or those wonders of creation as "signs".

This outwardness for the sake of inwardness which characterises Sufism[28] can be figured by a line joining the two apexes of the Seal of Solomon. The faculty of direct outward perception must be connected with the faculty of direct inward perception, and this connection is the already mentioned "chord of spiritual remembrance" which must be made to vibrate in order that the inward faculty may be awakened and that the "glorification" may be "understood"; and beyond that faculty, represented by the upper apex, the "chord" may be prolonged indefinitely, for the vibration does not stop short at the threshold of Heaven but is aimed at the Infinite. We are here once again at the very centre of our theme, for Sufism is the doctrine and method of this aim, nor is the vibration anything other than a variant of the ebbing wave which was our initial image. We may take up once more at this point the question "What is it that ebbs?", for the answer already given, that it is the centre of consciousness that ebbs, will now be clearer in the light of what has been said about the Heart, which always denotes the centre but which, because subjectively this centre is not stationary, may refer to the inward Moon or to the inward Sun or beyond this even to the Essence Itself.

Since everyone has always a centre of consciousness, everyone may be said to have a "heart". But the Sufis use the

[27] XVII: 44.

[28] This distinction, like many others made throughout this book, is relative and must not be exaggerated. It is a question of accent—as if each mysticism pronounced the same formula with a different intonation and different stresses.

term on principle in a transcendent sense to denote a centre of consciousness which corresponds at least to the inward Moon.

This principle has its roots in the Prophet's definition of *iḥsān* (excellence) which is directly related to Heart-knowledge: "Excellence is that thou shouldst worship God as if thou sawest Him; for if thou seest Him not, yet He seeth thee."

"As if thou sawest Him." As if man were still in full possession of his primordial faculties. The whole of one aspect of Sufi method lies in the word *ka' annaka* "as if thou..."; and this rule of idealism has many applications, some of which we shall see later. But it needs to be combined with the rule of actualism, the rule of "but in fact". No one is more acutely conscious of the fall of man than the mystic—so much so that a thing counts for him as positive according to the measure in which it is capable of setting up a vibration towards the Heart and clearing an access to it.

In principle, since *there is nothing which doth not glorify Him with praise,* everything has this capability. *Yet ye understand not their glorification.* It has to be admitted that the symbols which could penetrate the Heart of primordial man are prevented from being fully operative for fallen man by his obstructedness. In other words he cannot react to them powerfully enough to effect the necessary vibration; and if left to his own resources he would be impotent to achieve access to the Heart. The sight of a beautiful landscape, for example, arouses not only wonder and delight but also longing inasmuch as the subject cannot merge with the object; and this longing is no less than a degree of the already mentioned presentiment of one's higher possibilities, a degree of "remembrance" that in the archetypal world of the Spirit a merging of subject with object actually does take place. But such a presentiment would be, in almost every case, no more than a qualification for the spiritual path. In itself it would be hopelessly outmeasured. It is not for nothing that in most traditions the obstacle to be overcome is represented as a gigantic monster with supernatural powers. Nothing will serve short of a sword that has been forged and tempered in Heaven; but as an auxiliary to such a sword, the presentiment will be a precious strength in the soul; in other words, it needs to be consecrated by some Heaven-sent incantation, above all by the Divine Name itself.

It is important to remember here that *Dhikr Allāh* (Remembrance of God or Invocation of God) is a name of the Prophet, and that according to the Qur'ān this invocation is "greater" even than the ritual prayer. The word in question could also be translated "greatest", without the comparison, for both interpretations are linguistically possible; and in the present context it can be affirmed that calling on the Name of God, whether it be accompanied by some other experience or not, is the most positive thing in all the world because it sets up the most powerful vibration towards the Heart. The Prophet said: "There is a polish for everything that taketh away rust; and the polish of the Heart is the invocation of Allāh."

We are here anticipating the theme of the chapter on method; but like the unity which it aims at establishing, Sufism is so closely knit that it is impossible to isolate, in altogether separate chapters, the doctrine, the method, and the spiritual and psychic substance to which doctrine and method apply. To continue anticipating for a moment, it may be mentioned that although the invocation of the Supreme Name *Allāh* takes precedence over all the other practices of Sufism, the term *Dhikr Allāh* is also extended to other rites and in particular to the recitation or audition of the Qur'ān which is, as we have seen, of one substance with God; and in the context of causing vibration and of the passage from the outward to the inward, it is relevant to quote what the Revealed Book says of itself in virtue of the power of its own verses in this respect: *It causeth the skins of those that fear their Lord to thrill. Then their skins and their hearts grow pliant (or supple) unto the remembrance of God.*[29] The Sufis have here all the authority they need for using outward movement, such as the swaying of the body in the sacred dance, as a means to inward concentration.

The words *their hearts grow pliant* or, as it could be rendered, *their hearts soften,* can be glossed "their Hearts grow less hard". The barrier in question may be spoken of as hardness of heart or rust on the heart or clouds over the Moon or as a dragon that guards the access to the Fountain of Life. If it were not for this barrier, which is the direct result of the fall of man, there would be no need of religion in the ordinary sense, for Revelation could come directly to each man in his Heart which

[29] XXXIX: 23.

would then refract the Message to the mind and to the rest of the psychic substance. There would thus be a perpetual flow and ebb between the Self and the self. But as things are, a special Messenger has to be sent that he may transmit to others what his Heart receives. This does not mean however that all other souls are entirely cut off from the inward reception of spiritual light. It means that for so tremendous a descent as the Revelation, the Heart must be fully operative as is the case only with the Prophets and the Saints; but between these and the majority is the minority of mystics—"travellers" for whom by definition the barrier is or has become relatively transparent. They seek, as we have seen, to identify themselves with the Prophet and to ebb as he ebbs in response to the Revelation. In other words, it must be for the traveller as if the Revelation has come directly to him, in his Heart; and this *ka' anna*, like all the other "as ifs" of Sufism, is only possible on the basis of certainty.

What then is certainty? Or what is the difference between certainty and conviction? Conviction is indirect and belongs to the mind, being the result of purely mental processes such as argument. But certainty, being always direct, belongs to "the apex of the triangle". As such it can be the result of sensory perception; hearing or touch or sight can give certainty. But in its spiritual sense, when it has for object the Transcendent, certainty is the result of Heart-knowledge. Moreover, failing this knowledge in its fullest sense, those elements which are nearest the Heart at the summit of the soul must also be considered as faculties of direct perception, albeit in a fragmentary way; and through the light which these faculties of intuition receive in virtue of the transparency of the barrier, a soul may claim to be possessed of a faith which is no less than certainty.

Before closing this chapter, and as a preface to the doctrine which like all mystical doctrines presupposes at least a virtual certainty in the soul—otherwise the seed would "fall on stony ground"—let us consider the three degrees of certainty as Sufism defines them.[30] The Divine Truth is symbolised by the element fire. The three degrees, in ascending order, are the Lore of Certainty (*ʿilm al-yaqīn*), the Eye of Certainty (*ʿayn*

[30] *The Book of Certainty*, already mentioned, is based on the doctrine of these three degrees.

al-yaqīn) and the Truth of Certainty (*ḥaqq al-yaqīn*). The Lore is the certainty that comes from hearing the fire described; the Eye is the certainty that comes from seeing its flames; the Truth is the certainty which comes from being consumed in it. This last degree is the extinction (*fanā'*) of all otherness which alone gives realisation of the Supreme Identity. The second degree is that of Heart-knowledge, for the Eye which sees is the Heart. As to the Lore, it is a mental understanding which has been raised to the level of certainty by the faculties of intuition which surround the Heart; and it is one of the functions of the doctrine to awaken these faculties and make them operative.

Introduction to *Splendours of Qur'ān Calligraphy and Illumination*

The story of the spread of Islam has often been told, but it bears repeating; and it will not be irrelevant here to outline it briefly, for it is above all the story of an impact which directly caused, among other effects, the art that is the theme of this book.

In the sixth century AD the tribes of Arabia were poor, disunited, often at war with each other, and little known to the rest of the world. It was to a member of one of these tribes that the Divine Revelation was given, and some years later in 620 AD, having been rejected by the majority of his people, the new Prophet, in apparent danger of his life, left his home in Mecca with one companion and made his way to an unknown future in the eleven-camel-days distant township of Yathrib, soon to be known as Medina. One hundred and three years later the vanguards of his empire were crossing the Pyrenees into France, having conquered the whole of North Africa and most of Spain, while in the East that same empire had penetrated, through Persia and India, as far as the borders of China; and with subsequent losses outweighed by subsequent gains, Islam has remained in possession of most of those territories until the present day.

The force of the impact which produced this transformation was clearly such that it could scarcely have avoided striking, at the same time, other domains of human receptivity and potentiality; and another result of the Revelation, analogous to the more general one, was the birth of a new style of architecture, which showed, not in details but in total effect, an independence of anything that had gone before. In a relatively short space of time this new style of architecture was producing monuments such as have seldom been equalled and never surpassed.

There was yet another analogous "creation out of nothing", which cannot possibly be considered as the natural development of an already existing means. One of the great qualities of the pre-Islamic Arabs was what might be called an acute language-consciousness, centred upon poetry. But this love of poetry had not produced anything in the way of a sister art of calligraphy. On the contrary, rather than write down what they had composed, the Arab poets preferred to rely on the memory of two members of a younger generation specially chosen for the perpetuation of their lines. The somewhat rudimentary script, which few chose to master, was kept well in the background. Nor is this the only example that antiquity has to offer of an awareness of the negative aspects of writing. But that question has been amply considered elsewhere,[1] and it would be out of place to dwell on it here for obvious reasons.

The new religion was in more than one way a complement to Christianity, which preceded it by just over six hundred years and which is based on "the Word made flesh"; a man born of a virgin, with no earthly father. The Qur'ān defines Jesus as *His (God's) word which He delivered unto Mary*, and as *a spirit from Him* (IV, 171). Islam is based on "the Word made book", and Muḥammad, to whom it was revealed over a period of some twenty-two years, was "unlettered", having learned neither to read nor to write; a quality which in this context can be considered as analogous to the virginity of Mary. In virtue of its Divine substance, the Qur'ān is at the level of the Hebrew Pentateuch and the Psalms which are likewise revealed, unlike the other scriptures of Judaism which, like the Christian Bible,[2] are at the degree of inspiration. In Christianity the incomparably higher degree of Revelation had to be reserved for the foundation stone of the religion, the Word, in this case the Word made flesh, including by extension the Eucharist in virtue of its transubstantiation. The Qur'ān itself quotes Jesus as having prayed before the Last Supper that God would send

[1] See A. K. Coomaraswamy, *The Bugbear of Literacy* (Ghent, Sophia Perennis, 1979), ch. 1 and Martin Lings, *Ancient Beliefs and Modern Superstitions* (Cambridge, Archetype, 1999), ch. 1. [Included in this volume, pp. 81–93.—Ed.].

[2] A revelation is reduced by translation to the status of a commentary on the revealed text, a commentary more or less inspired as the case may be, but without the ritual efficacy that it possesses in the sacred language in which it came down from Heaven.

down to them *a banquet of food from heaven to be for us a feast, for the first of us and for the last of us, and a sign from Thee* (V, 114). Moreover the same word *āyah*, miraculous sign, is used of the verses of the Qur'ān itself; and in both Sunni and Shiʿi Islam, which accounts for the vast majority of Muslims, the orthodox view is that the text of the Qur'ān[3] is "not created".

Towards the end of the Prophet's mission the Archangel would visit him in the month of Ramaḍān to recite the whole Revelation with him, as much of it as had already been revealed, to make sure that nothing had been omitted or distorted; but in the last Ramaḍān of the Prophet's life, when he had already received the final Revelation, the Archangel came and went through the whole Qur'ān with him twice, which the Prophet took to be a sign of his own imminent death. This took place some five months later, in 632 AD/11 AH.[4]

[3] The whole book is a little shorter than the New Testament, and it contains 114 chapters, in Arabic *sūrah*, plural *sūwar*, of varying length. The first *sūrah*, of seven verses or "signs", by far the most often recited, is followed by the longest, of two hundred and eighty-six verses. After that come other long *sūwar* and there tends to be a gradual shortening of *sūrah* length as the book proceeds. The arrangement is in no sense chronological, and presumably it was determined by the Archangel and reflects, in this as in other respects, its celestial archetype.

[4] *Anno Hegirae*, the year of the Prophet's migration, *hijrah*, to Medina, which is year 1 in the Islamic calendar, corresponding to 620 AD. In what follows both dates will be given, AH/AD.

The Qur'ānic Art of Calligraphy

The need to record and hand down to succeeding generations every syllable of the Qur'ān with exactitude made it impossible to rely on anything so fallible as human memory, even though the memories in question were outstanding. But the point to be made here is not that a people ungiven to writing and building should have come to be, through the force of circumstances, both writers and builders. The analogy we are drawing is based on the change from almost nothing to almost everything; and in the case of calligraphy the change is perhaps even more striking than in that of architecture. It might even be said not only that the Arabs have never been surpassed as calligraphers,[1] but also that they have only been equalled by one other people, namely the Chinese, whose art has, however, developed along very different lines.

It cannot, however, be considered a paradox that the civilization of *the unlettered Prophet*[2] should have been destined to excel in the art of lettering. Even apart from the probable advantages of starting an enterprise uncluttered by previous experiences, the Arabs' disinclination to write down precious words had no doubt a very positive part to play in the genesis of Arabic calligraphy. These people were in love with the beauty of their language and with the beauty of the human voice. There was absolutely no common measure between these two summits on the one hand, and the ungainliness of the only available script on the other. Their disdain for writing showed a sense of values; and in the light of final results it is legitimate to suppose that it was the reverse side of an openness to calligraphic inspiration, as much as to say, "Since we have no choice but to write down

[1] With the Arabs must be included certain others of those peoples—pre-eminently the Persians and the Turks—for whom Arabic is the liturgical language. But the Arabs themselves were the pioneers.

[2] So Muḥammad is named in the Qur'ān (VII, 157-8) and, by extension, in many Islamic litanies.

the Revelation, then let that written record be as powerful an experience for the eye as the memorized record is for the ear when the verses are spoken or chanted."

The most usual explanation of the phenomenon we are now considering is that of human genius having been curbed from the art of sculpture, and from that of painting in most of its aspects, and made to flow with all its force into a relatively narrow channel. But this explanation, despite its elements of truth, is really more of a question than an answer, for it impels us to ask, "Where did that force come from? What was it doing before the outset of Islam? Or was it a dormant potentiality that the new Revelation awoke?"

It is impossible to deny that human genius has a vital part to play in sacred art; but there is genius and genius. In art that is related to religion, a distinction has to be made between sacred art in the strict sense and art that is religious without being sacred; and this means making a distinction between a genius which is dominated and penetrated by its own transcendent archetype, and a genius which is more or less cut off from that archetype and free to follow its own devices.

This distinction is one which Western Christendom has been trying not to see for almost the last five hundred years. It is none the less fundamental and becomes immediately clear in the light of a wider context. For if a sensitive and intelligent Christian be confronted with an ancient Egyptian wall-painting of Osiris, for example, or a sacramental statue of the Buddha, and if he be asked, "What has your religion produced that can measure up to these?" it is then that he is compelled to see the limitations of humanism, and to return, for an answer, to the theomorphic art of the Middle Ages. The Islamic answer to the same question would be in an altogether different mode – a prayer niche in one of the great mosques or perhaps, despite the smaller dimensions, something within the scope of this book. Miniature painting, in which the Persians excelled, is only on the periphery of Islamic art and does not come near to the central and sacred domain.[3]

[3] For one remarkable exception however, which is truly a work of sacred art, though it could never have a central place in the civilization of Islam, see Titus Burckhardt, *The Art of Islam* (London, World of Islam Festival Publishing, 1976), plate 13. The miniature in question depicts the Night Journey of the Prophet and a postcard of it is sometimes available at the British Library where the manuscript in question is (Or.2265.f.195).

In his concise yet far-reaching definition of what may be said to constitute a religion, Frithjof Schuon includes the presence of sacred art as one of the criteria of authenticity.[4] This will not seem surprising to anyone who bears in mind that the function of sacred art, always in the strictest sense of the term, is parallel to that of the Revelation itself as a means of causing repercussions in the human soul in the direction of the Transcendent. It is seldom, however, contemporary with the initial impact of a religion, and it is thus able to compensate for certain losses, above all as a means of expressing to later generations something of what the presence of the Messenger expressed to the first generation. The Qur'ān makes it clear that a Prophet must be considered as a Divine masterpiece. In one passage, God says to Moses what could be translated: *I have fashioned thee as a work of art for Myself* (XX, 41); and in another, Muḥammad is told: *Verily of an immense magnitude is thy nature* (LXVIII, 4).

To compensate for an absence is to be a prolongation of a presence; and this function is at once apparent in Christian sacred art, of which the icon is as it were the cornerstone. But it becomes also apparent as regards Qur'ān calligraphy and illumination when we remember that to be the vehicle of the Revelation was the primary function of the Prophet of Islam.

If sacred art comes as a half-miraculous sign that Providence has not abandoned the religion since its foundation, and if it therefore comes implicitly as a guarantee of that religion's Divine origin, it is also a criterion of authenticity in the way that a result is a criterion of its cause. To see this we have simply to remember that the function of religion is to bring about a restoration, if only a virtual one, of man's primordial state. Each new Revelation, whatever form it may take, is destined to precipitate a renewal of consciousness, in a particular people or group of peoples, that man was made in the image of God and that as His representative he is the mediator between Heaven and earth. The difference between man and all other creatures is that the latter merely reflect various Divine Qualities, whereas man reflects the Divine Essence, which comprises all the Qualities. The difference between man and man is that

[4] Frithjof Schuon, *Islam and the Perennial Philosophy* (London, World of Islam Festival, 1976), ch. 2 (opening).

though each reflects the Totality, one individual will have certain qualities as it were in the foreground of his nature, whereas another will have others in the foreground and so on, with a never exactly repeated variation. Each soul thus offers a differently ordered receptivity to the imprint of the Divine Nature, so that when that imprint is renewed by the pressure of the Revelation, the general excelling of oneself which results from it will be in different directions. As we learn from the Islamic litanies of the ninety-nine Divine Names, God is not only the King, the Just, the Wise, the Omniscient, the Almighty, the Victorious, the Irresistible. He is also the Beautiful, the Creator, the Former, the Marvellously Original, and the All-Holy; and here lies the metaphysical inevitability of sacred art as a result of the Revelation. Here also lie the roots of all artistic genius, and it is only from these roots that a tradition of sacred art can spring; a tradition which will eventually enable less gifted artists to participate in the consecrated genius of others and to excel themselves beyond all measure, whence the connection between sacred art and the traditional arts and crafts.

In other words, sacred art presupposes, somewhere, inspiration in the fullest sense. But the word "somewhere" is significant; for even where a definite name is attached to a masterpiece, there is always the possibility that the known artist worked under the influence of an unknown visionary; and there may be more than one generation between the perfector of any given style and the man who received the initial spiritual impetus. This possibility, which is in the nature of things, is nowhere more widely recognized than in the civilization of Islam. Thus, for example, when a celebrated fifteenth-century grammarian of Egypt, Khālid al-Azharī, is quoted as saying that he had been prompted to write one of his most important works by a great Sufi Sheikh of his day, the quoter adds the following note, "The good done by most of those who are famous for their outward science has been achieved through their frequenting the company of a saint, that is a man of inward science"; and he goes on to mention the founder of the Shādhilī Order of Sufis and his successor as eminent personifications of an outward-radiating inward science.[5]

[5] Ibn Ḥamdūn, *Sharḥ al-ājurrūmiyyah*

Moreover, apart from such possibilities, it must be remembered that sacred art is always strikingly impersonal[6] through its transcendence of the individual. All the more fitting therefore that it should be anonymous, as in fact so much of it is; and there can be no doubt that a large part of its anonymity has been deliberate, resulting from the consciousness of this or that artist that the work in question is not, ultimately speaking, "his".

To have one of its poles in Heaven and to have come into existence by a path that is something of a parallel to the process of creation, are essential conditions without which sacred art could never fulfil its ritual or liturgical function as a "Jacob's Ladder" of return. It is in virtue of its parallel "descent" that a great cathedral or mosque or other monument of sacred art has the privilege of being able to stand amidst the wilds of nature without the eye condemning it as an alien presence; and the rungs of these ladders of return offer the worshipper the relatively effortless means of taking a higher standpoint which, by repetition and by combination with other means, can even become more or less permanent. The way of creation is also the way of revelation, and in the particular art which is our theme the connection with revelation is very direct. Calligraphy and illumination are as it were compensations for such contingencies as ink and paper, a "step up" which makes it possible, in a flash of wonderment, to approach more nearly and penetrate more deeply the Divine Substance of the Qur'ānic text, and thus to receive a "taste", each soul according to its capacity, of the Infinite and the Eternal. The use here of the Sufi term "taste"— in Arabic *dhawq*—may be taken as a reminder of the close connection, in all traditions, between sacred art and mysticism.

As regards the earthly pole of sacred art, it is normal that a certain technical development should need to take place. It cannot be expected that Heaven should always dictate to man the details, as it did, exceptionally, in the case of Solomon's Temple; and the delay caused by the interval of man's apprenticeship is, as we have seen, in perfect harmony with the Providential function of a spiritual support which is needed far less

[6] See Frithjof Schuon, *Spiritual Perspectives and Human Facts* (Ghent, Sophia Perennis, 1969), pp. 29–33. See also, in general, Titus Burckhardt, *Sacred Art in East and West* (Ghent, Sophia Perennis, 1967).

at the outset of a new religion than in subsequent generations. Meantime the Revelation makes it clear that the Archetype of Qur'ān calligraphy already exists in Heaven, *in a hidden book* (LVI, 78), accessible only to angels. Nor can it be in the spiritual nature of things that its earthly manifestation should depend mainly on human initiative.

The Qur'ānic Art of Illumination

The art of Qur'ān illumination was bound to develop more slowly than that of calligraphy because it was not directly called for by the text. It was furthermore held in check by the fear of allowing anything to intrude upon that text. More positively, we can be certain that it was this same reverential awe, *haybah*, which guaranteed exactly the right channels for the flow of this development towards a result which is, by general agreement, marvellously right. "Fear of the Lord is the beginning of wisdom." This saying of Solomon, continually quoted in Islam, is itself a synthesis of wisdom which has its application at all levels. Sacred Art is "wise"; and from what has already been said about its anonymity, it follows that the Qur'ānic art of calligraphy itself, let alone that of illumination, was bound to start on a note of "reserve", a pious courtesy related to awe and to the artist's consciousness of the Divine Majesty.

The main features of Qur'ān illumination have been outlined more than once;[1] but to understand the significance of these features we have no alternative but to consult what was, beyond any doubt, the source of inspiration. Moreover, this source will give us a profound insight into the outlook, we might even say the psychic substance, of the artist himself. It is difficult for Christians, whose primary access to the Divine Presence is not through words, to imagine how deeply a book can penetrate a soul which deliberately invites such penetration. Many of the calligraphers and not a few of the illuminators would have known the Qur'ān by heart from beginning to end. But even when they did not know it all, the passages quoted in this and other chapters would have been so familiar as to be almost an organic part of their nature. "The verses of the Qur'ān are not only utterances which transmit thoughts; they are also, in a sense, beings, powers, talismans. The soul of

[1] Particularly important is Richard Ettinghausen's "Manuscript Illumination" in *A Survey of Persian Art*, Vol. III (London, Oxford University Press, 1939), pp. 1937–74.

the Muslim is as it were woven out of sacred formulae; in these he works, in these he rests, in these he lives, in these he dies."[2]

The Qur'ān itself may be said to hold out certain opportunities as it were in invitation to the illuminator. The most obvious of these are the *sūrah* headings, and the divisions between the verses. In addition, indications that five or ten verses have passed give an opportunity for a regularly repeated ornament in the margin, and the reader will find it helpful to know at what points in the text he is required to make a prostration, which also can be indicated ornamentally. It is, moreover, in the nature of things that if the opening of a *sūrah* admits of illumination, the opening of the first *sūrah* and therefore of the whole book should be treated with a particularly striking display of art.

Such arguments as these, however, would hardly have been able to overcome the calligraphers' scruples except on the understanding that ornamentation could, in fact, be a very positive means of heightening the effects they aimed at producing by the script. We have already seen that these effects are directly related to the nature of the Revelation itself; and it must be remembered in this connection that according to a fundamental point of doctrine, "the Qur'ān is uncreated", which means, however these words be interpreted, that the revealed book constitutes no less than a Divine Presence. How does this affect Qur'ān illumination? The answer is bound up with certain aspects of the Islamic perspective.

It has been said that the ancient Greeks were dominated by the idea of Perfection which, with the onset of that decadence from which no civilization can escape, tended more and more to exclude other aspects of Transcendence, with the eventual result that it took on the limitations of the untranscendent and finite. Now Islam also is dominated by the idea of Perfection. To see this, one has only to stand in the courtyard of one of the great mosques, or in front of a prayer-niche or an old city gate, not to mention examples which are closer to our theme. But Islam is also dominated by the idea of Infinitude. Perfection, *kamāl*, is here imbued with the idea of Totality. *He is the First and the Last and the Outward and the Inward* (LVII, 3).

[2] Frithjof Schuon, *Understanding Islam* (Bloomington, World Wisdom Books, 1998), p. 60.

One of the last *sūrahs* of the Qur'ān (CXII) is a definition of the Divinity, revealed in answer to a question about the nature of God. The two key Names with which it opens, *al-Aḥad* and *al-Ṣamad*, could be translated respectively "the Indivisible One-and-Only" and "the Totally Sufficing unto Himself in His Infinite Perfection". It is true that the definition implied by these Names is nothing other than sound metaphysics with regard to the Absolute. It is therefore universal and belongs as such to all religions. But what characterizes Islam is an unwillingness to leave this highest metaphysical plane except in passing and on condition of reverting, as soon as possible, from the relative to the Absolute. The differences between religions are always on the surface and never at the roots. In other words, one religion is implicit where another is explicit, and inversely, and it is these differences of emphasis which explain the immense variety of sacred art from one orthodoxy to another.

It is well known that Islam is a monotheistic religion. Less well known are some of the corollaries of this; and for the understanding of Islamic art it is essential not to forget the explicitness of Islam that the Absolute One defies not only addition and multiplication but also subtraction and division. Art in a sense depends on the Name the Outward, yet since the One is Indivisible, the Outwardness is always one with the Inwardness. In other words, when the Qur'ān says: *Wheresoever ye turn, there is the Face of God* (II, 115), no commentator can rightly say that this verse concerns only the Outward, for it also concerns, inseparably and mysteriously, the Inward and the First and the Last.

It is the function of sacred art in general to be a vehicle for the Divine Presence; and it follows from what has been said that the Islamic artist will conceive this function not as a "capturing" of the Presence but rather as a "liberation"[3] of its mysterious Totality from the deceptive prison of appearances. Islam is particularly averse to any idea of circumscribing or localizing the Divine, or limiting it in any way. But Totality is Wholeness, and Wholeness means Perfection; and on the visual plane perfection cannot be reconciled with formlessness, which leaves us no alternative but contour and therefore limitation.

[3] We are here at the very roots of the question, and it may be inferred from this that the relative absence of the "living" figural element in all the central arts of Islam has causes which are far more profound and more positive than is generally supposed.

What then is the answer? How can an art conform to a Presence that is explicitly conceived as a union of Qualities, when on the plane of forms these Qualities are scarcely compatible?

The answer partly lies in the domain of what might be called the first sacred art of all, inasmuch as it was, for man, the first earthly vehicle of the Divine Presence, namely nature itself; and it is, moreover, the Qur'ān which draws the artist's attention to this primordial "solution". There are few things that evoke more immediately the idea of perfection than a tree which has had time and space to achieve fullness of growth; and in virtue of the outward and upward pointing of its branches, it is not a closed perfection but an open one. The Qur'ān uses this very symbol of itself; that is, of the "good word", being itself the best of good words. *Hast thou not seen how God coineth a similitude? A good word is as a good tree, its root firm, its branches in heaven, giving its fruits at every due season by the leave of its Lord. And God coineth similitudes for men that they may remember* (XIV, 24-25). These last words bring us straight to our theme, for the truth to be remembered here, with the help of the tree as reminder, is precisely the non-finite nature of the Qur'ān. A Qur'ān recitation must not be thought of as limited to this world for it has repercussions up to the Heavens, where its "fruits" await the believer. Otherwise expressed, the Qur'ān uses the symbol of the tree so that it may liberate itself from being subject, in the awareness or in the subconsciousness of the believer, to the illusion that it is just one book among other books. It may thus be said to point a way for the illuminator,[4] telling him how to set free from the finite its

[4] It goes without saying that this reference here is not to every artist or craftsman but to the small minority of "founder-artists" whoever they may have been. Once the tradition had been established it would simply have been followed, with more or less understanding but without question, by generation after generation. Nor does this chapter claim, by putting certain trains of thought into the minds of its readers, to be reproducing the mental processes of the pioneers themselves. Inspiration tends to fold up thought; and all that the following paragraphs can presume to do is to note some of the more obvious relevancies of Qur'ān illumination to the Book it illuminates, in the knowledge that sacred art is providentially, by definition, the most strictly relevant art in the world. It would be beside the point and void of interest to say that such and such an artisan may well not have had some particular intention or other. At this artistic level, any correspondence that strikes the intelligence of one who contemplates the work in question is the proof of an intention *in divinis*.

Infinite Presence. We need not therefore be surprised that one of the most fundamental ornaments of Qur'ān illumination should be arboreal, namely the palmette, *shujayrah* or "little tree",[5] nor need we doubt that it is meant to stand for the good word. The *sūrah* heading consists of the title of the *sūrah*, the number of its verses, and the word *makkiyyah* or *madaniyyah* to show whether it was revealed in Mecca or Medina. Written in a script deliberately different from that of the Qur'ān itself, it is usually set in a wide rectangular panel, often richly framed with gold and other colours, and with an arabesque as background to the letters. This heading is prolonged into the outer margin by means of a palmette which points horizontally towards the paper's edge and which achieves for the eye the effect of a liberation of incalculable scope.[6]

The above quoted verse of the tree is immediately concerned with man's final ends, with the celestial "fruits" of the earthly action of reciting the holy book, which is considered here above all as a power of reintegration. This aspect of the *sūrah* palmette is often confirmed by an upward pointing marginal palmette which corresponds to the marginal "tree of life" in the Qur'ān manuscripts of Andalusia and North West Africa. But the ascending movements of return cannot be considered independently of the original descent. The Qur'ānic text is equally insistent upon both movements. In Arabic the word for revelation, *tanzīl*, means literally "a sending down"; and the reader is again and again reminded that what he is reading is no less than a Divine Message sent down directly to the Prophet.

[5] There are two main varieties of this symbol; the heavier and more complicated form with its cumbersome protruding petals or wings had a period of ascendancy, fortunately never exclusive, from the third/ninth to the fifth/eleventh century. But it was eventually superseded altogether by the simpler and more stylized palmette which is incomparably the more effective, and which itself may be subdivided into two varieties according to whether its roundness be suddenly or gradually tapered to its lobe. [For the original references to full-color plates meticulously supervised by the author, readers may want to refer to the original *Splendours of Qur'ān Calligraphy and Illumination.*—Ed.]

[6] The importance of this ornament is tragically demonstrated whenever, as is all too often the case, a binder in trimming the pages of an old manuscript has trimmed away the lobes of the palmettes. How little has been lost, and yet how much!

There are three main aspects which the artist has an obligation to convey if his art is to be relevant: the Qur'ān as a descending power of revelation; the Qur'ān as a mysterious Presence of the Infinite in the finite; and the Qur'ān as an ascending power of reintegration. The tree as we experience it on earth is a symbol of the last two of these aspects; but there is one verse in which the tree may be said to point in the direction of descent. *If all the trees in the earth were pens, and if the sea eked out by seven seas more were ink, the Words of God could not be written out to the end* (XXXI, 27). Here the tree plays a negative part; but to be chosen for mention in this context has its positive aspect. The verse tells us, generally speaking, that earthly things are as nothing compared with what they symbolize; but at the same time it implies inescapably that the tree, for the purpose of representing heavenly implements of transcription, is a supreme symbol. One of the chapters of the Qur'ān, *Sūrat al-Qalam* (LXVIII), is named after the Celestial Pen, which is also mentioned, in the very first verses (XCVI, 1-5) revealed to the Prophet, as the instrument through which the revelation was made.

The Prophet himself said, "The first thing God created was the pen. He created the tablet and said to the pen, 'Write!' And the pen replied, 'What shall I write?' He said, 'Write My knowledge of My creation till the day of resurrection.' Then the pen traced what had been ordained." There are thus three levels to be considered. The Qur'ān as men know it is an adapted form, reduced beyond all measure, of what is written on the Tablet, which itself only refers to creation and not to God's Self-Knowledge. It is to this highest level, that of the Divine Omniscience, that *the Words of God* refer in the above-quoted Qur'ānic verse. It is none the less an essential point of doctrine that the Qur'ān as revealed to men, not to speak of the Tablet, contains mysteriously everything, being no less than the Uncreated Word of God. We will come back later to this apparent contradiction.

From the point of view of descent, it is this instrument that the *sūrah* palmette may be said to portray. Nor does this constitute a change of meaning inasmuch as the Pen, no less than its "consort" the Guarded Tablet, is in the direct line of the descent of the Revelation and therefore virtually identical with it. It is simply a question of two directions, and the "neutral" horizontality of the palmette allows for its application to both.

The verse of the tree speaks of *its branches in Heaven.* The palmette in the margin is as near to a direct illustration as this art will allow. In other words, it is a reminder that the reading or chanting of the Qur'ān is the virtual starting point of a limitless vibration, a wave that ultimately breaks on the shore of Eternity; and it is above all that shore that is signified by the margin, towards which all the movement of the painting, in palmette, finial, crenellation and flow of arabesque is directed.

Another symbol which expresses both perfection and infinitude, and which is intimately, though not apparently, related to the "tree",[7] is the rayed sun. Again and again the Qur'ān refers to itself as light[8] or as being radiant with light; and many periods of Qur'ān illumination can give us examples of marginal verse counts inscribed in circles whose circumferences are rayed or scalloped. The solar roundels, *shamsah* or "little sun" is used also of stellar ornaments, occasionally replace the rosettes which divide the verses; and the rosettes themselves are often made luminous with gold. Sometimes the symbolism of light is directly combined with that of the tree, as when a solar roundel figures inside the *sūrah* palmette,[9] or when the palmette itself is rounded and rayed, with its lobe replaced by an outward pointing finial. There are other variants of the same combination; and what has already been said about the two directions applies equally here, for the Revelation is not only a shining of light from the next world, but it also throws its light towards the next world by way of guidance; nor can this reversed reintegrating light be separated from the soul's spiritual aspiration, which is likewise figured by everything that points to the beyond.

Related in more ways than one to the tree are the arabesques with which the palmettes, the roundels and other marginal ornaments are filled, and which often serve as a

[7] For this relationship, see René Guénon, *The Symbolism of the Cross* (London, Luzac, 1958), p. 52; and Martin Lings, *Symbol and Archetype* (Cambridge, Quinta Essentia, 1997), pp. 90–94.

[8] For example, *We have sent down to you a clear light* (IV, 174) and *We have made it a light whereby We guide whom We willI* (XLII, 52).

[9] These luminous palmettes are suggestive of another Qur'ānic tree, the one that feeds the lamp that is the symbol of the Divine Light of which the Qur'ān itself is an aspect: *a sacred olive tree that is neither of the East nor of the West; its oil well-nigh blazeth in splendour though the fire have not touched it* (XXIV, 35).

surrounding frame for the main part of the page. Being vineal rather than arboreal, the arabesque does not by its nature point out a way, though it can give a clear indication of tendency, and that is certainly one of its main functions in Qur'ān illumination. At the same time, in virtue of its elusiveness, it constitutes in itself a mysterious and supraformal presence. It is also, like the tree, a vital presence and, where it is a background for the script, it serves to heighten the effect of the letters as vehicles of the Living Word. Moreover, as a portrayal of rhythm, by its constant repetition of the same motives, in particular the small palmette, at regular intervals, it suggests rhythmic Qur'ān recitations, which take place, we are told, not only on earth but throughout all the degrees of the universe.[10]

In this context, mention must also be made of the symbolism of certain numbers and their geometrical equivalents. Nine and three, like the circle and the triangle, are worldwide symbols of Heaven, their earthly complements being the number four and the square or the rectangle. The rectangular setting of the Qur'ānic text thus signifies the terrestrial state which has been penetrated by the Revelation; and in most periods we find examples of a semicircular or triangular anse attached to the outer or "beyond" side of the rectangle, or to its summit. In either case it can only be the celestial dimension of the text which is indicated. The exact architectural equivalents are in the two varieties of *qubbah*, the hemispherical dome of the Eastern mosque and its pyramidal equivalent in the Maghrib.

It may be asked why, if the founders of the tradition desired certain effects, they did not use more directly imperative means. To give the impression of light, for example, why did they not surround their ornaments and the text itself with broad golden rays, instead of the delicate antenna like finials which, though occasionally red, are more often black or brown or blue? The answer is not only that the illuminator does not wish to "raise his voice" above that of the Qur'ān but also that he particularly wishes to avoid any such obviousness as might cause a premature crystallizing of the imagination and thus fatally arrest the soul from continuing to penetrate more

[10] The Qur'ān mentions the angels as reciting its verses (XXXVII, 3). For a profound and relevant comment on this passage, see René Guénon, "The Language of the Birds" in *Fundamental Symbols* (Cambridge, Quinta Essentia, 1995), p. 39.

deeply in the required direction. Inevitably, the more obvious impression of light has been attempted; analogously, there is a tenth/sixteenth century Western Qur'ān[11] in which the illuminator has replaced the palmettes by naturalistic tree branches. But such experiments merely serve to make one appreciate all the more the subtle and incalculable power of the traditional stylised symbol, which the craftsman has only to follow, "blindly" or not, as the case may be.

It must also be remembered that the whole purpose of illumination is to recall the higher or deeper dimension of the text. The relationship between the *hidden book* and the fully revealed Qur'ān is one of majesty to beauty, of contraction, or reserve, to expansion; and however paradoxical it may seem, illumination, being there to remind us of the *hidden book*, has an overall function of majesty in relation to the beauty of the text. This holds good[12] even when the illumination is at its most beautiful and when the text is written in a particularly majestic style. In plate 144,[13] by way of example, the Qur'ān itself is written in one of the larger cursive scripts. This is majesty in the domain of beauty, that is, of bountiful display. By contrast, the *sūrah* heading (after the four opening lines of the page) in the Eastern derivative of Kufic may be said to represent beauty in the domain of majestic reserve. As such, this inscription strikes the keynote not only of the rest of the illumination on the page but of Qur'ān illumination as a whole. No sacred art can be without its element of mystery; that cryptic, almost enigmatic reserve in virtue of which, while giving so much, it withholds more than it gives.

Colour is used towards the same ends as form. Gold was the initial element; and after a short period of fluctuation, that is, by the middle of the fourth/tenth century, blue had been given a marked precedence over both green and red, and it was soon raised to the level of parity with gold in the East, whereas in the West gold retained its original supremacy with blue as second. The importance of these two colours can be gauged by

[11] 1522 in the Chester Beatty Library, Dublin. See A. J. Arberry, *The Koran Illuminated* (Dublin, Hodges Figgis, 1967).

[12] It could almost be said that when it ceases to hold good, then is the beginning of decadence.

[13] [This reference is to folios 302v–303r of a Mamluk style Qur'ān of the 9th/15th century. Page dimensions: 46.5 × 34 cm.—Ed.]

the fact that whatever extra pigments might be added, it was nearly always in a subordinate capacity. Moreover, in almost every style and age one is likely to find a Qur'ān in which the illuminations consist exclusively of blue and gold, and this same exclusiveness is liable to be a feature of certain pages in any Qur'ān even where polychrome illuminations are to be found on other pages.

Blue is the colour of the Infinite, which is identical with Mercy, for *My Mercy embraceth all things* (VII, 156). The great symbol of this Infinitude is the all-surrounding sky. The relevant Divine Name, *al-Raḥmān*, the first of the two Names of Mercy, has been well translated "the Infinitely Good", for it expresses the essential "roots" of Mercy. At this level, Mercy, Revelation and Religion are one. We have here what might be called the "feminine" aspect of Providence[14] or more precisely the "maternal" aspect. Thus the supreme archetype of Revelation is termed the *mother of the book* (XIII, 39) and in this connection it may be noted that the most simple word formed from those letters which have the basic meaning of mercy, *rā', ḥā', mīm*, is *raḥim*, "womb".[15] Closely related to *al-Raḥmān* is the Name *al-Muḥīt*, the All-Embracing, and by extension, the word *muḥīt* also means "ocean".[16]

As a symbol of Infinite Mercy, the sea is, in fact, second only to the sky itself, whose colour it takes and assimilates; and in particular connection with the All-Embracing, another feature of Qur'ān illumination must be mentioned; so prevalent that many have suspected a "superstition", namely the use of blue for the outermost edge, both in individual ornaments and where there is a border to the text. One has the impression of an unwritten law that blue must have the last word; and enough has been said to make it clear why such a circumscription is no limitation.

[14] This manner of speaking must not be taken too exclusively since Truth and Wisdom belong to this aspect and blue is one of their symbols, but they cannot be called specifically "feminine".

[15] Not unanalogous is the iconographical connection in Christianity between the colour blue and the Virgin Mary, who may be considered as the supreme human manifestation of the Principle in question.

[16] Also relevant is the connection, we might almost say symbolic identity in certain respects, between Mary and the sea.

If blue liberates by Infinitude, gold liberates because, like the sun, it is a symbol of the Spirit and therefore virtually transcends the whole world of forms. Gold, by its very nature, "escapes" from form to the point that a calligrapher writing in gold has to outline his letters with black in order to make them formally effective. As the colour of light, gold is, like yellow, intrinsically a symbol of knowledge. Extrinsically, it means teaching or manifestation. Blue in the presence of gold is therefore Mercy inclined to reveal itself.

This brings us to the second Name of Mercy, *al-Raḥīm*, which signifies Mercy manifested and which we translate "the All-Merciful" since linguistically it is an intensive form of *rāḥim*, merciful, though less intensive than *raḥmān*. If it be asked why the illuminators did not revert from blue to green,[17] which is the colour of Mercy manifested (being the result of the mixture of the colours of intrinsic Mercy and of Light), it might be answered that the Qur'ānic text itself takes the place of green. This is no reason why green should not make a parallel appearance. But in his overall fidelity to blue, which takes religion back to its first origins, the illuminator assents to a typically Islamic ellipsis whereby the whole process of revelation is as it were folded back into its Principle, with nothing between primary cause and ultimate effect. Islam loves to dwell on the roots of things; the chapter that is named after the "cause" in question, *Sūrat al-Raḥmān*, begins with an ellipsis in the opposite direction: *The Infinitely Good taught the Qur'ān* (LV, 1-2). To say that blue and gold are the equivalents of the subject and the verb of this sentence is to sum up all that has so far been said about colour in Qur'ān illumination.

Blue and gold are opposite enough to enhance each other greatly. But in the triple domain of primary colour, perfect balance cannot come by two, but only by three. To take two of the colours and to leave out the third or to reduce it to being a mere auxiliary means that the scales will necessarily be tipped one way or another; but this can be a way of gaining or heightening a required effect. Gold has the exaltation to balance the depth of blue, but not being the hot colour, its mere

[17] Astrologically, the color blue corresponds to the planet Jupiter, "the greater benefic", and green to Venus, "the lesser benefic"; and there is a certain analogy between these two principles and the two Names of Mercy *al-Raḥmān* and *al-Raḥīm*.

warmth does not level out the coldness of blue. The resulting overall coolness does much to contribute to the total effect of holiness.[18]

Of all the features of illumination so far touched on, fine examples are to be found considerably before the close of the seventh/thirteenth century. That date is mentioned here chiefly because it marks the end of an era, or more precisely because the end which had in fact taken place some fifty years previously had had time by the turn of the century to make itself felt in the domain of art. Moreover, for reasons not unconnected with what brought the era to a close, the year 700/1300 or thereabouts forms a kind of barrier on the far side of which Qur'ān manuscripts are relatively rare. Inestimable treasures must have been destroyed by the Mongol invaders who sacked Baghdad[19] in 656/1258, perhaps even more than had already been destroyed in the course of the Crusades. But, as if by compensation, the new era seems to have brought with it a fresh impetus, which had its effect on Qur'ān calligraphy, but which made itself felt above all in illumination, particularly in illuminated frontispieces, a highly important feature which has been deliberately excluded from this chapter in order to be treated more fully later.

[18] The phrase "coolness of the eyes" means "delight" in Arabic and is especially connected with the joys of Paradise. But needless to say, red is also related to spiritual joy, and not unrelated to holiness. The predominance in question is simply a stress laid on a particular aspect. Nor can there ever have been a formal ruling on the subject. Sometimes the illumination on a page is almost entirely red and gold; but such an exception is usually made up for on other pages of the same manuscript.

[19] For just over five hundred years, since 132/750, Baghdad had been the cultural and administrative centre of the Islamic world, but after thirty-four days of destruction it never reached this status again. None the less, Islam was able to absorb its conquerors. Some remarkable Qur'āns currently in Istanbul were commissioned by a direct descendent of Genghis Khan, whose grandson Hūlāgū was the destroyer of Baghdad.

Selections from *Muhammad: His Life Based on the Earliest Sources*

I
The House of God

The Book of Genesis tells us that Abraham was childless, without hope of children, and that one night God summoned him out of his tent and said to him: "Look now towards heaven, and count the stars if thou art able to number them." And as Abraham gazed up at the stars he heard the voice say: "So shall thy seed be."[1]

Abraham's wife Sarah was then seventy-six years old, he being eighty-five, and long past the age of child bearing, so she gave him her handmaid Hagar, an Egyptian, that he might take her as his second wife. But bitterness of feeling arose between the mistress and the handmaid, and Hagar fled from the anger of Sarah and cried out to God in her distress. And He sent to her an Angel with the message: "I will multiply thy seed exceedingly, that it shall not be numbered for multitude." The Angel also said to her: "Behold, thou art with child, and shalt bear a son, and shalt call his name Ishmael; because the Lord hath heard thy affliction."[2] Then Hagar returned to Abraham and Sarah and told them what the Angel had said; and when the birth took place, Abraham named his son Ishmael, which means "God shall hear".

When Abraham had reached his hundredth year, and Sarah was ninety years old, God spoke again to Abraham and promised him that Sarah also should bear him a son who must be called Isaac. Fearing that his elder son might thereby lose favour in the sight of God, Abraham prayed: "*O that Ishmael*

[1] 15:5.

[2] 16:10-11.

might live before Thee!" And God said to him: "*As for Ishmael, I have heard thee. Behold, I have blessed him ... and I will make him a great nation. But My covenant will I establish with Isaac, which Sarah shall bear unto thee at this set time in the next year.*"[3]

Sarah gave birth to Isaac and it was she herself who suckled him; and when he was weaned she told Abraham that Hagar and her son must no longer remain in their household. And Abraham was deeply grieved at this, on account of his love for Ishmael; but again God spoke to him, and told him to follow the counsel of Sarah, and not to grieve; and again He promised him that Ishmael should be blessed.

Not one but two great nations were to look back to Abraham as their Father—two great nations, that is, two guided powers, two instruments to work the Will of Heaven, for God does not promise as a blessing that which is profane, nor is there any greatness before God except greatness in the Spirit. Abraham was thus the fountainhead of two spiritual streams, which must not flow together, but each in its own course; and he entrusted Hagar and Ishmael to the blessing of God and the care of His Angels in the certainty that all would be well with them.

Two spiritual streams, two religions, two worlds for God; two circles, therefore two centres. A place is never holy through the choice of man, but because it has been chosen in Heaven. There were two holy centres within the orbit of Abraham: one of these was at hand, the other perhaps he did not yet know; and it was to the other that Hagar and Ishmael were guided, in a barren valley of Arabia, some forty camel days south of Canaan. The valley was named Becca, some say on account of its narrowness: hills surround it on all sides except for three passes, one to the north, one to the south, and one opening towards the Red Sea which is fifty miles to the west. The Books do not tell us how Hagar and her son reached Becca;[4] perhaps some travelers took care of them, for the valley was on one of the great caravan routes, sometimes called "the incense route," because perfumes and incense and such wares were brought that way from South Arabia to the Mediterranean; and no doubt Hagar was guided to leave the caravan, once the place

[3] 17:20-21.

[4] According to the traditions of the Arabs, accepted by most Muslims, Ishmael was still a babe in arms when Hagar brought him to the valley of Becca.

was reached. It was not long before both mother and son were overcome by thirst, to the point that Hagar feared Ishmael was dying. According to the traditions of their descendants, he cried out to God from where he lay in the sand, and his mother stood on a rock at the foot of a nearby eminence to see if any help was in sight. Seeing no one, she hastened to another point of vantage, but from there likewise not a soul was to be seen. Half distraught, she passed seven times in all between the two points, until at the end of her seventh course, as she sat for rest on the further rock, the Angel spoke to her. In the words of Genesis: *And God heard the voice of the lad; and the angel of God called to Hagar out of heaven and said to her: What aileth thee, Hagar? Fear not, for God hath heard the voice of the lad where he is. Arise and lift up the lad and hold him in thy hand, for I will make him a great nation. And God opened her eyes, and she saw a well of water.*[5]

The water was a spring which God caused to well up from the sand at the touch of Ishmael's heel; and thereafter the valley soon became a halt for caravans by reason of the excellence and abundance of the water; and the well was named Zamzam.

As to Genesis, it is the book of Isaac and his descendants, not of Abraham's other line. Of Ishmael it tells us: *And God was with the lad; and he grew and dwelt in the wilderness and became an archer.*[6] After that it scarcely mentions his name, except to inform us that the two brothers Isaac and Ishmael together buried their father in Hebron, and that some years later Esau married his cousin, the daughter of Ishmael. But there is indirect praise of Ishmael and his mother in the Psalm that opens *How amiable are Thy tabernacles, O Lord of hosts*, and that tells of the miracle of Zamzam as having been caused by their passing through the valley: *Blessed is the man whose strength is in Thee; in whose heart are the ways of them who passing through the valley of Baca make it a well.*[7]

When Hagar and Ishmael reached their destination Abraham had still seventy-five years to live, and he visited his son in the holy place to which Hagar had been guided. The

[5] 21: 17–20.

[6] Ibid.

[7] Psalm 84: 5–6.

Qur'ān tells us that God showed him the exact site, near to the well of Zamzam, upon which he and Ishmael must build a sanctuary;[8] and they were told how it must be built. Its name, Kaᶜbah, cube, is in virtue of its shape which is approximately cubic; its four corners are towards the four points of the compass. But the most holy object in that holy place is a celestial stone which, it is said, was brought by an Angel to Abraham from the nearby hill Abū Qubays, where it had been preserved ever since it had reached the earth. "It descended from Paradise whiter than milk, but the sins of the sons of Adam made it black."[9] This black stone they built into the eastern corner of the Kaᶜbah; and when the sanctuary was completed, God spoke again to Abraham and bade him institute the rite of the Pilgrimage to Becca—or Mecca, as it later came to be called: *Purify My House for those who go the rounds of it and who stand beside it and bow and make prostration. And proclaim unto men the pilgrimage, that they may come unto thee on foot and on every lean camel out of every deep ravine.*[10]

Now Hagar had told Abraham of her search for help, and he made it part of the rite of the Pilgrimage that the pilgrims should pass seven times between Ṣafā and Marwah, for so the two eminences between which she had passed had come to be named.

And later Abraham prayed, perhaps in Canaan, looking around him at the rich pastures and fields of corn and wheat: *Verily I have settled a line of mine offspring in a tilthless valley at Thy Holy House.... Therefore incline unto them men's hearts, and sustain them with fruits that they may be thankful.*[11]

[8] XXII, 26.

[9] Saying of the Prophet, Tirmidhī VII, 49.

[10] Q. XXII: 26-27.

[11] Q. XIV: 37.

VIII
The Desert

It was the custom of all the great families of Arab towns to send their sons, soon after their birth, into the desert, to be suckled and weaned and spend part of their childhood amongst one of the Bedouin tribes. Nor had Mecca any reason for being an exception, since epidemics were not infrequent and the rate of infant mortality was high. But it was not only the desert's fresh air that they wished their sons to imbibe. That was for their bodies, but the desert had also its bounty for souls. Quraysh had only recently taken to the sedentary life. Until Quṣayy had told them to build themselves houses round the Sanctuary they had been more or less nomadic. Fixed settlements were perhaps inevitable, but they were dangerous. Their ancestors' way of life had been the nobler one, the life of tent-dwellers, often on the move. Nobility and freedom were inseparable, and the nomad was free. In the desert a man was conscious of being the lord of space, and in virtue of that lordship he escaped in a sense from the domination of time. By striking camp he sloughed off his yesterdays; and tomorrow seemed less of a fatality if its where as well as its when had yet to come. But the townsman was a prisoner; and to be fixed in one place—yesterday, today, tomorrow—was to be a target for time, the miner of all things. Towns were places of corruption. Sloth and slovenliness lurked in the shadow of their walls, ready to take the edge off a man's alertness and vigilance. Everything decayed there, even language, one of man's most precious possessions. Few of the Arabs could read, but beauty of speech was a virtue which all Arab parents desired for their children. A man's worth was largely assessed by his eloquence, and the crown of eloquence was poetry. To have a great poet in the family was indeed something to be proud of; and the best poets were nearly always from one or another of the desert tribes, for it was in the desert that the spoken language was nearest to poetry.

So the bond with the desert had to be renewed in every generation—fresh air for the breast, pure Arabic for the tongue, freedom for the soul; and many of the sons of Quraysh were kept as long as eight years in the desert, so that it might make a lasting impression upon them, though a lesser number of years was enough for that.

Some of the tribes had a high reputation for nursing and rearing children, and amongst these were the Bani Saʿd ibn Bakr, an outlying branch of Hawāzin, whose territory lay to the south-east of Mecca. Āminah was in favour of entrusting her son to the care of a woman of this tribe. They came periodically to Quraysh for nurselings, and some were expected shortly. Their journey to Mecca on this occasion was described in after-years by one of their number, Ḥalīmah, the daughter of Abū Dhuʿayb, who was accompanied by her husband, Ḥārith, and a recently born son of their own whom she was nursing. "It was a year of drought," she said, "and we had nothing left. I set forth on a grey she-ass of mine, and we had with us an old she-camel which could not yield one drop of milk. We were kept awake all night by our son who was wailing for hunger, for I had not enough in my breasts to feed him; and that ass of mine was so weak and so emaciated that I often kept the others waiting."

She told how they went on their way with nothing to hope for except a fall of rain which would enable the camel and the ass to graze enough for their udders to swell a little, but by the time they reached Mecca no rain had fallen. Once there they set about looking for nurselings, and Āminah offered her son first to one and then to another until finally she had tried them all and they had all refused. "That", said Ḥalīmah, "was because we hoped for some favour from the boy's father. 'An orphan!' we said. 'What will his mother and his grandfather be able to do for us?'" Not that they would have wanted direct payment for their services, since it was considered dishonourable for a woman to take a fee for suckling a child. The recompense they hoped for, though less direct and less immediate, was of a far wider scope. This interchange of benefits between townsman and nomad was in the nature of things, for each was poor where the other was rich, and rich where the other was poor. The nomad had the age-old God-given way of life to offer, the way of Abel. The sons of Cain—for it was Cain who built the first villages—had possessions and power. The advantage for the Bedouin was to make an enduring link with one of the great families. The foster-mother gained a new son who would look on her as a second mother and feel a filial duty to her for the rest of his life. He would also feel himself a brother to her own children. Nor was the relationship merely a nominal one. The Arabs hold that the breast is one of the channels of heredity and that a suckling drinks qualities into his nature from the nurse who suckles him. But little or nothing could be expected from the foster-child himself until he grew up, and meantime his father could normally be relied on to fulfil the duties of his son. A grandfather was too remote; and in this case they would have known that ʿAbd al-Muṭṭalib was an old man who could not reasonably be expected to live much longer. When he died, his sons, not his grandson, would be his heirs. As to Āminah, she was poor; and as to the boy himself, his father had been too young to have acquired wealth. He had left his son no more than five camels, a small flock of sheep and goats, and one slave girl. ʿAbd Allāh's son was indeed a child of one of the great families; but he was by far the poorest nurseling that these women were offered that year.

On the other side, though the foster-parents were not expected to be rich, they must not be too poverty-stricken, and it was evident that Ḥalīmah and her husband were poorer than any of their companions. Whenever the choice lay between her and another, the other was preferred and chosen; and it was not long before every one of the Bani Saʿd women except Ḥalīmah had been entrusted with a babe. Only the poorest nurse was without a nurseling; and only the poorest nurseling was without a nurse.

"When we decided to leave Mecca," said Ḥalīmah, "I told my husband: 'I hate to return in the company of my friends without having taken a babe to suckle. I shall go to that orphan and take him.' 'As thou wilt,' he said. 'It may be that God will bless us in him.' So I went and took him, for no reason save that I could find none but him. I carried him back to where our mounts were stationed, and no sooner had I put him in my bosom than my breasts overflowed with milk for him. He drank his fill, and with him his foster-brother drank likewise his fill. Then they both slept; and my husband went to that old she-camel of ours, and lo! her udders were full. He milked her and drank of her milk and I drank with him until we could drink no more and our hunger was satisfied. We spent the best of nights, and in the morning my husband said to me: 'By God, Ḥalīmah, it is a blessed creature that thou hast taken.' 'That is indeed my hope,' I said. Then we set out, and I rode my ass and carried him with me on her back. She outstripped the whole troop, nor could any of their asses keep pace with her. 'Confound thee!' they said to me, 'Wait for us! Is not this ass of thine the same ass that thou didst come on?' 'Yea by God,' I said, 'she is the very same.' 'Some wonder hath befallen her,' they said.

"We reached our tents in the Bani Saʿd country, and I know of no place on God's earth more barren than that then was. But after we brought him to live with us, my flock would come home to me replete at every eventide and full of milk. We milked them and drank, when others had no drop of milk; and our neighbours would say to their shepherds: 'Out upon you, go graze your flocks where he grazeth his,' meaning my shepherd. Yet still their flocks came hungry home, yielding no milk, while mine came well fed, with milk in plenty; and we ceased not to enjoy this increase and this bounty from God until the babe's two years had passed, and I weaned him.[1]

"He was growing well," she continued, "and none of the other boys could match him for growth. By the time he was two years old he was a well made child, and we took him again to his mother, although we were eager that he should stay with us for the blessings he brought us. So I said to her: 'Leave my little son with me until he grow stronger, for I fear lest he be stricken with the plague of Mecca.' And we importuned her until she gave him once more into our keeping and we brought him again to our home.

"One day, several months after our return, when he and his brother were with some lambs of ours behind our tents, his brother came running to us and said: 'That Qurayshite brother of mine! Two men clothed in white have taken him and have laid him down and opened his breast and they are stirring it with their hands.' So I and his father went to him and we found him standing, but his face was very pale. We drew him to us and said: 'What aileth thee, my son?' He said: 'Two men

[1] I.I. 105.

clothed in white came to me and laid me down and opened my breast and searched it for I know not what.'"[2]

Ḥalīmah and Ḥārith her husband looked this way and that, but there was no sign of the men; nor was there any blood or any wound to bear out what the two boys had said. No amount of questioning would make them take back their words or modify them in any respect. Yet there was not even the trace of a scar on the breast of their foster-child nor any blemish on his perfect little body. The only unusual feature was in the middle of his back between his shoulders: a small but distinct oval mark where the flesh was slightly raised, as it were from the impress of a cupping glass; but that had been there at his birth.

In after-years he was able to describe the event more fully: "There came unto me two men, clothed in white, with a gold basin full of snow. Then they laid hold upon me, and splitting open my breast they brought forth my heart. This likewise they split open and took from it a black clot which they cast away. Then they washed my heart and my breast with the snow."[3] He also said: "Satan toucheth every son of Adam the day his mother beareth him, save only Mary and her son."[4]

[2] Ibid.

[3] I.S. I/1, 96.

[4] B. LX, 54.

X
Baḥīrà the Monk

The fortunes of ʿAbd al-Muṭṭalib had waned during the last part of his life, and what he left at his death amounted to no more than a small legacy for each of his sons. Some of them, especially ʿAbd al-ʿUzzah, who was known as Abū Lahab, had acquired wealth of their own. But Abū Ṭālib was poor, and his nephew felt obliged to do what he could to earn his own livelihood. This he did mostly by pasturing sheep and goats, and he would thus spend day after day alone in the hills above Mecca or on the slopes of the valleys beyond. But his uncle took him sometimes with him on his travels and on one occasion when Muḥammad was nine, or according to others twelve, they went with a merchant caravan as far as Syria. At Bostra, near one of the halts where the Meccan caravan always stopped, there was a cell which had been lived in by a Christian monk for generation after generation. When one died, another took his place and inherited all that was in the cell including some old manuscripts. Amongst these was one which contained the prediction of the coming of a Prophet to the Arabs; and Baḥīrà, the monk who now lived in the cell, was well versed in the contents of this book, which interested him all the more because, like Waraqah, he too felt that the coming of the prophet would be in his lifetime.

He had often seen the Meccan caravan approach and halt not far from his cell, but as this one came in sight his attention was struck by something the like of which he had never seen before: a small low-hanging cloud moved slowly above their heads so that it was always between the sun and one or two of the travellers. With intense interest he watched them draw near. But suddenly his interest changed to amazement, for as soon as they halted the cloud ceased to move, remaining stationary over the tree beneath which they took shelter, while the tree itself lowered its branches over them, so that they were doubly in the shade. Baḥīrà knew that such a portent, though unobtrusive, was of high significance. Only some great spiritual presence could explain it, and immediately he thought of the expected Prophet. Could it be that he had at last come, and was amongst these travellers?

The cell had recently been stocked with provisions, and putting together all he had, he sent word to the caravan: "Men of Quraysh, I have prepared food for you, and I would that ye should come to me, every one of you, young and old, bondman and freeman." So they came to his cell, but despite what he had said they left Muḥammad to look after their camels and their baggage. As they approached, Baḥīrà scanned their faces one by one. But he could see nothing which corresponded to the description in his book, nor did there seem to be any man amongst them who was adequate to the greatness of the two miracles. Perhaps they had not all come. "Men of Quraysh," he said, "let none of you stay behind." "There is not one that hath been left behind," they answered, "save only a boy, the youngest of us all." "Treat him not so" said Baḥīrà, "but call him to come, and let him be present with us at this meal." Abū Ṭālib and the others reproached themselves for their thoughtlessness. "We are indeed to blame," said one of them, "that the son of ʿAbd Allāh should have been left behind and not brought to share this feast with us," whereupon he went to him and embraced him and brought him to sit with the people.

One glance at the boy's face was enough to explain the miracles to Baḥīrà; and looking at him attentively throughout the meal he noticed many features of both face and body which corresponded to what was in his book. So when they had finished eating, the monk went to his youngest guest and asked him questions about his way of life and about his sleep, and about his affairs in general. Muḥammad readily informed him of these things for the man was venerable and the questions were courteous and benevolent; nor did he hesitate to draw off his cloak when finally the monk asked if he might see his back. Baḥīrà had already felt certain, but now he was doubly so, for there, between his shoulders, was the very mark he expected to see, the seal of prophethood even as it was described in his book, in the selfsame place. He turned to Abū Ṭālib: "What kinship hath this boy with thee?" he said. "He is my son," said Abū Ṭālib. "He is not thy son," said the monk; "it cannot be that this boy's father is alive." "He is my brother's son," said

Abū Ṭālib. "Then what of his father?" said the monk. "He died," said the other, "when the boy was still in his mother's womb." "That is the truth," said Baḥīrà. "Take thy brother's son back to his country, and guard him against the Jews, for by God, if they see him and know of him that which I know, they will contrive evil against him. Great things are in store for this brother's son of thine."

XIII
The Household

The bridegroom left his uncle's house and went to live in the house of his bride. As well as being a wife, Khadījah was also a friend to her husband, the sharer of his inclinations and ideals to a remarkable degree. Their marriage was wondrously blessed, and fraught with great happiness, though not without sorrows of bereavement. She bore him six children, two sons and four daughters. Their eldest child was a son named Qāsim, and Muḥammad came to be known as Abū'l-Qāsim, the father of Qāsim; but the boy died before his second birthday. The next child was a daughter whom they named Zaynab; and she was followed by three other daughters, Ruqayyah, Umm Kulthūm, and Fāṭimah, and finally by another short-lived son.

On the day of his marriage, Muḥammad set free Barakah, the faithful slave he had inherited from his father; and on the same day Khadījah made him a gift of one of her own slaves, a youth of fifteen named Zayd. As to Barakah, they married her to a man of Yathrib to whom she bore a son, after whom she came to be known as Umm Ayman, the mother of Ayman. As to Zayd, he and some other youths had recently been bought at the great fair of ʿUkāẓ by Khadījah's nephew Ḥakīm, the son of her brother Ḥizām; and the next time his aunt visited him Ḥakīm had sent for his newly acquired slaves and invited her to choose one of them for herself. It was Zayd that she had chosen.

Zayd was proud of his ancestry: his father Ḥārithah was of the great northern tribe of Kalb whose territory lay on the plains between Syria and Iraq: his mother was a woman of the no less illustrious neighbouring tribe of Ṭayy, one of whose chieftains at that time was the poet-knight Ḥātim, famous throughout Arabia for his chivalry and his fabulous generosity. Several years had now passed since Zayd had been taken by his mother to visit her family, and the village where they were staying had been raided by some horsemen of the Bani

Qayn, who had carried the boy off and sold him into slavery. Ḥārithah, his father, had searched for him in vain; nor had Zayd seen any travellers from Kalb who could take a message from him to his parents. But the Kaʿbah drew pilgrims from all parts of Arabia, and one day during the holy season, several months after he had become Muḥammad's slave, he saw some men and women of his own tribe and clan in the streets of Mecca. If he had seen them the previous year, his feelings would have been very different. He had yearned for such an encounter; yet now that it had at last come it placed him in a quandary. He could not deliberately leave his family in ignorance of his whereabouts. But what message could he send them? Whatever its gist, he knew, as a son of the desert, that nothing less than a poem would be adequate for such an occasion. He composed some verses which expressed something of his mind, but implied more than they expressed. Then he accosted the Kalbite pilgrims and, having told them who he was, he said: "Speak unto my family these lines, for well I know that they have sorrowed for me:

> Though I myself be far, yet take my words
> Unto my people: at the Holy House
> I dwell, amidst the places God hath hallowed.
> Set then aside the sorrows ye have grieved,
> Weary not camels, scouring the earth for me,
> For I, praise be to God, am in the best
> Of noble families, great in all its line."

When the pilgrims returned home with their tidings, Ḥārithah at once set off for Mecca with his brother, Kaʿb; and going to Muḥammad they begged him to allow them to ransom Zayd, for as high a price as he might ask. "Let him choose," said Muḥammad, "and if he choose you, he is yours without ransom; and if he choose me, I am not the man to set any other above him who chooseth me." Then he called Zayd and asked him if he knew the two men. "This is my father," said the youth, "and this is mine uncle." "Me thou knowest," said Muḥammad, "and thou hast seen my companionship unto thee, so choose thou between me and them." But Zayd's choice was already made and he said at once: "I would not choose any man in preference to thee. Thou art unto me as my father and my mother." "Out upon thee, O Zayd!" exclaimed the men of

Kalb. "Wilt thou choose slavery above freedom, and above thy father and thine uncle and thy family?" "It is even so," said Zayd, "for I have seen from this man such things that I could never choose another above him."

All further talk was cut short by Muḥammad, who now bade them come with him to the Kaʿbah; and, standing in the Ḥijr, he said in a loud voice: "All ye who are present, bear witness that Zayd is my son; I am his heir and he is mine."[1]

The father and the uncle had thus to return with their purpose unachieved. But the tale they had to tell their tribe, of the deep mutual love which had brought about this adoption, was not an inglorious one; and when they saw that Zayd was free, and established in honour, with what promised to be a high standing amongst the people of the Sanctuary such as might benefit his brothers and other kinsmen in years to come, they were reconciled and went their way without bitterness. From that day the new Hāshimite was known in Mecca as Zayd ibn Muḥammad.

Among the most frequent visitors to the house was Ṣafiyyah, now Khadījah's sister-in-law, the youngest of Muḥammad's aunts, younger even than himself; and with her she would bring her little son Zubayr, whom she had named after her elder brother. Zubayr was thus well acquainted with his cousins, the daughters of Muḥammad, from his earliest years. With Ṣafiyyah came also her faithful retainer Salmā, who had delivered Khadījah of all her children, and who considered herself to be one of the household.

As the years passed there were occasional visits from Ḥalīmah, Muḥammad's foster-mother, and Khadījah was always generous to her. One of these visits was at a time of severe and widespread drought through which Halīmah's flocks had been seriously depleted, and Khadījah made her a gift of forty sheep and a howdah camel.[2] This same drought, which produced something like a famine in the Ḥijāz, was the cause of a very important addition to the household.

Abū Ṭālib had more children than he could easily support, and the famine weighed heavily upon him. Muḥammad noticed this and felt that something should be done. The wealthiest of

[1] I.S. III/I, 28.

[2] I.S. I/I, 71.

his uncles was Abū Lahab but he was somewhat remote from the rest of the family, partly no doubt because he had never had any full brothers or sisters amongst them, being the only child of his mother. Muḥammad preferred to ask for the help of ʿAbbās, who could well afford it, being a successful merchant, and who was close to him because they had been brought up together. Equally close, or even closer, was ʿAbbās' wife, Umm al-Faḍl, who loved him dearly and who always made him welcome at their house. So he went to them now, and suggested that each of their two households should take charge of one of Abū Ṭālib's sons until his circumstances improved. They readily agreed, and the two men went to Abū Ṭālib, who said when he heard their proposal: "Do what ye will, but leave me ʿAqīl and Ṭālib." Jaʿfar was now about fifteen, and he was no longer the youngest of the family. His mother Fāṭimah had borne yet another son to Abū Ṭālib, some ten years younger, and they had named him ʿAlī. ʿAbbās said he would take charge of Jaʿfar, whereupon Muḥammad agreed to do the same for ʿAlī. It was about this time that Khadījah had borne her last child, a son named ʿAbd Allāh, but the babe had died at an even earlier age than Qāsim. In a sense he was replaced by ʿAlī, who was brought up as a brother to his four girl cousins, being about the same age as Ruqayyah and Umm Kulthūm, somewhat younger than Zaynab and somewhat older than Fāṭimah. These five, together with Zayd, formed the immediate family of Muḥammad and Khadījah. But there were many other relatives for whom he felt a deep attachment, and who have a part to play, large or small, in the history which here is chronicled.

Muḥammad's eldest uncle, Ḥārith, who was now dead, had left many children, and one of the sons, his cousin Abū Sufyān, was also his foster-brother, having been nursed by Ḥalīmah amongst the Bani Saʿd a few years after himself. People would say that Abū Sufyān was of those who bore the closest family likeness to Muḥammad; and amongst the characteristics they had in common was eloquence. But Abū Sufyān was a gifted poet—perhaps more gifted than his uncles Zubayr and Abū Ṭālib—whereas Muḥammad had never shown any inclination to compose a poem, though he was unsurpassed in his mastery of Arabic, and in the beauty of his speech.

In Abū Sufyān, who was more or less his own age, he had something of a friend and a companion. A little closer by blood kinship were the numerous children of his father's full sisters, that is, of ʿAbd al-Muṭṭalib's five eldest daughters. Amongst the eldest of these cousins were the children of his aunt Umaymah who had married a man named Jahsh, of the North Arabian tribe of Asad.[3] He had a house in Mecca, and it was possible for a man who lived amongst a tribe other than his own to become, by mutual alliance, the confederate of a member of that tribe, into which he thus became partly integrated, sharing up to a point its responsibilities and its privileges. Ḥarb, now chief of the Umayyad[4] branch of the clan of ʿAbdu Shams, had made Jahsh his confederate, so that by marrying him Umaymah could almost be said to have married a Shamsite. Their eldest son, named after her brother ʿAbd Allāh, was some twelve years younger than Muḥammad, and the two cousins had a great affection for each other. Umaymah's daughter Zaynab, several years younger than her brother, a girl of outstanding beauty, was included in this bond. Muḥammad had known and loved them both from their earliest childhood; and the same was true of others, in particular of Abū Salamah, the son of his aunt Barrah.

The powerful attraction which centred on al-Amīn—as he was so often called—went far beyond his own family; and Khadījah was with him at that centre, loved and honoured by all who came within the wide circle of their radiance, a circle which also included many of her own relations. Particularly close to her was her sister Hālah whose son, Abū'l-ʿĀs, was a frequent visitor to the house. Khadījah loved this nephew as if he had been her own son; and in due course—for she was continually sought after for help and advice—Hālah asked her to find a wife for him. When Khadījah consulted her husband, he suggested their daughter Zaynab, who would soon be of marriageable age; and when the time came they were married.

The hopes of Hāshim and Muṭṭalib—the two clans counted politically as one—were set upon Muḥammad for the recovery of their waning influence. But beyond all question of clan, he had come to be considered by the chiefs of Quraysh as one of the most capable men of the generation which would

[3] Asad ibn Khuzaymah, a tribe to the north-east of Mecca, whose territory lay at the northern extremity of the plain of Najd. It is not to be confused with the Quraysh clan of Asad.

[4] Named after Ḥarb's father Umayyah, son of ʿAbdu Shams.

succeed them and which would have, after them, the task of maintaining the honour and the power of the tribe throughout Arabia. The praise of al-Amīn was continually upon men's lips; and it was perhaps because of this that Abū Lahab now came to his nephew with the proposal that Ruqayyah and Umm Kulthūm should be betrothed to his sons ʿUtbah and ʿUtaybah. Muḥammad agreed, for he thought well of these two cousins, and the betrothals took place.

It was about this time that Umm Ayman became once more a member of the household. It is not recorded whether she returned as a widow, or whether her husband had divorced her. But she had no doubt that her place was there, and for his part Muḥammad would sometimes address her as "mother", and would say of her to others: "She is all that is left me of the people of my house."[5]

[5] I.S. VIII, 162.

XV
The First Revelations

It was not long after this outward sign of his authority and his mission[1] that he began to experience powerful inward signs, in addition to those of which he had already been conscious. When asked about these he spoke of "true visions" which came to him in his sleep and he said that they were "like the breaking of the light of dawn."[2] The immediate result of these visions was that solitude became dear to him, and he would go for spiritual retreats to a cave in Mount Ḥirā' not far from the outskirts of Mecca. There was nothing in this that would have struck Quraysh as particularly strange, for retreat had been a traditional practice amongst the descendants of Ishmael, and in each generation there had been one or two who would withdraw to a solitary place from time to time so that they might have a period that was uncontaminated by the world of men. In accordance with this age-old practice, Muḥammad would take with him provisions and consecrate a certain number of nights to the worship of God. Then he would return to his family, and sometimes on his return he took more provisions and went again to the mountain. During these few years it often happened that after he had left the town and was approaching his hermitage he would hear clearly the words "Peace be on thee, O Messenger of God",[3] and he would turn and look for the speaker but no one was in sight, and it was as if the words had come from a tree or a stone.

Ramadan was the traditional month of retreat, and it was one night towards the end of Ramadan, in his fortieth year, when he was alone in the cave, that there came to him an

[1] [This refers to previous chapter, "The Rebuilding of the Kaʿbah", where Muḥammad plays a key role by being entrusted to put in place the sacred black stone on the corner of the Kaʿbah.—Ed.]

[2] B.I., 3.

[3] I.I. 151.

Angel in the form of a man. The Angel said to him: "Recite!" and he said: "I am not a reciter," whereupon, as he himself told it, "the Angel took me and whelmed me in his embrace until he had reached the limit of mine endurance. Then he released me and said: 'Recite!' I said: 'I am not a reciter,' and again he took me and whelmed me in his embrace, and again when he had reached the limit of mine endurance he released me and said: 'Recite!', and again I said 'I am not a reciter.' Then a third time he whelmed me as before, then released me and said: *Recite in the name of thy Lord who created! He createth man from a clot of blood. Recite; and thy Lord is the Most Bountiful, He who hath taught by the pen, taught man what he knew not.*"[4]

He recited these words after the Angel, who thereupon left him; and he said; "It was as though the words were written on my heart."[5] But he feared that this might mean he had become a jinn-inspired poet or a man possessed. So he fled from the cave, and when he was half-way down the slope of the mountain he heard a voice above him saying: "O Muḥammad, thou art the Messenger of God, and I am Gabriel." He raised his eyes heavenwards and there was his visitant, still recognisable but now clearly an Angel, filling the whole horizon, and again he said: "O Muḥammad, thou art the Messenger of God, and I am Gabriel." The Prophet stood gazing at the Angel; then he turned away from him, but whichever way he looked the Angel was always there, astride the horizon, whether it was to the north, to the south, to the east or to the west. Finally the Angel turned away, and the Prophet descended the slope and went to his house. "Cover me! Cover me!"[6] he said to Khadījah as with still quaking heart he laid himself on his couch. Alarmed, yet not daring to question him, she quickly brought a cloak and spread it over him. But when the intensity of his awe had abated he told her what he had seen and heard; and having spoken to him words of reassurance she went to tell her cousin Waraqah, who was now an old man, and blind. "Holy! Holy!", he said. "By Him in whose hand is the soul of Waraqah, there hath come unto Muḥammad the greatest Nāmūs,[7] even he that

[4] Qur'ān XCVI, 1–5. B.I., 3.

[5] I.I. 153.

[6] B.I., 3.

[7] The Greek *Nomos*, in the sense of Divine Law or Scripture, here identified with the Angel of Revelation.

would come unto Moses. Verily Muḥammad is the Prophet of this people. Bid him rest assured." So Khadījah went home and repeated these words to the Prophet, who now returned in peace of mind to the cave, that he might fulfil the number of days he had dedicated to God for his retreat. When this was completed, he went straight to the Kaʿbah, according to his wont, and performed the rite of the rounds, after which he greeted the old and the blind Waraqah whom he had noticed amongst those who were sitting in the Mosque; and Waraqah said to him: "Tell me, O son of my brother, what thou hast seen and heard." The Prophet told him, and the old man said again what he had said to Khadījah. But this time he added: "Thou wilt be called a liar, and ill-treated, and they will cast thee out and make war upon thee; and if I live to see that day, God knoweth I will help His cause."[8] Then he leaned towards him and kissed his forehead, and the Prophet returned to his home.

The reassurances of Khadījah and Waraqah were followed by a reassurance from Heaven in the form of a second Revelation. The manner of its coming is not recorded, but when asked how Revelation came to him the Prophet mentioned two ways: "Sometimes it cometh unto me like the reverberations of a bell, and that is the hardest upon me; the reverberations abate when I am aware of their message. And sometimes the Angel taketh the form of a man and speaketh unto me, and I am aware of what he saith."[9]

The Revelation, this second time, began with a single letter, the earliest instance of those cryptic letters with which several of the Qur'ānic messages begin. The letter was followed by a Divine oath, sworn by the pen which had already been mentioned in the first Revelation as the primary means of God's teaching men His wisdom. When questioned about the pen, the Prophet said: "The first thing God created was the pen. He created the tablet and said to the pen: "Write!" And the pen answered: "What shall I write?" He said: "Write My knowledge of My creation till the day of resurrection." Then the pen traced what had been ordained."[10] The oath *by the pen* is followed by a second oath, *by that which they write*; and amongst

[8] I.I. 153–4.

[9] B.I., 3.

[10] Tirmidhī 44.

what they, that is the Angels, write in Heaven with lesser pens on lesser tablets is the Qur'ān's celestial archetype, which subsequent Revelations refer to as *a glorious recitation* (*qur'ān*)[11] *on an inviolable tablet*[12] and as *the mother of the book.*[13] The two oaths are followed by the Divine reassurance: *Nūn. By the pen, and by that which they write, no madman art thou, through the grace of thy Lord unto thee, and thine shall be a meed unfailing, and verily of an immense magnitude is thy nature.*[14]

After the first Messages had come there was a period of silence, until the Prophet began to fear that he had incurred in some way the displeasure of Heaven, though Khadījah continually told him that this was not possible. Then at last the silence was broken, and there came a further reassurance, and with it the first command directly related to his mission: *By the morning brightness, and by the night when it is still, thy Lord hath not forsaken thee nor doth He hate thee, and the last shall be better for thee than the first, and thy Lord shall give and give unto thee, and thou shalt be satisfied. Hath He not found thee an orphan and sheltered thee, and found thee astray and guided thee, and found thee needy and enriched thee? So for the orphan, oppress him not, and for the beggar, repel him not, and for the bountiful grace of thy Lord, proclaim it!*[15]

[11] It is from this that the Divine Revelation on which Islam is based takes its name.

[12] LXXXV, 21–2.

[13] XIII, 39.

[14] LXVIII, 1–4.

[15] XCIII.

XXXVII
The Hijrah

Meantime the Prophet had returned to Abū Bakr, and losing no time they went out through a window at the back of his house where two camels, already saddled, were waiting for them. The Prophet mounted one of them, and Abū Bakr the other, with his son ʿAbd Allāh behind him. As they had planned, they made for a cave in the Mount of Thawr a little to the south, on the way to the Yemen, for they knew that as soon as the Prophet's absence was discovered search parties would be sent out to cover all the northern outskirts of the city. When they had gone a little way beyond the precincts of Mecca, the Prophet halted his camel, and looking back he said: "Of all God's earth, thou art the dearest place unto me and the dearest unto God, and had not my people driven me out from thee I would not have left thee."

ʿĀmir ibn Fuhayrah, the shepherd whom Abū Bakr had bought as a slave and then set free and put in charge of his sheep, had followed behind them with his flock to cover up their tracks. When they reached the cave, Abū Bakr sent his son home with the camels, telling him to listen to what was said in Mecca the next day when the Prophet's absence was discovered, and to bring them word of it the following night. ʿĀmir was to pasture his sheep as usual with the other shepherds during the day and to bring them to the cave at night, always covering up the tracks of ʿAbd Allāh between Thawr and Mecca.

The next night ʿAbd Allāh returned to the cave and his sister Asma' came with him, bringing food. Their news was that Quraysh had offered a reward of a hundred camels to anyone who could find Muḥammad and bring him back to Mecca. Horsemen were already following every normal route from Mecca to Yathrib, hoping to overtake them both—for it was assumed that Abū Bakr was with the Prophet, since he also had disappeared.

But others, perhaps unknown to ʿAbd Allāh, thought they must be in hiding, in one of the numerous caves in the hills round Mecca. Moreover, the Arabs of the desert are good trackers: even when a flock of sheep had followed in the wake of two or three camels, the average Bedouin would see at a glance the remains of the larger prints of the camel-hooves which the multitude of smaller prints had all but obliterated. It seemed unlikely that the fugitives would be to the south of the city; but for such a generous reward every possibility should be tried; and camels had certainly preceded the sheep on those tracks which led in the direction of Thawr.

On the third day the silence of their mountain sanctuary was broken by the sound of birds—a pair of rock doves they thought—cooing and fluttering their wings outside the cave. Then after a while they heard the faint sound of men's voices, at some distance below them but gradually growing louder as if the men were climbing up the side of the mount. They were not expecting ʿAbd Allāh until after nightfall, and there were still some hours to go before sunset, although in fact there was strangely little light in the cave for the time of day they supposed it to be. The voices were now not far off—five or six men at least—and they were still approaching. The Prophet looked at Abū Bakr, and said: "Grieve not, for verily God is with us."[1] And then he said: "What thinkest thou of two when God is their third?"[2] They could now hear the sound of steps, which drew nearer and then stopped: the men were standing outside the cave. They spoke decisively, all in agreement that there was no need to enter the cave, since no one could possibly be there. Then they turned back the way they had come.

When the sound of their retreating steps and voices had died away, the Prophet and Abū Bakr went to the mouth of the cave. There in front of it, almost covering the entrance, was an acacia tree, about the height of a man, which had not been there that morning; and over the gap that was left between the tree and the wall of the cave a spider had woven its web. They looked through the web, and there in the hollow of a rock, even where a man might step as he entered the cave, a

[1] IX, 40.

[2] B. LVII, 5.

rock dove had made a nesting place and was sitting close as if she had eggs, with her mate perched on a ledge not far above.

When they heard ʿAbd Allāh and his sister approaching at the expected hour, they gently drew aside the web that had been their safeguard, and taking care not to disturb the dove, they went to meet them. ʿĀmir had also come, this time without his flock. He had brought the Bedouin to whom Abū Bakr had entrusted the two camels he had chosen for their journey. The man was not yet a believer, but he could be relied on to keep their secret and also to guide them to their destination by such out-of-the-way paths as only a true son of the desert would know. He was waiting in the valley below with the two mounts, and had brought a third camel for himself. Abū Bakr was to take ʿĀmir behind him on his, to look after their needs. They left the cave, and descended the slope. Asma' had brought a bag of provisions, but had forgotten to bring a rope. So she took off her girdle and divided it into two lengths, using one to tie the bag securely to her father's saddle and keeping the other for herself. Thus it was that she earned the title "She of the two girdles".

When Abū Bakr offered the Prophet the better of the two camels he said: "I will not ride a camel that is not mine own." "But she is thine, O messenger of God." said Abū Bakr. "Nay," said the Prophet; "but what price didst thou pay for her?" Abū Bakr told him, and he said: "I take her at that price." Nor did Abū Bakr insist further on making it a gift, although the Prophet had accepted many gifts from him in the past, for this occasion was a solemn one. It was the Prophet's Hijra, his cutting off of all ties of home and homeland for the sake of God. His offering, the act of emigration, must be entirely his, not shared by another in any respect. The mount on which the act was accomplished must therefore be his own, since it was part of his offering. The camel's name was Qaṣwā', and she remained his favourite camel.

Their guide took them away from Mecca to the *west* and a little to the *south* until they came to the shore of the Red Sea. Yathrib is due north of Mecca, but it was only at this point that any north came into their direction. The coastal road runs north-west and for a few days they kept to this. On one of their first evenings, looking across the water towards the Nubian desert, they saw the new moon of the month of Rabīʿ

al-Awwal. "O crescent of good and of guidance, my faith is in Him who created thee."[3] This the Prophet would say when he saw the new moon.

One morning they were somewhat dismayed to see a small caravan approaching from the opposite direction. But their feelings changed to joy when they saw that it was Abū Bakr's cousin Ṭalḥah who was on his way from Syria where he had bought the cloth and other merchandise with which his camels were laden. He had stopped in Yathrib on his way, and intended to return there as soon as he had disposed of his wares in Mecca. The Prophet's arrival in the oasis, he said, was awaited with the greatest eagerness; and before bidding them farewell he gave them each a change of clothes from out of the fine white Syrian garments which he had intended to sell to some of the richer men of Quraysh.

Not long after their meeting with Ṭalḥah they turned due north, going slightly inland from the coast, and then north-east, now at last making directly for Yathrib. At one point of their journey the Prophet received a Revelation which told him: *Verily He who hath made binding upon thee the Qur'ān will bring thee home once more.*[4]

Shortly before dawn on the twelfth day after leaving the cave they reached the valley of ʿAqīq, and crossing the valley, they climbed up the rugged black slopes on the other side. Before they reached the top the sun was well up and the heat was intense. On other days they would have stopped for rest until the great heat of the day had passed; but they now decided to climb the final ridge of the ascent, and when at last they came within sight of the plain below there could be no question of holding back. The place that the Prophet had dreamed of, "the well watered land between two tracts of black stones," was lying before them, and the grey-green of the palm groves and the lighter green of orchards and gardens stretched at one point to within three miles of the foot of the slope they had to descend.

The nearest point of greenery was Qubā', where most of the emigrants from Mecca had first stayed, and where many of them still were. The Prophet told their guide: "Lead us straight

[3] A.H.V., 329.

[4] XXVIII, 85.

to the Bani ʿAmr at Qubāʾ, and draw not yet nigh unto the city"—for so the most densely inhabited part of the oasis was called. That city was soon to be known throughout Arabia, and thence elsewhere, as "the City", in Arabic *al-Madīnah*, in English Medina.

Several days previously news from Mecca of the Prophet's disappearance, and of the reward offered for him, had reached the oasis. The people of Qubāʾ were expecting him daily, for the time of his arrival was now overdue; so every morning, after the dawn prayer, some of the Bani ʿAmr would go out to look for him, and with them went men of other clans who lived in that village, and also those of the emigrant Quraysh who were still there and had not yet moved to Medina. They would go out beyond the fields and palm groves onto the lava tract, and after they had gone some distance they would stop and wait until the heat of the sun became fierce; then they would return to their homes. They had gone out that morning, but had already returned by the time the four travellers had begun their descent of the rocky slope. Eyes were no longer staring expectantly in that direction; but the sun shone on the new white garments of the Prophet and Abū Bakr which were set off all the more against the background of bluish-black volcanic stones, and a Jew who happened to be on the roof of his house caught sight of them. He knew at once who they must be, for the Jews of Qubāʾ had asked and been told why so many of their neighbours had taken to going out in a body into the wilderness every morning without fail. So he called out at the top of his voice: "Sons of Qaylah, he is come, he is come!" The call was immediately taken up, and men, women and children hurried from their houses and streamed out once more onto the strip of greenery which led to the stone tract. But they had not far to go, for the travellers had by now reached the most outlying palm-grove. It was a noon of great joy on all sides, and the Prophet addressed them, saying: "O people, give unto one another greetings of Peace; feed food unto the hungry; honour the ties of kinship; pray in the hours when men sleep. Even so shall ye enter Paradise in Peace."[5]

It was decided that he should lodge with Kulthūm, an old man of Qubāʾ who had previously welcomed both Ḥamzah and

[5] I.S. I/1, 159.

Zayd in his house on their arrival from Mecca. The Bani ʿAmr, Kulthūm's clan, were of Aws, and it was no doubt partly in order that both the Yathrib tribes might share in the hospitality that Abū Bakr lodged with a man of Khazraj in the village of Sunḥ which was a little nearer to Medina. After a day or two, ʿAlī arrived from Mecca, and stayed in the same house as the Prophet. It had taken him three days to return all the property which had been deposited with them to its various owners.

Many were those who now came to greet the Prophet, and amongst them were some Jews of Medina who were drawn more by curiosity than good will. But on the second or third evening there came a man who was different in appearance from any of the others, clearly neither an Arab nor a Jew. Salmān, for so he was named, had been born of Persian Zoroastrian parents in the village of Jayy near Isfahan, but he had become a Christian and gone to Syria as a very young man. There he had attached himself to a saintly bishop who, on his deathbed, recommended him to go to the Bishop of Mosul, who was old like himself but the best man he knew. Salman set off for the north of Iraq, and this was for him the beginning of a series of attachments to elderly Christian sages until the last of these, also on his deathbed, told him that the time was now at hand when a Prophet would appear: "He will be sent with the religion of Abraham and will come forth in Arabia where he will emigrate from his home to a place between two lava tracts, a country of palms. His signs are manifest: he will eat of a gift but not if it be given as alms; and between his shoulders is the seal of prophecy." Salmān made up his mind to join the Prophet and paid a party of merchants of the tribe of Kalb to take him with them to Arabia. But when they reached Wādi'l-Qurā near the Gulf of ʿAqabah at the north of the Red Sea they sold him as a slave to a Jew. The sight of the palms in Wādi'l-Qurā made him wonder whether this could be the township he was seeking, but he had his doubts. It was not long however before the Jew sold him to a cousin of his of the Bani Qurayẓah in Medina; and as soon as he saw the lie of the land, he knew beyond doubt that here was the place to which the Prophet would migrate. Salmān's new owner had another cousin who lived in Qubā'; and on the arrival of the Prophet this Jew of Qubā' set off for Medina with the news. He found his cousin sitting beneath one of his palms; and Salmān, who was working in the top of the tree, heard him say: "God curse the sons of Qaylah! They are even now gathered together at Qubā' about a man who hath come to them this day from Mecca. They claim him to be a Prophet." Those last words filled Salman with certainty that his hopes had been realised, and the impact was so great that his whole body was seized with trembling. He was afraid that he would fall out of the tree, so he climbed down; and once on the ground he eagerly began to question the Jew from Qubā', but his master was angry and ordered him back to his work in the tree. That evening however he slipped away, taking with him some of his food which he had saved, and went to Qubā', where he found the Prophet sitting with many companions, new and old. Salman was already convinced, but he none the less approached him and offered him the food, specifying that he gave it as alms. The Prophet told his companions to eat of it, but did not eat of it himself. Salman hoped that he would one day see the seal of prophecy, but to have been in the presence of the Prophet and to have heard him speak was enough for that first encounter, and he returned to Medina elated and thankful.

LXVII
"A Clear Victory"

It was during ʿUthmān's absence in Mecca[1] that there came over the Prophet a state which was comparable to that of receiving a Revelation but which left him in full possession of his faculties. He gave instructions to one of his Companions, who thereupon went through the camp proclaiming: "The Holy Spirit hath descended upon the Messenger and commandeth allegiance. So go ye forth in the Name of God to make your pledge."[2] Meantime the Prophet had seated himself beneath an acacia tree that was green with its spring foliage breaking into leaf; and one by one the Companions came and pledged allegiance to him. The first man to reach him was Sinān, who was of the same tribe as the Jaḥsh family, that is the Bani Asad ibn Khuzaymah. The crier had specified nothing about the nature of the pledge, so Sinān said "O Messenger of God, I pledge thee mine allegiance unto that which is in thy soul," and the others pledged themselves accordingly. Then the Prophet said "I pledge the allegiance of ʿUthmān," whereupon he put out his left hand, as the hand of his son-in-law, and grasping it with his right hand, pledged the pact. Only one man present failed to respond to the crier, and that was the hypocrite Jadd ibn Qays who tried to hide behind his camel but was none the less seen.

Quraysh now sent Suhayl to conclude a treaty, and with him were his two clansmen Mikraz and Ḥuwayṭib. They conferred with the Prophet, and the Companions heard their voices rise and fall according to whether the point in question was hard to agree upon or easy. When they had finally reached an agreement the Prophet told ʿAlī to write down the terms, beginning with the revealed words of consecration *Bismi Llāhi l-Raḥmāni l-Raḥīm, in the Name of God, the Good, the Merciful,*

[1] [This chapter begins with the Muslim pilgrims arrived from Medina, waiting outside Mecca on the outcome of ʿUthmān's embassy to the Quraysh.—Ed.]
[2] W. 604.

but Suhayl objected. "As to *Raḥmān*" he said, "I know not what he is. But write *Bismik Allāhumma,* In Thy Name, O God, as thou wert wont to write." Some of the Companions cried out "By God, we will write naught but *Bismi Llāhi l-Raḥmāni l-Raḥīm*" but the Prophet ignored them and said "Write *Bismik Allāhumma*" and he went on dictating: "These are the terms of the truce between Muḥammad the Messenger of God and Suhayl the son of ʿAmr"; but again Suhayl protested. "If we knew thee to be the Messenger of God," he said, "we would not have barred thee from the House, neither would we have fought thee; but write Muḥammad the son of ʿAbd Allāh." ʿAlī had already written "the Messenger of God," and the Prophet told him to strike out those words, but he said he could not. So the Prophet told him to point with his finger to the words in question, and he himself struck them out. Then he told him to write in their place "the son of ʿAbd Allāh," which he did.

The document continued: "They have agreed to lay down the burden of war for ten years, in which times men shall be safe and not lay violent hands the one upon the other; on condition that whoso cometh unto Muḥammad of Quraysh without the leave of his guardian, Muḥammad shall return him unto them; but whoso cometh unto Quraysh of those who are with Muḥammad, they shall not be returned. There shall be no subterfuge and no treachery. And whoso wisheth to enter into the bond and pact of Muḥammad may do so; and whoso wisheth to enter the bond and pact of Quraysh may do so." Now there were present in the camp some leading men of Khuzāʿah who had come to visit the pilgrims, whereas one or two representatives of Bakr had followed in the wake of Suhayl; and at this point the men of Khuzāʿah leaped to their feet and said: "We are one with Muḥammad in his bond and his pact." Whereupon the men of Bakr said: "We are one with Quraysh in their bond and their pact." And this agreement was subsequently ratified by the chiefs of both tribes. The treaty ended with the words: "Thou, Muḥammad, shalt depart from us this present year, and shalt not enter Mecca when we are present in despite of us. But in the year that is to come, we shall go out from Mecca and thou shalt enter it with thy companions, staying therein for three days, bearing no arms save the arms of the traveller, with swords in sheaths."[3]

[3] I.I. 747–8.

In virtue of the Prophet's vision, the Companions had been certain of the success of their expedition; and when they heard the terms of the treaty and realised that having reached the very edge of the sacred precinct they must now return home with nothing accomplished, it was almost more than they could endure. But worse was to come: as they sat there in sullen and explosive silence, the clank of chains was heard and a youth staggered into the camp with his feet in fetters. It was Abū Jandal, one of the younger sons of Suhayl. His father had imprisoned him on account of his Islam, fearing that he would escape to Medina. His elder brother ʿAbd Allāh was among the pilgrims and was about to welcome him when Suhayl caught hold of the chain that was round his prisoner's neck and struck him violently in the face. Then he turned to the Prophet and said: "Our agreement was concluded before this man came to thee." "That is true," said the Prophet. "Return him then unto us," said Suhayl. "O Muslims," shouted Abū Jandal at the top of his voice, "am I to be returned unto the idolaters, for them to persecute me on account of my religion?" The Prophet took Suhayl aside and asked him as a favour to let his son go free, but Suhayl implacably refused. His fellow envoys, Mikraz and Ḥuwayṭib, had been so far silent; but now, feeling that this incident was an inauspicious start for the truce, they intervened. "O Muḥammad," they said, "we give him our protection on thy behalf." This meant that they would lodge him with them, away from his father, and they held to their promise. "Be patient, Abū Jandal," said the Prophet. "God will surely give thee and those with thee relief and a way out. We have agreed on the terms of a truce with these people, and have given them our solemn pledge, even as they have done to us, and we will not now break our word."

At this point ʿUmar could no longer contain himself. Rising to his feet, he went to the Prophet and said "Art thou not God's Prophet?" and he answered "Yea." "Are we not in the right and our enemies in the wrong?" he said, and again the Prophet assented. "Then why yield we in such lowly wise against the honour of our religion?" said ʿUmar, whereupon the Prophet replied: "I am God's Messenger and I will not disobey Him. He will give me the victory." "But didst thou not tell us," persisted ʿUmar, "that we should go unto the House and make our rounds about it?" "Even so," said the Prophet, "but did I tell thee we should go to it this year?" ʿUmar conceded that he had not. "Verily thou shalt go unto the House," said the Prophet, "and shalt make thy rounds about it." But ʿUmar was still seething with indignation, and went to Abū Bakr to work off his feelings still further. He put to him exactly the same questions he had put to the Prophet; but though Abū Bakr had not heard the answers, he gave him the same answer to each question in almost exactly the same words; and at the end he added: "So cleave unto his stirrup, for by God he is right." This impressed ʿUmar, and though his feelings had not yet subsided, he gave no further vent to them, and when the Prophet summoned him to put his name to the treaty he signed it in silence. The Prophet also told Suhayl's son ʿAbd Allāh to put his name to it. Others of the Muslims who signed it were ʿAlī, Abū Bakr, ʿAbd al-Raḥmān ibn ʿAwf and Maḥmūd ibn Maslamah.

Some of the general bitterness seemed to have been smoothed over; but when Suhayl and the others left the camp, taking with them the tearful Abū Jandal, men's souls were stirred up again. The Prophet was standing apart, with those who had signed the document. He now left them, and went towards the main body of the pilgrims. "Rise and sacrifice your animals," he said, "and shave your heads." Not a man moved, and he repeated it a second and a third time, but they simply looked at him in dazed and bewildered silence. It was not a rebellion on their part, but having had their expectations shattered by the turn of events they were now genuinely perplexed by the command to do something which they knew to be ritually incorrect; for according to the tradition of Abraham the sacrifices had to be performed within the sacred territory, and the same applied to the rite of shaving the head. None the less, their apparent disobedience dismayed the Prophet, who withdrew to his tent and told Umm Salamah what had happened. "Go forth," she said, "and say no word to any man until thou hast performed thy sacrifice." So the Prophet went to the camel which he himself had consecrated and sacrificed it, saying in a loud voice, so that the men could hear: *Bismi Llāh, Allāhu Akbar*. At these words the men leaped to their feet and raced to make their sacrifices, falling over each other in their eagerness to obey; and when the Prophet called for Khirāsh—the man of Khuzāʿah he had sent to Mecca before ʿUthmān—to shave his head, many of the Companions set about shaving each other's heads so vigorously that Umm Salamah was afraid, as she afterwards remarked, that mortal wounds might be inflicted. But some of them merely cut locks of their hair, knowing that this was traditionally acceptable as a substitute. Meantime the Prophet had retired to his tent with Khirāsh; and when the rite had been accomplished he stood at the entrance with shaven scalp and said: "God have Mercy on the shavers of their heads!" Whereupon those who had cut their hair protested: "And on the cutters of their hair, O Messenger of God!" But the Prophet repeated what he had said at first, and the voices were raised in protest still louder. Then after another repetition and a third thunderous protest he added: "And upon the cutters of their hair!" When asked afterwards why he had first of all prayed only for the shavers of their heads, he answered: "Because they doubted not."

Returning to his tent, the Prophet gathered up his luxuriant black hair from the ground and threw it over a nearby mimosa tree, whereupon the men crowded round, each bent on taking what he could for its blessing. Nor was Nusaybah to be outdone by the men, and she also made her way to the tree, and was able to snatch some locks, which she treasured until her dying day.

The earth of the camp was strewn with the hair of the pilgrims. But suddenly there came a powerful gust of wind which lifted the hair from the ground and blew it towards Mecca, into the sacred territory; and everyone rejoiced, taking it as a sign that their pilgrimage had been accepted by God in virtue of their intentions, and they now understood why the Prophet had told them to perform their sacrifices.

After they had set off on the return journey to Medina, ʿUmar's conscience began to trouble him; and his anxiety was greatly increased when he rode up to the Prophet, seeking to enter into conversation with him, and the Prophet, so it seemed to him, was markedly distant and reserved. ʿUmar rode on ahead, saying to himself: "O ʿUmar, let thy mother now mourn her son!" He said afterwards that he was so troubled for having questioned the wisdom of the Prophet that he feared there would be a special Revelation condemning him. His fears reached their height when he heard behind him the hooves of a galloping horse, and the rider summoned him back to the Prophet. But his troubles vanished in an instant when he saw the Prophet's face radiant with joy. "There hath descended upon me a *sūrah,*" he said, "which is dearer to me than aught else beneath the sun."

The new Revelation left no doubt that the expedition from which they were now returning must be considered as a victorious one, for it opened with the words: *Verily We have given thee a clear victory.*[4] It also spoke of the recent pact of allegiance: *God was well pleased with the believers when they pledged allegiance unto thee beneath the tree. He knew what was in their hearts, and sent down the Spirit of Peace upon them, and hath given them the meed of a near victory.*[5] The Divine Good Pleasure referred to is no less than the promise of *Riḍwān*[6] for him who fulfilled his pledge, and so this beatific allegiance is known as the Pact of *Riḍwān*. The descent of the *Sakīnah,*[7] the Spirit of Peace, is mentioned also in another verse: *He it is who sent down the Spirit of Peace into the hearts of the believers that they might increase in faith upon their faith… that He may bring the believing men and the believing women into gardens that are watered by flowing rivers, gardens wherein they shall dwell immortal, and that He may take from them all guilt of evil. Triumph immense for them is that in the sight of God.*[8]

The Prophet's vision, which had prompted the expedition, is referred to as follows: God hath truly fulfilled for His Messenger the vision: *God willing, ye shall enter the inviolable mosque in safety, not fearing, with the hair of your heads shaven or cut. But He knoweth what ye know not, and before that hath He given you a near victory.*[9]

[4] XLVIII, 1.

[5] XLVIII, 18.

[6] The ultimate beatitude of *Riḍwān*, sometimes translated "Good Pleasure", is interpreted to mean God's final and absolute acceptance of a soul and His taking of that soul to Himself and His Eternal Good Pleasure therein.

[7] Hebrew *Shekinah.*

[8] XLVIII, 4–5.

[9] XLVIII, 27.

LXXV
The Conquest of Mecca

The tents had already been loaded on to the transport camels, and the Prophet had at last called for the standards and pennants to be brought to him. These he mounted one by one, placing each in the hand of the bearer he had chosen for it. He told ʿAbbās to accompany Abū Sufyān as far as the narrow end of the valley, and keep him there, so that he could see for himself the size of the army as it passed. There would be time enough for him then to return to Quraysh and deliver his message, for a single man could reach Mecca by a more direct way than the army would take.

"Who is that?" said Abū Sufyān, pointing to the man at the head of the host which now came in sight. "Khālid the son of Walīd," said ʿAbbās; and when he came level with them Khālid uttered three magnifications, *Allāhu Akbar*. With Khālid were the horse of Sulaym. They were followed by the yellow-turbaned Zubayr at the head of a troop of five hundred Emigrants and others. He likewise uttered three magnifications as he passed Abū Sufyān, and the whole valley resounded as with one voice his men echoed him. Troop after troop went by, and at the passing of each Abū Sufyān asked who they were, and each time he marvelled, either because the tribe in question had hitherto been far beyond the range of influence of Quraysh, or because it had recently been hostile to the Prophet, as was the case with the Ghaṭafānite clan of Ashjaʿ, one of whose ensigns was borne by Nuʿaym, the former friend of himself and Suhayl.

"Of all the Arabs," said Abū Sufyān, "these were Muḥammad's bitterest foes." "God caused Islam to enter their hearts," said ʿAbbās. "All this is by the grace of God."

The last of the squadrons was the Prophet's own, consisting entirely of Emigrants and Helpers. The glint of their steel gave them a greenish-black appearance, for they were fully armed and armoured, only their eyes being visible. The Prophet had given his standard to Sa'd ibn 'Ubādah, who led the van; and as he passed the two men at the side of the route he called out: "O Abū Sufyān, this is the day of slaughter! The day when the inviolable shall be violated! The day of God's abasement of Quraysh." The Prophet was in the midst of the troop, mounted on Qaṣwa', and on either side of him were Abū Bakr and Usayd, with whom he was conversing. "O Messenger of God," cried Abū Sufyān when he came within earshot, "hast thou commanded the slaying of thy people?"—and he repeated to him what Sa'd had said. "I adjure thee by God," he added, "on behalf of thy people, for thou art of all men the greatest in filial piety, the most merciful, the most beneficent!" "This is the day of mercy," said the Prophet, "the day on which God hath exalted Quraysh." Then 'Abd al-Raḥmān ibn 'Awf and 'Uthmān said to him, for they were close at hand; "O Messenger of God, we are not sure of Sa'd, that he will not make a sudden violent attack upon Quraysh." So the Prophet sent word to Sa'd to give the standard to his son Qays, a man of relatively mild temperament, and to let him lead the squadron. To honour the son was to honour the father, and in the hand of Qays the standard would still be with Sa'd. But Sa'd refused to hand it over without direct command from the Prophet, who thereupon unwound the red turban from his helmet and sent it to Sa'd as a token. The standard was immediately given to Qays.[1]

When the army had passed, Abū Sufyān went back to Mecca with all speed and standing outside his house he shouted at the top of his voice to a quickly gathering crowd: "O men of Quraysh, Muḥammad is here with a force ye cannot resist. Muḥammad is here with ten thousand men of steel. And he hath granted me that whoso entereth my house shall be safe." Hind now came out of the house and seized her husband by his moustaches. "Slay this greasy good-for-nothing bladder of a man," she cried. "Thou miserable protector of a people!" "Woe betide you," he shouted, "let not this woman deceive you against your better judgement, for there hath come unto you that which ye cannot resist. But whoso entereth the house of Abū Sufyān shall be safe." "God slay thee!" they said. "What good is thy house for all our numbers?" "And whoso locketh upon himself his door shall be safe," he answered, "and whoso entereth the

[1] W. 819–22.

Mosque shall be safe," whereupon the crowd that had gathered dispersed, some to their houses and some to the Mosque.

The army halted at Dhū Ṭuwā, which is not far from the city and within sight of it. This was the place where two years previously Khālid had been stationed to bar their approach. But now there was no sign of any resistance. It was as if the city were empty, as it had been at their visit the previous year. But this time there was no three-day limit to their stay; and when Qaṣwā' came to a halt the Prophet bowed his head until his beard almost touched the saddle, in gratitude to God. He then drew up his troops, putting Khālid in command of the right and Zubayr in command of the left. His own troop which was now in the centre he divided into two; half of it was to be led by Saᶜd and his son, and the other half, in which he himself would ride, was to be led by Abū ᶜUbaydah. When the order was given they were to divide and to enter the city from four directions, Khālid from below and the others from the hills through three different passes.

High above the gathered host, on the slopes of Mount Abū Qubays, were two figures which a keen sight could have distinguished as a somewhat bent old man with a staff, guided and helped by a woman. They were Abū Quḥāfah and Quraybah, the father and sister of Abū Bakr. That morning, when the news came of the Prophet's arrival in Dhū Ṭuwā, the blind old man had told his daughter to guide him up the mount and tell him what she could see. As a young and vigorous man he had climbed the hills on the other side of Mecca to see the army of Abrahah and his elephant. Now he was old, and had been blind for many years; but he would at least have a sight, through the eyes of his daughter, of this host of ten thousand in which were his son and two grandsons. Quraybah described what she could see as a dense mass of black, and he told her that those were the horsemen drawn up in close formation, waiting for orders. Then she saw the black mass spreading out until it became four distinct divisions, and her father told her to take him home with all speed. They were still on their way when a troop of horse swept past them, and one man leaned over from his saddle and snatched the silver necklace that Quraybah was wearing. Otherwise they suffered no harm and reached home in safety.

They had not been alone on Abū Qubays. At another part of the mount ᶜIkrimah, Ṣafwān and Suhayl had gathered a force of Quraysh together with some of their allies of Bakr and Hudhayl. They were determined to fight; and when they saw Khālid's troop making for the lower entrance to the city they came down and attacked them. But they were no match for Khālid and his men, who put them to flight, having killed some thirty of them with the loss of only two lives on their own side. ʿIkrimah and Ṣafwān escaped on horseback to the coast; Suhayl went to his house and locked the door.

The fight was almost at an end when the Prophet entered through the pass of Adhākhir into Upper Mecca. Looking down towards the market-place, he was dismayed to see the flash of drawn swords. "Did I not forbid fighting?" he said. But when it was explained to him what had happened he said that God had ordained it for the best.

He could see his red leather tent which Abū Rāfiʿ had now pitched for him not far from the Mosque. He pointed it out to Jābir who was at his side; and after a prayer of praise and thanksgiving he made his way down to the hollow. "I shall not enter any of the houses," he said.

Umm Salamah, Maymūnah and Fāṭimah were waiting for him in the tent; and just before his arrival they had been joined by Umm Hāni'. The law of Islam had made it clear that marriages between Muslim women and pagan men were dissolved, and this applied to her marriage with Hubayrah, who had foreseen the fall of Mecca and gone to live in Najrān. But two of her kinsmen by marriage, one of them the brother of Abū Jahl, had taken part in the righting against Khālid and had afterwards fled to her house for refuge. Then ʿAlī had come to greet her, and seeing the two Makhzūmites he drew his sword and would have killed them despite the formal protection she had given them; but she threw a cloak over them, and stepping between him and them she said: "By God, thou shalt slay me first!", whereupon he left the house. And now, having locked the door upon them, she had come to intercede with the Prophet. She found Fāṭimah no less stern than ʿAlī. "Dost thou give protection to idolaters?" she said. But Fāṭimah's reproaches were cut short by the Prophet's arrival. He greeted his cousin with great affection, and when she told him what had happened he said: "It shall not be. Whom thou makest safe, him we make safe; whom thou protectest, him we protect."

He performed the rite of the greater ablution and prayed eight cycles of prayer, after which he rested for an hour or more. Then he called for Qaṣwa', and having put on his coat of mail and his helmet, he girt on his sword; but in his hand he carried a staff, and his visor was up. Some of those who had ridden with him that morning were already in line outside the tent, and they made an escort for him as he went to the Mosque, talking to Abū Bakr, who was at his side.

He rode straight to the south-east corner of the Kaᶜbah and reverently touched the Black Stone with his staff, uttering as he did so a magnification. Those who were near him repeated it, *Allāhu Akbar, Allāhu Akbar*, and it was taken up by all the Muslims in the Mosque and the whole of Mecca resounded with it, until the Prophet motioned them to silence with his hand. Then he made the seven rounds of the Holy House with Muḥammad ibn Maslamah holding his bridle. At the Lesser Pilgrimage that honour had been given to a man of Khazraj. It was therefore fitting that this time it should go to a man of Aws.

The Prophet now turned away from the Kaᶜbah towards the idols which surrounded it in a wide circle, three hundred and sixty in all. Between these and the House he now rode, repeating the verse of the Revelation: *The Truth hath come and the false hath vanished, Verily the false is ever a vanisher*[2] and pointing at the idols, one by one, with his staff; and each idol, as he pointed at it, fell forward on its face. Having completed the circle he dismounted and prayed at the Station of Abraham, which was at that time adjoining the Kaᶜbah. Then he went to the Well of Zamzam where ᶜAbbās gave him to drink; and he confirmed for ever the traditional right of the sons of Hāshim to water the pilgrims. But when ᶜAlī brought him the key of the Kaᶜbah, and when ᶜAbbās asked him to give their family also the right of guarding it, he said: "I give you only that which ye have lost, not that which will be a loss for others." Then he called for the man of ᶜAbd al-Dār who earlier had come to him in Medina with Khālid and ᶜAmr, ᶜUthmān ibn Ṭalḥah; and handing him the key he confirmed for ever his clan's traditional right of guardianship. ᶜUthmān reverently took the key and went to open the door of the Holy House, followed by the Prophet. Usāmah and Bilāl were close behind,

[2] XVII, 81.

and bidding them enter after him the Prophet told ʿUthmān to lock the door behind them.

Apart from the icon of the Virgin Mary and the child Jesus, and a painting of an old man, said to be Abraham, the walls inside had been covered with pictures of pagan deities. Placing his hand protectively over the icon, the Prophet told ʿUthmān to see that all the other paintings, except that of Abraham, were effaced.[3]

He stayed awhile inside, and then, taking the key from ʿUthmān, he unlocked the door; and standing on the threshold with the key in his hand, he said: "Praise be to God, who hath fulfilled His promise and helped His slave and routed the clans, He alone." The Meccans who had taken refuge in the Mosque had since been joined by many of those who had at first taken refuge in their homes and they were sitting in groups, here and there, not far from the Kaʿbah. The Prophet now addressed them, saying: "What say ye, and what think ye?" They answered: "We say well, and we think well: a noble and generous brother, son of a noble and generous brother. It is thine to command." He then spoke to them in the words of forgiveness which, according to the Revelation, Joseph spoke to his brothers when they came to him in Egypt: "Verily I say as my brother Joseph said: *This day there shall be no upbraiding of you nor reproach. God forgiveth you, and He is the most Merciful of the merciful.*"[4]

Abū Bakr had left the Mosque in order to visit his father, and he now returned leading Abū Quḥāfah by the hand, followed by his sister Quraybah. "Why didst thou not leave the old man in his house," said the Prophet, "for me to go to him there?" "O Messenger of God," said Abū Bakr, "it is more fitting that he should come unto thee than that thou shouldst go unto him." The Prophet gave him his hand and drawing him down to sit in front of him, he invited him to make the two testifications of Islam, which he readily did.

Having given orders that Hubal, the largest of the fallen idols, should be broken to pieces and that all of them should be burned, the Prophet had it proclaimed throughout the city

[3] W. 834; A.I., 107. But other accounts say "all" without mention of these two exceptions.

[4] XII, 92.

that everyone who had an idol in his house must destroy it. He then withdrew to the nearby hill of Ṣafā, where he had first preached to his family. Here he received the homage of those of his enemies who now wished to enter Islam, both men and women. They came to him in hundreds. Amongst the women was Hind, the wife of Abū Sufyān. She came veiled, fearing that the Prophet might order her to be put to death before she had embraced Islam; and she said: "O Messenger of God, praise be to Him who hath made triumph the religion which I choose for myself." Then she unveiled her face and said: "Hind, the daughter of ʿUtbah"; and the Prophet said: "Welcome." Another of the women who came to Ṣafā was Umm Ḥakīm, the wife of ʿIkrimah. When she had entered Islam she begged the Prophet to give her husband immunity. He did so, although ʿIkrimah was still at war with him; and Umm Ḥakīm found out where he was, and went after him to bring him back.The Prophet looked round at the gathering in front of him, and turning to his uncle he said: "O ʿAbbās, where are thy brother's two sons, ʿUtbah and Muʿattib? I see them not." These were the two surviving sons of Abū Lahab. It was ʿUtbah who had repudiated Ruqayyah under pressure from his father, and it seemed that they were afraid to appear. "Bring them to me," said the Prophet, so ʿAbbās fetched his nephews, who entered Islam and pledged their allegiance. Then the Prophet took them each by the hand, and walking between them, he led them to the great place of supplication which is named al-Multazam and which is that part of the Kaʿbah wall which lies between the Black Stone and the door. There he made a long prayer, and noticing the joy on his face, ʿAbbās remarked on it. He was answered: "I asked my Lord to give me these two sons of mine uncle, and He hath given me them."[5]

The nearest to Mecca of the three most eminent shrines of paganism was the temple of al-ʿUzzā at Nakhlah. The Prophet now sent Khālid to destroy this centre of idolatry. At the news of his approach the warden of the temple hung his sword on the statue of the goddess and called upon her to defend herself and slay Khālid or to become a monotheist. Khālid demolished the temple and its idol, and returned to Mecca. "Didst thou see nothing?" said the Prophet. "Nothing," said Khālid. "Then

[5] I.S. IV/1, 41–2.

thou hast not destroyed her," said the Prophet. "Return and destroy her." So Khālid went again to Nakhlah, and out of the ruins of the temple there came a black woman, entirely naked, with long and wildly flowing hair. "My spine was seized with shivering," said Khālid afterwards. But he shouted "ʿUzzā, denial is for thee, not worship," and drawing his sword he cut her down. On his return he said to the Prophet: "Praise be to God who hath saved us from perishing! I was wont to see my father set out for al-ʿUzzā with an offering of a hundred camels and sheep. He would sacrifice them to her and stay three days at her shrine, and return unto us rejoicing at what he had accomplished!"[6]

Meantime most of the Meccans had pledged their allegiance. Suhayl was an exception; but having taken refuge in his house, he sent for his son ʿAbd Allāh to ask him to intervene with the Prophet on his behalf. For despite the general amnesty he could scarcely believe that it would apply to him. But when ʿAbd Allāh spoke to the Prophet he immediately answered: "He is safe, under the protection of God, so let him appear." Then he told those about him: "No harsh looks for Suhayl, if ye meet him! Let him come out freely, for by my life he is a man of intelligence and honour, not one to be blind to the truth of Islam." So Suhayl came and went as he pleased; but he did not yet enter Islam.

As to Ṣafwān, his cousin ʿUmayr obtained for him a two months' respite from the Prophet, whereupon he set out after him and found him waiting for a boat at Shuʿaybah, which was in those days the port of Mecca. Ṣafwān was suspicious and flatly refused to change his plans, whereupon ʿUmayr went again to the Prophet, who gave him his turban of striped Yemeni cloth to take to his cousin as a token of his safety. This convinced Ṣafwān, who decided to return and seek further assurances for himself. "O Muḥammad," he said, "ʿUmayr telleth me that if I agree to a certain thing"—he meant the entry into Islam—"well and good, but that if not, thou hast given me two months' respite." "Stay here," said the Prophet. "Not until thou givest me a clear answer," said Ṣafwān. "Thou shalt have four months' respite," said the Prophet; and Ṣafwān agreed to stay in Mecca.

[6] W. 873–4.

ʿIkrimah was the last of the three to come into the presence of the Prophet after the victory of Mecca. Yet he was the first of them to enter Islam. He had decided to take a boat from the coast of Tihāmah to Abyssinia, and as he was about to step on board the captain said to him: "Make good thy religion with God." "What shall I say?" said ʿIkrimah. "Say: there is no god but God" was the answer, and the man made it clear that for fear of shipwreck he would accept no passenger who did not so testify. The four words *lā ilāha illa Llāh* entered into the soul of ʿIkrimah, and he knew at that moment that he could have uttered them with sincerity. Yet he did not embark, for his sole reason for wishing to do so had been to escape from those words, that is from the message of Muḥammad which was summed up in *lā ilāha illa Llāh*. If he could accept that message on board boat, he could accept it on shore. "Our God at sea is our God on land," he said to himself. Then his wife joined him and told him that the Prophet had guaranteed his safety in Mecca, and they returned forthwith. The Prophet knew he was coming and said to his Companions: "ʿIkrimah the son of Abū Jahl is on his way to you, as a believer. Therefore revile not his father, for the reviling of the dead giveth offence unto the living and reacheth not unto the dead."

On his arrival in Mecca ʿIkrimah went straight to the Prophet, who greeted him with a face full of gladness, saying to him, after he had formally entered Islam: "Thou shalt not ask of me any thing this day but I will give it thee." "I ask thee," said ʿIkrimah, "that thou shouldst pray God to forgive me for all mine enmity against thee," and the Prophet prayed as he had asked. Then ʿIkrimah spoke of the money he had spent and the battles he had fought to bar men from following the truth, and he said that he would henceforth spend the double of it and fight with doubled effort in the way of God; and he kept his promise.

LXXXI
The Degrees

Spiritual motives were poorly represented in many of the conversions which now took place; and it was not long before there came the following further Revelation: *The Arabs of the desert say: We have faith. Say thou: Faith ye have not, but say "we submit", for faith hath not yet entered your hearts. And if ye obey God and His Messenger, He will in no wise withold from you your meed for what ye do.*[1]

This verse completed the hierarchy of Islam, submission without faith being the lowest degree. The higher degrees, that is the degrees of faith, are the theme—or rather one of the themes—of the Verse of Light which had been revealed to the Prophet some months before the truce of Ḥudaybiyah. God is *the Light*, and this Name is partly equivalent to His Names *the Truth* and *the Knower*. Truth is the object of Knowledge, and both are Light as opposed to the darkness of error and ignorance. The Light is One, but it is manifested with different degrees of intensity throughout creation, degrees of guidance which radiate from Truth and degrees of faith which radiate from Knowledge.

The Qur'ān constantly affirms, both of itself and other revealed messages, that they are "Light", and it could indeed be named "the Book of Light" in virtue of its continual reference to the ilumination of guidance which it gives, and to the ilumination of faith which it kindles in the souls of men. The Verse of Light, which describes a series of receptacles lit by the Divine Light, may be interpreted as a definition of four degrees of enlightenment: *God is the Light of the heavens and of the earth. His light is as a niche wherein is a lamp. The lamp is in a glass; the glass is as it were a shining planet. It is kindled from a blessed tree, an olive neither of the east nor of the west. The oil thereof wellnigh blazeth in splendour even though the fire have not touched it. Light*

[1] XLIX, 14.

upon light. God guideth to His light whom he will; and God citeth symbols for men; and God is of all things the Knower.[2]

There is firstly, in ascending order, the niche, that is illuminated but not in itself luminous. Then there is the crystalline glass, above which is the splendour of the oil; and finally there is the flame itself. The mention of symbols recalls another verse which begins with the same sentence: *God citeth symbols for men*, but which adds the reason: *that they may meditate.*[3]

Many of the commentators of the Qur'ān, including some of the earliest, have said that the niche is the breast of the believer and that the glass is his heart. ʿAbd Allāh, the son of ʿAbbās, possibly repeating something that his father had heard from the Prophet himself, is quoted as having said: "God's guidance in the heart of the believer is like pure oil which shineth before the fire hath touched it and when the fire hath touched it increaseth in splendour upon splendour. Even so is the heart of the believer: he acteth by guidance until knowledge come to him."[4]

In the Verse of Light the different degrees are indicated symbolically rather than directly. But elsewhere, starting from some of the earliest revelations, the Qur'ān is quite explicit. In one of these[5] mankind is divided into three groups, *those of the right, those of the left* and *the foremost. Those of the right* are the saved, *those of the left* the damned. As to *the foremost*, that is, those of the highest degree, who are also called *the slaves of God,*[6] it is said of them that they are *brought near to God,* this epithet being also used of the Archangels to distinguish them from the Angels. Other early Revelations introduced a third degree into the hierarchy of the faithful, *the righteous,* who are between *the foremost* and *those of the right.* The relationship between these three degrees may be inferred from what the Qur'ān says about their blessings in Paradise. Whereas *those of the right* are given *pure flowing water* to drink, it is *the foremost*

[2] XXIV, 35.

[3] LIX, 21.

[4] Tabarī, *Tafsīr*.

[5] LVI, 7–40.

[6] LXVI, 6; LXXXIX, 29. The Qur'ān uses the term *slaves of God* in two senses, one altogether inclusive—even Satan is His slave—and the other exceedingly exclusive, as in the above verses, and also in the following, which is addressed to Satan: *As to My slaves, over them thou hast no power* (XVII, 65).

alone who have direct access to the highest fountains, but *the righteous* are given a draught which has been blended at one or another of these fountains,[7] which suggests that they are those who follow in the footsteps of *the foremost.*

Degrees of superiority are also implied by the Revelation in its mention of the heart. In speaking of the majority, it says: *Not blind are the eyes, but blind are the hearts within the breasts.*[8] The Prophet on the other hand, like Prophets before him, said that his heart was awake, which means that its eye was open; and the Qur'ān indicates that this possibility can be shared, if only in some measure, by others also, for it sometimes addresses itself directly to *those who have hearts.*[9] It is reported that of Abū Bakr the Prophet said: "He surpasseth you not through much fasting and prayer but he surpasseth you in virtue of something that is fixed in his heart."[10]

The Prophet often spoke of the superiority of some of his followers over others; and in Mecca, at the time of the victory, when in his presence Khālid retorted angrily against ʿAbd al-Raḥmān ibn ʿAwf, who had rebuked him, he said: "Gently Khālid, let be my Companions; for if thou hadst Mount Uḥud all in gold and didst spend it in the way of God thou wouldst not attain unto the merit of any man of my Companions."[11]

According to the Revelation the differences between one degree and another are vaster in the next world than in this: *Behold how We have favoured some of them above others; and verily the Hereafter is greater in degrees and greater in hierarchic precedences.*[12] And the Prophet said: "The people of Paradise will behold the high place that is above them even as they now

[7] LXXVI, 5; LXXXIII, 27.

[8] XXII, 46. In this connection was revealed one of the many verses which refer to the heart as the faculty by which man has sight of supernatural realities. The eye of the heart, though closed in fallen man, is able to take in a glimmering of light and this is faith. But an evil way of living causes a covering like rust to accumulate over the heart so that it cannot sense the Divine origin of God's Message: *When Our Revelations are recited unto him, he saith: Tales of the men of old. Nay, but their earnings are even as rust over their hearts* (LXXXIII, 13–14).

[9] XII, 111; XIII, 19, etc.

[10] al-Ḥakīm al-Tirmidhī, *Nawādir al-uṣūl.*

[11] I.I. 853.

[12] XVII, 21.

behold the bright planet[13] on the eastern or western horizon."[14] The disparities between man and man were also reflected in the manner of his teaching, some of which was reserved for the few who would understand it. Abū Hurayrah said: "I have treasured in my memory two stores of knowledge which I had from the Messenger of God. One of them have I divulged; but if I divulged the other ye would cut this throat,"[15] and he pointed to his own throat.

During the return march to Medina after the victories of Mecca and Ḥunayn the Prophet said to some of his Companions: "We have returned from the Lesser Holy War to the Greater Holy War." And when one of them asked: "What is the Greater Holy War, O Messenger of God?" he answered: "The war against the soul."[16] The soul of fallen man is divided against itself. Of its lowest aspect the Qur'ān says: *Verily the soul commandeth unto evil.*[17] The better part of it, that is the conscience, is named *the ever-upbraiding soul;*[18] and it is this which wages the Greater Holy War, with the help of the Spirit, against the lower soul.

Finally there is *the soul which is at peace,* that is the whole soul no longer divided against itself, after the battle has been won. Such are the souls of those who have reached the highest degree, at the level of *the foremost, the slaves of God, the near.* The Qur'ān addresses this perfect soul in the words: *O thou soul which art at peace, return unto thy Lord with gladness that is thine in Him and His in thee.*[19] *Enter thou among My slaves. Enter thou My Paradise.*[20] The twofold nature of this blessing recalls the Qur'ān's promise of two Paradises for the blessed soul, and also the Prophet's reference to his own ultimate state as "The meeting with my Lord and Paradise". For *the soul which is at peace,* the entry into *My paradise* corresponds to "the meeting with my Lord", whereas the entry *among My slaves* corresponds

13 Venus.

14 M. LI, 4.

15 B. III, 42.

16 Bayḥaqī, *Zuhd.*

17 XII, 53.

18 LXXV, 2.

19 That is, with mutual *Riḍwān.*

20 LXXXIX, 27–30.

to "Paradise", that is the second accompanying Paradise. The Supreme Paradise, that of God, "the meeting with my Lord", is none other than *Riḍwān*. The following verse had recently been revealed: *God hath promised the believers, the men and the women, gardens that are watered by flowing rivers wherein they shall dwell immortal, abodes of excellence in the Paradises of Eden. And Riḍwān from God is greater. That is the Infinite Beatitude.*[21]

The Prophet also spoke of the supreme degree insofar as it can be reached during life on earth, and this saying is one of those which are called holy traditions because they transmit the direct words of God: "My slave ceaseth not to draw near unto Me with devotions of his free will until I love him; and when I love him I am the hearing with which he heareth and the sight with which he seeth and the hand with which he graspeth and the foot on which he walketh."[22]

The chief of the voluntary devotions is *dhikr Allāh*, which may be rendered "remembrance of God" or "calling upon God". In one of the first Revelations the Prophet was commanded: *Invoke in remembrance the Name of thy Lord, and devote thyself to Him with an utter devotion.*[23] A later Revelation says: *Verily the ritual prayer preserveth from iniquity and abomination; but the remembrance of God is greater.*[24] With reference to the heart's blindness and its cure the Prophet said: "For everything there is a polish that taketh away rust, and the polish of the heart is remembrance of God."[25] And when asked who would rank highest in God's esteem on the Day of Resurrection he answered: "The men and the women who invoke God much in remembrance." And when asked if they would rank even above the man who had fought in God's path he answered: "Even though he wielded his sword amongst infidels and idolaters until it was broken and smeared with blood, yet would the rememberer of God have a more excellent degree than his."[26]

[21] IX, 72.

[22] B. LXXX1, 37.

[23] LXXIII, 8.

[24] XXIX, 45.

[25] Bayhaqī, *Daʿawāt.*

[26] Tirmidhī XLV.

LXXXIV
The Choice

The Prophet continually spoke of Paradise, and when he did so it was as a man who sees what he describes. This impression was confirmed by many other signs, as for example when he once stretched out his hand as if to take something, and then drew it back. He said nothing, but some of those who were with him noticed his action and questioned him about it. "I saw Paradise," he said, "and I reached out for a cluster of its grapes. Had I taken it, ye would have eaten of it as long as the world endureth."[1] They had grown accustomed to thinking of him as one who is already in a sense in the Hereafter. Perhaps it was partly for this reason that when he spoke of his death, and when he inferred indirectly, as sometimes now he did, that it might be imminent, his words made little impression on them. Moreover, despite his sixty-three years, he still had the stature and grace of a much younger man, his eyes were still bright, and there were only a few white hairs in his black hair. Yet on one occasion a remark of his when he was with his wives was sufficiently ominous to prompt the question as to which of them would be the first to rejoin him in the next world. He replied: "She of the longest reach will be the soonest of you to join me,"[2] whereupon they set about measuring their arms, one against another. Presumably, though it is not recorded, Sawdah was the winner of this contest, for she was the tallest of them and in general the largest. Zaynab, on the other hand, was a small woman, with an arm to match. But it was Zaynab who died first of them all, some ten years later. Only then did they realise that by "she of the longest reach" the Prophet had meant the most giving, for Zaynab was exceedingly generous, like her predecessor of the same name who had been called "the mother of the poor".

[1] B. XVI, 8.

[2] I.S. VIII, 76–7.

One night, not long after the Prophet had ordered preparations for the Syrian campaign and before the army had left, he called to a freedman of his in the small hours, Abū Muwayhibah, and said: "I have been commanded to pray forgiveness for the people of the cemetery, so come thou with me." They went out together, and when they reached the Baqīᶜ the Prophet said: "Peace be on you, O people of the graves. Rejoice in your state, how much better it is than the state of men now living. Dissensions come like waves of darkest night, the one following hard upon the other, each worse than the last." Then he turned to Abū Muwayhibah and said: "I have been offered the keys of the treasuries of this world and immortality therein followed by Paradise, and I have been given the choice between that and meeting my Lord and Paradise." "O dearer than my father and my mother," said Abū Muwayhibah, "take the keys of the treasuries of this world and immortality therein followed by Paradise." But he answered him saying: "I have already chosen the meeting with my Lord and Paradise." Then he prayed for forgiveness for the people of the Baqīᶜ.[3]

It was at dawn that day, or perhaps the next day, that his head ached as he had never known it to ache, but he none the less went to the Mosque and after leading the prayer he mounted the pulpit and invoked blessings on the martyrs of Uḥud, as if—so it was said afterwards—he were doing it for the last time. Then he said: "There is a slave amongst the slaves of God unto whom God hath offered the choice between this world and that which is with Him, and the slave hath chosen that which is with God." When he said this Abū Bakr wept, for he knew that the Prophet was speaking of himself and that the choice meant imminent death. The Prophet saw that he had understood, and telling him not to weep, he said: "O people, the most beneficent of men unto me in his companionship and in that which his hand bestoweth is Abū Bakr; and if I were to take from all mankind an inseparable friend he would be Abū Bakr—but companionship and brotherhood of faith is ours until God unite us in His Presence." It was on that occasion that he said, looking round at the multiple entrances into the Mosque from the private houses which surrounded it: "Behold these doors that intrude upon the Mosque. Let them be walled

[3] I.I. 1000.

up, save only the door of Abū Bakr."[4] Before leaving the pulpit he said: "I go before you, and I am your witness. Your tryst with me is at the Pool,[5] which verily I behold from here where now I stand. I fear not for you that ye will set up gods beside God; but I fear for you this world, lest ye seek to rival one another in worldly gains."[6]

From the Mosque he went back to the apartment of Maymūnah, whose turn it was to house him. The effort of speech to the congregation had increased his fever; and after an hour or two, wishing to let ʿĀ'ishah know that he was ill, he went briefly to visit her. She also was suffering from a headache, and when he entered her room she moaned: "Oh my head!" "Nay, ʿĀ'ishah," said the Prophet, "it is oh *my* head!" But he looked at her searchingly, as if to seek some sign of mortal sickness in her face, and finding none he said: "I wished that it might be"—he meant her death—"whilst yet I was alive, that I might ask forgiveness for thee and invoke mercy upon thee and shroud thee and pray over thee and bury thee." ʿĀ'ishah could see that he was ill and she was alarmed at the tone of his voice, but she tried to make light of it, and succeeded in bringing a brief smile to his face. Then he repeated: "Nay, but it is oh *my* head,"[7] and returned to Maymūnah.

He tried to do as he did when he was well, and continued to lead the prayers in the Mosque as usual; but his illness increased, until the hour came when he could pray only in a sitting position, and he told the congregation that they also should pray seated. On his return to the apartment of the wife whose day it was, he asked her "Where am I tomorrow?" and she named the wife to whom he would go. "And where the day after tomorrow?" he asked. Again she answered; but struck by his insistence, and sensing that he was impatient to be with ʿĀ'ishah, she told the other wives, whereupon they all came to him and said: "O Messenger of God, we have given our days with you unto our sister ʿĀ'ishah."[8] He accepted their gift, but

[4] I.I. 1006.

[5] Fed by Kawthar, the celestial river given to the Prophet, the Pool is a lake where the believers quench their thirst on their entry into Paradise.

[6] B. LXIV, 17.

[7] I.S. II/2, 10.

[8] I.S. II/2, 30.

was now too weak to walk unaided, so ʿAbbās and ʿAlī helped him to ʿĀ'ishah's apartment.

Word came to him that there was much criticism of his choice of so young a man as Usāmah to command the army for the Syrian campaign, and that there was in consequence a certain slackening in the preparations. He felt the need to answer his critics, but his fever was intense, so he said to his wives: "Pour over me seven skins of water from different wells that I may go out unto the men and exhort them." Ḥafṣah brought a tub to ʿĀ'ishah's room and the other wives brought water, and he sat in the tub while they poured it over him. Then they helped him to dress and bound up his head, and two of the men took him between them to the Mosque, where he sat in the pulpit and addressed those who were assembled there, saying: "O people, dispatch Usāmah's troop, for though ye question his leadership even as ye questioned the leadership of his father before him, yet is he worthy of the command,[9] even as his father was worthy of it." He descended from the pulpit and was helped back to ʿĀ'ishah's house. Preparations were hastened on, and Usāmah went out with his army as far as Jurf, where they encamped, about three miles to the north of Medina.

At the next call to prayer the Prophet felt he could no longer lead it even though he remained seated, so he said to his wives: "Tell Abū Bakr to lead the people in prayer." But ʿĀ'ishah feared that it would greatly pain her father to take the place of the Prophet. "O Messenger of God," she said, "Abū Bakr is a very sensitive man, not strong of voice and much given to weeping when he reciteth the Qur'ān." "Tell him to lead the prayer," said the Prophet, as if she had not spoken. She tried again, this time suggesting that ʿUmar should take his place. "Tell Abū Bakr to lead the prayer," he reiterated. ʿĀ'ishah had thrown a glance of appeal at Ḥafṣah, who now began to speak, but the Prophet silenced her with the words: "Ye are even as the women that were with Joseph.[10] Tell Abū Bakr to lead the people in prayer. Let the blamer find fault and let the ambitious aspire, God and the believers will not have it

[9] When, after some delay, the campaign took place, Usamah proved the truth of these words.

[10] Referring to Potiphar's wilful wife and her friends; see Q. XII, 31–3.

otherwise."[11] He repeated the last sentence three times, and for the rest of his illness Abū Bakr led the prayer.

The Prophet lay much of the time with his head resting on ʿĀ'ishah's breast or on her lap; but when Fāṭimah came ʿĀ'ishah would withdraw a little to allow the father and daughter some privacy together, and at one of these visits ʿĀ'ishah saw him whisper something to his daughter, who thereupon began to weep. Then he confided to her another secret and she smiled through her tears. As she was leaving, ʿĀ'ishah asked her what he had said, and she answered that they were secrets she could not divulge. But later she said to her: "The Prophet told me he would die in that illness whereof he died, and therefore I wept. Then he told me that I would be the first of the people of his house to follow him, and therefore I laughed."[12]

He suffered much pain in his illness, and one day when it was at its worst his wife Ṣafiyyah said to him: "O Prophet of God, would that I had what thou hast!" whereupon some of the other wives exchanged glances and whispered one to another that this was hypocrisy. The Prophet saw them and said: "Go rinse your mouths." They asked him why, and he said: "For your maligning of your companion. By God, she speaketh the truth in all sincerity."[13]

Umm Ayman was in constant attendance, and she kept her son informed. He had already resolved to advance no further and to remain in his camp at Jurf until God should decide. But one morning the news was such that he came to Medina and went in tears to the Prophet, who was too ill that day to speak, though he was fully conscious. Usāmah bent over him and kissed him, and the Prophet raised his hand, palm upwards, to ask and to receive blessings from Heaven. Then he made a gesture as if to empty the contents of his hand upon Usāmah, who returned sadly to his camp.

The next day was Monday the twelfth of Rabīʿ I in the eleventh year of Islam, that is, the eighth day of June in the year AD 632. Early that morning the Prophet's fever abated, and although he was exceedingly weak the call to prayer decided him to go to the Mosque. The prayer had already begun when

[11] I.S. II/2, 20.

[12] B. LXII, 12.

[13] I.S. VIII, 91.

he entered, and the people were almost drawn away from it for joy at the sight of him, but he motioned them to continue. For a moment he stood to watch them and his face shone with gladness as he marked the piety of their demeanour. Then, still radiant, he made his way forward, helped by Faḍl and by Thawbān, one of his freedmen. "I never saw the Prophet's face more beautiful than it was at that hour," said Anas. Abū Bakr had been conscious of the stir throughout the ranks behind him. He knew that it could only have one cause, and that the man he now heard approaching must be the Prophet. So without turning his head, he stepped back, but the Prophet placed his hand on his shoulder and pressed him forwards again in front of the congregation, saying "Lead thou the prayer," while he himself sat on the right of Abū Bakr and prayed seated.

Great was the rejoicing at this apparent recovery, and not long after the prayer Usāmah arrived again from his camp, expecting to find the Prophet worse and overjoyed to find him better. "Set forth, with the blessings of God," said the Prophet. So Usāmah bade him farewell, and rode back to Jurf, where he told his men to make ready for the northward march. Meantime Abū Bakr had taken leave to go as far as Upper Medina. Already before his marriage to Asmā', he had long been betrothed to Ḥabībah, the daughter of Khārijah, the Khazrajite with whom he had lodged ten years ago on his arrival in the oasis, and they had recently been married. Ḥabībah still lived with her family at Sunḥ, where he now went to visit her.

The Prophet returned to ʿĀ'ishah's apartment helped by Faḍl and Thawbān. ʿAlī and ʿAbbās followed them there, but did not stay long, and when they came out some men who were passing asked ʿAlī how the Prophet was. "Praise be to God," said ʿAlī, "he is well." But when the questioners had gone on their way ʿAbbās took ʿAlī's hand and said: "I swear I recognise death in the face of God's Messenger, even as I have ever been able to recognise it in the faces of our clansmen. So let us go and speak with him. If his authority is to be vested in us, then we shall know it; and if in other than us, then will we ask him to commend us unto the people, that they may treat us well." But ʿAlī said: "By God, I will not, for if the authority be withheld from us by him, none after him will ever give it us."[14]

[14] I.I. 1011.

The Prophet had now returned to his couch and was lying with his head upon ʿĀ'ishah's breast as if all his strength had been used. None the less, when her brother ʿAbd al-Raḥmān entered the room with a tooth-stick in his hand, she saw the Prophet looking at it in such a way that she knew he wanted it. So she took it from her brother and gnawed upon it to soften it. Then she gave it to the Prophet, who rubbed his teeth with it vigorously despite his weakness.

Not long afterwards he lost consciousness, and ʿĀ'ishah thought it was the onset of death, but after an hour he opened his eyes. She then remembered his having said to her: "No Prophet is taken by death until he hath been shown his place in Paradise and then offered the choice, to live or to die." And she understood that this had been accomplished, and that he had returned from a vision of the Hereafter. "He will not now choose us!" she said to herself. Then she heard him murmur: "With the supreme communion in Paradise, *with those upon whom God hath showered His favour, the prophets and the saints and the martyrs and the righteous, most excellent for communion are they.*"[15] Again she heard him murmur: "O God, with the supreme communion,"[16] and these were the last words she heard him speak. Gradually his head grew heavier upon her breast, until the other wives began to lament, and ʿĀ'ishah laid his head on a pillow and joined them in lamentation.

[15] Q. IV, 69.

[16] I.S. II/2, 27.

ART & POETRY

Hamlet

The basic theme of Hamlet is summed up in the Prince's own words: "Virtue cannot so inoculate our old stock but we shall relish of it." (III, I, 118–20). This means: "It is no use plastering one or two superficial virtues over our old stock, that is, the original sin which permeates our nature, since in spite of all such virtues, we shall still continue to reek of the old stock." But in order to express fully what is in Hamlet's mind here we must add: "There is only one thing which can effectively wipe out the stench of our old stock and that is the complete reversal of the Fall, total liberation from the grip of the enemy of mankind, in other words, the slaying of the dragon, or more simply, in the language of this play, revenge."

As to Hamlet's manner of expression, Shakespeare allows himself here, under cover of the prince's "madness", to come within close range of divulging esoteric secrets. Initiation into the Mysteries is nothing other than the inoculating or grafting of a scion of man's primordial nature onto the old stock of his fallen nature which will thus be effaced, stench and all, provided that the new primordial scion be duly tended and implacably protected against any suckers that the old stock may put forth in an attempt to re-establish itself. That tending and that protection are the rites and disciplines of the Lesser Mysteries, the path of purification from original sin and the recovery thereby of man's Edenic state. This complete reversal of the Fall is precisely what is meant according to the play's deepest meaning, not only by "revenge" but also by "honour", the symbolism of which is bound up with that of revenge. No revenge, no honour: for men of understanding, the subhuman plight of fallen man is a state of global dishonour.

In its immediate impact upon us sacred art[1] is like a stone thrown into water. The ever widening ripples illustrate the

[1] Shakespeare's plays cannot be considered as sacred art in the full and central sense of the term, but they can be considered as an extension of it, and as partaking both of its qualities and its function.

limitless repercussions that are made, or can be made, upon the soul by this impact, fraught as it is with several meanings at different levels. One meaning can, as we have seen, open out onto another deeper meaning[2] that lies beyond it. In this way sacred art often conveys far more than it appears to convey, far more sometimes even than the mind in question is conscious of or could take in by way of ordinary didactic teaching.

Needless to say, the initial impact itself captivates the mind and the emotions. According to the literal meaning of *Hamlet*, we are given many strong and obvious reasons why Hamlet should kill Claudius, enough at any rate even to make us forget for the moment that revenge is un-Christian. None the less, it would be true to say that there is no common measure between the literal meaning of this play and the deep sense of urgency that Shakespeare instils into us. So long as we are in the theatre we are not far from feeling that revenge is the most important thing in the world; and we are right, for there *is* nothing more important, and indeed nothing more Christian, than what revenge stands for here.

The allegorical meaning serves to universalise the literal meaning and thus to guarantee its spiritual significance. Both are at the same cosmic level; but though the allegory does not transcend the human plane, it none the less expands it, sometimes even to its full extent. The discords of Shakespeare's great plays are often suspended more or less explicitly between two harmonies which in certain cases have to be identified, allegorically speaking, with the Edenic Age and the Millennium. When that is so the Fall of man is to be seen through a deliberately transparent veil which is never more transparent than it is in *Hamlet*. The Ghost's revelation to the Prince is, as regards the allegoric meaning, like a puzzle with a few missing pieces which it is not difficult for us to supply in the light of those pieces which we are given—the garden with its fruit trees, the serpent, the guilty woman, whose guilt has something mysteriously unfathomable about it. The *Genesis* narrative is undoubtedly here. There is also, explicitly, the first-fruit of the Fall, the sin of fratricide.[3] But the Fall itself was in fact a

[2] Not that every detail in the text has a deeper meaning. Conversely, there are some details which only make good sense on the deepest plane of all.

[3] The murderer himself says: "Oh, my offence is rank, it smells to heaven;|It hath the primal eldest curse upon't|A brother's murder!" (III, 3, 36–8)

murder also, the slaying or making mortal of Adam by the serpent, and the forbidden fruit was the "poison" through which that murder was effected.

The Queen is not merely Hamlet's mother; she is his whole ancestral line going back to Eve herself; and inasmuch as she is Eve, she represents, in general, the fallen human soul, especially in its passive aspect. In other words, she represents that passivity which in man's primordial state was turned towards Heaven and which after it lost contact with the Spirit has come more or less under the sway of the devil or, in the words of the play, having "sated itself in a celestial bed" has come to "prey on garbage". No doubt in foresight of her repentance the Ghost says to Hamlet:

> Leave her to heaven,
> And to those thorns that in her bosom lodge,
> To prick and sting her. (I, 5, 86–8)

So meantime the Prince takes upon himself to personify those thorns in the hope, we may conclude, of finally waking her conscience which she has lulled to sleep.

According to the letter of the law, the Queen is altogether innocent of the murder of King Hamlet and indeed altogether ignorant of it. But the fact that she was willing to marry a monster of a man almost immediately after having been widowed of his opposite makes her eminently qualified to personify the initial guilt of fallen humanity, for however the Fall may be represented, it amounts essentially to exchanging a "celestial" treasure for earthly "garbage". Moreover, since the Fall, as we have seen, may be considered as a murder, to personify the Fall is to personify its guilt in that respect also, which makes Gertrude in a way the accomplice of Claudius. Nor can it be denied that her consent to marry him meant that she had stifled within herself the memory of her first husband's outstanding qualities, and to stifle is to kill, which to a certain extent gives Hamlet the right to accuse her of having killed his father, as he does, albeit indirectly and under cover of madness, when he puts into the Player Queen's mouth the lines:

> In second husband let me be accurst!
> None wed the second but who kill'd the first. (III, 2, 191–92)

Unlike the writer of epic, the dramatist has a very limited space at his disposal. Consequently he often chooses to build a house of more than one storey. In *Hamlet* the soul is not only represented by the Prince and his mother; its state is also reflected in the condition of the country. Not that there is actually a sub-plot of civil war as in *Henry IV*, but none the less "Something is rotten in the state of Denmark" and "The time is out of joint" and needs to be "set right".

Fallen man stands between two perfections, one past and one future, that which was lost and that which is to be gained. In this play it is the dead King Hamlet who stands for the past perfection and its loss, whereas Fortinbras represents the perfection which is to come. It is he whom the dying Hamlet is to name as his heir. The analogy between the symbolism of this play and that of *Henry IV* is by no means exact in every detail; but the dead King Hamlet, at any rate as regards legitimacy, corresponds to the dead King Richard II, whereas Queen Gertrude and her son correspond to King Henry IV and his son, while Fortinbras in a sense corresponds to that son regenerated as King Henry V. It would be a mistake however to seek to establish a precise correspondence here between parent and parent and between son and son. It is true that Gertrude is burdened with guilt towards King Hamlet just as Henry IV is burdened with guilt towards King Richard; but Prince Hamlet, the censurer of self and others, also has much in common with Henry IV, whereas in some respects, as we shall see, Gertrude may be said to come closer symbolically, to the repentant prodigal Prince Hal.

As a parallel to the whole action of the Danish play, a parallel that powerfully underlines its deepest meaning, the soul of King Hamlet is being purified in Purgatory. But the dead King has also another aspect. Just as Adam was not only the man who fell but also the most perfect of all creatures, made in the image of God, so also King Hamlet, who in a sense corresponds to Adam, is not only a purgatorial pilgrim but also a symbol of man's lost Edenic state. It is in virtue of this that he refers to his own marriage with Gertrude as a "celestial bed", and is spoken of by Hamlet in terms of human perfection:

> A combination and a form indeed
> Where every god did seem to set his seal
> To give the world assurance of a man. (III, 4, 60–2)

It is also in virtue of this aspect that he acts as spiritual guide to his son.

There can be no problem here for any member of the audience, since we are all accustomed to thinking and speaking of Adam in these two different ways. Nor is there any contradiction between the general impression of great majesty made by the Ghost and his having, at cockcrow,

> started like a guilty thing
> upon a fearful summons. (I, 1, 148–49)

For Shakespeare had enough imagination to know that a soul in Purgatory is by definition preoccupied by a sense of the magnitude of his imperfections which, as regards himself, the Ghost describes as "the foul crimes done in my days of nature" (I, 5 12). The purgatorial aspect of King Hamlet can none the less be said to unite in him the two Adams, for his status as a soul in Purgatory means that he is already saved and on his way to Paradise. It is thus that the Catholic church speaks of souls in Purgatory as *animae sanctae*, holy souls.

The difference between simple piety and mysticism might almost be summed up by saying that the averagely pious man looks at the story of the Garden of Eden for the most part objectively, whether he takes it literally or allegorically. The mystic, on the other hand, looks at it subjectively as something which intensely, directly and presently concerns himself. Again, the averagely pious man is aware of the existence of the devil, but in fact, if not in theory, he imagines him to be more or less harmless and has little idea of the extent of his own subservience to him. In general he is extremely subject to the illusion of neutrality. But the mystic knows that most of what seems neutral is harmful, and that "one may smile and smile and be a villain" (I, 5, 108). The Ghost initiates Hamlet into the Mysteries by conveying to him the truth of the Fall not as a remote historical fact but as an immediate life-permeating reality, an acute pain which will not allow his soul a moment's rest; and every man in fact is in exactly the same situation as the Prince of Denmark, did he but know it, that is, if he were not

> Duller ... than the fat weed
> That roots itself at ease on Lethe wharf. (1, 5, 32–3)

What the Ghost says to Hamlet could almost be paraphrased: "Latterly you have been feeling that 'all is not well'. I come to confirm your worst suspicions and to show you the remedy. Since man has been robbed by the devil of his birthright, there is only one way for him to regain what is lost and that is by taking revenge upon the robber."

With all the ardor of the novice, in answer to his father's last injunction "Remember me!" the Prince replies :

> Remember thee?
> Yea, from the table of my memory
> I'll wipe away all trivial fond records,
> All saws of books, all forms, all pressures past,
> That youth and observation copied there;
> And thy commandment all alone shall live
> Within the book and volume of my brain,
> Unmixed with baser matter. (I, 5, 95–104)

He is true to his word in the sense that from now on the thought of the task that has been laid upon him remains uppermost in his mind. But that does not make any the less ironical his earlier words when the Ghost first told him the bare fact that he had been murdered without yet having told him who the murderer was:

> Haste me to know it, that I, with wings as swift
> As meditation or the thoughts of love
> May sweep to my revenge (I, 5, 29–31)

Yet Hamlet, unlike Othello and Lear, is a supreme psychologist, and knows himself as well as he knows others. Moreover if he is slow to act he is quick to think, and it does not take him long to replace the momentary impulse of sweeping to his revenge with the consciousness that the mandate laid on him by Heaven constitutes an almost unbearably difficult task. The scene ends with his couplet:

> The time is out of joint; O cursed spite
> That ever I was born to set it right! (I, 5, 189–90)

We have, however, been promised that he will succeed, for at the end of the preceding scene, when Marcellus says: "Something is rotten in the state of Denmark," Horatio immediately adds: "Heaven will direct it" (1,4,90–1).

Dante mentions the different meanings of a work of art, literal, allegorical, moral, anagogical, in an order which rightly suggests a hierarchy, leading up to the anagogical or esoteric meaning which is the highest. As to that which comes second to it, the ethical aspect of dramatic art may be said to concern the spectators insofar as they are drawn to identify themselves, in varying degrees, with whatever increase of beauty of soul is set before them on the stage, and to dissociate themselves from all movements in the opposite direction. The simile used earlier of the widening ripples caused by a stone cast into water may serve to illustrate not only the opening out of the literal meaning onto the further meanings but also, subjectively, the gradual heightening and deepening of the receptivity of spectator and reader insofar as they are capable of spiritual growth. The same simile is also apt for the moral message as a whole, since unlike the three others this message is present at every level. In its highest reaches it is absorbed into the supreme message: to portray, as Shakespeare constantly does in his maturer plays, the dazzling plenitude of virtue, without which there can be no perfection and therefore no passage through the Mysteries, is to trace out a dimension which is truly anagogical, a necessary aspect of the steep ascent of the mysterial way. Otherwise expressed, this message, like virtue itself, is as it were suspended between human goodnesses and their supreme archetypes, that is, the Divine Qualities. "Be ye perfect, even as your Father in Heaven is perfect." The phrase "to excel oneself," if properly used, indicates that the virtue in question partakes in some degree of the transcendent. Shakespeare is explicit in this respect, for example, as regards the virtues of Duncan in *Macbeth* which have power to "plead like angels, trumpet-tongued" (I, 7, 19). Another outstanding example is Cordelia's self-sacrifice in *King Lear*, a sacrifice upon which "the Gods themselves pour incense" (V, 3, 20–1).

It must be remembered that the closely knit brevity of the dramatic form calls for simplicity and speed; and when the theme of a play is the Mysteries, something can be gained by making it begin not too far from the threshold of fulfilment. Shakespeare by no means always avails himself of this possibility, but when he chooses to do so, as in this play and in certain others, he makes his audience conscious, sometimes even from the very start, of a virtual perfection of moral substance in his heroes and heroines, a virtuality that is almost already an actuality except for what the drama itself is destined to actualise. Upon our first contact with Hamlet and Othello, for example, we are immediately aware of a magnanimity that has a touch of the absolute, a grandeur of soul which enthralls and edifies. From his first entry Othello confronts us with a majesty which is maintained throughout; and Hamlet, in his own very different way, is a no less striking example. In this latter case the initial effect is strengthened by contrast: against the foil of the extreme hypocrisy of Claudius and of the flatterers who pander to him, the profound sincerity of Hamlet is overwhelming. It is all the more so, when seen on the stage, for being visual, with the Prince himself in black and everyone else dressed for festive merrymaking, a contrast which is held at considerable length before our eyes and doubled in its effect by the mourner's prolonged unbroken silence matched by the unchanging solemn sadness of his face, all leading up to his words, when he finally does speak in answer to his mother's query as to why, since death is a common occurrence, it should seem so particular to him in the case of his father:

> Seems, madam! Nay, it is; I know not "seems".
> 'Tis not alone my inky cloak, good mother…
> Together with all forms, modes, shows of grief,
> That can denote me truly; these indeed "seem",
> For they are actions that a man might play;
> But I have that within which passeth show;
> These but the trappings and the suits of woe. (I, 2, 76–82)

Then when he is left alone, and in scenes that closely follow, other aspects of perfection become manifest. We have before us a brilliantly gifted and highly sensitive prince, brought up to be King, a youth endowed with a vast and probing intelligence that is implacably objective, the severest of critics but without a trace of arrogance, being himself his first object of criticism, a man dedicated to truth and allergic to falsity in any form, a soul that reverberates with love of good and abhorrence of evil.

Fie on't! O fie! 'Tis an unweeded garden
That grows to seed; things rank and gross in nature
Possess it merely. (I, 2, 135–37)

This heartfelt disgust at the corruption of the Danish court under Claudius is balanced by the heartfelt joy that radiates from him at any manifestation of the opposite. It is remarkable how impressive Hamlet's gratitude is for the existence, despite this corruption, of one or two individuals whom he can trust, in particular Horatio and Marcellus. It is they who witnessed the appearance of the Ghost and have sworn to keep that, and all things connected with it, a secret; and these lines, which immediately follow their oath, are intensely moving for the depth and nobility of soul from which they spring:

So, gentlemen,
With all my love I do commend me to you;
And what so poor a man as Hamlet is
May do, to express his love and friending to you,
God willing, shall not lack. (I, 5, 183–87)

We may quote also, from Hamlet's praise of Horatio in another scene:

Give me that man
That is not passion's slave, and I will wear him
In my heart's core, ay, in my heart of heart,
As I do thee. (III, 2, 79–82)

Hamlet is also quick to recognise, in others, a virtue which he himself needs to perfect. The example which comes first to mind is that of Fortinbras, who is the theme of Hamlet's soliloquy which begins: "How all occasions do inform against me!" (IV, 4, 32). But this reflection might also have been made on another somewhat later "occasion" which much more directly "informs" against Hamlet; and though he himself is not present to take note of it, the audience can do so for themselves. This "occasion" concerns Laertes, who is also, like the Prince of Norway, an object of Hamlet's esteem: "That is Laertes, a very noble youth" (V, 1, 24–6), he says to Horatio as the mourners enter for the funeral of Ophelia; and later in the scene he protests to Laertes himself:

> What is the reason that you use me thus?
> I loved you ever.

Now both Hamlet and Laertes were absent from Denmark at their fathers' respective deaths; and Laertes was given to understand, through various rumours, that his father had died at the hand of Claudius. Immediately he goes back to Denmark, gathers round himself a multitude of supporters, overcomes the royal guards, and to the accompaniment of shouts "Laertes shall be king, Laertes king!" (IV, 5, 107) he breaks into the palace, confronts Claudius, and says to him:

> O thou vile king,
> Give me my father! (IV, 5, 114–15)

Hamlet, for his part, is also given, together with the news of his father's death, an imperative reason for taking action against Claudius, namely that Claudius has usurped the throne, or, to use the Prince's own words, that he has shown himself to be a thief, a "cut-purse",

> That from a shelf the precious diadem stole
> And put it in his pocket! (III, 4, 100–1)

If Hamlet had set about doing what Laertes did, he would no doubt have found himself very soon at the head of a powerful host which would almost certainly have been joined by rapidly increasing sections of the army itself; and if, in preference to Claudius, there had been cries of "Laertes shall be king," how much more would the people have shouted for their beloved Prince! It is true that Hamlet's failure to take action can be partly attributed to one of his virtues, that he is totally devoid of worldly ambition. But that does not excuse him for neglecting his responsibilities and leaving his country in the hands of a man whom he knows to be utterly debased, even though he does not yet know him to be a regicide. The weakness that Hamlet has to overcome, and does overcome in the end, is shown up very clearly in the light of Laertes' strength in that particular respect. Nor is Hamlet deceived, as we shall see, in judging him to be "a very noble youth".

In accordance with world-wide tradition it could be said that to regain what was lost at the Fall is to become once more in all fullness a priest-king which is what man was created to be, king because he was placed at the centre of this earthly state to be there the viceregent of God, priest because his centrality has also a vertical aspect, that of being mediator between Heaven and earth. This definition is relevant to many of Shakespeare's greater plays, and it is nearly always the priestly dimension which most needs to be developed and perfected. At the outset of Hamlet however the Prince is more priest than king. Not that he has not already also a wealth of royalty in his nature, but it falls short of fullness in one direction, and his growth to adequacy in that respect is the main theme of the drama.

The texture of many of the plays, and of none more than Hamlet, provides a favourable setting for the simultaneous presence of more than one meaning. On the one hand, to go back to Shakespeare's mastery of his art, he partly achieves his extraordinary dramatic concentration by not wasting words. He never fails to tell us explicitly everything that we really need to know; but apart from the essential, he not infrequently challenges us to open, with the keys of what he has given us in the way of implications, the doors which he has not opened himself. His economy in leaving many things unsaid thus serves not only to increase the tension but to introduce an enigmatic element which can have a subtly galvanising effect upon the audience. This is akin to the use of paradox in aphorisms: if we say, for example, that divinity is the most truly human feature of man, the barbed shaft of what seems like a contradiction in terms can spur the intelligence to abandon the habitual channels of thought and to transcend itself. In this connection it should also be remembered that perplexity is universally recognised in mysticism as a possible stepping-stone to intellection; nor can it be denied, with regard to enigma, that the mysterious may open out onto the mysterial—to use this latter word in the sense of that which is related to the Mysteries.

If the play is somewhat haunted by enigma, it is also haunted by madness, first of all the feigned madness of Hamlet, then the unfeigned madness of Ophelia; and madness is, like the use of paradox, yet another example of escape from the rut of ordinary mental processes. The fact that madness is in most actual cases an escape in a downward direction is altogether irrelevant to what we are considering here. As to the feigned madness of the Prince, one of the play's lesser enigmas is that Shakespeare, despite his lavish use of soliloquy, never lets his protagonist explain why he has come so immediately to the decision that it is an imperative necessity for him to pretend to be mad. But in this case we can easily take up the Bard's challenge and fill the gap ourselves. The pretence might seem at first a contradiction of Hamlet's sincerity, of his "I know not 'seems'," whereas in fact it finds in these very words part of its explanation. His new-found knowledge of how his father died makes it impossible to continue as before. His words, "I do not set my life at a pin's fee" (I, 4, 65), are no longer true, for his life has now a purpose to it and must therefore be protected from the danger which besets it. How much easier it would be for Claudius to kill him than it is for him to kill Claudius! Perhaps he is already under a secret sentence of death. If not, he will be under sentence as soon as the suspicions of Claudius are aroused; and he knows that his sincerity, combined with his ultra-sensitivity, would make it impossible, if he continues to behave normally, for him to hide his loathing for his uncle. Moreover a regicide is bound to be suspicious of others and always on his guard. So is a usurper, and Claudius is both of these at once. But madness, at any rate of the kind that Hamlet would feign, might serve to disarm him somewhat, as far as the madman was concerned; and the mad are usually humoured, which would give him more liberty and perhaps more opportunity of fulfilling the task imposed on him. Another reason for the pretence, albeit a secondary one, is that it would relieve the tension for himself. He said, at the end of his first scene: But break, my heart, for I must hold my tongue! (I, 2, 159) He will now be able to talk, and even to say many pertinent things. So much for the literal meaning.

As to what lies above it, since spiritual wisdom, from a worldly point of view, is a kind of madness, madness can be made to serve, in certain contexts, as a symbol of spiritual wisdom. Shakespeare avails himself of this possibility more than once in his plays; and in Hamlet, in addition to its more outward meaning as a stratagem and a blind, the "antic disposition" which the Prince puts on serves above all to underline the drastic change that has taken place in his life. In his soliloquies he shows no trace of madness; but as soon as he has to face the world, that is, when Horatio and Marcellus enter, shortly after the exit of the Ghost, the new-found spiritual outlook which fills his soul almost to bursting point has to find an outlet in what Horatio describes as "wild and whirling words". It is under cover of this "wildness" that Shakespeare momentarily allows the deeper meaning of the play to come to the surface, for what Hamlet says is:

> And so without more circumstance at all,
> I hold it fit that we shake hands and part;
> You, as your business and desire shall point you;
> For every man hath business and desire,
> Such as it is; and, for mine own poor part,
> Look you, I'll go pray. (I, 5, 127–32)

And prayer, which in the widest sense of the word may be said to comprise all forms of worship, is in fact man's chief weapon of "revenge".

In connection with madness, it may be recalled that the already quoted line: "Let me wipe it (my hand) first; it smells of mortality," which brings the deeper meaning of *King Lear* to the surface, is spoken by Lear when he is mad. The fact that Hamlet's madness is feigned whereas Lear's is not makes no difference to its symbolism. Another kind of "madness" which has the same significance is the "folly" of the professional fool, and it may in fact be wondered whether the Prince has not partly taken his cue, for his own play of madness, from his memories of Yorwick. Many of the darts that he throws are more akin to the sallies of a jester than to the ineptitudes of a lunatic, as when, for example, Claudius says to him after Polonius's death: "Where's Polonius?" and he replies: "In heaven; send thither to see; if your messenger find him not there, seek him i' the other place yourself" (IV, 3, 35–8). Hamlet almost immediately takes Horatio and Marcellus into his confidence as to his intention to feign madness, and later he takes Horatio altogether into his confidence. Later still he confides everything to his mother. There is yet another person on whom, in the nature of things, he would like to unburden his heavily laden soul, and that is Ophelia. But when in his first scene, summing up his mother's guilt, he says: "Frailty, thy name is woman!" (I, 2, 146) the generality of this remark not only serves to clinch still further the allegorical equation of Gertrude with Eve, but it may also be taken, as regards the literal meaning of the play, to indicate that in addition to his mother Ophelia has likewise come into his mind, if only in the form of the question, "Is she perhaps equally frail?" And when later he comes and gazes into her face, is he not trying to find with his eyes the answer to the question: "If I tell her everything as a secret, would she be capable of not telling her father?" We, wise after all the events, might be inclined to say "Yes". But "No" is evidently the answer that his eyes must have given him. Moreover he had no right to take any risks; and she had already shown evidence of the considerable degree of her subjection to her father by repelling the Prince's letters and refusing to give him access to her. So he leaves her without a word, for the only utterance he could have made to her at that moment would have been to tell her the whole truth.

Hamlet is not a drama of love, but of spiritual warfare, of renunciation, and of death and rebirth. The task laid upon the Prince by his father is something of a death sentence. It is not easy to kill a king, especially when that king is of the nature of Claudius. Still less is it easy to kill a king and to escape with one's own life, and Hamlet, far from being an optimist, is an implacable realist. He therefore cannot help wondering what will happen to Ophelia after he is gone. As to the present, despite his love for her, it is clearly no time for marriages; and it is in any case clear to the priestlike Hamlet that everything must be sacrificed to "the one thing necessary". For Ophelia, therefore, the best solution would no doubt be to enter a convent, which would protect her, after his almost certainly imminent death, from the "things rank and gross in nature" which are all that is left in the "unweeded garden" that the world has now become.

In the "nunnery scene", where we first see them together, Shakespeare once more allows the deeper meaning of the play to rise to the surface under cover of Hamlet's "madness". The first part of the spiritual path is "the descent into Hell". The deeper meaning of Dante's *Inferno*[4] is the descent of Dante

[4] The references here and elsewhere to Dante do not mean to suggest that Shakespeare owes anything to him directly. Of this we know nothing. *The Divine Comedy* can none the less help to throw light on certain aspects of these plays because it is based on principles with which no intellectual of Shakespeare's time could fail to be familiar.

into the hidden depths of his own soul. The novice has first to learn the meaning of "original sin"; he must come to know the evil possibilities which lie, almost unsuspected, beneath the surface illusion of being "indifferent honest". But in *The Divine Comedy* the discovery of the soul's worst possibilities and purification from them are treated separately. The *Inferno* and the *Purgatorio* correspond to an altogether exhaustive Confession followed by a full Absolution. The "architecture" of Dante's poem demands this separate treatment, as also the fact that it has an eschatological as well as a mystical meaning. Occasionally, as we shall see, Shakespeare also treats the two phases separately, but more often, as in Hamlet, he represents them as taking place simultaneously. The killing of Claudius will mean reaching not only the bottom of Hell but also the top of the Mountain of Purgatory, for revenge means purification.

Hell and Purgatory together constitute what Greco-Roman antiquity knew as the Lesser Mysteries (*mysteria parva*). Hamlet has now fully entered into these Mysteries and is thus in a situation parallel to that of his father—hence his preoccupation with sin. Very significant are the words he says to himself when he sees Ophelia approaching:

> Nymph, in thy orisons
> Be all my sins remember'd. (III, 1, 88–9)

And the gist of all that he says to her is in the following speech:

> Get thee to a nunnery; why wouldst thou be a breeder of sinners? I am myself indifferent honest; but yet I could accuse me of such things that it were better my mother had not borne me. I am very proud, revengeful, ambitious; with more offences at my beck than I have thoughts to put them in, imagination to give them shape, or time to act them in. What should such fellows as I do crawling between heaven and earth? We are arrant knaves all; believe none of us. Go thy ways to a nunnery. (III, 1, 122–32)

What mysticism terms "the descent into Hell", that is, the discovery of sinful propensities in the soul which were hitherto unknown, sometimes takes the form of actually committing the sins in question, as happens, for example, with Angelo in *Measure for Measure* and with Leontes in *The Winter's Tale*. The case of *Macbeth* is, as we shall see, quite different, for that is a descent without return, unrelated to the Mysteries.

When Hamlet, on his way to speak with his mother, suddenly comes upon Claudius praying and is about to kill him, he refrains from doing so on the grounds that to kill him while at prayer would amount to sending him to Heaven, which would be "hire and salary, not revenge". To be truly revenged he must send him to Hell. We have here a perfect example of how action of great importance can be paralysed by too much mental business, as he has said in the most famous of his soliloquies:

> And thus the native hue of resolution
> Is sicklied o'er with the pale cast[5] of thought,
> And enterprises of great pitch and moment
> With this regard their currents turn awry
> And lose the name of action. (III, 1, 84–8)

His words are, as he enters upon his uncle:

> Now might I do it pat, now he is praying;
> And now I'll do't: and so he goes to heaven;
> And so am I revenged. (III, 3, 73–5)

His "now I'll do it" shows "the native hue of resolution" which immediately, in what follows, "Is sicklied o'er with the pale cast of thought" (I, 5, 83). The "cast" is indeed "pale", for the given pretext is pitifully unconvincing. It is not to be imagined that a man of Hamlet's spiritual intelligence could sincerely believe that it is so easy to go to Heaven and that a man as wicked as Claudius could do so simply for having died when his knees were bent in prayer; nor, in all justice, did the regicide wish to send his victim to Hell, nor did he do so; and worst of all, the pretext throws to the winds one of the chief reasons for killing Claudius:

> Let not the royal bed of Denmark be
> A couch for luxury[6] and damned incest. (I, 5, 82–3)

[5] Vomit.

[6] *Luxuria*, the Latin term for the deadly sin of lust.

Thus, from the literal point of view, that is, according to Hamlet as a morality play, the Prince's inability to take decisive action makes him ready to snatch at any pretext for procrastination. A blind eye has therefore to be turned to the actual pretext given, the more so in that if taken seriously, to represent weighed thoughts, it would be in flagrant contradiction with the character of its speaker. What sin can compare with the implacable determination to send a soul to Hell?[7] And how is such appalling malevolence, worse than anything that Claudius the man is guilty of, to be reconciled with Hamlet's nobility of character? These considerations do not however apply to the pretext if we bear in mind the mystical significance of revenge.

To be more explicit, the different levels of interpretation are in agreement that it is Hamlet's spiritual immaturity which prevents him from taking action. But whereas at the lower level the pretext he gives has to be rejected by the audience as nonsense, that is, as the proverbial "straw" at which a drowning man will clutch, at the highest level the pretext makes profound sense which is perfectly compatible with the Prince's goodness. To see this we have only to consider the significance of Claudius at the different levels.

According to the literal meaning Claudius is an evil man on his way to Hell. Allegorically, as the killer of King Hamlet, he is the "Serpent" who was responsible for the making mortal of Adam and who thereby gained a hold over the entire human race. Anagogically Claudius is that very hold itself, and to kill him is to set oneself free from it and so eliminate "original sin" which results from the satanic grip. Now in Claudius the man, to go back to the literal meaning, the evil fluctuates somewhat—as Iago's evil never does in *Othello*—and it is only in the last two acts of the play that it has become a fixation. Until then there are moments when the regicide's allegorical significance is, as it were, suspended. The prayer scene is one

[7] As answer to this question we may quote from *Measure for Measure* (written about the same time as *Hamlet*) what the Duke says about sending a soul to Hell. He has been trying to prepare Barnardine for death, a criminal justly sentenced to be executed for murder. When asked if Barnardine is ready to die, the Duke replies:

> A creature unprepar'd, unmeet for death;
> And to transport him in the mind he is
> Were damnable... (IV, 3, 66–8)

of these brief respites, and on such rare occasions, Satan's manifestation of himself in Claudius recedes. To kill him then would only constitute a perfect revenge in the literal sense. It would also root out the rottenness from Denmark and "set right" what is "out of joint"; but it could not bear the weight of allegory, let alone that of anagogy, and this is just what the words of the pretext must be interpreted as saying.

Revenge on the devil must be absolute. It requires no apologies. There must be no scruples and no compromise. But the time is not yet ripe. There would be no revenge, and therefore no self-purification, in killing Claudius at that moment because Claudius is not himself. Sometimes the soul's worst possibilities may manifest themselves only partially, in such a way that it would be quite easy to overcome them. But nothing final could be hoped for from resisting them on such an occasion; it is only when those possibilities really show themselves for what they are, when they are rampant in all their iniquity, only then is it possible, by stifling them, to give them the death-blow or mortally wound them. As Hamlet says:

> When he is drunk asleep, or in his rage,
> Or in the incestuous pleasure of his bed,
> At gaming, swearing, or about some act
> That has no relish of salvation in't;
> Then trip him, that his heels may kick at heaven
> And that his soul may be as damn'd and black
> As hell, whereto it goes. (III, 3, 89–95)

In this scene the devil is far from manifesting himself fully in Claudius. The dragon has not yet come out into the open. Or in other words, Hamlet has not nearly reached the bottom of Hell. He has not even had yet any direct experience of the full villainy of Claudius. All that he has learnt so far is relatively indirect compared, for example, with what he finds when he opens the letter to the King of England and reads Claudius' instructions to have him beheaded immediately on arrival; but the very bottom of Hell is only reached when the Queen lies dead and Hamlet's own body has tasted the poison. Meantime, before he can kill the great devil he has first of all to account for the lesser devils, Rosencrantz and Guildenstern, for whose death in England, "No shriving time allowed" (V, 2, 47), he is responsible; and like Dante's "cruelty" towards some of the sufferers he sees in Hell, who are really elements in his own soul, Hamlet's attitude becomes immediately understandable and acceptable and reconcilable with his nobility of nature if we realize that all the victims of his revenge are in a sense part of himself.

Rosencrantz and Guildenstern are indeed nothing but prolongations of Claudius. They would not be there at all if they had not been expressly sent for by him, to act as his spies; and Shakespeare makes it clear, in the last speeches of any length that he puts into their mouths (III, 3), that they have found their true element in the regicide's corrupt court, where they have quickly developed into monsters of flattery and hypocrisy. As to Polonius, despite his extreme subservience to Claudius, the worst we can do is to reserve our judgement and leave his case undecided as Hamlet appears to leave it in his recently quoted gibe at Claudius. But Hamlet also says, this time in all seriousness, pointing to the old man's body:

> For this same lord,
> I do repent …
> and will answer well
> The death I gave him. (III, 4, 172–77)

Nor is it permissible to forget the last line that we hear Ophelia sing before she makes her final exit: "God ha' mercy on his soul" (IV, 6, 198) which may no doubt be said to outweigh all other considerations.

The great bedroom scene which follows the prayer scene is as it were the centre of the play. The Queen instinctively equates her son with her conscience, and she has been holding him at a certain distance. Even now, when the two are to be alone together at last, she has contrived, or rather let us say willingly consented, to have a third party present, hiding behind the arras. The presence of Polonius at the beginning of this scene means the presence, in the soul, of the determination to brazen things out. The Queen's first words to Hamlet referring to Claudius as his "father", are shameless in their effrontery: "Hamlet, thou has thy father much offended" (Ill, 4, 9.). But when Hamlet's sword pierces the body of Polonius, the way is opened for conscience to pierce through the soul's mask of self justification. The sword itself may be said to represent the truth which pierces through the foolish blindness of which Polonius is the embodiment; and it is immediately after his death that Gertrude comes to know at last the truth about Claudius.

The word "immediately" is by no means pointless. The audience, ever since the first appearance of Hamlet and his mother, have had an increasing desire to see them alone together on the stage. Shakespeare has kept them waiting; but now that longed for moment has come. What they want above all is the satisfaction of hearing the Prince tell the Queen how his father died, and of seeing how far it will change her attitude to her second husband. Now it is true that she, as well as Claudius, has witnessed the poisoner's crime re-enacted in some detail by the players under Hamlet's guidance, and she has also witnessed the overwhelming impact of that episode upon Claudius. This experience serves the purpose of enabling her to grasp the whole truth in an instant when the time comes for her to be told, but meantime it amounts to no more than a subconscious preparation. Her brazen words to Hamlet as he joins her make it clear both to him and to the audience that she has not yet drawn any conclusions either from the play itself or from the King's reaction to it. She therefore needs to be informed; nor is it nearly enough, from the point of view of dramatic art, that Hamlet, in listing his uncle's vices, should simply include the word "murderer", as he does later in the scene. That merely implies that he has already conveyed to her the facts of the murder; and so indeed he has, but with such marvellous economy that in the performances of Hamlet that we are accustomed to seeing on the stage or on the screen it does not come across to the audience, and they are denied the satisfaction they have been waiting for.

This shortcoming is too great a violation of the unwritten laws of drama to be blamed on Shakespeare. It is not possible that the consummate dramatist could have made such a blunder at so vital a moment in the play. But editors can easily go astray, and that is what has happened here, initially through some editor's clumsy insertion of a stage direction which is lacking in both the Quarto and Folio editions of *Hamlet*. At what point precisely does the Prince lift the arras and reveal the body of Polonius? As we shall see, the text itself makes it clear when this should take place; but the editor in question has timed it four lines too late; and unfortunately he has been followed, with one exception,[8] by all subsequent editors—at least, all whose work I have seen—including Edward Dowden, the editor of the 1928 Arden edition. The apparent reason for the general acceptance of this delay is that it makes the lifting of the arras, when it comes, more "dramatic"; and so, for the sake of a somewhat paltry effect, one of the most truly dramatic moments in Shakespeare has been sacrificed, a moment which any actors would be glad to exploit for the display of their talent, and, what is more, the very moment that the audience have been waiting for with such expectation.

Let us briefly consider the action as it takes place from the entry of the Prince. The Queen, seeing almost at once that she can no longer control her son in virtue of her parental authority, makes a move as if to go in search of others. Hamlet, no doubt taking her by the arm, says:

> Come, come and sit you down; you shall not budge;
> You go not till I set you up a glass
> Where you may see the inmost part of you. (III, 4, 18–20)

Still thinking him to be mad, the Queen is not unnaturally afraid, and cries for help. Polonius echoes her, presumably as loud as possible in the vain hope that there might be someone within earshot. A shout can disguise a voice; and who indeed could be expected to be, at night, behind the arras in the Queen's closet, except the King? Hamlet assumes that it must be him, and making a pass through the arras he kills Polonius who with his last breath, groans or sighs: "Oh, I am slain!" (III, 4, 25). Admittedly, a dying utterance will also tend to disguise the voice, but probably less than a shout. At any rate it seems to be at this moment that Hamlet begins to doubt the identity of his victim; and when the Queen exclaims: "Oh me, what hast thou done?" he replies: "Nay, I know not; is it the king?" Having put this urgent question, it would be unnatural if he did not then and there give himself the answer by lifting the arras. It is moreover necessary that he should do so precisely then as a cue for the Queen's cry of dismay when she sees the dead and

[8] The editor of the current Arden edition, Harold Jenkins, times it right. His interpretation of the spoken words, however, does not seem to differ from that of the other editors.

bleeding body of Polonius: "Oh, what a rash and bloody deed is this!" (III, 4, 25–7) It is the crucial passage which immediately ensues; and if it be played more or less as follows, all problems vanish, no loose thread is left hanging and the audience are more than satisfied.

At first Hamlet is appalled: for anyone of his sensitivity, it is not nothing to have killed a relatively innocent man by mistake, a man who is moreover his beloved Ophelia's father whom, whatever his limitations, she dearly loves, as the Prince knows. He slowly and solemnly echoes the Queen's words: "A bloody deed!" He is for the moment disconcerted: altogether contrary to his purpose, he has put himself instead of his mother in the wrong. Then he proceeds to redress the balance; and since it is imperative that she should take him seriously and not continue to think him mad, he must seek to convince her of his perfect sanity both by the way he looks at her and by his slow recollected and impressive manner of speech as he adds:

> almost as bad, good mother,
> As kill a king, and marry with his brother. (III, 4, 28–9)

There must be a pause at "king", since the two halves of the line have to be taken separately in that they concern two different persons. Admittedly, by reason of its syntax, the whole line might seem at first sight to concern the Queen and to accuse her of murder as well as of incest; and we have already seen that her subservience to the regicide makes her in a sense his accomplice. None the less the line cannot be passed over lightly as a mere echo of the Player Queen's "None wed the second but who killed the first." There are overwhelming reasons for us to take "as kill a king" to be nothing other than an accusation against Claudius alone. Firstly, the context demands mention of a killing in the ordinary sense such as can serve as a parallel to the Prince's killing of Polonius. "Almost as bad" is a typically Hamlettian ironic equivalent of "nothing like so bad". Secondly, the context also demands that Hamlet shall not speak to his mother, at this juncture, in anything but clear terms. Such indeed is his express purpose, "I will speak daggers to her but use none" (III, 2,415), and the daggers must not be blunted by anything enigmatic. Moreover, in order to convince her of her guilt, he would have been on his guard against including in his accusations any blame that she could easily deny. Thirdly, for his "daggers" to make their full impact, that is, for her to be fully vulnerable to their thrust, it is necessary for her to know that the man to whom she has given herself, body and soul, is the murderer of her first husband; and if in those four words "as kill a king" and his subsequent corroboration of them Hamlet is not telling her exactly how his father died, then he never does tell her, and that would be, we repeat, too great a violation of dramatic art to be attributed to Shakespeare. But in fact Shakespeare is here displaying his art of the stage to its full.

The slow emphatic delivery of the four key words with a pause at "king" not only gives time for Hamlet to speak with his eyes as well as his tongue, but also for the truth to dawn on the Queen. We may suppose that she scarcely hears "and marry with his brother" which Hamlet throws in so as not to leave her for a moment without blame. She too must let her eyes speak and perhaps draw closer to him. Looking into his face as she queries his words with her own "As kill a king?", at first half incredulous, but then convinced by the certitude conveyed to her from Hamlet and, in retrospect, by the guilty reaction of Claudius to the players' enactment of the poisoning in the garden. Her questioning echo of his words means: "Was the king your father in fact killed, not by a snake as we were told, but by a man?" Yet she herself knows the answer almost as she puts the question, and Hamlet sees that she knows it and that there is no need for him even to name the man, so he simply caps her query with his implacable "Ay, lady, 'twas my word" (III, 4, 30). Seldom can a dramatist have portrayed such intimacy between characters as Shakespeare does here between mother and son; and intimacy, telepathic almost by definition, has power to replace the spoken thought by the unspoken thought. In fact, such is the verbal thrift at this point that Hamlet is able to convince his mother of the whole iniquitous truth in less than one line.

He now speaks to Polonius:

> Thou wretched, rash, intruding fool, farewell!
> I took thee for thy better; take thy fortune;
> Thou find'st to be too busy is some danger. (III, 4, 31–3)

When the play is acted in obedience to the printed text, that is, to the editors, Hamlet does not raise the arras until just before he utters these words. We are accustomed to hearing them declaimed as an outburst of savage exasperation; and this violence is often kept up long enough to be turned against his mother and to set a feverish temperature for the dialogue that follows. But in fact, when the Prince addresses the dead man, he has already had time to adjust himself to the shock of the unforeseen accident. He has moreover already achieved something with his mother, enough to give him a presentiment of his mastery of the situation. Violence is therefore not called for. He can well afford to bid farewell to his victim with solemnity, stern no doubt, but not without a touch of pity. Then, all the more terrible for his calm weighing of words, he makes ready to speak his "daggers" to the Queen:

> Leave wringing of your hands. Peace! sit you down,
> And let me wring your heart; for so I shall
> If it be made of penetrable stuff,
> If damned custom have not braz'd it so
> That it is proof and bulwark against sense.

She makes a last vain effort to resist her conscience by taking refuge in her innocence of the murder and her ignorance of it. There should be a stress on 'I' in the line which follows:

> What have I done that thou dar'st wag thy tongue
> In noise so rude against me? (III, 4, 31–40)

But this serves to give Hamlet the best possible cue for overwhelming her with what she inescapably knows to be true, and she is eventually driven to say:

> O Hamlet, speak no more;
> Thou turn'st mine eyes into my very soul,
> And there I see such black and grained spots
> As will not leave their tinct.[9] (III, 4, 88–91)

It is often the case in Shakespeare's greater plays that there should be more than one "purgatorial pilgrim", more than

[9] Nothing I can say to myself will make them leave their black tint to take on a lighter colour.

one "Everyman"; and although the part of Gertrude is short in words, from her first appearance she holds the audience in the grip of an intense interest which is only second to their interest in Hamlet. Her repentance signifies her qualification to follow her son and enter upon the path of purification. It is at this moment that the Ghost, unseen by her, reappears to Hamlet and delegates him to be the spiritual guide of his mother; and under the inspiration of his father's words:

> Oh, step between her and her fighting soul ...
> Speak to her, Hamlet, (III, 4, 113–115)

he tells his mother what she must do. In this scene the literal meaning itself is drawn up to the mysterial level. The Prince speaks to his new disciple with an exalted penetration worthy of a master who has years of practical experience of the mystic path behind him. The spiritual dialogue ends with her solemn oath:

> Be thou assured, if words be made of breath,
> And breath of life, I have no life to breathe
> What thou hast said to me. (III, 4, 197–99)

The two lines which immediately follow have in themselves no direct spiritual significance, but they are spiritually most moving as expressive of a profound norm of human relationship which had been torn asunder and is now perfectly restored. This is the first time that we have seen the mother and the son at ease together, and the extraordinary effect of their words upon us is enhanced by the very ordinariness of his question and her answer:

> I must to England; you know that?
> Alack,
> I had forgot; 'tis so concluded on. (III,4, 200–1)

To judge from the cuts in the First Folio edition of *Hamlet*, published only seven years after Shakespeare's death, we may assume that the full text of this play was considered then, as now, too long for the requirements of theatrical performance. Unfortunately, one of the passages nearly always sacrificed today is Act IV, scene 4, without which the balance of the play as a whole is seriously upset. In this scene Hamlet, on his way to the Danish coast to set sail for England, has a glimpse of Fortinbras, the young Prince of Norway, who is leading his army through Denmark to fight against the Poles; and this glimpse reveals to Hamlet a hero endowed with the virtue which he himself most needs to develop. The scene where Fortinbras first appears is needed above all in that it marks a stage in the development of Hamlet, who drinks a new strength into his soul from his vision of Fortinbras. In the soliloquy which is prompted by his foretaste of his own true self there is a ring of confidence and resolution which we have not heard before.

> From this time forth,
> My thoughts be bloody, or be nothing worth! (IV, 4, 65–6)

Objectively of course the word "bloody" must be taken to mean "concerned with slaughter", that is with the killing of Claudius. But subjectively it means "from the heart", that is, penetrated by resolution. No longer shall "the native hue of resolution" be "sicklied o'er with the pale cast of thought". He promises us, and convinces us, that from now on the process will be reversed: instead of imposing its own pallor on other faculties, thought shall borrow resolution's own natural colour, which is blood-red inasmuch as it springs from the heart. It must be remembered, in this connection, that the word "heart", which in its ordinary sense refers to the central organ of the body, has universally also the mystical sense of centre of the soul, witness such terms as "Eye of the Heart"[10] which are common to all traditions; and Shakespeare is in line with the whole ancient world in assigning resolution to the Heart. Intellect and resolution, the crowns of intelligence and will respectively, are both, according to the esoterisms of West as well as East, enthroned in the Heart, the gateway to the Spirit, the "narrow gate" which alone allows passage from this world to the Beyond. It is significant that one of the great Sufi poets terms the path of the Mysteries as "the way of resolution".[11]

[10] The capitals here denote the transcendent sense of the organs in question.

[11] ʿUmar ibn al-Fāriḍ in his poem *al-Khamriyyah* (the Winesong). See my annotated translation in *Sufi Poems: A Mediaeval Anthology*, Cambridge, Islamic Texts Society, 2004. The term in question is there rendered "the path of firm resolve".

The spirituality of the mystic is magnetic for all other souls which are of the right metal; and the Prince draws in his wake not only his mother but also Ophelia. Her madness takes us by surprise; it is not difficult however to imagine the reasons for it—Hamlet's supposed loss of his sanity, her own supposed loss of his love, his madly precipitate departure, her father's sudden unaccountable disappearance, then (we do not know how long afterwards) news of his death and burial, *all without any explanation whatsoever*, and all in the absence of her brother on whom she might have leaned for support. But at a higher level of meaning her gains are far greater than her losses. She can be said in a sense to have followed Hamlet's behest "Get thee to a nunnery" inasmuch as her madness is indeed a retreat in which she has renounced all worldliness. For her there are only two categories of persons, the dead and the dying:

> And will he not come again?
> And will he not come again?
> No, no, he is dead,
> Go to thy death bed.
> He never will come again. (IV, 5, 189–93)

Her great supports are hope and patience: "I hope all will be well. We must be patient" (IV, 5, 177). Lear's madness is likewise a spiritual retreat, and he too preaches patience. There is also a sharp discernment in both madnesses, an insight which enables Ophelia, with regard to others, to know *what* they are, even if she fails to know *who* they are.

In her last scene, when she distributes her flowers, it is natural that she should go first to Laertes as the nearest and dearest of those present. But she does not know who he is and speaks to him rather as if he were her beloved Hamlet. Rosemary for remembrance, and pansies for loving thoughts, are the flowers she gives him. His comment, "A document in madness", that is instruction in the guise of madness, is a clear indication that her distribution is not without significance. To Claudius, who is standing next to Laertes, she gives fennel, the symbol of insincerity and flattery, together with columbines which are a sign of cuckoldom, and which are apt in the sense that his wife has been "seduced" from him by the Spirit. The Queen she recognises as a fellow traveller upon the path of repentance and purification which leads, in good time, to grace: "There's rue for you; and here's some for me; We may call it herb of grace o'Sundays" (IV, 5, 177). To the unnamed gentleman, no doubt typical of the new Danish court, she gives a daisy, which is associated with dissembling and with being an upstart; and to Horatio she says: "I would give you some violets but they withered all when my father died." The violet is the flower of fidelity (IV, 5, 180–1).

Also authoritative is Ophelia's serenity: she has found peace in her retreat, without a trace of bitterness; and her last words, in which she extends to "all Christian souls" (IV, 5, 199) her already quoted prayer for mercy on her father, are in perfect keeping with her "nunnery", for to renounce worldly life is to renounce particularity and to take on a more universal responsibility. In the same way her final "God be wi' you" must be pronounced, not as a mere formality, but as a solemn blessing. It anticipates the words of Laertes at her burial: "A ministering angel shall my sister be" (V, 1, 263).

In that same churchyard scene, before the funeral procession enters, Hamlet who is himself to die the next day, has the inevitable certainty of death brought home to him with a concrete realism which makes his bones ache, and those of the audience too. He is made to hear death in the knocking together of dead men's bones as the grave-digger throws down one against another; he sees, touches and smells death as he takes the jester's skull in his hands; he even almost tastes death as he remembers how often as a child he had put his lips against what is now no more than two rows of teeth set in two jawbones: "Here hung those lips that I have kissed I know not how oft" (V, 1, 201–8).

There is yet another sign that his days are numbered, for it comes out that the grave-digger had taken up his profession on the day that Hamlet was born, thirty years previously; and for him the Prince is already almost a thing of the past, one who has not only come but gone. A strange and sudden chill emanates from the words, spoken with the objectivity of a chronicle: "It was the very day that young Hamlet was born; he that is mad, and sent into England" (V, 1, 160–2). Moreover the scene is to end with the actual burial of everything that had represented, for Hamlet, the possibility of earthly happiness, and he himself finally leaps into the grave, where the convulsive violence of his outburst is indeed suggestive of a death agony.

We learn from hagiographies that more than one mystic has sought before now to familiarise himself with death by laying himself out in a coffin; and this scene amounts to that for Hamlet. It leads up to his speech in the final scene where he expresses his readiness to die at any time. What does it matter if a man die young, since no man really ever possesses any of the things he leaves behind him at death? "Since no man has aught of what he leaves, what is't to leave betimes?" (V, 2, 233–34). We have come a long way from the attitude towards death that is expressed in the most famous of his soliloquies.

The Mysteries are a pact between the Divine and the human, and they lay on man the obligation of perseverance, that is, resolution faithfully maintained. Hamlet's fulfilment of his pact lies in his perpetual preoccupation with "honour" and "revenge". As to the Divine part of the pact, Horatio's already quoted promise, "Heaven will direct it", may be said to have its fulfilment in various ways, most of them no doubt hidden, but some of them manifest, like the appearance of the Ghost in the Queen's closet immediately after the Prince has won over his mother to repentance. A subsequent example is his glimpse of Fortinbras, which was nothing other than a grace, for there was no human intention behind the encounter. Next, and most direct of all, there is the inspiration which saves him from Claudius' plot to have him killed in England. This is inextricably identified, as far as his spiritual development is concerned, with the clearly providential churchyard episode, which comes after the inspiration but which precedes it for the reader and the spectator. It is only in the last scene of the play that we hear of Hamlet's inspired activity on board the boat and that we see the effect of that grace upon him, interwoven with the effect of his foretaste of death. He ascribes, with considerable insistence, every detail of his escape to Divine intervention, and his account of what happened enables trust in Providence to take its place as cornerstone in the remarkable image of kingliness which Shakespeare gives us in Hamlet at the beginning of this scene. His now full-grown royalty of nature causes Horatio to exclaim: "Why, what a king is this!" (V, 2, 62). It is significant also that only here, for the very first time, does Hamlet mention, among Claudius' other iniquities that he has robbed him of the crown that he himself had hoped to wear; and when Horatio implies that there is no time to be lost because news of what has happened will shortly come from England, and when Hamlet replies:

> It will be short; the interim is mine;
> And a man's life's no more than to say "One." (V, 2, 73–4)

we are certain that Claudius has not long to live.

"Everyman" now knows that he has almost come to the end of his journey and that the end will be victory but also, necessarily, death. The spiritual station of Hamlet at this moment is comparable to that of Henry IV who, on hearing of his victory against the rebels, sinks down in mortal sickness, with the words: "And wherefore should these good news make me sick? (Pt 2: IV, 4, 102). As to Hamlet's foreboding of death, it is just before the entry of the King and Queen and Laertes for the fencing match that he intimates to Horatio his premonition that he is going to die. Horatio begs to be allowed to postpone the match, but Hamlet will not hear of it. His refusal is perhaps the greatest speech of the play, and we have already quoted the essence of it:

> Not a whit; we defy augury; there's a special providence in the fall of a sparrow. If it be now, 'tis not to come; if it be not to come, it will be now; if it be not now, yet it will come; the readiness is all; since no man has aught of what he leaves, what is't to leave betimes? Let be. (V, 2, 229–35)

To be ready for death when it comes is all that matters; and in telling us this, Hamlet tells us that he himself is ready. As such, he is spiritually even more magnetic than before; and in addition to the souls of the Queen and Ophelia, there is yet another soul that is destined to be drawn in his wake. In speaking to Horatio about the fate of Rosencrantz and Guildenstern he remarks that it is dangerous for men of "baser nature" to insinuate themselves between two "mighty opposites", that is, in this case, between Claudius and himself. Claudius is mighty because he is on the throne albeit as a usurper, but Hamlet himself is mighty with the Divine right of kings which is his in virtue of his now fulfilled kingliness of nature or, in other words, in virtue of his now being up to the mandate laid on him, or yet again because, since all Heaven is on his side as he now knows beyond doubt, the clash is ultimately between Michael and Lucifer. It is his serenely objective application of the word "mighty" to himself which in fact prompts Horatio's already quoted exclamation "Why, what a king is this!" But Rosencrantz and Guildenstern are not the only ones whose destiny brings them into this zone of danger. Claudius manoeuvres also Laertes into the same fatal situation, and at first it seems that the son of Polonius will prove to be the perfect tool for the end towards which he is being manipulated. He has merely to be told whose hand it was that struck his father down; and the madness of Ophelia followed by her death adds timely fuel to the fire of Laertes' anger.

It is in a state of raging hatred of Hamlet that Laertes, having invoked curses on his head, jumps into Ophelia's grave; and he adds, when the Prince jumps in after him: "The devil take thy soul!" (V, 1, 280). Yet within less than twenty-four hours it is Claudius who is the object of Laertes' hatred, whereas Hamlet is the object of his esteem almost to the point of brotherly love, without there being any direct explanation in the text or indeed any indication that a change is taking place, except for the "aside" of Laertes shortly before he wounds Hamlet: "And yet 'tis almost gainst my conscience" (V, 2, 307). This is yet another example of enigma resulting from the extreme concentration of Shakespeare's art. But here again, as always, he has given us the keys to open the doors he has not opened for us expressly.

He has however explicitly affirmed Laertes' nobility of nature through the mouth of Hamlet himself; and that weighty judgement cannot but mean that Laertes is qualified for the way of the Mysteries since, in the eyes of a man like the Prince, the fact of being "very noble" could not possibly mean anything less. This estimate is moreover confirmed when Hamlet avows his regret for his share of the clash in the graveyard:

> But I am very sorry, good Horatio
> That to Laertes I forgot myself;
> For by the image of my cause, I see
> The portraiture of his; I'll court his favours. (V, 2, 75–8)

Literally this means: we are both sons of slain fathers whose deaths make us in honour bound to avenge them. But beyond that it places Laertes side by side with Hamlet also as regards the supreme significance of honour and revenge.

The outset of Laertes' spiritual path is when he starts out from France to Elsinore to wreak his vengeance upon Claudius and we may assume that it is for this purpose that he bought the poison from the mountebanke. By nature he would shrink from being a poisoner, but with regard to the enemy of mankind such scruples are out of place, witness the words of Hamlet, when he finally uses this very same poison against that enemy: "Then venom to thy work" (V, 2, 333). Nor has Laertes set off on the wrong track, as he is later led to believe, since the regicidal act of Claudius is truly responsible for both of Laertes' bereavements, his father's death and his sister's madness leading to her death. If King Hamlet had not been murdered there could have been no question of Polonius hiding behind the arras in the Queen's closet, and the loves of Hamlet and Ophelia would presumably have flowered into a harmonious marriage. It is thus clear that Claudius is in a sense doubly qualified for his allegorical significance. The main theme of the tragedy equates him at that level, as we have seen, with the serpent who "poisoned" our first ancestor, and he retains this significance throughout. But as the action proceeds there is a piling up of wrong; and towards the end, in what we might call the Laertes theme, the stress is rather on the global responsibility of Claudius, his quantitative guilt, which qualifies him to bear, allegorically, the guilt for all the evil that exists herebelow. Laertes himself never in fact learns the full extent of the iniquity in question; but in his final summing up to Hamlet there is none the less a ring of totality in his denunciation of Claudius: "The king, the king's to blame" (V, 2, 331).

As to what lies above and beyond allegory, let it be said once again that whereas Claudius must be seen allegorically as the contriver of man's fall and as the gainer thereby of a hold over all mankind, anagogically or mysterially he personifies that hold itself; and the path of Laertes, like that of Gertrude, affords us a very direct image of the Lesser Mysteries. In the purgatorial process of which these Mysteries are woven, it is always initially a question of loosening, with a view to finally throwing off, the grip of Satan who, for his part, will seek to tighten his hold, as Claudius succeeds in doing at first when he persuades Laertes to turn his revengeful animosity in another direction on the grounds that he, Claudius, is not to blame. At first the bare fact that it was Hamlet and not Claudius who killed Polonius seems on the surface to support Claudius' claim; but other facts subsequently come to light, as we shall see, and these enable the better nature of Laertes, momentarily overcome by the deceiver, to reassert itself. Claudius, not being able to see in depth, is blind to his nobility; but he can see his surface, the plane of temperament; and given the circumstances, Laertes' temperament suits to perfection the plot of Claudius, who rightly senses that once the young man has been set in impetuous motion upon a course, it will indeed be difficult for anything to turn him aside. That difficulty was none the less to be overcome by his nobility, too late to save Hamlet's life, but in time to reverse, for himself, the process of the fall of man.

As to the way towards that end, it seems probable that even before they all leave the graveyard, Claudius has begun to lose something of his hold over Laertes, whose mistaken attitude towards the Prince may well have begun to waver, having reached its climax in his already quoted curse "the devil take thy soul!" At any rate, for the rest of the scene, Laertes remains totally silent, which in itself is not conclusive either way. But during that silence two facts, hitherto unknown to him, are impressed upon him. We may assume that Claudius, in seeking to augment Laertes' thirst for revenge against the killer of his father, had taken care to say nothing about Hamlet's madness lest it should seem to exonerate him and thus take the edge off Laertes' hostility. But in the graveyard Claudius is, despite himself, obliged by circumstances to beg Laertes to excuse Hamlet's behaviour there on the ground of his madness. The Queen likewise strenuously affirms her son's madness. Thus doubts of Hamlet's full responsibility for Polonius' death will at least have crossed Laertes' mind even before the Prince himself pleads his innocence, as he does so disarmingly the next day. The other unknown fact which is suddenly and powerfully brought to light in the graveyard is the depth and sincerity of Hamlet's love for Ophelia, and Laertes may well have suffered some stabs of conscience, remembering how he had so emphatically warned his sister against taking Hamlet's professions of love seriously. Was he altogether innocent, he may have wondered, of having sowed seeds which might have contributed to the madness of both these lovers?

Enough has perhaps been said to explain the already quoted aside of Laertes: "But yet 'tis almost gainst my conscience." That aside however is merely a milestone on a way which leads far beyond the domain of "almost". That the violent collision on Ophelia's grave should come to be transformed into harmonious union can no doubt best be explained, as has already been intimated, by the powerful magnetism of spirituality on Hamlet's side and, on the side of Laertes, his being of just the right metal to be drawn by the magnet in question. Nor is it to be doubted that when the King and Queen and their courtiers enter, together with Laertes, for the fencing match, the spiritual maturity of Hamlet, which has just evoked Horatio's exclamation of wonderment, would be bound to have at least some effect upon any other sensitive man. Moreover the Mysteries are always fraught with a choice which, in the case of Gertrude, was put explicitly before her; but Laertes does not have to be told: "Look here upon this picture, and on this" (III, 4, 53), for the two "mighty opposites" are there, standing before him in the flesh. Birds of a feather flock together; and when Laertes sees his "enemy", the kingly Hamlet, side by side with his "ally", the depraved usurper, it is scarcely possible that he should not be assailed by discomforting thoughts of being on the wrong side. Unlike Rosencrantz and Guildenstern, he himself is very definitely not of the feather of Claudius.

The actor who plays Laertes must therefore make it clear, almost from his entry in this final scene, that he is a man divided against himself, that is, until his dissociation from Claudius and his union with Hamlet have been completed. Meantime, by a meagre residue of his initial impetus, he continues to move on in the course in which he is set, and mechanically picks out, according to plan, an unbated foil from among the bated ones. But his dividedness robs his fencing of all its brilliance, as we may gather from remarks made by both Hamlet and Claudius.

As soon as Hamlet's wound tells him that his adversary's weapon is unbated, he closes with him and snatches from him the misdirected bloodstained blade. In doing so he pulls the man himself altogether free from the grip of their common enemy. Then he confirms this freedom by handing him his own innocence in the form of the bated foil. Laertes' last links with Claudius are snapped. That sudden reversal of the weapons and with it his own sudden vulnerability, like a dazzling manifestation of Divine justice, completely overwhelm him with a sense of his need to atone for his blindness; and his brief but full purgatory may be said to take place while he desperately fences for his life with no more than the bated foil in his hand against the now fatally armed Prince. When he in his turn is wounded he says to Osric: "I am justly killed with mine own treachery" (V, 2, 318), and then to Hamlet:

> The treacherous instrument is in thy hand,
> Unbated and envenom'd; the foul practice
> Hath turned itself on me; lo, here I lie,
> Never to rise again; thy mother's poison'd:
> I can no more. (V, 2, 327–31)

But he is to die victorious, having had his share in Hamlet's slaying of the Dragon, for which he now gives the signal: "The king, the king's to blame" (V, 2, 331). And when Hamlet thereupon kills Claudius by stabbing him and pouring the deadly drink down his throat, Laertes applauds the justice of the deed, for which he himself had supplied the blade and indicated the poisoned cup. His victory is sealed by his dying words:

> Exchange forgiveness with me, noble Hamlet:
> Mine and my father's death come not upon thee,
> Nor thine on me! (V, 2, 339–42)

And it is above all sealed by the Prince's answering absolution: "Heaven make thee free of it! I follow thee" (V, 2, 343).

Laertes' participation in Hamlet's victory is also apparent from another angle. We have already seen in *Henry IV*, as we shall also see in considering some of the later plays, that as regards the deepest meaning there are two harmoniously coexisting and mutually corroborating modes of interpretation, one of which might be called analytical and the other synthetic. According to the first of these there is, in *Henry IV*, more than one Everyman, each with his own individual way, the King and the Prince; according to the second, Everyman is a synthesis of father and son taken together. But the synthesis may consist of more than two elements, as in fact it does in other plays: a varying number of subordinate characters may be taken to personify different aspects of the central character, and Everyman will then consist of the protagonist together with the subordinates in question. To interpret *Hamlet* in this way, with the Prince as the sole Everyman, and to revert now to Laertes, we have already seen that, like Fortinbras, he personifies precisely those qualities which are as yet only virtual in Hamlet and of which the development is an essential aspect of the main theme. The absence of Laertes for most of the play is thus very significant, and so is his return just at the moment when all that he represents has been brought to life in the Prince by his vision of Fortinbras. Also significant is Ophelia's already mentioned confusing of Laertes with Hamlet—we might say her fusion of Laertes into Hamlet—when she says to him: "There's rosemary, that's for remembrance; pray you, love, remember" (IV, 5, 174–5). A phase of the same fusion is their grappling with each other in her grave, an antagonism destined to become a union and perhaps furthered in that direction by her angelic presence. The union is also prefigured by the interpenetration of their weapons as they fence, and then, even more, by their interchange of weapons. Laertes' rapier can be said, symbolically, to sum up all that the Prince has needed to develop in himself. His having already developed it gives him the right to that mortally effective blade and empowers him to take possession of it. When he does so, it is as if he had absorbed Laertes into himself and taken him with him upon his own victorious way.

From the same synthetic standpoint Ophelia personifies all the love and happiness which Hamlet has sacrificed in this life with a view to the next life whither she herself has already been transferred before the end of the play; and we have also seen that Gertrude is in a sense the fallen soul of Hamlet, a significance which is confirmed by her allegorical equation with Eve, he himself being its faculties of intelligence, conscience and will. But this synthetic mode of interpretation is less called for here than it is in some other plays. Rather to the contrary, the vast canvas upon which the tragedy of the Prince of Denmark is woven has almost epic dimensions which favour a recognition of more than one Everyman, each with his or her own individual way; and it remains for us to complete what has already been said about the way of the Queen.

Here again we are compelled to use our imaginations, along the definite lines laid down for us by the dramatist. If the great bedroom scene is the first time we see her alone with her son, it is also the last. That scene is prolonged and confirmed in a brief aside (IV, 5, 17–20) in which she simply expresses her consciousness of her guilt, thus showing a preoccupation which is characteristic of a novice upon the way. But apart from this we never again see her in circumstances which enable her to speak freely. Claudius is nearly always there and when he is not, his place is taken by Ophelia, whose presence is also inhibiting, albeit in a different way. In this respect, what is generally accepted today as the final text is almost certainly more elliptical than Shakespeare originally intended it to be when he conceived the play. After the King and Laertes withdraw together at the end of Act IV, scene 5, the First Quarto has a scene in which Horatio tells the Queen of Claudius' unsuccessful attempt to have Hamlet killed in England and of Hamlet's return. When the Queen learns that her son is back in Denmark, she tells Horatio:

> Bid him awhile
> Be wary of his presence, lest he fail
> In that he goes about

which means, freely paraphrased: "Tell him to make quite sure that Claudius does not kill him before he kills Claudius". But although this scene is left out in all the later editions of the play, according to the final text a letter is brought from Hamlet to his mother, presumably telling her everything. Moreover, on the basis of Claudius' remark at the end of the churchyard scene: "Good Gertrude, set some watch upon your son" (V 1, 318), we may imagine that mother and son have ample time to discuss the whole situation.

As to the last scene, since she knows that Claudius is determined to kill her son and that he has spent much time talking to Laertes who is determined to avenge his father's death, it is more than probable that she has fears of a plot between them, whence perhaps her message to Hamlet that he should speak to Laertes in a friendly way before the fencing match. Certainly—and the playing of her part should be based on this—she knows her son's life to be in the very greatest danger. She therefore watches Claudius' every move; nor can there be any doubt that when he calls for a glass of wine, drinks from it to the sound of trumpets and cannon, then offers it to Hamlet, having thrown the priceless pearl he speaks of into it, she suspects or even assumes that he has at the same time surreptitiously inserted something else besides, or that the "pearl" itself is not what it appears to be. Hamlet refuses the drink, but only for the moment, whereupon she herself decides to put it to the test, and suddenly takes up the cup to drink her son's health. The King forbids her to drink, but she is not to be stopped: "I will, my lord, I pray you pardon me" (V, 2, 302). Nor, when she realises that her fears were altogether justified, will she allow her sacrifice to be in vain, and when Claudius seeks to make light of her collapse: "She swounds to see them bleed" (V, 2, 319), she finds the strength to protest:

> No, no, the drink, the drink—O my dear Hamlet—
> The drink, the drink!—I am poison'd. (V, 2, 320–1)

These farewell words, and especially their most moving interjection, must be taken as an expression of her total gift of soul to Spirit. As such they may assure us that her death, like that of Laertes, is a dying into life.

As to Hamlet's last words, it is significant that they are a message to Fortinbras. This, together with the entry of Fortinbras immediately after Hamlet's death marks a certain continuity between the dead prince and the living one. There is a suggestion—nothing more—that Hamlet is mysteriously reborn in Fortinbras, though Shakespeare does not indicate this "alchemy" explicitly here as he does in *Henry IV*. At the end of *Hamlet* the stress lies rather on the fruit of rebirth, that is, not on an earthly horizontal succession, but on an upward celestial continuity. If the play as a whole corresponds to an interpenetration of Dante's *Inferno* and *Purgatorio*, the *Paradiso* is none the less not merely implicit. It is expressly anticipated in Horatio's farewell prayer for Hamlet:

> Good night, sweet prince,
> And flights of angels sing thee to thy rest! (V, 2, 345)

The Meeting Place

O blessèd meeting place of land and sea,
Of earth and water, rock and ocean wave,
What is thy secret, that we find in thee,
From the first hour, the home that exiles crave?
Intimate art thou, yet mysterious,
And though thy welcome unreserved we have,
We must to thee confirm, not thou to us.

For thou art agèd with surpassing eld,
Wherefrom to us a majesty is lent;
And thou art ever young: who hath beheld
Thy beauty without joy of wonderment?
Our souls beneath its spell are purified,
Content with little, childlike, innocent,
O world new-born at every ebb of tide.

It is enough to cast off clothes and wear
The sunlight as we walk upon the strand,
Enough to hear the surge, to breathe the air,
To feel beneath our naked feet the sand,
To give thanks for the great and for the small,
For the vast ocean, towering heads of land,
And gathered shells and pebbles, rich in all.

A cloud hath thrown its shadow to our side
Of this calm haven; all beyond is bright:
See through the cleft, where the dark rocks divide,
The splendour of that cliff face in full light
Of dazzling sun. It beckons; we draw near,
And gulls upon its ledges, grey and white,
Open their wings and voice our presence here.

Many fly out, each in its orbit wheeling.
Their cries that on the rocks reverberate,
Unearthly strange, thy secret half revealing,
Proclaim to us that shores are ultimate,

That sea cliffs are the edge of the unknown.
But we, not they, thy secret bear innate
Within our hearts in fullness, we alone.

For man's first nature is a meeting place
Where two worlds intermingle, yet are not joined:
Towards the Infinite is turned his face,
And winged ones from the soul fly out beyond,
Nor come they back save yet again to go,
Drawn by the inward Deep. The Heavens respond:
Tides of the Spirit flow and ebb and flow.

Translations from the Arabic

Al-Ghazālī
Deathbed Poem[1]

Say unto brethren when they see me dead,
And weep for me, lamenting me in sadness:
"Think ye I am this corpse ye are to bury?
I swear by God, this dead one is not I.
I in the Spirit am, and this my body
My dwelling was, my garment for a time.
I am a treasure: hidden I was beneath
This talisman of dust, wherein I suffered.
I am a pearl; a shell imprisoned me,
But leaving it, all trials I have left.
I am a bird, and this was once my cage;
But I have flown, leaving it as a token.
I praise God who hath set me free, and made
For me a dwelling in the heavenly heights.
Ere now I was a dead man in your midst,
But I have come to life, and doffed my shroud."[2]

[1] Presumably Ghazālī wrote this poem towards the end of his life, and it is said by some to have been found under his pillow after his death.

[2] Brit. Mus. Add. 76561; M. al-Murtaẓā, *Itḥāf as-Sāda*, Cairo, 1311 AH, p. 43. There is a full translation in Margaret Smith, *Al-Ghazālī the Mystic* (London, Luzac & Co., 1944, p. 36), evidently from a different recension. Although the poem is also attributed to others, in particular to Abū Ḥāmid's brother, Aḥmad al-Ghazālī (d. 520 AH/1126 AD), and to Abū'l-Ḥasan ʿAlī as-Sibṭī (d. 600 AH/1203 AD), Pedersen remarks that the weight of manuscript authority is strongly in favour of the attribution to Abū Ḥāmid ("Ein Gedicht al-Ghazālīs", *Le Monde Oriental*, 1931, XXI).

ʿUmar Ibn al-Fāriḍ
The Wine-Song (*Al-Khamriyya*)[3]

Rememb'ring the belovèd, wine we drink
Which drunk had made us ere the vine's creation.
A sun it is; the full moon is its cup;
A crescent hands it round; how many stars
Shine forth from it the moment it be mixed!
But for its fragrance ne'er had I been guided
Unto its tavern; but for its resplendence
Imagining could no image make of it.
Time its mere gasp hath left; hidden it is.
Like secrets pent in the intelligence,
Yet if it be remembered in the tribe,[4]
All become drunk—no shame on them nor sin.
Up hath it fumed from out the vessel's dregs.
Nothing is left of it, only a name;
Yet if that name but enter a man's mind,
Gladness shall dwell with him and grief depart.
Had the boon revellers gazed upon its seal,[5]
That seal, without the wine, had made them drunk.
Sprinkle a dead man's grave with drops of it,
His spirit would return, his body quicken.
If in the shadow of the wall where spreads
Its vine they laid a man, mortally sick,
Gone were his sickness; and one paralysed,
Brought near its tavern, would walk; the dumb would speak,
Did he its savour recollect. Its fragrance,
If wafted through the East, even in the West,
Would free, for one berheumed, his sense of smell;

[3] This poem, here translated into blank verse, was translated into prose by Nicholson in his *Studies in Islamic Mysticism*, Cambridge, Cambridge University Press, 1921, pp. 184–88, and by Arberry in *The Mystical Poems of Ibn al-Fārid* (Chester Beatty Monographs 4, London, Emery Walker, 1952), pp. 81–84. For the Arabic, see Arberry *ibid.*, pp. 39–41, edited in transcription from the oldest manuscript, and *Dīwān Ibn al-Fāriḍ*, an undated Cairo edition probably from the first half of the twentieth century, annotated and published by Maḥmūd Tawfīq, pp. 82–84.

[4] The reference is to the *dhikr*, the remembrance or invocation of the Name of God, the basic rite of Islamic mysticism. It is to this Name that every mention of the wine's name refers throughout the poem. The tribe is the brotherhood.

[5] The Prophet is not only the cup, but also, as Seal of the Prophets, the seal upon the wine-jar.

And he who stained his palm, clasping its cup,
Could never, star in hand, be lost by night.
Unveil it like a bride in secrecy[6]
Before one blind from birth: his sight would dawn.
Decant it, and the deaf would hearing have.
If riders rode out for its native earth,[7]
And one of them were bit by snake, unharmed
By poison he. If the enchanter traced[8]
The letters of its name on madman's brow,
That script would cure him of his lunacy;
And blazoned on the standard of a host,[9]
Its name would make all men beneath it drunk.
In virtue the boon revellers it amends,
Makes perfect. Thus by it the irresolute
Is guided to the path of firm resolve.
Bountiful he, whose hand no bounty knew;
And he that never yet forbore forbeareth,
Despite the goad of anger. The tribe's dunce,
Could he but kiss its filter, by that kiss
Would win the sense of all its attributes.
"Describe it, well thou knowest how it is",
They bid me. Yea, its qualities I know:
Not water and not air nor fire nor earth,
But purity for water, and for air
Subtlety, light for fire, spirit for earth—
Excellencies that guide to extol its good
All who would tell of it, and excellent
Their prose in praise of it, excellent their verse.
So he that knew not of it can rejoice[10]

[6] Literally "unveil her", for *khamr* (wine) is feminine. As Arberry remarks in the notes to his translation, the comparison of the unveiling of the becobwebbed wine-jar with the unveiling of a bride is frequent "in bacchic poetry".

[7] The riders are the advanced initiates, *sālikūn* (travellers), who are immune from the effects of poison which, according to Nābulusī, is the passionate attachment to worldly things.

[8] Again according to Nābulusī, the enchanter is the Spiritual Master and the madman is one who takes appearances for reality.

[9] Another reference to the brotherhood, this time as an army whose warriors are engaged in the Greater Holy War (*al-jihād al-akbar*), "the war against the soul".

[10] Every human being is in love with the wine even if he be not conscious of it. The descriptions of it serve to awaken that latent love. Nuʿm, like Laylā, is one of those women's names by which Sufis denote the Divine Essence. Love of Nuʿm and love of the wine may therefore be said to coincide.

To hear it mentioned, as Nu'm's lover doth
To hear her name, whenever Nu'm is named.
Before all beings, in Eternity
It is, ere yet was any shape or trace.
Through it things were, then it by them was veiled,
Wisely, from him who understandeth not.
My spirit loved it, was made one with it,
But not as bodies each in other merge.
Wine without vine: Adam my father is.
Vine without wine, vine mothereth it and me.[11]
Vessels are purer for the purity
Of truths which are their content, and those truths
Are heightened by the vessels being pure.[12]
Things have been diff'renced, and yet all is One:
Our spirits wine are, and our bodies vine.[13]
Before it no before is, after it
No after is; absolute its privilege
To be before all afters. Ere time's span
Its pressing was, and our first father's age[14]

[11] At the level of my oneness with the principial wine in Eternity—wine which, being absolutely independent, is therefore in no need of grape or vine for its existence—I am a true son of Adam who, as Logos, prefigures my union by his. The vine is *Nafas al-Raḥmān* (the Breath of the All-Merciful) which is also termed *al-Ṭabīʿah* (Universal Nature), the feminine or maternal source of all manifestation.

[12] Reading *tasmū* as in the oldest manuscript. It is for the mystic to ensure, by the ritual means at his disposal, that his soul is filled with spiritual presences or truths. These presences have a purifying effect upon the soul, which is their vessel, and this increase of purity qualifies the vessel to endure a heightening of the truths. If we read *tanmū*, "have increase", as in the other manuscripts, the meaning is not basically changed.

[13] But, as Nābulusī remarks, the vine contains the spiritual juice which will ultimately be transmuted into wine. We may compare the lines of Ibn al-Fāriḍ's younger contemporary, ʿAlī al-Shushtarī:

> Behold My beauty, witness of Me
> In every man,
> Like the water flowing through
> The sap of branches.
> One water drink they, yet they flower
> In many hues.

[14] It is not the spiritual or "winal" nature of Adam which is referred to here but his human or "vineal" nature, of which the Prophet said: "I was a Prophet when Adam was yet between water and clay," while nonetheless having to speak of his own spiritual nature in answer to the question "When did you become a Prophet?"

Came afterwards — parentless orphan it!
They tell me: "Thou hast drunk iniquity".
Not so, I have but drunk what not to drink
Would be for me iniquitous indeed.
Good for the monastery folk, that oft
They drunken were with it, yet drank it not,
Though fain would drink. But ecstasy from it
Was mine ere I existed, shall be mine
Beyond my bones' decaying. Drink it pure!
But if thou needs must have it mixed, 'twere sin
To shun mouth-water from the Loved One's lips.[15]
Go seek it in the tavern; bid it unveil
To strains of music. They offset its worth,
For wine and care dwelt never in one place,
Even as woe with music cannot dwell.
Be drunk one hour with it, and thou shalt see
Time's whole age as thy slave, at thy command.
He hath not lived here, who hath sober lived,
And he that dieth not drunk hath missed the mark.
With tears then let him mourn himself, whose life
Hath passed, and he no share of it hath had.

[15] If you have not the spiritual strength for oneness with the Divine Essence Itself, then let the water that you mix the wine with be nothing less than "the saliva of God", that is, the Supreme Spirit, which, if it be not fully Him, is not other than Him. The mixing of the wine thus signifies the emergence of the Logos, *al-Rūḥ al-Muḥammadī*, and this explains the mention of stars in line 4. The manifestation of the Spirit of Muḥammad precipitates the existence of the Spirits of his Companions, whom he likened to stars: "My companions are even as the stars. Whichsoever of them ye follow, ye shall be rightly guided." By extension the words "how many stars" may be taken to include those Saints who are heirs of the Companions in subsequent generations.

Aḥmad al-ʿAlawī
The Path[16]

Will the seeker of God be content to be far?
Nay, for he needeth no less than Union.
The true seeker hath a sign on his face,
A light shineth gleaming upon his forehead.
Ever near is he, courteous, reverential,
Resolute, forbearing before censure, true friend
Honouring. His purpose all purposes transcendeth:
Naught can prevent him, the steep he seeth as level.
He hath no aim aside from his mark.
Longing for family diverteth him not, nor blame.
Fair his description, he needeth no other
But this, most excellent, that he seeketh the Truth.
Whoso is Its seeker, he maketh his quest
Sole object of his eyes. Then strippeth he his soul
Of all faults he can detect, and when stripped, robeth it
In their opposites. God's slave at each time and place,
His bounden debt of worship fulfilling,
He addeth thereunto of his own free will,
Until the Truth is his Hearing, Sight,
Tongue and Utterance, and Hands and Feet.
He dieth before his death to live in his Lord,
Since after this death is the supreme migration.
He calleth himself to account ere he be called,
He herein most fitted to act for the Truth.
The Truth's Being he seeth before his own,
And after it, and wheresoever he turn.
Alone God was, and with Him naught else.
He is now as He was, lastly as firstly,
Essentially One, with naught beside Himself,
Inwardly Hidden, Outwardly Manifest,
Without beginning, without end. Whate'er thou seest,
Seest thou His Being. Absolute Oneness
No "but" hath and no "except." How should God's Essence
Be confined with a veil? No veil there but His Light.

[16] *Dīwān*, p. 10.

The Wine[17]

Friends, if the truth of my state ye have understood,
Here lies your path before you: follow in my footsteps,
For by Heaven, here are no doubts, no vague imaginings:
I know God, with a knowledge part secret, part proclaimed.
I drank the cup of love, and then possessed it,
And it hath become my possession for all time.
God reward him who lavished[18] his Secret upon me,
For bounty, true bounty, is to bestow the Secret.
I hid the Truth on a time, and screened It well,
And whoso keepeth God's Secret shall have his reward.
Then when the Giver vouchsafed that I might proclaim It,
He fitted me—how I know not—to purify[19] souls,
And girded upon me the sword of steadfastness,
And truth and piety, and a Wine He gave me,
Which all who drink must needs be always drinking,
Even as a drunk man seeketh to be more drunk.
Thus came I to pour It—nay, it is I that press It.
Doth any other pour It in this age?
Marvel not that I speak thus, for our Lord
Himself hath said that He singleth out for Grace
Whomso He will and giveth unsparingly.
This is God's Grace: He giveth It whom He will.[20]
Surpassing Praise and Glory and Thanks be His!

Lord, with the Spirit of the Beloved,[21] Thy Spirit,
With the Spirit of Holiness help me, *make easy my task.*[22]
Untie my tongue, Lord. *Let one share my burden*
From Thy true helpers, and confound me not
The Day of the Gathering.[23] Lord, whelm with Thy Presence
And greet with Peace, bless, magnify, extol,
The Beloved's Spirit, in the Abode of the Secret.

[17] *Dīwān*, p. 35.

[18] The Shaykh Al-Būzīdī.

[19] *Tajrīd*, literally "abstraction," "disentanglement".

[20] Qur'ān, V, 54.

[21] The Prophet.

[22] This and the following quotations are from the prayer which Moses uttered on being told to go to Pharaoh. (Qur'ān, XX, 25–35).

[23] The Day of Judgement.

Laylā[24]

Full near I came unto where dwelleth
Laylā, when I heard her call.
That voice, would I might ever hear it!
She favoured me, and drew me to her,
Took me in, into her precinct,
With discourse intimate addressed me.
She sat me by her, then came closer,
Raised the cloak that hid her from me,
Made me marvel to distraction,
Bewildered me with all her beauty.
She took me and amazed me,
And hid me in her inmost self,
Until I thought that she was I,
And my life she took as ransome.
She changed me and transfigured me,
And marked me with her special sign,
Pressed me to her, put me from her,
Named me as she is named.
Having slain and crumbled me,
She steeped the fragments in her blood.
Then, after my death, she raised me:
My star shines in her firmament.
Where is my life, and where my body,
Where my wilful soul? From her
The truth of these shone out to me,
Secrets that had been hidden from me.
Mine eyes have never seen but her:
To naught else can they testify.
All meanings in her are comprised.
Glory be to her Creator!

Thou that beauty wouldst describe,
Here is something of her brightness.
Take it from me. It is my art.
Think it not idle vanity.
My Heart lied not when it divulged
The secret of my meeting her.
If nearness unto her effaceth,
I still subsist in her subsistence.

[24] *Dīwān*, p. 22. Laylā, a woman's name meaning "night", here represents the Divine Essence.

List of Sources

Oneness of Being: *A Sufi Saint of the Twentieth Century: Shaikh Aḥmad al-ʿAlawī: His Spiritual Heritage and Legacy*. Cambridge, UK: Islamic Texts Society, 1993, pp. 121–30.

The Symbolism of the Letters of the Alphabet: *A Sufi Saint of the Twentieth Century*, pp. 148–57.

The Truth of Certainty: *The Book of Certainty: The Sufi Doctrine of Faith, Vision, and Gnosis*. Cambridge, UK: Islamic Texts Society, 1992, pp. 1–11.

The Fall: *The Book of Certainty*, pp. 28–34.

The Symbol: *The Book of Certainty*, pp. 35–40.

The Seal of Solomon: *The Book of Certainty*, pp. 59–66.

The Tree of the Knowledge of Good and Evil: *The Book of Certainty*, pp. 67–9.

What is Symbolism?: *Symbol and Archetype: A Study of the Meaning of Existence*. Louisville, KY: Fons Vitae, 2005, pp. 1–11.

The Decisive Boundary: *Symbol and Archetype*, pp. 12–6.

The Symbolism of the Pairs: *Symbol and Archetype*, pp. 17–25.

The Past in the Light of the Present: *Ancient Beliefs and Modern Superstitions*. London: Archetype, 2001, pp. 1–14.

The Spirit of the Times: *The Eleventh Hour: The Spiritual Crisis of the Modern World in the Light of Tradition and Prophecy*. London: Archetype, 2002, pp. 53–83.

Do the Religions Contradict One Another?: *A Return to the Spirit: Questions and Answers*. Louisville, KY: Fons Vitae, 2005, pp. 20–28.

The Secret of Shakespeare: *The Secret of Shakespeare: His Greatest Plays Seen in the Light of Sacred Art*. Cambridge, UK: Quinta Essentia, 1996, pp. 177–83.

Why "With All Thy Mind"?: *A Return to the Spirit*, pp. 29–43.

The Spiritual Master: *A Sufi Saint of the Twentieth Century*, pp. 79–101.

The Originality of Sufism: *What is Sufism?* Cambridge, UK: Islamic Texts Society, 1993, pp. 11–16.

The Universality of Sufism: *What is Sufism?* pp. 17–24.

The Heart: *What is Sufism?* pp. 45–62.

Introduction to *Splendours of Qur'ān Calligraphy and Illumination*. Vaduz, Liechtenstein: Thesaurus Islamicus Foundation, 2005, pp. 13–14.

The Qur'ānic Art of Calligraphy: *Splendours of Qur'ān Calligraphy and Illumination*, pp. 15–19.
The Qur'ānic Art of Illumination: *Splendours of Qur'ān Calligraphy and Illumination*, pp. 20–29.
Selections from *Muhammad: His Life Based on the Earliest Sources.* Cambridge, UK: Islamic Texts Society, 1991.
I The House of God: pp. 1–3.
VIII The Desert: pp. 23–26.
X Baḥīrà the Monk: pp. 29–30.
XIII The Household: pp. 37–40.
XV The First Revelations: pp. 43–45.
XXXVII The Hijrah: pp. 118–22.
LXVII "A Clear Victory": pp. 252–56.
LXXV The Conquest of Mecca: pp. 299–305.
LXXXI The Degrees: pp. 328–31.
LXXXIV The Choice: pp. 340–44.
Hamlet: *The Secret of Shakespeare*, pp. 20–56.
The Meeting Place: *Collected Poems: Revised and Augmented.* London: Archetype, 2002, pp. 55–56.
Al-Ghazālī, Deathbed Poem: *Sufi Poems: A Mediaeval Anthology*. Cambridge, UK: Islamic Texts Society, 2004, pp. 56–57.
ʿUmar Ibn al-Fāriḍ, The Wine-Song (*Al-Khamriyya*): *Sufi Poems*, pp. 68–74.
Aḥmad al-ʿAlawī, The Path: *A Sufi Saint of the Twentieth Century*, pp. 216–17.
Aḥmad al-ʿAlawī, The Wine: *A Sufi Saint of the Twentieth Century*, p. 224.
Aḥmad al-ʿAlawī, Laylā: *A Sufi Saint of the Twentieth Century*, p. 225.

Bibliography

The Book of Certainty: The Sufi Doctrine of Faith, Vision, and Gnosis. London: Rider, 1952; New York: Samuel Weiser, 1970; second edition: Cambridge, UK: Islamic Texts Society, 1992.

A Moslem Saint of the Twentieth Century: Shaikh Aḥmad al-ʿAlawī: His Spiritual Heritage and Legacy. London: Allen & Unwin, 1961; second edition: *A Sufi Saint of the Twentieth Century: Shaikh Aḥmad al-ʿAlawī: His Spiritual Heritage and Legacy*. London: George Allen & Unwin, 1971; Berkeley, CA: California University Press, 1971; third edition: Cambridge, UK: Islamic Texts Society, 1993.

Ancient Beliefs and Modern Superstitions. London: Perennial Books, 1964; second edition: London & Boston: Unwin Paperback, 1980; Cambridge, UK: Quinta Essentia, 1991; third edition: London: Archetype, 2001.

Shakespeare in the Light of Sacred Art. London: Allen & Unwin, 1966; New York: Humanities Press, 1966; second edition: *The Secret of Shakespeare: His Greatest Plays Seen in the Light of Sacred Art*. Wellingborough: The Aquarian Press, 1984; New York: Inner Traditions, 1984; third edition: Cambridge, UK: Quinta Essentia, 1996; fourth edition: *The Sacred Art of Shakespeare: To Take Upon Us the Mystery of Things*. Rochester, VT: Inner Traditions, 1998; fifth edition: *Shakespeare's Window Into the Soul: The Mystical Wisdom in Shakespeare's Characters*. Rochester, VT: Inner Traditions, 2006.

The Elements, and Other Poems. London: Perennial Books, 1967.

The Heralds, and Other Poems. London: Perennial Books, 1970.

What is Sufism? London: George Allen & Unwin, 1975; Berkeley, CA: University of California Press, 1975; London & Boston: Unwin Paperbacks, 1977; Cambridge, UK: Islamic Texts Society, 1993.

The Qur'ānic Art of Calligraphy and Illumination. London: World of Islam Festival Publishing, 1976; second edition: *Splendours of Qur'ān Calligraphy and Illumination*. Vaduz, Liechtenstein: Thesaurus Islamicus Foundation, 2005.

Muhammad: His Life Based on the Earliest Sources. London: Allen & Unwin, 1983; Rochester, VT: Inner Traditions, 1983; second edition: Cambridge, UK: Islamic Texts Society, 1991; third edition: Rochester, VT: Inner Traditions, 2006.

Collected Poems. London: Perennial Books, 1987; second edition: *Collected Poems: Revised and Augmented*. London: Archetype, 2002.

The Eleventh Hour: The Spiritual Crisis of the Modern World in the Light of Tradition and Prophecy. Cambridge, UK: Quinta Essentia, 1987; second edition: London: Archetype, 2002.

Symbol and Archetype: A Study of the Meaning of Existence. Cambridge, UK: Quinta Essentia, 1991; second edition: Louisville, KY: Fons Vitae, 2005.

Mecca: From Before Genesis Until Now. London: Archetype, 2004.

Sufi Poems: A Mediaeval Anthology. Cambridge, UK: Islamic Texts Society, 2004.

A Return to the Spirit: Questions and Answers. Louisville, KY: Fons Vitae, 2005.

The Underlying Religion: An Introduction to the Perennial Philosophy, edited by Martin Lings and Clinton Minnaar. Bloomington, IN: World Wisdom, 2007.

The Holy Qur'ān: Translations of Selected Verses. Cambridge, UK: The Royal Aal al-Bayt Institute for Islamic Thought & The Islamic Texts Society, 2007.

Shakespeare's Spirituality: A Perspective: An Interview with Dr. Martin Lings (DVD), produced and directed by Ira B. Zinman. Bloomington, IN: Mt. Washington II Entertainment, 2007.

Circling the House of God: Reflections of Martin Lings on Hajj (DVD), produced and directed by Ovidio Salazar. London: Archetype, 2009.

Enduring Utterance: Collected Lectures (1993–2001), edited by Trevor Banyard. London: The Matheson Trust, 2014.

To Take Upon Us the Mystery of Things: The Shakespeare Lectures of Martin Lings, edited by Ira B. Zinman. London: The Matheson Trust, 2014.

Biographical Notes

MARTIN LINGS (1909–2005) was a leading member of the perennialist school and an acclaimed author, editor, translator, scholar, Arabist, and poet. After a classical education he read English at Oxford where he was a pupil and later a close friend of C. S. Lewis. In 1935 he went to Lithuania where he lectured on Anglo-Saxon and Middle English; subsequently he went to Egypt and lectured mainly on Shakespeare at Cairo University. In 1952 he returned to England and took a degree in Arabic and in 1955 he joined the staff of the British Museum where from 1970–73 he was Keeper of Oriental Manuscripts. He is the author of several award-winning books on subjects ranging from Sufism to Shakespeare, including *A Sufi Saint of the Twentieth Century: Shaikh Aḥmad al-ʿAlawī*, the best-selling *Muhammad: His Life Based on the Earliest Sources* (translated into over a dozen languages), and *Shakespeare in the Light of Sacred Art*. In addition, he is also the author of the chapter "Mystical Poetry" in Volume 2 of *The Cambridge History of Arabic Literature*, and the chapter on "The Nature and Origin of Sufism" in Vol. 19 of World Spirituality, as well as numerous articles for *Studies in Comparative Religion*, *Sophia*, *The New Encyclopaedia of Islam*, and the *Encyclopaedia Britannica*.

REZA SHAH-KAZEMI (b. 1960) is an author in the fields of Islamic studies and Comparative Religion. He obtained a Ph.D. in Comparative Religion from the University of Kent. He is a Senior Research Associate at the Institute of Ismaili Studies, London, and has been involved in important interfaith initiatives for the last two decades. He has edited, translated, and written numerous books and articles, including *Paths to Transcendence according to Shankara, Ibn Arabi & Meister Eckhart*, *The Spirit of Tolerance in Islam*, the award-winning *Justice and Remembrance: Introducing the Spirituality of Imam Ali*, *The Other in the Light of the One: Qur'ānic Perspectives on Interfaith Dialogue*, and *Common Ground Between Islam and Buddhism*, which was prefaced and launched by HH The Dalai Lama. Shah-Kazemi lives in Westerham in the south of England.

Index of Names

210, 270. *See also* Christ
Jīlī, ʿAbd al-Karīm al-, 7, 13, 14, 19, 21, 60
Jossot, ʿAbd al-Karīm, 165
Justin Martyr, 149

Kaʿb, 243
Kalki, 37, 110
Kāshānī, ʿAbd al-Razzāq al-, 199
Khadījah, 242, 244, 245, 246, 249, 250, 251
Khālid, 265, 267, 268, 269, 271, 272, 276
Kharrāz, Al-, 10, 11
Krishna, *xv*, 71, 72, 110, 149

Laertes, 297, 298, 315, 316, 318, 319, 320, 321, 322, 323, 324, 325, 326
Lakshmī, 71
Lear, King, 133, 137, 138, 139, 294, 295, 301, 315

Marcellus, 294, 297, 301
Massignon, Louis, *xii*, 4, 7, 8, 9
Maymūnah, 268, 281
Michelangelo, 134
Milton, 134
Moses, *xv*, 27, 28, 45, 92, 121, 129, 147, 153, 193, 194, 198, 214, 250, 335
Muḥammad, *ix*, *xiii*, 4, 5, 14, 19, 21, 28, 32, 45, 121, 122, 123, 127, 129, 147, 148, 151, 152, 153, 154, 159, 163, 166, 168, 230, 239, 240, 242, 243, 244, 245, 246, 247, 248, 249, 250, 252, 260, 261, 265, 266, 269, 272, 273, 333. *See also* Prophet, the

Nābulusī, ʿAbd al-Ghanī al-, 16, 331, 332
Nicholas of Cusa, St, 115
Nicholson, R.A., *xii*, 3, 8, 174, 330
Noah, 153

Ophelia, 297, 299, 301, 302, 303, 307, 310, 315, 316, 318, 319, 320, 321, 322, 324, 325
Othello, 138, 294, 296, 305

Parvati, 71
Perry, Whitall, 114
Pharaoh, 67, 335
Pius XI, Pope, 161
Polonius, 301, 307, 308, 309, 310, 311, 319, 320, 321
Prophet (Muhammad), the, *ix*, *xi*, *xiii*, 6, 7, 12, 13, 14, 21, 22, 28, 29, 31, 32, 33, 39, 41, 53, 56, 122, 123, 127, 128, 129, 155, 161, 163, 165, 167, 168, 171, 173, 174, 175, 177, 178, 180, 181, 193, 194, 195, 200, 203, 205, 206, 207, 211, 213, 214, 222, 223, 233, 249, 250, 251, 252, 253, 254, 255, 256, 257, 258, 259, 260, 261, 262, 263, 264, 265, 266, 267, 268, 269, 270, 271, 272, 273, 274, 275, 276, 277, 278, 279, 280, 281, 282, 283, 284, 285, 332. *See also* Muḥammad
Prospero, 140

Qabbalah, 118
Qays, 259, 266
Qouraybah, 267, 270

Rābiʿah al-ʿAdawiyyah, 7
Rama, *xv*, 71, 110
Ramana Maharshi, 160
Ruqayyah, 242, 245, 247, 271
Ruysbroeck, 115

Saʿd, 235, 236, 237, 245, 266,

Index of Foreign Terms

Other Titles in the Perennial Philosophy Series by World Wisdom

The Betrayal of Tradition: Essays on the Spiritual Crisis of Modernity, edited by Harry Oldmeadow, 2005

Borderlands of the Spirit: Reflections on a Sacred Science of Mind, by John Herlihy, 2005

A Buddhist Spectrum: Contributions to Buddhist-Christian Dialogue, by Marco Pallis, 2003

A Christian Pilgrim in India: The Spiritual Journey of Swami Abhishiktananda (Henri Le Saux), by Harry Oldmeadow, 2008

Emir Abd el-Kader: Hero and Saint of Islam, by Ahmed Bouyerdene, 2012

The Essential Ananda K. Coomaraswamy, edited by Rama P. Coomaraswamy, 2004

The Essential René Guénon, edited by John Herlihy, 2009

The Essential Seyyed Hossein Nasr, edited by William C. Chittick, 2007

The Essential Sophia, edited by Seyyed Hossein Nasr and Katherine O'Brien, 2006

The Essential Titus Burckhardt: Reflections on Sacred Art, Faiths, and Civilizations, edited by William Stoddart, 2003

Every Branch in Me: Essays on the Meaning of Man, edited by Barry McDonald, 2002

Every Man An Artist: Readings in the Traditional Philosophy of Art, edited by Brian Keeble, 2005

Figures of Speech or Figures of Thought? The Traditional View of Art, by Ananda K. Coomaraswamy, 2007

A Guide to Hindu Spirituality, by Arvind Sharma, 2006

Introduction to Traditional Islam, Illustrated: Foundations, Art, and Spirituality, by Jean-Louis Michon, 2008

Introduction to Sufism: The Inner Path of Islam, by Éric Geoffroy, 2010

Islam, Fundamentalism, and the Betrayal of Tradition: Essays by Western Muslim Scholars, edited by Joseph E.B. Lumbard, 2004, 2009

Journeys East: 20th Century Western Encounters with Eastern Religious Traditions, by Harry Oldmeadow, 2004

Light From the East: Eastern Wisdom for the Modern West, edited by Harry Oldmeadow, 2007

Living in Amida's Universal Vow: Essays in Shin Buddhism, edited by Alfred Bloom, 2004

Maintaining the Sacred Center: The Bosnian City of Stolac, by Rusmir Mahmutćehajić, 2011

The Mystery of Individuality: Grandeur and Delusion of the Human Condition, by Mark Perry, 2012

Of the Land and the Spirit: The Essential Lord Northbourne on Ecology and Religion, edited by Christopher James and Joseph A. Fitzgerald, 2008

On the Origin of Beauty: Ecophilosophy in the Light of Traditional Wisdom, by John Griffin, 2011

Outline of Sufism: The Essentials of Islamic Spirituality, by William Stoddart, 2012

Paths to the Heart: Sufism and the Christian East, edited by James S. Cutsinger, 2002

Remembering in a World of Forgetting: Thoughts on Tradition and Postmodernism, by William Stoddart, 2008

Returning to the Essential: Selected Writings of Jean Biès, translated by Deborah Weiss-Dutilh, 2004

Science and the Myth of Progress,
edited by Mehrdad M. Zarandi, 2003

Seeing God Everywhere: Essays on Nature and the Sacred,
edited by Barry McDonald, 2003

Singing the Way: Insights in Poetry and Spiritual Transformation,
by Patrick Laude, 2005

The Spiritual Legacy of the North American Indian: Commemorative Edition, by Joseph E. Brown, 2007

Sufism: Love & Wisdom,
edited by Jean-Louis Michon and Roger Gaetani, 2006

The Timeless Relevance of Traditional Wisdom,
by M. Ali Lakhani, 2010

Touchstones of the Spirit: Essays on Religion, Tradition & Modernity,
by Harry Oldmeadow, 2012

The Underlying Religion: An Introduction to the Perennial Philosophy,
edited by Martin Lings and Clinton Minnaar, 2007

Universal Aspects of the Kabbalah and Judaism,
by Leo Schaya, 2014

Unveiling the Garden of Love: Mystical Symbolism in Layla Majnun and Gita Govinda,
by Lalita Sinha, 2008

What Does Islam Mean in Today's World: Religion, Politics, Spirituality,
by William Stoddart, 2012

The Wisdom of Ananda Coomaraswamy: Selected Reflections on Indian Art, Life, and Religion,
edited by S. Durai Raja Singam and Joseph A. Fitzgerald, 2011

Wisdom's Journey: Living the Spirit of Islam in the Modern World,
by John Herlihy, 2009

Ye Shall Know the Truth: Christianity and the Perennial Philosophy,
edited by Mateus Soares de Azevedo, 2005